The Barthian Revolt in Modern Theology

Also by Gary Dorrien
from Westminster John Knox Press

The Remaking of Evangelical Theology

The Word as True Myth:
Interpreting Modern Theology

The Barthian Revolt in Modern Theology

Theology without Weapons

GARY DORRIEN

Westminster John Knox Press
Louisville, Kentucky

Book design by Sharon Adams
Cover design by PAZ Design Group

First edition
Published by Westminster John Knox Press
Louisville, Kentucky

This book is printed on acid-free paper that meets the American National Standards Institute Z39.48 standard. ♾

PRINTED IN THE UNITED STATES OF AMERICA

00 01 02 03 04 05 06 07 08 09—10 9 8 7 6 5 4 3 2 1

Library of Congress Cataloging-in-Publication Data

Dorrien, Gary J.
The Barthian revolt in modern theology : theology without weapons / Gary Dorrien.
p. cm.
Includes bibliographical references and index.
ISBN 0-664-22151-3 (alk. paper)
1. Barth, Karl, 1886–1968. 2. Dialectical theology. I. Title.
BX4827.B3D57 1999
230′.044′092—dc21 99-38148

For Pam Sotherland
and
Becca Kutz-Marks.
Cherished friends and colleagues.

Let this point therefore stand: that those whom the Holy Spirit has inwardly taught truly rest upon Scripture, and that Scripture indeed is self-authenticated; hence, it is not right to subject it to proof and reasoning. And the certainty it deserves with us, it attains by the testimony of the Spirit.—John Calvin

Knowledge of God is the expression of religious experience wholly without weapons.—Wilhelm Herrmann

CONTENTS

INTRODUCTION

Neoorthodoxy Reconsidered

The giant figures compel later generations to explain them. To the extent that they have any say in the matter, they also usually resist the labels assigned to them. The preeminent theologian of the twentieth century, Karl Barth, offers a striking example on both counts. As a field-shaping interpreter of the modern meaning of Christianity, Barth's historical stature in modern theology is rivaled only by the figure that he defined himself against, Friedrich Schleiermacher, whose writings between 1799 and 1834 established and epitomized the modern liberal approach to theology. Barth's theological career began during World War I and ended with his death in 1968. Over the past generation, however, it is Barth who has seemed more remote from the field that he dominated in the 1930s and 1940s. Much of the liberal theology of the past generation has carried on Schleiermacher's project of experiential interpretaton with only slight departures from his theological method and only a modest range of debates about how Schleiermacher should be interpreted. On the other hand, the field of theology is rife with disputes about how Barth should be interpreted; relatively few theologians claim to be Barthians, and most of those who do think of themselves as Barthians interpret Barth through categories that he vehemently rejected.

Throughout his later intellectual career Barth sharply denied that his theology should be called "neoorthodox" or "dialectical" or even "Barthian." He was not part of any movement to create a new or modernized orthodoxy, he insisted, nor did he want any school of followers. It appalled him when the term "neoorthodoxy" became the conventional signifier for the theological movement that he inspired and more or less represented. As a continental European, the word carried historical associations for Barth that it did not bear for most British or American theologians. He associated the term with the kind of stuffy Lutheran conservatism taught at Erlangen. He wanted no place in the history of orthodox confessionalism or scholasticism. He countered that he was a church theologian in the ongoing tradition of Luther and Calvin who sought to express the faith of the Reformation in forms of expression suitable to the twentieth century. He wanted to be categorized under no other marker than "church theologian of God's free and sovereign Word."

Most of the other major architects of "neoorthodox theology" did not care for their movement-labels, either. In the 1920s, Barth and his chief theological collaborators called their perspective "crisis theology" or "dialectical theology." They included Eduard Thurneysen, Friedrich Gogarten, Emil Brunner, and Rudolf Bultmann. Paul Tillich was an occasional ally. In the 1930s these thinkers and numerous others, notably Dietrich Bonhoeffer, Reinhold Niebuhr, H. Richard Niebuhr, Regin Prenter, Gustav Aulen, and Helmut Thielicke worked out their own forms of theologically postliberal thinking while highlighting their differences from Barth and each other. Some of these thinkers were more deeply rooted in the tradition of theological liberalism than they acknowledged, but even the more conservative figures among them were wary of identifying with a movement that earned such tags as "neo-supernaturalist" and "Barthian." As represented by these influential figures, theological neoorthodoxy was always too diverse and contentious to be a genuine movement, and the term itself was disowned by all of them.

So-called "neoorthodoxy" was not well named, notwithstanding the hordes of Barthians, Brunnerians, Niebuhrians and others who readily embraced this term in the 1940s and 1950s. Among the major "neoorthodox" theologians of the past century, only Barth was decisively shaped by the dogmatic tradition of seventeenth-century Protestant orthodoxy. "New Reformationist" theology would have been a better name for the kind of perspective that he and Brunner pioneered in the 1920s, though Barth undoubtedly would have rejected this label also. By whatever name, however, the constellation of theologies that grew out of the crisis theology movement of the early 1920s effected a stunning reorientation of the field of Christian theology. Twentieth-century theology begins with Barth's revolt against his liberal teachers during World War I. I shall argue that the nature of this revolt and its continuing legacy cannot be comprehended without understanding that Barthian theology was a highly creative blend of Reformationist, orthodox, and liberal modernist elements. The latter elements were crucial to its character as a theology of the self-authenticating Word of Christ. More broadly, for all of their blistering rhetoric against Schleiermacher's children, all of the major proponents of theological neoorthodoxy remained importantly rooted in the tradition of nineteenth-century theological liberalism.

This argument would be relatively easy to press with regard to Tillich, Bultmann, or Reinhold Niebuhr, but I shall press it with regard to its hardest case. Barth denounced the liberal tradition with a vehemence that was matched only by Brunner. He charged that liberal theology betrayed Christ in its eagerness to accommodate modern consciousness and the culture of modernity. He insisted that modern Protestant theology could recover its authentically Christian basis only by returning to the Reformationist way of revelation and faith alone. He drank more deeply from the well of Protestant orthodoxy than any of his counterparts, a fact that ultimately set him apart from most of them. It is equally significant, however, that Barth also distinguished himself from most of his counterparts and even many Barthians by keeping alive certain crucial aspects of his Herrmannian liberal past. The present interpretation of the making and legacy of his theology emphasizes his refashioning of these nineteenth-century liberal motifs into a neo-Calvinist theology of Word and Spirit that reclaimed ancient orthodox ways of speaking of Christ as Logos and of God as Triune mystery.

Barth's theological rhetoric was immensely powerful and nearly equally divisive. I shall argue that both of these qualities were chiefly attributable to his uncompromising insistence on doing theology as exegesis of the Spirit-illuminated Word without any resort to philosophical preunderstandings or apologetic stopgaps or demythologized worldviews. Against the long-dominant reading of Barth as the theorist of the most conservative wing of the neoorthodox tradition, I shall emphasize the radically open character of Barthianism as a theology without weapons. Barth disdained all descriptive labels for his perspective because, among lesser reasons, he had no interest in defending an abstract position or belief system. With Paul, Calvin, and Wilhelm Herrmann, but in a way that made him a more distinctive thinker than he ever acknowledged, he demonstrated the possibility of doing theology as a Word-following dialectic of divine hiddenness and presence that trusted in the sufficiency of the revealed object of faith.

The notion that Barth relinquished his dialectical approach to theology in the early 1930s is one of the chief conventions of modern theology, partly because Barth had reasons to encourage this exaggeration. The notion that he became the dogmatist of a conservative "revelational positivism" in his later career is equally entrenched among theologians, despite Barth's vehement protests against it. Neither of these interpretations is completely wrong, but, joined together, they have created an impression of Barth's theological significance that is almost entirely mistaken. Though he renounced the tag of "dialectical theologian" in the early 1930s and thus confused a host of theological interpreters to the present day, Barth's theology remained a dialectical rhetoric of freedom throughout his later career. The dialectic of divine veiling and unveiling remained crucial to his thought. Unlike some of the neoorthodoxies that his work inspired, he persistently refused to treat God's presence or absence undialectically. He avoided the false objectivism that derives from an undialectical emphasis on presence, but he also refused to fossilize his own crisis theology slogans about God's wholly otherness. I shall argue that his perspective therefore has more to contribute to the possibility of a compelling postmodern theology of Word and Spirit than much of the neoorthodox movement that his work engendered.

INTERPRETIVE TRADITIONS: READING BARTH

The story of how Barth rebelled against his eminent liberal teachers and became the leader of the "crisis theology" revolt against a liberal theological establishment is the founding narrative of twentieth-century theology. Despite its central importance to modern theology and its frequent retellings, this story is usually told in a way that exaggerates Barth's various reversals of position. The key reversals in question are his break from liberal theology and his later adoption of an analogical dogmatic method. For reasons that served his theological and political purposes, Barth was inclined to portray his theological development as a series of dramatic conversions. This emphasis on conversion motifs was heightened in the influential accounts of his development offered by Hans Urs von Balthasar and Thomas F. Torrance, who described Barth's ostensible conversion "from dialectical to dogmatic thinking" as the key to the greatness of his mature theology.[1] In both cases, the picture of the "mature" Barth that emerged was the picture that most Barth interpreters across the theological spectrum have reproduced. It is the picture of Barth as the dogmatician of a conservative neoorthodox positivism.

The present work belongs to the generational reinterpretation of Barth's development and perspective pioneered by Eberhard Mechels, Ingrid Spieckermann, Michael Beintker, Trutz Rendtorff, and Eberhard Jüngel.[2] In the United States and England this reinterpretive project has been advanced most notably by Bruce L. McCormack, George Hunsinger, Walter Lowe, Graham Ward, William Stacy Johnson, and various proponents of Yale-school "narrativist" or "postliberal" theology.[3] The descriptions of Barth's thinking that these interpreters present are different enough from each other to falsify almost any generalization that one might put forth about their work, especially if Jüngel is included. As a high-level generalization, however, it is safe to say that all of them question or reject the still-prevailing image of Barth as essentially a conservative dogmatist. More specifically, most of them take exception to the long-prevailing notion that Barth discarded dialectical thinking in his belated embrace of an objectivistic dogmatic method.

Mechels, Beintker, and Spieckermann variously broke down the dialectic-to-analogy schematism that dominated Barthian interpretation under von Balthasar's and Torrance's influence. In the mid-1980s, Spieckermann and Beintker independently developed an argument, first outlined by Mechels in 1974, that Barth already used analogical modes of argument in his crisis theology writings and that he continued to employ dialectical arguments in the *Church Dogmatics.* To a similar effect, though more cautiously, Jüngel contended in the early 1980s that the only decisive break in Barth's theology was away from theological liberalism during World War I. In a different vein, Rendtorff argued in 1972 that Barth's dogmatic theology should not be viewed as a form of updated orthodoxy, but rather as a form of liberal theology that sought to free the divine object of theology from ecclesiastical and academic control. During the same period, Friedrich-Wilhelm Marquardt set off an interpretive controversy of a different kind by contending that Barth's lifelong commitment to democratic socialism and his various engagements with pressing political issues, especially the Cold War, were crucially defining aspects of his theological position.[4]

In recent years numerous North American and British theologians have amplified all of these arguments and proposed new lines of interpretive inquiry. McCormack argues that Barth's adoption of a divine object-oriented critical realist epistemology was the key to his theological development and that Barth's later work remained a type of dialectical theology. Various postliberal narrativist theologians point to Barth's later emphasis on narrative interpretation as evidence against the picture of Barthianism as a form of objectivizing dogmatism. One influential figure in this school of interpretation, Hunsinger, contends that Barth's employment of multiple interwoven patterns of thought falsifies all essentialist readings of his theology. Moving beyond the narrativist claim that Barth was the key forerunner of a nonfoundationalist approach to theology, interpreters such as Lowe, Ward, and Johnson play up the postmodern or even deconstructionist implications of Barth's dialecticism, rhetorical pluralism, and epistemological antifoundationalism.

The present work cuts across all of these readings. It contains numerous points of difference with Jüngel's neoorthodox-leaning interpretation of Barthian theology, but it shares Jüngel's emphasis on Barthianism as a theology of the Word of God. It contains numerous points of agreement with McCormack, but it differs from McCormack on important points of emphasis and interpretation. I shall argue that the key to the possibility and character of Barth's theology was his commitment to the primacy of the Spirit-illuminated Word. My emphasis on Barth's epistemological nonfoundationalism, his dialecticism, and his insistence on doing theology without weapons all flow from this fundamental interpretive assertion. I shall argue that Barth understood even his controversial turn to church dogma in the mid-1920s as an outgrowth of his determination to recover and express the spiritual depth of the inscripturated Word.

For the same reason that Barth took a wary attitude toward philosophy, I am wary of attributing a systematic theory of religious knowledge to Barth. McCormack's recent attempt to give such a systematic coherence to Barth's thinking gets most of the pieces right, but I believe that it does not take with sufficient seriousness Barth's insistence that the Spirit-illuminated Word of Christ subverts and transcends the authority of all theoretical systems, philosophical categories, and historical judgments. In the process of recounting how Barth struggled to recover the voice and authority of the Word for theology in the wake of the discrediting of German liberal theology, the present work will maintain that it was Barth's reworking of the Herrmannian themes of revelation as self-revealing and self-authenticating that gave the Barthian revolt its immense spiritual power.

With equal emphasis I shall argue that the implications of these themes also made Barthianism a decidedly curious phenomenon. The irony of Barth's legacy is that his towering stature and achievements persuaded relatively few theologians to follow his way of doing theology. No theological movement in Christian history has effected a more dramatic transformation of its inherited intellectual and spiritual landscape than the movement that Barth set into motion in the early 1920s. Even at the height of his influence in the late 1930s, however, only a relative handful of theologians embraced Barth's thoroughgoing Herrmannianism of the Word. Barth was reasonably sincere in not wanting followers who merely adopted his positions on matters of theological interpretation, but he did try to convince theologians to adopt his way of doing theology. At the height of his field-dominating stature in 1938, when he was already being compared to Thomas Aquinas and Augustine as a theological Father of the church, Barth acknowledged that his lifework appeared to lack "a certain accumulative power" and that it even seemed to contain "a certain explosive" effect.[5] The middle chapters of the present work will examine his debates with Bultmann, Brunner, Tillich, Reinhold Niebuhr, Bonhoeffer, and others to discern how his theology could be enormously influential and yet lack accumulative influence at the same time.

"NEOORTHODOXY" AS SIGNIFIER AND PROBLEM

To make a case for the continuing significance of Barth's dialectic of the self-authenticating Word is to fight off the lingering odor and weight of a long-dominant neoorthodoxy. One way to deal with this problem is to claim that Barth's theology actually had very little to do with the neoorthodox movement or even the self-described Barthian tradition within it. Some of the best recent work on Barth's theology takes this tack. McCormack sweepingly dismisses what he calls "the myth of the neo-orthodox Barth," while Hunsinger disposes of several neoorthodox interpretations of Barth before putting forth his own "multiple pattern" reading of Barth's dialectic.[6] For the most part my reading of Barth's relation to neoorthodoxy is congruent with the main arguments presented by McCormack and Hunsinger. I share their conviction that Barth's theology was more complex, more dialectical, and far less domesticated than much of the Barthian literature produced by neoorthodox theologians. This judgment is heightened in the present work by my emphasis that Barth pursued theology without weapons or foundations as church-embedded exegesis of the Word. Barth's vigorous reworking of themes that he inherited from Wilhelm Herrmann made his theology significantly different from the Barthianism of the midcentury neoorthodox establishment. The closing section of Chapter five contains a pointed critique to this effect, a critique of the kind of neoorthodox Barthianism represented by Thomas Torrance.

At the same time I believe that the project of seeking to gain a new hearing for Barth's approach to theology, or at least for some aspect of it, is inescapably bound up with the broader problem of neoorthodoxy. As I shall emphasize in Chapter five, Barth's theology did contain crucially-defining, orthodox doctrinal elements that he derived from his studies of patristic theology and the dogmatic systems of Reformed and Lutheran orthodoxy. As a descriptive signifier, "neoorthodoxy" was too constricted and connotatively misleading to serve as a sufficient name for Barth's approach to theology, but it did convey the truism that Barth's theology blended modern and classical orthodox elements. More pertinently to the interpretive focus of the present study, it is not possible to extricate Barth's position from the legacy of the Biblical Theology movement or related neoorthodox theologies without acknowledging that, at the height of their influence, these theologies were widely perceived as having saved and reformulated the most credible aspects of Barth's dogmatic project. Neoorthodoxy derived from the Barthian revolt and built a substantial theological tradition upon it. In several of its forms, it made a serious claim to having carried out the indispensable aspects of Barth's teaching. In its chief currents it differed from Barthian teaching mainly on those points on which Barth is still widely rejected today.

Neoorthodoxy is usually defined as the theology of the schools of Barth and Brunner, and sometimes Niebuhr, which reasserted the principles of Reformation teaching in modern forms. This conventional definition suffices for the present work as long as one bears in mind that most neoorthodox theologians took modern forms for granted and that most of them took their "orthodox" elements from Luther and Calvin, not from later Protestant orthodoxy. The dialectical "but" was indispensable to neoorthodox rhetoric. Barth recovered the classical Reformationist language of sin, redemption, transcendence, and grace for Protestant theology, but the movement that his work inspired was not a mere throwback to any premodern tradition. It made traditional-sounding appeals to the Word of God and the authority of scripture, but it redefined the nature of these appeals in distinctively modern terms. Barth replaced the liberal emphasis on natural reason and experience with an orthodox-sounding appeal to revelation, but his conception of revelation derived from the distinctively modern tradition of Hegelian idealism. It was from G. W. F. Hegel, the nineteenth-century tradition of right-Hegelian theology, and more directly, Herrmann, that Barth adopted the idea of revelation as non-propositional divine *self*-revelation.[7]

After Barth cut his ties to the dialectical theology movement (for reasons that this study will examine closely), "neoorthodoxy" became the identifying term for the theological orientation that Barth, Brunner, Bultmann, and Reinhold Niebuhr were said to represent. In 1958, Langdon Gilkey aptly described neoorthodoxy as "a new synthesis of two widely divergent interpretations of the Christian religion, that of the Reformation and that of nineteenth-century liberalism."[8] This definition was better than much of the literature that second-generation neoorthodoxy produced. Unlike many of his liberal-bashing neoorthodox colleagues, Gilkey recognized that neoorthodoxy was a type of liberal modernist theology. Like many of his American and British counterparts, however, he conceived neoorthodoxy as a blend of Brunner, Niebuhr, and Tillich. Second-generation neoorthodoxy in England and the United States derived only indirectly from Barth, whose dogmatics were presumed to be impossible to understand and (often) not worth the effort. The prevailing image of Barth, even among many followers of Brunner and Niebuhr, was that of a dogmatizing scholastic who refused to defend the truth of Christian teaching.

In this reading, Barth's theology represented a step back from the gains of a liberal tradition informed by modern science, historical criticism, and Enlightenment philosophy. Liberal theology established credible starting points for its theorizing by appealing variously to moral reason (as in Immanuel Kant) or religious experience (as in Friedrich Schleiermacher) or metaphysical reason (as in Hegel) or faith-informed historicism (as in Adolf von Harnack). By contrast, Barth overturned all appeals to the authority of experience or reason. His critics protested that by appealing exclusively to the self-authenticating authority of a non-objective divine Word, Barth established a secure ground for theological affirmations at the cost of consigning theology to a religious never-never land of critically immunized revelation. Barth's methodological fideism left theology without any basis on which it could defend its claims or compare its claims to those of rival traditions.

This verdict has been pressed by theologians as different as Charles Raven, Gordon Clark, Wolfhart Pannenberg, and David Tracy over the past century.[9] More significant for the present study is the fact that most of the major architects of what came to be called neoorthodoxy rendered some variation of the same judgment. From Brunner to Thomas Torrance, neo-orthodox theologians sought to evade the charge of revelational positivism or fideism by establishing stronger philosophical or historical grounds for Christian claims than Barth's approach allowed. Brunner embraced an existential epistemology and a program of apologetic "eristics," Gogarten developed a grounding "states of life" theophilosophy, Bultmann translated demythologized Christian claims into the language of Heideggerian existentialism, Tillich constructed a neo-Protestant religious ontology, Reinhold Niebuhr insisted that the truth in Christian myth must be validated in experience against the claims of other religious traditions, and various leaders of the Biblical Theology movement appealed to the foundational historicity of the "mighty acts of God" in scripture. Though Torrance otherwise epitomizes the Barthian stream of theological neoorthodoxy, even he argues that Barth's objectivism properly leads to Torrance's own science-claiming epistemological realism and natural theology.

In each of these cases, some of the offense was drained from Barth's uncompromising commitment to the way of faith and revelation alone. Niebuhr and Tillich repeatedly charged that Barth's "neo-supernaturalist" theology was merely a sophisticated form of the old Protestant dogmatism.[10] In most of its forms, neoorthodoxy took on the appearance of being more relevant, better established, and easier to understand than Barth's massive scholastic tomes. By the late 1950s, at the height of its theological dominance, mainstream neoorthodoxy in England and the United States generally acknowledged its debts to Barth only in passing. Neoorthodoxy was a compound of Brunner's and Tillich's theologies, Niebuhr's emphasis on sin and political realism, and the biblical scholarship of the Biblical Theology movement, or, more radically, the Bultmannian school. These sources appeared to be more than enough to sustain what seemed like a triumphant religious movement. In Germany, theologians such as Hermann Diem, Otto Weber, and Helmut Thielicke gave more attention to Barth than their Anglo-American counterparts, but like such counterparts as Alan Richardson, William Hordern, and Paul Minear, they expressed the generational confidence that a dominant "New Reformationist" tradition had established a secure basis by improving upon its Barthian origins.[11] Young theologians such as Gilkey and William Hamilton aggressively promoted neoorthodoxy while feeling little or no compulsion to read Barth.[12]

By committing itself to various philosophical fads and a complex of claims about the historicity of the biblical "acts of God," an ascending neoorthodox movement opened itself to the possibility of devastating refutation. Virtually all of the movement's major theologians routinely attacked the liberal tradition for giving up the substance of Christian faith and hope. Brunner, both Niebuhrs, and the leaders of the Biblical Theology movement repeatedly charged that liberal Protestantism was fatally compromised by its devotion to the culture of modernity. Biblical Theology leaders such as G. Ernest Wright, H. H. Rowley, and Alan Richardson claimed that their movement recovered the spirit and historically-grounded foundation of authentic biblical faith. In the early 1960s, these claims were subjected to withering criticism by Gilkey, James Barr, and several others. Gilkey pressed the Biblical Theologians to explain exactly how their interpretations of biblical  narrative differed in principle from the historiocriticism of liberal scholarship. Barr dismantled Biblical Theology claims about the distinctiveness of Hebrew thought patterns and semantics.[13]

The force of these critiques and the pressure from a secularizing trend in American culture brought about a remarkably swift end to the Biblical Theology movement. An imposing intellectual and institutional structure crashed to the ground, marking the end of the reign of neoorthodox biblical scholarship and, soon afterward, the end of neoorthodox domination in theology as well. Various offshoots of the neoorthodox episode secured a place in a fragmented theological spectrum, but the epigones of Barth, Bultmann, Wright, and the Niebuhrs found themselves increasingly marginalized by the emergence of "death of God" theologies and the first wave of liberation theologies. Some of these thinkers recycled the slogans of crisis theology or Biblical Theology; some of them (notably Hamilton) became God-is-dead theologians; some made links to the new liberationist movements; some (notably Gilkey) tried to make theology make sense to a secular-drifting culture by returning to a Schleiermacher-style phenomenology of religious experience. Liberation theology never achieved the kind of domination over the fields of theology, ethics, and biblical scholarship that neoorthodoxy attained at midcentury, but by the mid-1970s the ascendancy of liberationism did make the neoorthodox generation look very stodgy and compromised indeed.

Niebuhr was routinely pilloried by liberationists as an apologist for the

Cold War capitalist establishment; Biblical Theology was criticized for its provincialism and religious conservatism; Brunner's once-influential works were simply ignored. Barth's theology generally received more respectful treatment in the new German "hope theologies" of Jürgen Moltmann and Wolfhart Pannenberg, but, even here, sizable pieces of the passing neoorthodox establishment were sharply criticized. Moltmann maintained what he later called "at best, a highly problematic" intellectual relationship to Barth.[14] He blasted the Bultmannian and more conservative neoorthodox schools for their individualism and political conformism, while Pannenberg denounced Barth and most neoorthodox thinkers for failing to rationally defend Christian truth claims. Neoorthodoxy acquired a distinct odor along the way. Its faint attic smell became offensive to all manner of liberationists, liberals, futurist theologians, and others who promoted their alternatives to it.

Today this impression lingers among many theologians who otherwise celebrate the pluralization of theology in a postmodern cultural context. As the last perspective to attain anything like a hegemonic position over the field of Christian theology, neoorthodoxy continues to elicit a distinctive wariness or sense of threat among many theologians. To a theological generation that prizes multicultural difference and diversity above all other values, the very term carries unattractive associations. The neoorthodox model is remembered chiefly as the last theologically serious attempt to shore up a declining modern Protestant establishment. It imposed a layer of dogmatic asphalt over a disintegrating, mainline cultural religion (to use Sidney Ahlstrom's image), but today the Protestant churches in Europe are nearly empty and in North America the formerly mainline churches are struggling to sustain even a small public role in the margins of the dominant culture.[15]

All of this historical legacy stands in the way of gaining a new hearing for whatever pertinent truth the theology of Karl Barth may be said to contain for contemporary theology. I have no interest in defending the kind of neoorthodoxy that paved a decomposing Christendom with asphalt. I am not a Barthian or an advocate of any existing form of neoorthodoxy. My reasons for not being a Barthian begin with Barth's antifeminism, his doctrinal dogmatism on several subjects, his frequently demeaning attacks on his theological opponents, and his complete disinterest in interreligious dialogue.[16] My reasons for not identifying with neoorthodoxy begin with the stigmatizing rhetoric that neoorthodoxy inherited from Barth and its presumption in claiming a secure doctrinal basis apart from theological liberalism. The major theorists of neoorthodoxy and their epigones exaggerated their break from theological liberalism. Most of them made claims to a qualitative alternative while failing to acknowledge that their key assumptions derived from the liberal tradition. They brushed off occasional warnings that their attacks on liberalism could be self-devouring. On various occasions during the 1930s and afterward, Wilhelm Pauck cautioned that orthodox theologies give rise only to more orthodoxies. He urged his neoorthodox and liberal colleagues to recognize that neoorthodoxy was conceivable only as a child of theological liberalism. With rare discernment, he perceived that even Barth remained deeply indebted to his liberal past.[17] But the chief theorists of first- and second-generation neoorthodoxy invested too much significance in their antiliberal polemics to acknowledge the significance of their own liberalism. As advocates of a triumphant theological perspective, many of them also fell into the very trap of cultural accommodation that they found so devitalizing in the liberal tradition.

On both counts, their theologies tended to be less coherent than those of their liberal opponents. Liberal theology was clear about its fundamental principles and its desire to enhance the cultural prestige of Christianity. From Schleiermacher onward, liberals sought to defend religion from its cultured despisers by explaining very clearly which aspects of traditional Christianity they did not take literally. By contrast, neoorthodox thinkers rarely acknowledged that their own forms of Christendom theology were fueled by similar concerns about the cultural status of Christianity and the disciplinary status of theology. More importantly, they denounced liberal biblical scholarship while practicing an inconsistent form of it. These weaknesses exposed neoorthodoxy to pulverizing criticism in the early 1960s and abruptly ended its theological preeminence.

For most of the past generation, the neoorthodox model has appeared exhausted. Various surveys of theological options have barely mentioned neoorthodoxy; major neoorthodox works by Torrance and Eberhard Jüngel have received little attention. Many theologians concur with David Tracy that neoorthodoxy achieved its religious gains by refusing to submit Christian claims to critical analysis.[18] Neoorthodoxy was too comfortable with the language of paradox and mystery, Tracy judges. It was especially too inclined to speak of God as ineffable mystery. Like many others, Tracy calls for a new revisionist model that would make theology more credible to a pluralized and increasingly secular academic culture. He warns that theology will never be taken seriously again, in the modern university, if theologians make their discipline impervious to outside criticism. Neoorthodoxy was content to exploit the existential power of its critically-untouchable symbols, he explains, but what is needed is a revisionist philosophical theology that critically correlates Christian texts with common human experience and language. For all of its undoubted religious power, the model of assertion that neoorthodoxy inherited from Barth reduced theology to the language of revealed mystery.[19]

This is a plausible objection to the project of reconsideration that I am proposing. Despite their various attempts to avert this fate, the theologians of modern neoorthodoxy were apparently fated to share, with Barth, the dismissive charge of "revelational positivism." From his wartime Nazi prison cell, Dietrich Bonhoeffer famously protested that Barth's "revelational positivism" reduced theology to a "like it or lump it" enterprise.[20] Many interpreters before and after Bonhoeffer have similarly charged that Barth placed unbelievable teachings beyond critical reach and compelled assent to them.

I shall argue that in the narrow sense of its meaning, however, the charge of *Offenbarungspositivismus* does not do justice to the way Barth argued theologically. For all of his situational peculiarities in speaking to a theological crisis that is not our crisis, Barth thought about Christianity in a way that often remarkably prefigured the insights of Thomas Kuhn, Alasdair MacIntyre, and various postmodern critics of the Enlightenment quest for universal reason.[21] The postmodern thesis that all theoretical and practical reasoning occurs within some intellectual tradition became a staple of neoorthodox teaching through Barth's influence. I shall argue that this recognition of the tradition-dependent character of reason made Barthian theology more critically conscious in a crucial sense than its various critics acknowedged. It also makes Barth's dialectic of the Word instructive to those who seek to discern the meaning of Christian faith under postmodern conditions.

Like contemporary postmodernists, Barth rejected every kind of philosophical and historical foundationalism. He refused to reduce God to one element of a system. He insisted that Christian theology can be healthy and free only if it remains open to a multiplicity of philosophies, worldviews, and forms of language. For many years his arguments on these themes were widely read as evidence of his reactionary positivism or dogmatism, but these arguments read very differently if one does not presume that Christian claims must be judged by a modernist ideal of disinterested reason. When most theologians were trying to make theology respectable by accommodating Christianity to modernist cultural trends, Barth warned that this strategy compromised the truth of the gospel and elevated modernist theorizing to an unwarranted position of authority. He insisted that theologians should not tie the gospel to any worldview or philosophy or political ideology.

The crisis of modernity that Barth's early theology warned against is our inheritance. We live in a time that has lost its shared religious and even its shared secular memories and meanings. One symptom of the sense of moral confusion and disorder that pervades our culture is the utter fragmentation of contemporary theology. In recent years the high tide of liberation theology as a religious movement has clearly passed, but no alternative vision has captured the imagination or even the attention of a critical mass of religious thinkers. In this situation, the possibility of a new kind of neoorthodoxy is getting a second look by a small but wide-ranging assortment of theologians. Many of them are rereading Barth or the writings of Yale-school "postliberals" or both.[22] Some of them emphasize the connections between Barthian and postmodern antifoundationalism.

A word of caution about this project is needed at the outset. I believe it would be a new form of the modernist mistake to present some kind of "new neoorthodoxy" merely as the solution to a postmodernist problem. The appropriate test of Christian theology is not whether it conforms to or confirms any independent theory of reality, but whether it makes present the narrated Word of Christ in all of its sovereign freedom. The postmodern turn in our culture provides a novel opening for a reconsideration of the best insights of the Barthian and neoorthodox projects, but postmodernism as a philosophy warrants no more regard as the criterion of Christian truth than existentialism, Enlightenment rationalism, or Platonic idealism. This was a defining Barthian theme. In crucial respects it was a theme that Barth appropriated from his teacher, Wilhelm Herrmann. Barth's dialectic of the open Word merits our reconsideration chiefly because he struggled to be true to this theme and to work out its implications. This book is a narrative-style reconsideration of that project.

I shall argue that the problem of neoorthodoxy as a school is exemplified by the limitations of the Biblical Theology movement and by the ways that Barth's theological legacy was carried out by some of his ostensibly closest followers. In both cases the neoorthodox tendency was conservative and domesticating. Neoorthodox theologians turned Barth's dialectical rhetoric of freedom and grace into a school theology containing all manner of historical foundations, apologetic stopgaps, and claims to scientific objectivity. Some of them justified these strategies by exaggerating the objectivizing turn in Barth's later theology. Without denying that Barth did add certain objectivizing elements to his later theology—sometimes rightly—I shall argue that his theological vision was always more subversive, open, and dialectical than the school-movement he inspired. At the same time, one reason that neoorthodoxy became a rather stodgy school was that Barth's theology was too biblicist and dogmatic. The next generational attempt to refigure Word and Spirit must take more from Barth than from his neoorthodox followers and critics, but it must also be open to movements of the Spirit that Barth's house of authority shut out.

1

TWILIGHT OF THE GODS

Liberal Theology and the Barthian Revolt

Near the end of his last seminar as a university professor at Harvard University, Paul Tillich told his students that the best way to become a theologian is to learn the best available theological system "inside and out," and then turn against it. Certainly that is how the Barthian "crisis theology" movement came into being. Karl Barth was the son of a conservative Reformed pastor and theological professor at the University of Berne, Fritz Barth, but in the early years of the twentieth century the younger Barth converted to the liberalism of his teachers at Berlin and Marburg. He later described the experience as a spiritual innoculation. "One of the best remedies against liberal theology and other kinds of bad theology is to take them in bucketsful," he explained. "On the other hand, all attempts to withhold them by stratagem or force only causes people to fall for them even more strongly, with a kind of persecution complex."[1]

Barth's determination to study the wrong kind of theology occurred during the high tide of German theological liberalism. At the turn of the century the liberal descendants of Friedrich Schleiermacher and Albrecht Ritschl controlled most of the prestigious theological chairs at German universities. From his position as rector of the University of Berlin, Adolf von Harnack towered over the fields of church history, history of doctrine, and historical theology. He also served as director-general of the Royal Library and as a close advisor to Kaiser Wilhelm II. His best-selling lectures on the essence of Christianity epitomized for many the triumph of the liberal historicist approach to theology.[2] In the winter semester of 1906–1907, one of his students was young Karl Barth.

With deep admiration Barth listened to Harnack lecture on the history of dogma. He joined Harnack's seminar on early church history and listened to Herman Gunkel's lectures on Old Testament theology with nearly equal excitement. The possibility of understanding Christianity in terms of the history of religion was, at first, intoxicating to him. He also bought and treasured his first copies of Wilhelm Herrmann's *Ethik* and Schleiermacher's *Über die Religion.* By the time that he returned to the University of Berne the following semester, his father was alarmed at his enthusiasm for liberal theology, especially liberal historicism. Fritz Barth's idea of a good theological school was Halle or Greifswald. His own seminary at Berne had been founded in 1876 to combat the University of Berne's commitment to liberal theology. Following the Continental custom of attending several universities, Karl wanted to study next at Marburg, but his father vehemently refused. They settled on Tübingen, where the younger Barth could get a strong dose of positive theology from Adolf Schlatter.

Barth soon hated Tübingen, however. He found Schlatter evasive and irritating. He sneered at Schlatter's conservatism and despaired that Tübingen was a "low dive" and a "wretched hole." Even the systematized Ritschlian liberalism of Theodor Häring (a friend of his father's) was too dogmatic for him. He pleaded for the opportunity to study at Marburg, where Herrmann taught theology and Adolf Jülicher lectured on New Testament theology and criticism. Finally Fritz Barth relented and saved his son from a persecution complex. The younger Barth went to Marburg and found the guide he was looking for.[3]

Herrmann was a prominent former disciple of Ritschl's who appealed to the "inner life of Jesus" as the historical ground of faith. He told his students that the first four speeches in Schleiermacher's *Speeches on Religion* were the most important texts to have been written since the closing of the New Testament canon. Having resolved at Berlin to follow Schleiermacher's liberal experientialism "blindly all along the line," Barth found a home at Marburg. Harnack had assured him that liberal theology recovered the simple and beautiful religion of Jesus; Herrmann convinced him that liberal theology retained the essential gospel faith through its insistence that the living Christ could be known personally. At Marburg, Barth found the greatest contentment and inspiration of his student career. "Herrmann was *the* theological teacher of my student years," he later recalled, adding elsewhere, "I absorbed Herrmann through every pore."[4]

RESISTING HISTORICISM: HERRMANN AND THE RITSCHLIAN SCHOOL

To a significant degree this was a defensive resort. Herrmann and Harnack were products of the dominant Ritschlian school of liberal theology, but in the closing years of the nineteenth century an offshoot of the Ritschlian school began to compete for influence and authority. This was the *Religionsgeschichtliche Schule* led by Ernst Troeltsch. A former student and disciple of Ritschl's, Troeltsch argued that the historicism of the mainstream Ritschlian school was compromised by its dogmatic Christian assumptions. Though he allowed that Ritschl and Harnack practiced a form of historical criticism, he contended that their historical arguments were firmly controlled by their fundamental belief in the superiority of Christianity.

This critical judgment challenged the Ritschlian school at its core. Harnack and other Ritschlians claimed to provide a critical historical foundation for dogmatic Christian teaching, but Troeltsch's school countered that true historicism is not compatible with any religious claim to dogmatic absoluteness or finality.[5] To understand Christianity historically is to locate its emergence within the widest possible context of religious history, they argued. A truly critical historiocriticism must pay attention not only to factors that make Christianity distinctive, but especially to aspects of Christian myth and ritual that are common to other religious traditions. In its early years the history of religions school was led by Troeltsch, Gunkel, William Wrede, Wilhelm Bousset, and Johannes Weiss. Later converts to its approach included Julius Wellhausen, Rudolf Otto, Ulrich von Wilamowitz-Moellendorff, and Albrecht Dieterich.[6] By 1897 the church-oriented Ritschlians and the insurgent *Religionsgeschichtliche* group were factional rivals, as Gustav Ecke documented in his book of that year, *Die theologische Schule Albrecht Ritschls.* The Ritschlian school produced other factional disputes as well, as Ecke observed, but this one challenged Ritschlian theology in its fundamental, gospel-centered character.[7]

In the same year Troeltsch observed with a tinge of boasting that "the rise of a comparative history of religion has shaken the Christian faith more deeply than anything else."[8] His school of interpreters argued that cult and liturgy (not theology) form the experiential center of every religious tradition. They taught that religions can be understood scientifically only if they are examined by historiocritical criteria that do not belong to or derive from any particular religious tradition. They judged that most religions are syncretistic blends of various sources and traditions. Like earlier generations of mythical-school theorists, but with the authority of a more comprehensive and purportedly scientific approach to religion, they argued that Christian scripture is pervaded with mythical teaching and narrative.[9]

Both Barth and Rudolf Bultmann studied at Berlin and Marburg during the ascendancy of this intellectual movement. Though Bultmann adopted much of the movement's intellectual apparatus in his historiocritical scholarship, both of them looked for a theological alternative within liberalism that put a brake on the relativizing effects of *Religionsgeschichtliche* criticism. In other words, both of them were well suited to become Herrmann's disciples. For most of the foregoing century liberal theologians had claimed that historical criticism was their friend, but with the emergence of a Ritschlian offshoot that lurched all the way to a thoroughgoing historicism, some liberals questioned whether their tradition had not ceded too much authority to historiocritical reason in the first place.

Under Herrmann's influence, Barth became one of them. As a student at Marburg he could see that despite Harnack's unmatched prestige and scholarly accomplishments, the history of religions school was surpassing Ritschl's church-oriented followers. With impressive, if troubling, plausibility, the *Religionsgeschichtliche* scholars claimed that they were carrying out the logical implications of the Tübingen-school historical approach to religion in which Ritschl was trained. In the late 1890s, their movement gained effective control over the flagship journal of German theological liberalism, *Die Christliche*

Welt, which had been a stronghold of the Ritschlian school.[10] The prospect of a triumphant historical relativism in theology drove Barth to embrace Herrmann's alternative to it. He later recalled that the *Religionsgeschichtliche* standpoint was never a possibility for him. "Troeltsch was only an onlooker, not a religious thinker," he explained. "Herrmann was better; and Herrmann and Troeltsch were always at swords' points."[11] From Herrmann he drew confidence that Christian theology had its own disciplinary work to do.

Herrmann was the son of an evangelical Prussian pastor from Melkow. He studied under Julius Müller at Halle, where he also became personal secretary to the legendary neopietist theologian and preacher Friedrich August G. Tholuck. At Tholuck's home he first met Martin Kähler and also met Ritschl, whose close associate he became. At the height of Ritschl's theological influence in the late 1870s, Herrmann was his prize disciple. In effect, he was the founder of the Ritschlian school. Through his early writings and personal influence, he significantly influenced Ritschl's later thinking. By the time that Barth became his student at Marburg, however, Herrmann represented to him not only the possibility of a serious alternative to Troeltsch, but also to Ritschl.[12]

Herrmann's early writings focused on the role of metaphysics in theology. *Die Metaphysik in der Theologie* (1876) and *Die Religion im Verhältnis zum Welterkennen und zur Sittlichkeit* (1879) criticized the variable tendency within Catholicism, Protestant orthodoxy, and theological liberalism to make theology dependent on metaphysical arguments. Against the often-implicit assumption that theologians must ground their religious statements in some kind of metaphysical system, Herrmann contended that metaphysical reasoning is not a way into true religion but rather a way of evading or losing the life of faith that constitutes true religion.[13]

This argument became a touchstone of the Ritschlian school, though it was Herrmann, and not Ritschl, who first made a sustained neo-Kantian case for it. By the early 1870s, Ritschl's creative blend of Tübingen-school historicism and neo-Kantian moralism had made him the dominant figure in Continental Protestant theology, a stature that was secured in 1874 by the completion of his three volume magnum opus, *Die christliche Lehre von der Rechtfertigung und Versöhnung.* Along neo-Kantian lines, he argued that religious knowledge belongs to the realm of value judgments and that the heart and goal of true religion is the attainment of the highest possible good. He taught that true knowledge of this good as defined by Christianity is attainable through historical critical research.[14]

In the 1870s, Ritschl's rise to a position of preeminent influence in Protestant theology made him a prominent target for defenders of various orthodoxies, especially Pietist conservatives and confessional Lutherans. His liberalism was bitterly attacked by Lutherans Christoph Ernst Luthardt (of Leipzig) and Franz Hermann Frank (of Erlangen), and by the Pietist theologian Hermann Weiss (of Tübingen). Ritschl could be short-tempered and imperious toward his followers—Herrmann later recalled that he demanded deference from them—but he was poorly suited for partisan conflict.[15] He took controversial positions on religious subjects, but tried to avoid controversy. His presumption that this was a sustainable approach to theological debate reflected, to some degree, his socially privileged status as the son of a prominent bishop. In the early 1880s, however, Herrmann and other followers convinced Ritschl that he was obliged to defend their position from outright attacks. An especially vigorous attack on one of Ritschl's close followers, Hermann Schultz, finally drove Ritschl to enter the lists against his critics.

His polemical touchstone came from Herrmann's recent writings. Herrmann had noted that virtually every critic of the Ritschlian school identified some type of metaphysical position with the Christian message. Every orthodoxy foisted a host of assumptions about the nature of reality or the propositional nature of religion onto the gospel faith. In this regard, he added, most forms of liberal theology were equally misguided. Virtually all of the recent theologies deriving from Kant, Schleiermacher, and Hegel committed Christianity to some particular theory of knowledge. Herrmann was quite careful in later years to explain what this critique did not mean, but in the early 1880s his broadsides against the prevailing theological tendency to enmesh Christianity in general theories of knowledge gave Ritschl a polemical weapon that he used less discriminately. Ritschl charged that all of the confessionalist and Pietist attacks on his theology featured an "unseemly mingling of metaphysics with revealed religion." He judged that this unseemly procedure contaminated all of the biblical exegesis on which various guardians of orthodoxy were basing their theological formulations and attacking his position. "When they allege that they surpass me in their concern for Christianity, it is only a deception which mirrors their unexamined faith in a false epistemology," he claimed.[16]

This polemic against any theological resort to metaphysics obscured Ritschl's own reliance on Kantian epistemology. Ritschl and Herrmann both assumed Immanuel Kant's account of the limitations of pure reason and the qualitative distinction between pure and practical reason. Both of them used Kantian arguments to secure an independent ground for religious claims. Following Kant, Ritschl assumed that science describes the way things are, or appear to be, while theology (as a function of moral reason) is properly about the way things should be. It followed for him that religious knowledge is never disinterested, for religion consists always of value judgments about reality. Though Ritschl and especially Herrmann held out for a higher view of the importance and integrity of theological language than Kant, they secured their claims for the independence of theology on grounds that derived from Kantian arguments.[17]

Herrmann was clearer about what this did not mean. It did not mean that theologians had no business dealing with the problems of epistemology. More precisely than Ritschl, he delineated the boundaries of philosophical theorizing for theology and acknowledged that Kant's distinctions helped him conceptualize these boundaries. His thinking on this subject was sharpened by his debates with Marburg colleagues Hermann Cohen and Paul Natorp, both of whom were neo-Kantian philosophers.[18] Kant's critiques of pure, practical, and aesthetic reason had divided the field of knowledge into the fields of science (logic), ethics, and aesthetic judgment. For Kantian theologians and philosophers, one of the crucial questions that this schematism raised for the interpretation of religion was the place of religion itself. Kant reduced religion entirely to the sphere of moral reason, but various religious thinkers otherwise influenced by Kant provided different accounts of the nature of religious knowledge. Schleiermacher maintained that religious feeling *(Gefühl)* is a deeper aspect of human experience than any kind of reason or even sensation. True religion is rooted in a deep prereflective awareness of reality that underlies all thought and sensation, he proposed. Natorp defended a reformulation of this approach, while Cohen followed Kant in relegating religion to the sphere of moral reason.[19]

Insofar as Kantian philosophy sought to account for the kinds of knowledge attained in natural science, ethics, and aesthetic judgment, Herrmann was a straightforward neo-Kantian. Though he pressed Ritschl to affirm the independence of theology from every kind of metaphysics, his own commitment to a neo-Kantian epistemology within its appropriate boundaries was clearer and stronger than Ritschl's. More importantly, his thinking was also less Kantian than Ritschl's in this crucial respect. Ritschl polemicized against the mingling of metaphysics with theology without clarifying the boundaries of his own considerable dependence on Kantian philosophy. Herrmann adopted an outright Kantian account of the kinds of knowledge knowable to philosophy while insisting that the reality known to true religion is another kind of knowledge. Kantian philosophy saved a place for religion by reducing faith to a postulate of morality, but this strategy rendered the reality known to religious faith as an object of human creation.[20]

This is exactly the outcome that theology must never endorse, Herrmann contended. To incorporate religion into a general theory of knowledge is to treat being as a function of thinking. In biblical terms, it is to commit idolatry. Kant viewed religion as a postulate of moral reason, but Herrmann countered that true religion is an independent power through which a lost human being is saved by God. He did not deny that morality has a crucial role to play in the inner drama of salvation. In his *Ethik,* Herrmann affirmed that it is through morality that a lost soul comes to discover that he or she is lost. The experience of inner moral conflict is a necessary precondition for every saving encounter with Christ. But moral experience itself is not saving, he cautioned. We are saved by faith, as Martin Luther taught, not by moral achievement. Through faith we learn that God is unique, mysterious, and transcendent. Because the reality known to true faith is knowable only to faith, and not to any other kind of cognition, the religious way and kind of knowing is fundamentally different from all other forms of knowledge. The crucial reason that metaphysics must be eliminated from theology, he taught, is that the kind of knowing that occurs in science and logic "absolutely does not reach to the reality of our God." Since philosophy and science have no access to divine reality, theology must not seek any kind of support from these disciplines or any other discipline.[21]

Long after he gave up on theological liberalism, Barth lauded this aspect of Herrmann's thinking as his greatest contribution to theology. "Herrmann was certainly at his best when he was engaged in battle against apologetics, both the old and the new, the modest and the arrogant," he remarked. "His theological science was definitely determined through his knowledge of what the ancients called 'autopistia,' that is by the conviction of Christian truth as based on itself. This knowledge is rat-poison to all intellectualizing subtleties in theology."[22] At Marburg some of his classmates dismissed Herrmann's courses as "advanced confirmation instruction," but Barth's desire to become a theologian was confirmed by Herrmann's warm-hearted devotion to Christ and by his insistence that Christian truth requires no basis outside itself. Herrmann was not ashamed of the gospel and not impressed with outside criticisms of its truth.

This insistence on the independence and self-authenticating character of revelational experience played a crucial role in Barth's later theology, but it was a related issue that played a stronger decisive role in attracting him to Herrmann's version of liberal Protestantism in the first place. This was the slippery question of what it means to affirm the historical character of Christian truth. Barth later recalled that, during his career as a theology student, German theology was fixated on the challenges posed by the *Religionsgeschichtliche Schule.* Were critical theologians obliged to adopt Troeltsch's historicizing relativism? One of Troeltsch's favorite maxims was that as soon as one concedes an inch to historical criticism, it takes a mile. Barth worried that because Ritschl and Harnack conceded much more than an inch to historical criticism, their theologies were vulnerable to being devoured by it. On all other counts he was a convinced liberal. He thought he had acquired a sufficient theological foundation by virtue of having studied Kant and Schleiermacher. It was only the devouring logic of recent liberal historicism that he resisted. "The name of Troeltsch, then at the heart of our discussions, signified the limit beyond which I thought I must refuse to follow the dominant theology of the age," he explained. "In all else I was its resolute disciple."[23]

He was thus perfectly disposed to become Herrmann's disciple. Herrmann had begun his career as Ritschl's prize epigone, but in the late 1880s he began to make a prolonged and often carefully subtle turn away from Ritschl's historical orientation. Ritschl taught that Christianity is fundamentally concerned with the attainment of the highest possible good. He reasoned that the content of this good in Christianity must be derived from what he called the "apostolic circle of ideas" as established by historical critical research. The object of the constructive historical task of theology is not so much to establish what Jesus actually said or did, he reasoned. Rather, the object of historically-grounded critical theology is to establish the collective Christian experience of value that was inspired by Jesus. Ritschl's dogmatic system thus asserted, at the outset, that "it would be a mistaken purism were anyone, in this respect, to prefer the less developed statements of Jesus to the forms of apostolic thought."[24]

There is no deeper foundation of Christian belief than the apostolic circle of ideas that Jesus inspired. As the highest form of true religion, Christianity is concerned essentially with value. This theme derived from Ritschl's Kantianism, but in Ritschl's system it was blended with his Tübingen-school resolve to secure a historical basis for Christian teaching. He assumed that to call anything "historical" is to affirm that it passes the tests of historicity established by the discipline of critical history. He assured his many followers that the essence of Christian teaching is historical in precisely this sense. The reliable verdict of historical research is that the essence of Christianity is the kingdom of God as valued by the early Christian community.

Herrmann's later theology remained a variation within this approach to Christianity. Like Ritschl, he never doubted that Christianity is founded historically in what he called "the fact of Jesus." Like Ritschl, he did not invest much religious significance in the results of historical criticism pertaining to the life of the historical Jesus. What was important to Herrmann, as for Ritschl, was not the historicity of any particular details in the gospel narratives, but the historicity of Christ's redeeming and reconciling action in the life of the Christian community. Christ called people to saving faith by calling them to himself as Lord and Savior. Whatever the truth may be about the historicity of the sayings or miracles of Jesus recorded in the gospel narratives, they contended, the historicity of the deeper core of Christian faith is securely established.

Liberal theology in the Ritschlian mode insisted that Christian truth is historical by virtue of its relation to "the man Jesus," who inspired the kingdom-bearing community of value that constitutes the historical body of Christ. To Ritschl this meant that Christian faith is grounded in historical facts that are open to historical criticism and confirmed by it. Ritschl and his followers gave ultimate importance to the value of the life and teaching of Jesus. With the publication of his soon-famous work in 1886, *Der Verkehr des Christen mit Gott* (hereafter, *The Communion of the Christian with God),* Herrmann introduced a variation on this theme that eventually drove his theology into a different direction. He argued that it was not so much the history-making life and teaching of Jesus that was crucial, but rather the inner life of Jesus that is knowable only to faith. To call Christianity "historical" is not to claim that Christian faith is founded on historical facts confirmed by historical criticism, he reasoned. It is rather to claim that Christianity is grounded in an experience of Christ-mediated communion with God that comes about only in history. Christianity is historical in the sense that it bears the kind of spiritual reality and power that makes history. As historical reality, it can be understood only by those who participate in its effects, not by Troeltschian onlookers.[25]

ANOTHER KIND OF RITSCHLIANISM

Many of Ritschl's critics mistakenly understood him to base his theology on a version of the story of Jesus constructed by historical criticism. Some of them noted that strategies of this kind were vulnerable to being falsified by historical criticism. Virtually all of Ritschl's critics in the *Religionsgeschichtliche Schule* charged that his judgments about Christian history were controlled by dogmatic presuppositions. Herrmann wrote *The Communion of the Christian with God* partly to defend the Ritschlian school from these lines of criticism. His first edition made a strong appeal to the inspiring personality of Jesus as the basis of Christian faith. It offered numerous Ritschlian assurances about the historicity of the gospel picture of Jesus. Even the book's later editions continued to speak of Jesus as "the historical fact" through which God's love has been made known to people of faith. Herrmann's original shift from the life and teaching of Jesus to the inner life of Jesus was meant to secure a stronger basis for Ritschlian theology against its critics.

Ritschl immediately grasped that this move constituted something deeper than a mere shift in emphasis, however. He told Herrmann that he could scarcely find himself in the book. He had to read it several times before he could convince himself that it contained anything of value.[26] Over the next several years Herrmann gradually acknowledged that his position owed as much to Schleiermacher as to Ritschl. Though his thinking was also different from Schleiermacher's at crucial points, he told his students that Schleiermacher marked a new stage in the history of religion and that it was Schleiermacher who freed him from authoritarian faith. Ritschl's historical core was the kingdom-bringing effect of Christ's life and teaching, but Herrmann moved away from the very notion of a critically-established historical core. The rise of the history of religions movement spurred him to clarify his conception of a liberal alternative to it. He noted that the vigorous historicism of the *Religionsgeschichtliche Schule* restricted its advocates to mere spectator-knowledge about Christianity. Troeltsch had nothing meaningful to say about that which is most deeply constitutive of Christian truth because his method bracketed out the life of faith by which Christian truth can be known.[27]

At the same time Herrmann perceived that there was something about Ritschl's appeal to historical science that created obstacles to the proclamation and hearing of the gospel. The problem was not merely that Ritschl's appeal to history was often misunderstood. The deeper problem was that Ritschl's reliance on history took on the character of an apologetic device that diminished the power of the claim to truth made by gospel faith. At Herrmann's urging, Ritschl had finally repudiated the strategy of committing Christianity to any metaphysical system, but he was still using historical science as an apologetic crutch. He sought to bring people into Christianity by convincing them that his historical arguments about it were correct.

Herrmann's withering polemic against apologetics fueled the negative side of his distinctive alternative. His central work, *The Communion of the Christian with God,* censured all forms of Christian mysticism, orthodox confessionalism, and metaphysical theology for obscuring or detracting from the essential gospel faith. Herrmann judged that mysticism makes the historical Jesus peripheral to its quest for unmediated communion with God. He argued that orthodoxy overloads Christian teaching with legalistic doctrines that are alien to genuine Christian faith. He contended that metaphysical theologies invariably distort the gospel by turning it into an abstraction.[28]

Herrmann recognized that the historical character of Christianity posed special problems for his opposition to historical apologetics. For this reason, and because his own position retained several key Ritschlian elements, he was careful not to attack Ritschl directly in his polemic against apologetic resorts to history. He believed that his own position recognized the historical character of Christianity in a way that saved (by reformulating) the Ritschlian approach to history. He held fast to the historical "happenedness" of the "fact" of Jesus.[29] Even in the first edition of *The Communion of the Christian with God,* however, Herrmann saved his most biting remarks for those who understood Christianity as "historical facts that require faith." In the book's later editions, he heightened his polemic against all forms of historical foundationalism. He observed that many defenders of Christianity persisted in believing that the power that saves us lies in the gospel narratives about Jesus. Many gospel defenders understood the Christian message to be an invitation to believe in a list of facts about Jesus narrated in the gospels and systematized in church dogma.

But no one has ever been saved by information, Herrmann objected. What saves us is never any kind of information about Jesus, but rather the person of Jesus himself as we encounter and experience him as a fact. Put differently, it is not the historical Jesus sought by historians whom we meet through faith, but rather the living presence of the personality of Jesus. Christian faith is founded on the inner life of Jesus that becomes knowable to us by faith. It has no basis outside itself. Herrmann readily acknowledged that this conception of the "essence of faith" bore a close kinship to Pietism at its best. His theology embraced Tholuck's neopietist claim that Christianity is founded on a specific experience of sin and regeneration. Like Tholuck, he insisted that regeneration is the necessary precondition of all theological knowledge. Herrmann's view of the Pietist tradition as a whole was mostly disapproving, however. He repeatedly blasted its tendency to degenerate into some variant of doctrinal conservatism. Pietist preachers and theologians nearly always sought to provide a systematic or genetic account of the phenomenon of faith, he observed. They tried to explain the basis of faith and how faith comes about. This doctrinalizing tendency obscured the pure individuality of faith and thus betrayed the defining religious truth of Pietist Christianity.[30]

To Herrmann this was another form of the apologetic/metaphysical mistake. He spared no terms of reproach in condemning it. His alternative blended the experiential approaches of Schleiermacher and Tholuck within a revised Ritschlian framework. At the same time, like Tholuck and Ritschl,

Herrmann regarded himself as a good Lutheran. He was anxious to claim Luther for his side. He was not seeking to create a new kind of Protestantism cut off from its Reformation roots, he explained. His aim was rather to recover the deepest religious truths of the Reformation in forms of understanding that were appropriate to a modern educated sensibility. In Herrmann's case, this crucial appeal to a Reformationist heritage centered on Luther's doctrine of justification by faith.

He argued that this doctrine is the refutation of all religious creedalism and legalism. Rightly understood, it stands against every attempt to make any other doctrine essential to Christianity. It also stands against every attempt to establish or provide support for Christian faith on some basis outside the experience of faithful communion with God itself. "The basis of faith can only be what produces faith as the inward experience of pure trust," Herrmann contended. The gospel faith does not invite people to make up their minds about whether certain biblical narratives and doctrines are true. He charged that those who presented the faith in this way were "making themselves faith's executioners." In the name of defending biblical truth "they do not notice that they themselves are profaning it when they lay upon others as a ceremonial law what is in truth a gift of God's grace." By God's grace and through the mediation of Christ, Christians are brought into a saving communion of the soul with the living God. That is the gospel faith, Herrmann urged: "True religion, the blessed life of the spirit, is given to us only when we are willing to obey the simplest demand of the moral law, namely, to know ourselves."[31]

He acknowledged that Luther himself was not entirely true to this understanding of salvation by faith alone. "Luther lived in an age when the authority of Holy Scripture as the Infallible Word of God and the authority of the dogma of the ancient Church enjoyed unquestioning recognition," he allowed. "And Luther held these views, these mental possessions of his time, more firmly than any other man." If we are to be true to the deepest meaning of the Reformation, Herrmann taught, we must distinguish between Luther's Christianity and Luther's theology. Luther's theology was built on the dogmatic assumptions of medieval Catholicism, but his Christianity broke through these assumptions to disclose the creed-subverting possibility of living by faith alone through grace. Luther described the new life that is created in the Christian through God's unmerited love and grace. Though he wedded his description of this new life to the dogmatic framework of Catholic theology, "in reality they had nothing to do with each other." To take Luther seriously is not to perpetuate or revise the outmoded mental possessions of his time, Herrmann urged. It is rather to hold fast without conditions or weapons to the new life in Christ that Luther described.[32]

The same lesson applies to the New Testament. "The authority of the New Testament, which gives the needed and safe guidance to every Christian, has for its sphere something quite different from fixity of doctrine, namely, the communion of the Christian with God which is mediated through Jesus Christ." It would be ridiculous to claim that a Christian must accept "all the various doctrines uttered in the New Testament," Herrmann judged. The common notion that this is what Christianity teaches is "to put it plainly, a monstrous fiction." The authority of the New Testament is diminished whenever it is identified with New Testament doctrines. Herrmann countered that the New Testament bears genuine authority entirely by virtue of its capacity to bring Christians into communion with God: "If, however, we have learned to fix our eyes on that which God's revelation produces in the inner life of a Christian, then, in our reading of Scripture, we shall constantly meet with an authority by which we shall be safely led and wonderfully uplifted."[33]

Because Christian truth is "a secret in the soul," it cannot be handed from one person to another. It is not possible to prove to an unbeliever that Christianity is true, Herrmann argued, because Christian knowledge "is grasped in its truth only by those who occupy already the standpoint of faith." Actual communion with God is the only nourishment on which faith can be fed. To call for assent before faith is to suppose that an act of intellectual decision apart from faith can be saving. This is a ridiculous notion that has harmed Christianity greatly, Herrmann contended. One does not become a Christian by accepting doctrines about God or Christ, for the doctrines of the church are themselves expressions of a life of faith. The doctrines cannot be true for someone who is not in a faith-relation to God. "The thoughts of others who are redeemed cannot redeem me," he explained. "If I am to be saved, everything depends on my being transplanted into that inner condition of mind in which such thoughts begin to be generated in myself, and this happens only when God lifts me into communion with Himself."[34]

Herrmann insisted that this was not religious subjectivism. The Christian tradition has produced various theologies that seek to secure objectivity by appealing to reasons or evidences outside the faith-relation, but Herrmann warned that this strategy inevitably distorts the true objectivity of Christian knowledge. In faith we lay hold of a certain objective reality, he taught. This reality, the reality of God, is knowable only by grace through faith. To push aside the knowledge that is obtainable only through faith is to be cut off from that which makes reality possible. It is to be cut off from objective reality itself. "The objective reality of which we are thinking is something quite different from the thoughts of faith which are formulated in the common doctrine," he explained. "These thoughts have no power to generate the communion of the Christian with God; they are only the expression of that sense of new life which comes with such communion. But everything depends on being able clearly to grasp the objective reality which, by its sheer bulk, produces in the Christian the certainty that he is not without God in the world."[35]

What the church has traditionally called "revelation" must be redefined to conform with this understanding of salvation by faith. Revelation is precisely that which brings us into actual communion with God, Herrmann taught. It is not propositional, but occurs as event. It is not to be identified with the thoughts of faith, though faith does produce certain true thoughts. Revelation occurs as events of grace that produce true thoughts of faith. Put differently, he explained, "we can regard as the thoughts of our own faith only what comes home to us as truth within the sphere of our actual communion with God." Herrmann affirmed that this made Christian truth entirely a matter of religious experience: "All that can be the object of Christian doctrine is summed up in religious experience."[36]

His point was not that a person's confidence in God is entirely a matter of subjective feeling. What saves us is not our yearning for God, he explained, but God's actual communion with us that is mediated through Christ. This was Herrmann's reply to Ludwig Feuerbach's claim that "God" is merely the wish-being of religious desire. We know in faith that God is real because we know "the man Jesus" whom God sent to us. Herrmann counseled that when a critic objects that liberal Protestantism is subjective, "we can only suppose that for him Jesus is not objective." Herrmann took his stand on the affirmation that Jesus himself is God's Word to us: "We are Christians because, in the human Jesus, we have met with a fact whose content is incomparably richer than that of any feelings which arise within ourselves."[37]

And how is knowledge of Christ mediated to us? Herrmann cautioned that "the mere historian" is of little help. "It is a fatal error to attempt to establish the basis of faith by means of historical investigation," he warned. The basis of any true faith must be something fixed, he explained, but the results of historical research are constantly changing. In the eighteenth century G. E. Lessing famously questioned how a merely probable truth could serve as the basis for eternal happiness. Herrmann concurred that because historical reason renders merely probable verdicts, "it is impossible to attach religious conviction to a mere historical decision." Those who base their faith on the historical reliability of the biblical record are bound to look upon the enterprise of biblical criticism with considerable anxiety, but the person who knows Christ himself does not fear science or historiocriticism: "We have no such anxiety; on the contrary, we declare that the historical appearance of Jesus, in so far as it is drawn into the sphere of this attempt to establish the probable truth, cannot be a basis of faith. It is only a part of that world with which faith has to wrestle."[38]

Herrmann allowed that every reader inevitably asks whether various events actually occurred in the way that the Gospel texts describe. He granted that historical criticism rightly seeks to attain the best possible answers that historical reason can give to such questions. But the crucial problem of religious truth lies beyond the scope of historical reason, he argued. The crucial religious question is not what we make of the gospel story, but what the content of the story makes of us. "And the one thing which the Gospels will give us as an overpowering reality which allows no doubt is just the most tender part of all: it is the inner life of Jesus itself." Through faith and the fellowship of the Christian community we are led into Christ's presence and receive a picture of his inner life. The inner life of Jesus becomes part of our reality in the same way that any historical personality meaningfully enters our lives: "The inner content of any such personality is laid open only to those who become personally alive to it, and feel themselves aroused by contact with it and see their horizon widened."[39]

Thus it was not to the kingdom-bringing power of Christ's resurrection or his unique presence in the Holy Spirit that Herrmann took his stand. For him, as for liberal Protestantism generally, Christianity centered on the person of "the man Jesus" known to faith. Herrmann took this approach a step further than Ritschl and Harnack, who still proposed to use scripture and historical reason to establish the content of faith that Christians should believe. In the year before Barth arrived at Marburg, Herrmann judged that this lingering dogmatism made Ritschl the "last great representative of orthodox dogmatics." Ritschl never quite relinquished the traditional conception of scripture as a source of prescriptive ideas about the content of faith.[40]

Herrmann's alternative gave witness to a locus of divine revelation that is knowable only from within. Jesus brings us to communion with God not because of anything in particular that he said or did, but through his inner life that is knowable through the effects of its spiritual history: "Only he who yearns after an honest fulness for his own inner life can perceive the strength and fulness of that soul of Jesus, and whenever we come to see the Person of Jesus, then, under the impress of that inner life that breaks through all the veils of the story, we ask no more questions as to the trustworthiness of the Evangelists. The question whether the portrait of Jesus belongs to history or fiction is silenced in every one who learns to see it at all, for by its help he first learns to see what is the true reality of personal life."[41]

Barth later recalled that there was a ring in Herrmann's voice, "the ring of prophetic utterance." He was the prophet of religious experience expressed wholly without weapons. To Herrmann the tragedy of Roman Catholicism was epitomized in its mistaken equation of revelation with doctrine. He condemned this error ferociously, calling it "dishonest," "immoral," "seductive evil," and the like—and his students cheered when he reminded them that he wasn't speaking only of Catholicism. Barth recalled that "we listened gladly when traditionalism on the right, rationalism on the left, mysticism in the rear were thrown to the refuse dump, and when finally 'positive and liberal dogmatics' were together hurled into the same pit." By the early twentieth century, the Ritschlian school had produced an ample supply of liberal dogmatics that met this judgment. To Herrmann the more free-spirited Ritschlians owed their confidence that theology had its own thriving basis, its own work to do, and even its own professional fervor.[42]

PREACHING HERRMANNIAN THEOLOGY

Armed with these assurances, Barth entered the ministry. He was not oblivious to the problems that his acquired theology might create for him as a pastor. Barth was ordained by the church of Bern in 1908, but he spent the following year at Marburg working with Ritschlian school theologian Martin

Rade as an assistant editor of *Die Christliche Welt.* He was in no hurry to begin his parish career, for reasons that he plainly expressed in an article on "Modern Theology and Work for the Kingdom of God." Barth explained that it was "incomparably more difficult" for people like himself to move into parish ministry than it was for students from conservative institutions like Halle or Greifswald. Conservative students took the old doctrines of the church for granted when they assumed their pastoral positions, he noted. They repeated the creeds in good conscience and prescribed them as normative for others, to the approval of most parish communities.

But this approach to the language of faith was not open to graduates of modern institutions like Marburg and Heidelberg, Barth observed. The reason was that modern theology is critical in two crucial ways. It teaches a worldview of religious individualism and it compels an acceptance of the relativizing implications of historical criticism. Modern critical consciousness does not accept as valid any ethical norms that are imposed upon an individual from without, he noted. From a modern standpoint, a moral norm can obtain authenticity only if it is generated by an individual's willing activity. Barth noted that, for the same reason, modern theology is obliged to face up to historical criticism. Modern theologians accept that for historical science there are no privileged religious traditions. All religions are relative historically. For this reason all religions must be studied with the same methods of analysis. Modern theology recognizes that the New Testament must be analyzed with the same critical methods by which the historian analyzes Zoroastrianism.[43]

This is why the conservative "flight into pastoral work" is not open to the authentic student of Herrmann or Harnack, Barth explained. Harnack's children understood the historical relativity of Christianity and the impossibility of imposing genuine religious faith upon anyone. Having learned to read the Bible and the creeds with the tools of modern historiocriticism, they no longer read the same Bible and creeds as the traditionalists. Barth also had an explanation for the fact that so many graduates of Marburg and Heidelberg later became fake conservatives. The genuinely modern pastor has to negotiate a narrow personal path between "the Scylla of clericalism" and "the Charybdis of agnosticism," he observed. This path is very demanding in its spiritual and intellectual challenges, which explained why mediocre students at good institutions tended to become dogmatists after they entered the ministry. Faced with the difficulties of keeping the gospel faith alive among churchpeople who didn't want to hear about modern biblical criticism, Barth explained, those who were mere "schoolboys" in their student careers were usually tempted to throw off their education and preach like conservatives. Barth could tolerate the genuine conservatives, but he was contemptuous of those who pretended not to know better. He urged that the only way worth taking was the difficult road that negotiated between agnosticism and the old dogmatism.[44]

This exhortation was given partly to himself. It was written only a few weeks before he began to serve as *Vikar* of a German-speaking congregation in Geneva. Was there an element of wistfulness in this last declaration of his student phase, as Hans Frei later thought? Did Barth envy the conservative students for their orthodoxy and self-assuredness? Bruce McCormack rightly counters that Barth was too imbued with a sense of superiority over conservatives to feel envious of them. Barth later remarked to Rade that "the picture of the perplexed candidate who [stands] at the edge of despair . . . does not suit me."[45] There is another element in his youthful essay of 1909 that does not quite fit with Barth's later presentation of his development, however. He always described himself as a committed disciple of Herrmann who unequivocally embraced Herrmann's experiential alternative to Troeltsch's historicism. "Troeltsch's thinking was pure historicism," he explained. "I was from the beginning a systematic thinker."[46] From the beginning of his formative identification with Herrmann's theology at Marburg, he set himself against Troeltsch's historical approach to religion. Herrmann appealed to him most importantly because he offered a faith-saving alternative to Troeltsch's historical relativism.

Yet Barth described and embraced historical relativism as one of the two indispensable features of modern theology. Was this the argument of a convinced Herrmannian? In his way, Herrmann did accept historical relativism on its own terms, but he argued that for Christianity the devouring threat of historical relativism was disarmed precisely by the deeper religious reality known to faith. By seeking to ground faith in the science of history, he contended, Troeltsch negated the only possible ground of religious certainty, which is faith. Troeltsch nullified the possibility of faithful thinking by seeking to base his faith on probable arguments. Herrmann insisted that historical criticism becomes a threat to faith only when the nature of genuine faith itself is misunderstood.[47]

Young Karl Barth clearly allied himself with this side of the defining theological debate of his time. He viewed his teacher as a faith-keeping bulwark against a *Religionsgeschichtliche* onslaught. The centrality and emphasis that he gave to historical relativism in his first theological article suggests that he was not completely convinced, however, that Herrmann had disarmed the threat of historical relativism to Christian theology. Barth could have argued that one of the two distinguishing characteristics of theological liberalism was its openness to historical criticism or its use of historiocritical methods, but he lurched instead all the way to identifying liberal theology with historical *relativism.* He noted that liberal theologians like Harnack and Herrmann applied the scalpel of historical relativism to their own theologies. They recognized that liberal Protestantism represented merely one form of Christian truth among other religious forms. This willingness to face up to the relativizing implications of historical criticism is the shining strength of liberal theology, Barth affirmed, but it is also the source of the vulnerability of liberal theology. Liberal theology secured a strong ground for Christian claims by understanding religion as experience "in rigorously individual terms," he explained, but theological liberalism also opened the door to the misunderstanding that Christian truth claims were not to be taken seriously.[48] Faced with the imminent prospect of preaching to ordinary people, Barth's depiction of the religious dilemma faced by young pastors surely reflected his apprehension that Herrmann's liberalism would not wear well in most parishes.[49]

In August 1909 he moved to Geneva to begin his service as a *pasteur suffragant* at a German-speaking Reformed church pastored by Adolf Keller. Speaking from the very pulpit at which John Calvin and John Knox had preached, Barth exhorted his twentieth-century congregants to think seriously about themselves and "try to become valuable." He told them that "before I can know God, I must know myself." He assured them that "Calvin's view of the authority of the Bible would be quite wrong for us." On one occasion he devoted an entire sermon to the argument that that Sunday's text from the letter of James was written in a weak moment. "There I was, one hundred percent a Marburg product," he later recalled. "I knew everything, and knew it better than anyone else. And I entered the ministry and stumbled up the steps of Calvin's pulpit with an inexperience and awkwardness and unshakeable confidence reminiscent of the behavior of a young St. Bernard."[50]

His major piece of theological reflection during this period brought him back, not surprisingly, to the problem of the relation of faith and history. This time Barth showed no sign of doubting that Herrmann had solved the problem. Speaking to a pastors' conference in Neuchatel, he argued that the faith/history problem was solvable as long as one kept Herrmann's definitions of both terms in mind. Following Herrmann, he defined faith as experience of God or, more technically, as "an immediate awareness of the presence and efficacy of the power of life." Following Herrmann and Cohen, he set the experience of faith against all forms of knowing subsumed within the fields of pure, practical, and aesthetic knowledge. Christian theology does not rightly claim to have "knowledge" of God in any ordinary sense of the term, Barth explained. To affirm that theology is based upon faith (that is, upon experience of God) is to rule out the notion that theology should also find some basis in science or practical reason or aesthetics. It followed for Barth, as for Herrmann, that Troeltsch's program of historical theology was not theological at all. Barth allowed that *Religionsgeschichtliche* criticism had performed a vital service in debunking various attempts to establish an objective historical ground for Christian claims. By clearing the ground of various orthodox and Ritschlian halfway houses, he explained, the history of religions school had made the true choices clear. As a form of discourse that made its own religious claims, however, Troeltsch's method operated outside the boundary of Christian knowledge. The Troeltschian historicists sought to "cultivate history only as history" and, therefore, "lost sight of the revelation."[51]

Barth countered that genuinely Christian theology engages the inner life of Jesus as it shines forth in the writings of the biblical writers and a subsequent history of witnesses. Through a kind of faithful spiritual empathy, he explained, the modern Christian sees and experiences what the biblical authors saw and experienced. The point of theology is not to judge the historicity of the biblical narratives, but to come into contact with the spiritual reality to which the biblical writers gave witness. Faith is the historical moment par excellence because it stands outside the forms of understanding that assess validity in science, morality, and aesthetics. That is, in Herrmann's language explicitly, Barth asserted that the experience of faith marks the birth of the individual as an individual. It is not a quality in human nature, "something presupposed in the essence of humanity," for the Christ made known to faith transcends the human condition. But for those who live in the experience of faith, he assured, history and faith come together: "Christ outside of us=Christ in us, history=faith." Moreover, if the presence of Christ in us brings history and faith together, it must follow that the righteousness of Christ becomes my righteousness: "Christ's piety becomes my piety. He becomes I."[52]

This was the religious worldview that Barth translated into sermons for two years in Calvin's pulpit. He later reflected that his sermons did little harm, having been heard by so few people. During his time in Geneva, the women's section of the sanctuary was rarely filled on Sundays, and Barth hardly ever saw a man. Not many people came to church in the first place, and few took any interest in Barth's moralizing or in the logic of his Christmonism. He later remarked that he never regretted "having tried to foist all that historicism and individualism on the people in Geneva, but in any case, they weren't having any."[53] The experience of preaching to a mostly-empty sanctuary apparently gave him few qualms about the meaningfulness of the liberal gospel. He assured himself that Herrmann's inner Jesus was really the Christ of Christian faith and that Christianity has no other credible basis.

But the problem of the sermon weighed far more heavily upon Barth after he became pastor to a small farming and industrial community in Safenwil. Church attendance in the canton of Aargau was not much stronger than it had been in Geneva, but now he was preaching to his own congregation. Barth worked hard to give the people of Safenwil something worth listening to. He prepared diligently and preached long, demanding sermons that struggled (and mostly failed) to make contact with his parishioners. His style was vigorous and direct. Barth plainly admitted to his congregation that he often found his sermon texts to be alien or perplexing. He was more comfortable speaking on themes that he shared with Herrmann. In his early years at Safenwil, he gave topical sermons on themes such as "Reformation," "Mission," or "The Life of William Booth." He equated God with that which is "highest and best in our souls" and lauded Schleiermacher as "the brilliant leader of a new reformation." He taught that Christianity is rooted in the individual's experience of Christ and that Christ's victory over death lay in his calm acceptance of his impending crucifixion. Jesus was resurrected long before he died, Barth assured his congregation. As he had anticipated before his parish ministry began, however, most of Barth's congregation did not find these assurances to be nearly as edifying or inspiriting as he had when he first heard them from Herrmann. He later recalled that he and the people of Safenwil always seemed to be looking at each other through a pane of glass.[54]

The differences between his congregation and the academic audiences that Berlin and Marburg provided for Harnack and Herrmann were chastening to him. Barth recognized that his congregation's lack of response to him owed something to his inner disquiet. He was characteristically direct in speaking to the problem, often speaking freely from the pulpit about his inner doubts and sense of restlessness. These attempts to gain greater rapport with his congregation generally had the effect of making his parishioners even more wary of him. He later remarked that he was sorry "for everything that my congregation had to put up with." In 1935, when he revisited his former congregation as a renowned theologian, he apologized for not having preached the gospel clearly to them. "I have often thought with some trepidation of those who were perhaps led astray or scandalized by what I said at that time, or of the dead who have passed on and did not hear, at any rate from me, what by human reckoning they ought to have heard," he confessed. Elsewhere he confessed that he was tormented "by the memory of how greatly, how yet *more* greatly, I *failed* as a pastor of Safenwil."[55]

These judgments on his ten-year ministry at Safenwil were made in the aftermath of a completed theological transformation, however. Barth was genuinely repentant for having subjected his congregation to what later seemed to him a series of substitutes for the gospel of Christ. In his early years at Safenwil, he preached a liberal gospel of culture-affirming religiosity; later his thinking and preaching took a Socialist turn; still later—during the Great War—he cast about in various directions, seeking the best means to explicate what he called "the strange new world within the Bible." By the time that he judged that his ministry at Safenwil had been a failure, he was appalled that he could ever have written or preached that "He becomes I." It was the personal transformation that the people of Safenwil witnessed, however, that changed the course of twentieth-century Christian theology. The course that Barth followed in making this transformation could not have made much sense to the Safenwilers at the time, for it began with his conversion to religious socialism.

THE SOCIALIST DIFFERENCE: POLITICS AND THEOLOGY

From his standpoint this was hardly a strange or novel development. In 1903 a highly-regarded Zurich pastor, Hermann Kutter, published an electrifying manifesto for Christian socialism titled *They Must; or, God and the Social Democracy,* which inspired a group of Swiss pastors to organize the Swiss Religious Socialist movement. Leonhard Ragaz and Hans Bader were among them. Kutter was well-known in Swiss Reformed circles for his inspiring preaching and social activism. In 1898, he was elected to the ministry of the Neumünster in Zurich; six years later, his reelection amounted to a popular endorsement of radical Christian social democracy. Kutter wrote in a flaming, impassioned style that made him a highly effective preacher and movement pamphleteer. "Our society makes a parade of morality because it has none; it grows furious over a little scandal to hide its own great scandal," he pronounced with typical righteousness. "Its morality is the painted shield of its immortality."[56]

By the time that Barth returned to his native Switzerland from Germany, religious socialism was sweeping the churches. The movement had its own journal (*Neue Wege,* edited by Ragaz) and a powerful charismatic leader. Barth later recalled that its influence was not only appealing, but unavoidable. "Every young Swiss pastor who was not asleep or living somehow behind the moon or for whatever reason errant, was at that time in the narrower or the wider sense a 'Religious Socialist.' We became—in negative things more certain to be sure than in the positive—powerfully *antibürgerlich.*"[57]

This was not a development for which Barth's theological education provided any preparation. Swiss Christian socialism was radically social democratic, but in Germany the only Christian socialist movement was conservative. The German Evangelical Social Congress was founded in 1890 by Adolf Stöcker (among others), and from 1902 to 1912 its president was Harnack—who taught that the gospel is above politics. Harnack explained that Christianity is based on the "purely religious" teaching of Jesus. Though Jesus was clearly concerned about the moral and spiritual life of individuals, he was no political reformer: "The Gospel makes its appeal to the inner man, who, whether he is well or wounded, in a happy position or a miserable, obliged to spend his earthly life fighting or quietly maintaining what he has won, always remains the same," he wrote. It followed for Harnack that beyond its concerns about individual morality, the church has no business getting involved in political issues: "The Gospel is above all questions of mundane development; it is concerned not with material things, but with the souls of men."[58]

Herrmann similarly taught that the ethical implications of Christian teaching applied mostly to individual moral life. He argued that the aim of Jesus was "to help men in their moral needs." This meant something quite different to Jesus than it usually means to modern people, he cautioned. Modern people are greatly concerned about commerce and politics, but there is no evidence that Jesus attributed any importance to these forms of work. Jesus knew about the work done by merchants and bankers and laborers, but he never appears to have thought "that the worth of a man is, as a rule, dependent upon his serving the community in some such way."[59]

Herrmann's point was not that modern people should not care about such matters, but rather that they should not appeal to Christianity when they take positions upon them. Jesus believed many things that we cannot possibly believe, he cautioned. To be a follower of Christ today is not to adopt all or even part of his worldview, but to live in his spirit and share his inner life:

"Anything in Jesus that we cannot understand as triumphant personal life is not for us part of a complete Christianity, but at the very most of a bygone Christianity." An important example was the apocalypticism of Jesus. Herrmann noted that Jesus took an eschatological worldview for granted and that, on the basis of this worldview, he preached an ethic of indifference to the world. Centuries later many Christians still felt obliged to adopt the eschatology of Jesus, Herrmann wryly continued, yet very few of these people treated the present world with indifference. He shared the judgment of the prominent social Christian leader, Friedrich Naumann, that modern Christians needed to stop making Christianity look ridiculous in this way. The church needed to stop making outdated ideas central to Christianity. Herrmann took this contention a step further, urging that the church needed to stop making *any* ideas central to Christianity. "With regard to these utterances of Jesus, we confess that we cannot possibly comply with them, since we do not share His conception of the universe, and so are living in a different world," he explained. "On the other hand, the mind which they reveal should be present also in us; that is, the will really to act in accordance with our own convictions."[60]

Harnack and Herrmann were not oblivious to the moral power of the more radicalized forms of social gospel Christianity that arose in the 1890s. Both of them opposed the "Godless" ideology of laissez-faire capitalism, which they called "Manchesterism." Both of them taught that any gospel-rooted civilization should curb the worst abuses of its prevailing economic order, which included the abuses of an increasingly industrialized order in Germany. Their arguments about how such Christian influence should be exerted centered almost entirely on individual morality, however. They took no interest in structural considerations and they denied outright that the church has any business seeking to transform the social order. With more than a hint of patronizing ridicule they dismissed the "well-meant performances" of figures like Kutter and Ragaz, who promoted Christian socialism with the aim of "providing Jesus with a defense and a recommendation."[61]

Barth came to a very different view of Christian socialism in Safenwil. The majority of his parishioners worked in a large knitting mill or in a group of weaving mill and dye works factories that were owned by two highly-respected local families. Wages were very low, working conditions were often dangerous and grueling, and the workers had no trade union to protect them. The fact that only the Socialists seemed to care about the misery of common working people made a deep impression on him. Barth later recalled that "in the class conflict which I saw concretely before me in my congregation, I was touched for the first time by the real problems of real life." Chastened by "real life" problems, which included the death of his father in 1912, he found little time for theology. He joined the Religious Socialist movement and became a student of political economics. "What I really studied were factory acts, safety laws, and trade unionism, and my attention was claimed by violent local and cantonal struggles on behalf of workers," he later recalled.[62] While braving protests from upper-class parishioners who insisted that he should stay out of politics, Barth gave numerous speeches to workers' groups and otherwise gave his voice and energy to the union movement. When the area's leading industrialist, Walter Hüssy, publicly ridiculed him as an ignorant idealist, Barth made a strong reply that revealed his considerable knowledge of labor/capital issues.[63]

The significance of Religious Socialism for Barth was more deeply and lastingly religious than it was socialist. His political activist phase lasted only a few years, but from Kutter he learned a religious lesson that reverberated through all of his later work. Kutter truly believed that God was real and at work in history. His preaching vividly communicated this faith. "Yes, God is speaking today," he proclaimed. "God is working miracles, but of a different kind from what your traditional Christian formulas and your 'inward' piety can understand—mightier, more elemental, more real. For God is a God of reality. His life cannot be woven out of systems of doctrines."[64]

This was theological liberalism, but with a huge difference from the cultured individualism that Barth learned at Marburg. The Religious Socialists were religiously serious in a way that was new to him. They spoke and behaved as though it made all the difference in the world whether one believed in God. "From Kutter I simply learned to speak the great word 'God' once again seriously, responsibly, and forcibly," Barth later reflected. He recalled elsewhere that "with a force like that of no one near him," Kutter's inspiring preaching and writing taught him "that the realm of God's power is greater than the realm of the church."[65] Kutter never tired of reminding his followers that God is not a God of the Christians or even the Social Democrats alone: "He gives the Spirit to whomsoever He will. Let not the Church forget that."[66]

In his activist phase, Barth embraced the Religious Socialist credo that the Christian and socialist movements needed each other. Though Kutter steered clear of involving himself with outside political or trade union movements, Barth agreed with Ragaz and other Christian socialists that Religious Socialism should not be restricted to the sphere of the church. At the high tide of the Swiss and American Christian socialist movements (in 1911), he declared that true socialism is "the true Christianity for our time." Because Jesus identified in a special way with those who were poor and oppressed, he asserted, the church has no right to call itself Christian if it does not preach and practice a gospel of social justice for the poor. On the other hand, he argued, there was no prospect that a secularized Socialist movement would be either desirable or successful. "I regard socialist demands as an important part of the application of the gospel, though I also believe that they cannot be realized without the gospel," he explained.[67]

The quality that Barth admired most in Herrmann was that he was not ashamed of the gospel. Barth recognized the same quality in the Religious Socialists, while judging that their Christianity reclaimed much more of the authentic ethical spirit of the gospel than Herrmann's individualism. Harnack and Herrmann adjusted the gospel to fit the values of modern educated German culture, but the Religious Socialists were not impressed with the economic or cultural achievements of modernity. German theological liberalism secured a place for a culture-affirming religion of inwardness, but Kutter stridently condemned its role in sacralizing a social order based upon the pervasive idolatry of mammon. The actual religion promoted by modern culture is the religion of mammon, he protested, which commodifies everything that it touches.[68]

Herrmann viewed religion in almost exclusively positive terms, but Barth's participation in the Religious Socialist movement drove him to adopt a more critical perspective on religion, especially the bourgeois religiosity of his teachers. In the two years that preceded the outbreak of World War I, his sermons became increasingly critical of the modernist tendency to accommodate the gospel to modern values. He cautioned his congregation that the Holy Spirit is not to be confused with the spirit of the times. He began to speak of God as "wholly other." God is not in our possession, he cautioned; the "true life" to which God calls us is "wholly other" than we can imagine. With a righteous fire that resembled Kutter's prophetic sermonizing, he preached that God is neither the guardian of bourgeois civilization nor merely the "inner light" within. The Father of Jesus Christ is the wholly other God of righteousness who commands justice and a world made new. Without a commitment to a kingdom-bringing social justice, Barth warned his congregation, their religion was nothing but a pack of lies.[69]

At the time, these themes were woven into a basically Herrmannian theology. This was hardly a novel phenomenon. Most of the American social gospelers were theologically liberal, as were most Swiss Religious Socialists. Walter Rauschenbusch provided a striking example at the time of how a commitment to radical social democracy could be blended with German theological liberalism.[70] Like Rauschenbusch, Barth sought to blend the most attractive aspects of liberal theology with the prophetic gospel of Christian socialism. He still assumed, with Schleiermacher and Herrmann, that religious experience is the generative ground of theology. He still believed, with Herrmann, that the basis of Christian faith is personal experience of the inner life of Jesus. He still followed the Ritschl/Herrmann line on what it means to affirm one's salvation in Christ.

THEOLOGY AND THE GREAT WAR

On the eve of the Great War, Barth's thinking and preaching still belonged wholly to the nineteenth century. Twentieth-century theology begins with his wartime judgment that he did not believe in the same god as his revered teachers. On various occasions in Barth's later life he told the story of how his break from liberal theology came about at the outset of the war. He usually got the dates wrong and he often exaggerated the immediacy and extent of his wartime break with theological liberalism. It actually took him six years to accept that he no longer belonged to a tradition that included

Schleiermacher. For all of his exaggerations in recounting the story, however, there is no question that the war was dramatically life-changing for Barth. Though he was not surprised by the outbreak of the war itself, the reaction of his German teachers to it shocked him profoundly.

For more than a year he had warned and lamented that the war was coming. He warned repeatedly that the world was in crisis, a catastrophe was building, and the abyss was in sight. He later recalled that he felt obliged "to let the war rage through all my sermons" until a parishioner finally asked him if he could please for once speak about something else.[71] Then, fatefully, on 1 August 1914, in a public address written by Harnack, Kaiser Wilhelm II called the German nation to war. Three days later, while Germany invaded Belgium, the German Social Democrats in the Reichstag voted unanimously to support the war effort. Barth was disgusted that the German Socialists failed to uphold their purported opposition to war for even a week. In the early weeks of the war, he also complained bitterly to Martin Rade that his former teachers were trying to sacralize their nation's war effort as a religious experience. Rade was not as effusive in his war-boosting as many of his colleagues. He carefully stopped short of claiming that God had willed the war. In three successive issues of *Die Christliche Welt,* however, he and other German theologians did claim that God was the "only possible ground and author" of the surge of war enthusiasm that the German people were experiencing.[72]

This appeal to the phenomenon of a "religious war experience" was familiar in a sickening way to Barth. To see it employed as a sacralizing warrant for German militarism made him doubt the entire theology of experience that he had learned from Schleiermacher and Herrmann. In September he told his closest friend, Eduard Thurneysen, that the truths of the gospel were being "simply suspended for the time being and in the meantime a German war-theology is put to work, its Christian trimming consisting of a lot of talk about sacrifice and the like." This spectacle made him doubt whether the gospel had ever been anything more than a "surface varnish" for German theology. "It is truly sad! Marburg and German civilization have lost something in my eyes by this breakdown, and indeed forever." On 1 October 1914, he told Rade that his long-held respect for the "German character" was being destroyed. The Christian part of German liberal theology is breaking to pieces under the pressure of a war psychosis, he charged.[73] Barth resisted the verdict that he no longer belonged to a tradition that included Harnack and Herrmann, but he already felt, at best, a deep ambivalence toward his teachers.

Two days later, on 3 October, ninety-three prominent German intellectuals issued a ringing manifesto of support for the German war policy. Their statement repudiated the distinction (sometimes drawn by English academics) between the spirit of German science and Prussian militarism. "There is no spirit in the German army that is different from that of the German nation, for both are one and we, too, are part of it," the intellectuals declared. The German army was presently making use of German science to wage a battle for Germany's freedom "and, therefore, for all the benefits of peace and morality not only in Germany." With supreme confidence in the righteousness of their cause, the intellectuals assured that the salvation of European culture itself depended upon a German victory in the war: "We believe that for European culture on the whole salvation rests on the victory which German 'militarism,' namely manly discipline, the faithfulness, the courage to sacrifice, of the united and free German nation will achieve."[74]

The signatories included virtually all of Barth's theological teachers except Rade. The experience of reading it was shattering to him. "For me it was almost worse than the violation of Belgian neutrality," he later recalled. It seemed to him that his revered teachers had become "hopelessly compromised" by the claims of the state and its ideology of war. The moral failure of Harnack, Herrmann, and the rest even to raise the question of national idolatry proved to him that "their exegetical and dogmatic presuppositions could not be in order." He later recalled that "I suddenly realized that I could not any longer follow either their ethics and dogmatics or their understanding of the Bible and of history."[75] On 4 November, he wrote an open letter to Herrmann that sharply asked for his position on the "war experience" argument. Barth assured Herrmann that he continued to feel deep gratitude to him as a person and teacher, but on the issues that mattered, he declared, he felt only a "complete antithesis."

Rade tried to explain the basic problem between Barth and his German teachers. The problem was that Barth's Swiss citizenship made him incapable of understanding the German position. As a citizen of a neutral country, Rade observed, Barth lacked the singular experience that all Germans presently knew as a deeply binding reality. He lacked the German war experience. Barth countered that this was a nationalistic warrant that had nothing to do with Christianity. If liberal theology is so easily turned into an instrument of patriotic hubris, he objected, how can it claim to be Christian? He was appalled that his teachers were so deeply compromised by their ties to the dominant order that they could not imagine any other response to the war. He was repulsed by their appeal to a religious war experience, which was "supposed to bring us to silence, if not demand reverence from us."[76] The manifesto drove him to the realization that he could take no more instruction from his teachers: "An entire world of theological exegesis, ethics, dogmatics, and preaching, which up to that point I had accepted as basically credible, was thereby shaken to the foundations, and with it everything which flowed at that time from the pens of the German theologians." With some exaggeration he later recalled that for him, from this moment onward, "19th-century theology no longer held any future."[77]

From this moment onward he would no longer take theological guidance from Harnack and Herrmann, though he still imagined that he belonged to Schleiermacher's tradition at its best. Neither could he believe any longer that Socialism was the answer to the problems of injustice and war, though he joined the Social Democratic Party at this seemingly unlikely moment.

Barth was appalled that the German Social Democrats ditched their commitment to international solidarity as soon as Germany went to war. It grieved him that Socialists throughout Europe were similarly taking sides with their national governments on the war issue. This revulsion drove him to finally join the (neutral) Social Democratic Party of Switzerland in January 1915. As Barth explained to Thurneysen, he became a dues-paying Socialist in order to demonstrate "that faith in the Greatest does not exclude but rather includes within it work and suffering in the realm of the imperfect."[78] Because Socialists were betraying Socialism throughout Europe, he reasoned that it was imperative at that precise moment to take a stand in solidarity with the idea of true Socialism and those who upheld it.

Barth's first impulse was to muddle through the war and his theological confusion by standing up for true Christian socialism. He was soon thrown into doubt about what even this should mean. The Swiss Religious Socialists had long been divided between those who wanted to "Christianize" the Social Democratic movement and those who wanted Christian socialism to stay out of secular politics. The former group, led by Ragaz, argued that Christian socialists were obliged by their theology and their ethical commitments to transform society into the kingdom of God. The latter group, led by Kutter, argued that Christian socialists would lose their distinctively Christian character if they sought to compromise with or attain power over the social order. Kutter's group was more quietist-leaning in its politics, but it was also more militant in its commitment to a radical Socialist identity. In the defining German Socialist debate between Karl Kautsky's radical Marxism and Eduard Bernstein's social democratic revisionism, Kutter sided with Kautsky. By contrast, the Ragaz activists were ethical idealists. They sought to infuse a new spirit of cooperation and fellow-feeling in society by working with Social Democrats to create a democratic socialist order.[79]

The same conflict of visions simmered among most democratic socialist movements of the time, but, with the outbreak of World War I, this split in Swiss Religious Socialism nearly tore the movement apart. Ragaz insisted that Swiss Socialists should condemn the war unequivocally, but Kutter's faction urged that such an action would be presumptuous. Speaking for Kutter's group, *Freie Schweizer Arbeiter* editor Gustav Benz contended that the moment called for silence and quiet listening for the voice of God. Many of the Socialists in Kutter's wing, especially Kutter himself, were chastened by their sympathy for Germany and their devotion to German culture. Kutter believed that German civilization was more advanced spiritually and culturally than the capitalist powers of the West. On the other hand, Ragaz's near-pacifism was challenged by his fervent conviction that true religious socialism could not advance without the defeat of German militarism and nationalistic hubris. While he continued to oppose the war, Ragaz clearly hoped that Germany would lose it. While he urged his Socialist brethren to keep quiet, Kutter apologized to his German readers for the Swiss Socialists who blamed Germany for the war.[80]

Barth was torn between them. Politically he tended to side with Ragaz. He shared Ragaz's conviction that it made no sense to call for Socialism and then refuse to work with unions and Socialist parties. He believed, with Ragaz, that Socialists were obliged to oppose the wars of nation states. For all of his filial regard for certain German theologians and universities, he did not share Kutter's pieties about the spiritual superiority of German culture. Calvin and Rousseau were given to the world by France, he noted, and Tolstoy was Russian. More consistently than Ragaz, whose animus against German nationalism blended uneasily with his opposition to the war, Barth's early view held out for the prewar ethical socialist line against the wars of nation states and for the international solidarity of workers. He told Thurneysen that a clear victory by either Germany or the Entente Powers would probably engender another cycle of chauvinism and revenge, and thus reproduce the outcome of the Franco-Prussian war of 1870. He therefore hoped that the war would cease without a clear victory by either side.[81]

But his closest friend and colleague was decidedly more sympathetic to Kutter's side of the argument. Thurneysen cautioned Barth against writing off Kutter as a pro-German quietist. He argued that Kutter's emphasis on "waiting for God" contained a deeper spiritual wisdom than Ragaz's eagerness to see signs of the kingdom in the antiwar opposition or the Socialist movement. Kutter understood that every hearing of the Word in the present situation was problematic. In the early months of 1915, Barth resisted the political choices that seemed to come from this outlook while conceding to Thurneysen that Kutter's spiritual sensibility was more deeply grounded than Ragaz's. He was intrigued by the possibility that Kutter's greater independence and radicalism derived from his deeper communion with God. An extended visit with the charismatic Christian socialist Christoph Blumhardt deepened Barth's interest in developing a more God-centered way of thinking.

He and Thurneysen had journeyed to Marburg to attend the wedding of Barth's younger brother Peter to Martin Rade's daughter. On the way back from Marburg they spent five days in Bad Boll talking to Blumhardt. The son of a famous Lutheran preacher and healer, Johann Christoph Blumhardt (1805–1880), the younger Blumhardt had been the first Lutheran pastor in Germany to join the Social Democratic Party (SDP). The following year, in 1900, he was elected to serve as a deputy representing the SPD in the provincial parliament, and for six years he represented the party as principal spokesperson for the five opposition parties in the Stuttgart *Landtag.* More than any other figure, he had sparked the current movement in German Lutheranism toward a social understanding of the church's mission. His followers included Kutter and Ragaz. Like his father, the younger Blumhardt had grown up with and later rejected the Pietist tradition, arguing that Pietism fostered a spirituality of self-preoccupation. He taught that Christians are not supposed to obsess over the signs of their piety, but are meant rather to give witness to the reality of Christ's kingdom-bringing Spirit. To Barth he was a giant figure, but the most striking aspect of Blumhardt's persona was his fervent sense of God's active presence in the world. As Barth later explained, "Blumhardt always begins right away with God's presence, might, and purpose: he starts out from God; he does not begin by climbing upwards to Him by means of contemplation and deliberation." From this prophetic figure who embodied so much of Barth's ideal of Christianity, Barth drew the lesson that good theology attends first to what God is doing in the world. Genuinely Christian thinking is oriented not to the subject of religious experience, but to God's initiatives and purpose in the world.[82]

This perception had the immediate effect of moving Barth closer to Kutter. He explained in September 1915 that while he continued to respect the integrity of Ragaz's political idealism, he was moving to the view that the Christianity in Christian socialism needed its own language, sphere, and basis. It especially needed to focus and wait upon a God who does not submit to human plans. In his reading (drawing on a lecture by Hans Bader), Ragaz emphasized social needs and the ethical demands of faithful living, but Kutter emphasized experience of God and the kingdom of God as promise. Ragaz believed in social development and the politics of social democracy, but Kutter believed that people are enslaved without God. As long as they remained non-Christian, he warned, the Social Democrats would never comprehend why Christian Socialists chose to be Christians. Ragaz wanted to form a Religious Socialist Party that appealed to workers, opposed the war, opposed the church, and adopted a spirit of martyrdom. Kutter countered that pastors should be the focus of Religious Socialist organizing, that the movement should concentrate on developing spiritual fellowship groups, and that the movement should seek to prepare the church for its long-range future in a hostile world. In brief, Ragaz emphasized an activist agenda for building the kingdom while Kutter called for formative spiritual communities that waited upon the movement of God's Spirit in the world. [83]

Barth felt considerable ambivalence about moving in Kutter's direction. He still doubted that Religious Socialism made sense if it did not make alliances with unions and social democratic parties. He disliked Kutter's anti-intellectualism, especially his disregard for academic theology. He was suspicious of Kutter's affection for Germany, especially after Kutter published his wartime speeches to the German nation that apologized for Swiss criticism of Germany.[84] But on the crucial points of religious orientation and emphasis Barth came to the verdict, somewhat to his surprise, that Kutter was right. Ragaz-style activists presumed that the kingdom was being built through their idealism, but with Kutter's help Barth began to question whether any particular group represented the inbreaking of God's kingdom. He began to appreciate the otherness and mystery of the biblical idea of the kingdom. He thanked Thurneysen for making Kutter accessible to him on this point.[85] In the name of seeking to live out the true Christian socialism of Kutter and Blumhardt, Barth resolved to open himself to God's "Wholly Other" reality. McCormack and Ingrid Spieckermann rightly argue that this was the crucial turning point in his development.[86] McCormack calls the new position that Barth adopted "critically realistic dialectical theology." Though I believe that he overstates Barth's commitment to a critical realist epistemology, McCormack is right that in the year after the German theologians endorsed the Kaiser's war as a Christian cause, Barth became a dialectical theologian. More importantly, in a crucial sense he never ceased being a divine Object-oriented dialectical theologian afterward.

THE BARTHIAN TURN: GIVING UP SCHLEIERMACHER

His first attempts to find a new theological basis lurched in various directions, sometimes within a single essay. Kutter's witness to the "living God" and the younger Blumhardt's spirituality of Christian socialist hope were helpful to him, but neither of them was a theologian. Barth and Thurneysen considered turning to Hegel, but never quite went through with it. They studied scripture more seriously than before and read "huge amounts of Dostoevsky," as Barth later recalled. Barth gave special attention to Kant, who "spoke in a remarkably new and direct way to me in those years."[87] At his brother Heinrich's urging he took up a serious study of Plato, which influenced the argument of his first edition of *Der Römerbrief.* In the years that followed the publication of his first edition of *The Epistle to the Romans* (*Romans*), he was also greatly influenced by the writings of Soren Kierkegaard and the Swiss church historian Franz Overbeck.

Throughout this period Barth was clear that he needed to find a new basis for his preaching and religious thinking, but he was slow to accept that this would require leaving Schleiermacher behind. For more than six years he struggled with the question whether Schleiermacher had launched German theology down a fatal sub-Christian path. He was slow to render a verdict on the question because he wanted so desperately to remain linked to Schleiermacher. In 1920 Barth was still assuring himself that Schleiermacher would have approved of the redirection in his thinking. Like many interpreters, notably Herrmann, he believed that the early Schleiermacher's understanding of Christianity was not derived from a general theory of religious consciousness. Several years after he had openly broken ranks with Harnack and Herrmann, Barth continued to assure himself that at least he was still linked to the younger Schleiermacher.[88]

This self-assurance had to be fought for in the face of considerable contrary evidence. In 1915 the question at issue was far from abstract or merely academic. Schleiermacher's ostensible heirs were using an appeal to religious experience to promote the German war effort. Was this a distortion of Schleiermacher's apologetic? Barth later recollected that from the outset he had worried that it was not. The younger Schleiermacher wrote sharply insulting things about the British and French. He was a leading Prussian partisan who made outright patriotic appeals from the pulpit of Trinity Church (Berlin). In 1813 he exhorted hundreds of his students from the University of Berlin to join the onslaught against a retreating Napoleon in Breslau.[89]

Moreover, the purpose of Schleiermacher's apologetic was to awaken the "cultured despisers of religion" to their repressed or wrongly-named religious feelings. Barth understood that this strategy assumed that the meaning of Christianity must be adjusted to accommodate the beliefs and values of modern culture. Schleiermacher took it for granted that the truth and moral worth of Christian teaching must be judged by modern norms.

The German theologians of Barth's time took it for granted that their nation was defending the spiritual heritage of Christian civilization from the godless materialism of England and its allies. Did this mean that Harnack's war-boosting was a logical outgrowth of the tradition of modernist religious conformism initiated by Schleiermacher? Would Schleiermacher have signed the 1914 manifesto of the German intellectuals? For the rest of his life, Barth refused to believe that Schleiermacher would have gone this far. Long after he set his theology squarely against Schleiermacher's, he persisted in the belief that Schleiermacher never would have signed "that horrible manifesto."[90] In the early 1920s, however, he did begin to voice the verdict that the fatally compromised Christianity of the manifesto was a logical outgrowth of Schleiermacher's theology. He told Thurneysen in May 1921 that the muzzle of his gun was trained upon Schleiermacher and that he was ready to declare war upon him.[91] Later that year, his second edition *Epistle to the Romans* blasted Schleiermacher for turning the gospel into a religion. Liberal theology treated the gospel of Christ as one human possibility among others, Barth explained: "Since Schleiermacher, this attempt has been undertaken more consciously than ever before in Protestant theology—and it is the betrayal of Christ."[92]

This stunning reproach was the culmination of Barth's half-dozen years of straining not to believe that the problem began with Schleiermacher. He later explained that he was finally unable to resist the verdict that the corrupted culture-Protestantism of his teachers "was grounded, determined, and influenced decisively" by Schleiermacher.[93] In 1923, barely two years after he had begun his career as a professor of theology at Göttingen, Barth told his students that they needed to study Schleiermacher in order to understand themselves. "If anyone still speaks today in Protestant theology as though he were still among us, it is Schleiermacher," he explained. "We *study* Paul and the reformers, but we *see* with the eyes of Schleiermacher and think along the same lines as he did." Virtually all modern academic theology simply assumed that the subject of theology is religion, he noted. Historical and systematic theologians alike presumed to understand the meaning of Christianity by studying the phenomenon of religious self-consciousness.[94]

Barth pressed his students to recognize the immensity of Schleiermacher's influence upon them. It was from Schleiermacher (usually indirectly) that they took their governing assumptions about the nature of Christianity and how it should be studied. Barth allowed that Schleiermacher inspired a wide range of liberal theologies. He conceded that various offshoots of the older Pietist, confessionalist, rationalist, and mediationist theologies could be found here and there at the better universities. He granted that the nineteenth century produced a smattering of outright dissenters from liberal theology that included Kierkegaard, Gottfried Menken, J. T. Beck, both Blumhardts, and a few others. In other contexts Barth included his own father in this list. But the latter figures made little impact in their time, he judged, and all of the other modern theological currents were forced to accommodate themselves to the overwhelming influence of liberal theology. "Theologically the 'genius' of the major part of the church is that of Schleiermacher," Barth lectured. "All the so-to-speak official impulses and movements of the centuries since the Reformation find a center of unity in him: orthodoxy, pietism, the Enlightenment. All the official tendencies of the Christian present emanate from him like rays: church life, experiential piety, historicism, psychologism, and ethicism."[95]

In 1822 Joachim Christian Gass told Schleiermacher that his dogmatics had launched a new epoch in theological studies.[96] A decade later, on the day of Schleiermacher's death, the distinguished church historian August Neander pronounced that Schleiermacher had inaugurated a new period in church history. Barth pressed his students to recognize that they were living in what was still Schleiermacher's period of church history. "When we learn to know Schleiermacher we learn to know ourselves and the main characteristics of the theological situation today," he told them. He recalled that the last significant theological movement to propose a break from Schleiermacher's focus on religious consciousness was quickly absorbed by it. Albrecht Ritschl proposed to place liberal theology on a historical basis, but his movement soon produced theologies that were "more easily conceivable without Ritschl than without Schleiermacher." The problem of historical relativism that Ritschl's historicism unleashed drove Herrmann to set faith against history. Barth noted that it also produced the kind of psychologized religious theorizing that his colleague, Georg Wobbermin, was currently teaching in Göttingen theology classes.[97]

With the full weight and meaning of what this implied, Barth implored his students to imagine the possibility that the present century-long period of church history could be brought to an end. This possibility must be imagined, he urged, because the road taken by Schleiermacher and followed by nearly every theologian afterward had led to a dead end. In the past year both Herrmann and Troeltsch had died. Barth judged that the present situation in theology amounted to a standoff between their epigones. He further judged that neither side deserved to call itself a legitimate heir of the Reformers. He further judged that the problem began with Schleiermacher. He told Thurneysen that he often had to resist the urge to cry out that Schleiermacher's theology was "just one gigantic swindle."[98] With only slightly less restraint he told his class at the end of the semester that his course preparations had been "fairly shattering" to him.

"When I embarked with you on this material, which I had not examined closely for many years, I was prepared for something bad," he explained to his class. "But I was not prepared to find that the *distortion* of Protestant theology—and we have to speak of such in view of the historical importance of the man—was as deep, extensive, and palpable as it has shown itself to be." Schleiermacher's thinking was worst on the most important issues, he judged. It was precisely on the questions of the nature of revelation, the Bible as holy scripture, miracles, God, and immortality that Schleiermacher had departed the furthest from authentic Christian teaching and thus damaged the cause of Protestant theology.[99]

Barth confessed that as a Protestant he found this verdict to be "an oppressive and almost intolerable thought." He worried that Protestantism would be unable to regain any confidence in the power of its truth. He fretted that the spiritual ravages of theological liberalism made it very difficult to affirm the doctrine of the providence of God ruling over the church. He urged that the church needed to make an honest appraisal of these ravages, however. Nothing worthy of the name "Protestantism" would otherwise emerge from the ashes of the past century of Protestant theology. Liberal theology interpreted the doctrine of divine providence in accord with its faith in historical progress, but Barth cautioned that providence is also rendered in history as divine judgment. His second edition *Romans* had recently described history as the footprint of God's wrath.[100] This is the meaning of the Schleiermacher period in church history, he declared: The dead end at which liberal theology had arrived was a sign of the wrathful judgment of God on modern Protestantism itself. In this situation, he exhorted, anything less than revolutionary resistance was insufficient. Faithfully Christian thinking could only take the form "of a *theological revolution,* a basic No to the whole of Schleiermacher's doctrine of religion and Christianity, and an attempted reconstruction at the *very* point which we have constantly seen him hurry past with astonishing stubbornness, skill, and audacity."[101]

Barth recognized in the early 1920s that the moment was ripe for much of this attack on theological liberalism. In the aftermath of the Great War, no European could believe that the world was getting better. His second edition *Romans* had already caused a sensation, falling, as Karl Adam remarked, "like a bomb on the playground of the theologians."[102] Paul Tillich assured him that the book was a prime symptom of the dawning of a history-changing "kairos."[103] Barth cautioned that there was no occasion for triumphant superiority at the tomb of Schleiermacher, however. If it was now becoming painfully evident that Schleiermacher and his children had distorted Christian teaching in order to accommodate it to nineteenth-century German idealism, romanticism, moralism, and historicism, it was not nearly as clear how theology should be done otherwise. "Schleiermacher undoubtedly did a good job," he remarked. "It is not enough to know that another job has to be done; what is needed is the ability to do it at least as well as he did his."[104]

This was the sizable project that he assigned to himself and his movement, all the while protesting with apparent justification that his lack of intellectual preparation made him nowhere near suitable for the task. Barth formally repudiated the liberal tradition in the early 1920s and only rarely looked back afterwards, usually to rehearse his case against Schleiermacher. Always he contended that theological liberalism made the human subject the subject of theology and turned Christ into a mere predicate. The powerful force with which he and others wielded this critique created a dominant new theological movement.

This movement never quite became the "theological revolution" that Barth was seeking, however. Barth lacked the essential qualities of a movement leader and he eventually disavowed all of the movement-labels assigned to him. More importantly, his theology and the movements it inspired contained too many liberal elements to become a genuinely third way in Protestant thinking. Barth left Herrmann behind in the late 1920s, even as a foil for his own position-taking, but he took for granted a cluster of Herrmannian themes and positions that crucially defined his theological outlook. He blasted the anthropocentrism of liberal theology while retaining some of its key underpinnings. The field-changing theological movement that he inspired shared both of these characteristics. For movement reasons the Barthians exaggerated their break from the logic of theological liberalism, but today there is no movement to puff up or defend. There is only the opportunity to make sense of what used to be called neoorthodoxy in a theological situation that bears little resemblance to the contexts in which the liberal and neoorthodox movements were once dominant.

2

DIALECTICS OF THE WORD

Crisis Theology

The first name given to the Barthian revolt was "crisis theology." Barth wrote in 1920 that before the kingdom of God can become real to modern Christians "there must come a crisis that denies all human thought."[1] Crisis theology was a reaction against the slaughter and destruction of the Great War and the complicity of Barth's teachers in sacralizing the German war effort. More pointedly, to its original proponents it was a response to the ferocious judgment on European cultural pretension that the war appeared to deliver. Liberal German theologians had long conveyed the impression of being comfortable with God and proud of their own sophistication, but crisis theology was about shattered illusions and the experience of emptiness before a hidden God. More importantly, it was also about the unexpected world of spiritual meaning that Barth found in what he called "the strange new world within the Bible."[2]

This discovery marked the critical turning point of twentieth-century theology.[3] In January 1916 Barth remarked to Thurneysen that his thinking was becoming "frightfully indifferent" to historical questions. He allowed that "of course this is nothing new for me." His attraction to Wilhelm Herrmann in the first place had rested largely upon Herrmann's presentation of a liberal alternative to an ascending liberal historicism. Like Herrmann, Barth thought of historical criticism as merely a means of attaining intellectual freedom in relation to traditional doctrine. He still believed that Herrmann's approach (on this subject) was basically right. Without reflecting on the fact that Herrmann's recent thinking had moved further in the same direction, however, Barth told Thurneysen that his opposition to historical reasoning in theology was becoming deeper and more categorical. As he put it, the "antithesis" between himself and Paul Wernle-style liberalism was becoming sharper.[4]

For several years Barth had conducted a friendly ongoing debate with Wernle, an influential liberal theologian at Basel who belonged to the *Religionsgeschichtliche* wing of the Ritschlian school. Though he greatly respected Wernle, Barth was disturbed by his claim that the future of liberal theology belonged to the history of religions school. He questioned Wernle's assurance that Ritschlian school theology had a promising future as a form of thoroughgoing historicism. Barth doubted that Wernle or any theologian could embrace a thoroughgoing historicism without being devoured by it. He judged that Troeltschian-style historicism made Christianity secondary to its own comparativist historical methodology. This fear was confirmed for him by Troeltsch's acceptance of a chair in philosophy (not theology) at Berlin in 1915. The disciples of Wernle and Troeltsch liked to talk about "how history can enrich one," Barth observed, but his own impression was that the history of religions approach made theology weak and shallow. In November 1915, his lecture on "Wartime and the Kingdom of God" emphasized God's absence from contemporary secular life. Wernle reached for his most dismissive epithet—"apocalyptic"—in dismissing Barth's argument. Two months later Barth told Thurneysen that the day was coming when they would have to "strike a great blow against the theologians."[5]

The following July he mentioned to Thurneysen that he was beginning to assemble a "copy-book" of comments on Paul's letter to the Romans that summarized Paul's message in modern language. He also noted that he had discovered a "gold mine" that was helping him decipher Paul's meaning. The gold mine was a collection of biblical commentaries authored by his father's spiritual exemplar and favorite teacher, the Württemberg biblical scholar Johann Tobias Beck. "As a biblical expositor he simply towers far above the rest of the company, also above Schlatter," Barth enthused. Beck had taught biblical interpretation to Barth's father and grandfather. His respect for the divine inspiration and canonical integrity of scripture gave his scholarship a spiritual depth that Barth missed in liberal historiocriticism. It also brought Barth closer in feeling to the memory of his recently-deceased father. He told Thurneysen that Beck's old-style approach to biblical theology was "in part directly accessible and exemplary for us." It disclosed a world of religious meaning—the spiritual world of the Bible—that liberal scholarship never managed to find. "The older generation may once more have some pleasure in us, but a bit differently from what it intended," he remarked.[6]

OPENING TO THE WORLD OF GOD

Out of these beginnings Barth set upon the course that ignited the crisis theology movement. In 1916 he declared that the gospel message is "much too strong for our ears" because modern preaching had reduced the gospel to its own "weak, pitiably weak tones." Modern biblical criticism seeks to establish the meaning of scripture by deconstructing the Bible's literary and religious history, he observed, but this procedure obscured the spiritual truth of scripture. It negated the driving spiritual force that makes the Bible holy scripture. "If we wish to come to grips with the contents of the Bible, we must dare to reach far beyond ourselves," Barth exhorted. "The Book admits of nothing less." It is the Bible itself that "drives us out beyond ourselves and invites us, without regard to our worthiness or unworthiness, to reach for the last highest answer." The answer that scripture gives us is its own strange new world, "the world of God." There is a rushing stream in the Bible "that carries us away, once we have entrusted our destiny to it—away from ourselves to the sea," Barth urged: "The Holy Scriptures will interpret themselves in spite of all our human limitations. We need only dare to follow this drive, this spirit, this river, to grow out beyond ourselves toward the highest answer."[7]

And what is it that takes us into the spiritual world of the Bible? Barth gave Herrmann's answer. It is faith that opens the strange new world of the Bible to us. We cannot enter the world of scriptural truth by reading the Bible with false modesty or academic restraint, he cautioned, for these are passive qualities. Faith is precisely a form of spiritual daring, and the invitation to dare and "reach toward the highest" is the expression of divine grace that scripture contains. "The Bible unfolds to us as we are met, guided, drawn on, and made to grow by the grace of God," Barth explained. By the grace of God's Spirit, through faithful openness to the Word that scripture contains, a new world enters and suffuses our old ordinary world. "We may reject it. We may say, 'It is nothing; this is imagination, madness, this God,' " Barth allowed. "But we may not deny nor prevent our being led by Bible 'history' far out beyond what is elsewhere called history—into a new world, into the world of God."[8]

The kingdom of God is not a second world standing apart from the existing "real" world, he proclaimed. God's kingdom is, rather, this existing world made new through the inbreaking power of the Spirit. This argument was soon developed at length in Barth's first edition *Der Römerbrief.* His wartime writings also made heavy use of organic metaphors (some of them borrowed from Beck) in expressing the kingdom hope of a new world. "We are offered the magnificent, productive, hopeful life of a grain of seed, a new beginning, out of which all things shall be made new," he declared. "One can only let it live, grow, and ripen within him. One can only believe—can only hold the ground whither he has been led. Or not believe. There is no third way." The Bible repeatedly makes straight for the point at which one must decide whether to accept God's sovereignty or reject it. There is no third alternative. To accept it is to enter the new world of the Spirit of truth.[9]

Barth cautioned that the Bible often does not answer the questions that people bring to it. Many people approach the Bible with the expectation that it will offer pertinent guidance on various moral and practical questions, but this is not what scripture is about. Scripture is about the new world of God's reign. It is about God's glory and sovereignty. The Bible is not about how we should find our way to God, Barth explained. Scripture is always about how God has sought and found the way to us. This was the crucial biblical truism that the old conservatives rightly fought for when they opposed Schleiermacher's anthropocentric revisionism. By giving up any genuine appeal to revelation, he implied, Schleiermacher gave up the spiritual heart of the biblical witness. "And our fathers were right when they guarded warily against being drawn out upon the shaky scaffolding of religious self-expression."[10]

The fathers that he had in mind included some of the better theologians of nineteenth-century Pietism, especially Beck, Friedrich August G. Tholuck, and C. H. Rieger. These were Barth's principal guides as he worked through Paul's letter to the Romans, in addition to commentaries by Calvin and Johannes Bengel. He also drew upon his father's unpublished lecture book on Romans and upon Kutter's *Kirchenfreund* articles on Romans. Barth's emphasis on spiritual decision and the spiritual meaning of scripture reflected the considerable influence of Pietist thinking upon him. For Barth, as for Herrmann, however, there were sharp limits to the usefulness of the Pietist tradition as a resource for theology. Much of the religious witness and theology that derived from Pietism were repulsive to him. At its worst, Pietist preaching was crude, mechanical, and obsessed with hellfire and blood atonement. Even at its best, Pietist preaching on the "regenerated heart" was easily turned into a stopgap for the kind of experiential liberalism that Barth was trying to overcome. Shortly before he began to write his commentary on Romans, he read Ritschl's history of Pietism "and scented in it something of the air that Wernle breathes."[11]

Later that year, Barth got an extended dose of popular Pietist Christianity when the evangelist Jakob Vetter conducted a week-long revival at his church. It was a chastening experience. Vetter was invited to Safenwil by members of Barth's congregation. Some of them were apparently moved by the evangelist's incessant warnings about the consuming fires of hell, but Barth was appalled. He shook his head at Vetter's mechanical psychologizing, which traced the journey of the soul through "an awakening, a conversion, a sealing, then five different levels of resistance to the Holy Spirit, then the blood of Christ flows as medicine for the soul." Despite all of these splendors that awaited the Christ-choosing soul, Barth observed, Vetter always came back to "the open jaws of hell." Pietist revivalism was very long on soul experiences and "gruesome thundering about sin," he judged. In Vetter's preaching it also turned a promising approach to Christianity into an ugly form of fear-mongering religious mechanics. "If *this* were 'pietism,' we would never again believe that there was even the slightest point of contact between us and the pietists," he remarked.[12] As it was, though he was soon to be tagged as some kind of pietistic revivalist by his former teachers, the experience of listening to Vetter reinforced Barth's resolve that he could drink only very selectively from the well of Pietism.

Shortly before he began to write his commentary on Romans, Barth told Thurneysen that when the moment came to "strike the great blow against the theologians," they would have to untangle the web of Pietist and historicist influences that they had imbibed from their liberal teachers. His subsequent commentary on Romans made several blistering asides against the self-absorbed spiritual intensity of Pietism, "in which the demons do their work." It was harder for Barth to imagine during this period, however, that his project of theological rethinking would also require him to give up Herrmann's Kantian understanding of conscience as the repository of God's righteous will. In 1916 he was still appealing to the individual conscience as the single indispensable source of knowledge about God's will. Though conscience may be reduced to silence or led astray, he allowed, "it remains forever the place, the only place between heaven and earth, in which God's righteousness is manifest." Throughout every rise and fall in feeling about it, he explained, conscience speaks of a will that unfailingly remains true to itself. This steadfast will is the righteousness of God. We live by the conscience-given knowledge that the "deepest essence of all things" is God's righteous will. "We forget it often, to be sure; we overlook it; we spurn it," Barth allowed. "And yet we could not even keep on living, did we not profoundly know that God is righteous."[13]

The method of his argument and much of its spirit were still thoroughly liberal. The fact that Barth was beginning to focus on the Pauline theme of God's righteousness, however, reflected a decisive theological shift. The Bible was driving him back to the theme of God's sovereignty and righteous will as distinguished from the liberal emphasis on religious feeling and experiences of value: "We have found in the Bible a new world, God, God's sovereignty, God's glory, God's incomprehensible love. Not the history of man but the history of God! Not the virtues of men but the virtues of him who hath called us out of darkness into his marvelous light! Not human standpoints but the standpoint of God!" In the excitement of this spiritual and intellectual turn, Barth explicated the Word that Paul's letter from another age was speaking to him. In the closing weeks of the war, after he had finished his commentary, Barth fretted that his conversion to a biblically-oriented revelationism had come too late. "If only we had been converted to the Bible *earlier* so that we would now have solid ground under our feet!" he sighed to Thurneysen.[14]

But in fact, his turn against his teachers was perfectly timed. The war had destroyed much of the proud cultural heritage that it was said to have been about. Amid the colossal carnage, the memory of "war experience" theology was abhorrent to many. As a pastor during the war Barth preached numerous sermons that sought to give hope to Swiss congregants who feared that the war would never end or that it would spill into their country. After February 1917 some of them feared that the Bolshevik revolution would spill into their country. By 1917 nearly all of them were pressed hard by commodity shortages and inflated living costs that were caused by the war. Barth was never the type of preacher who indulged his congregation with flattery or easy religion, even in this difficult period. One of his wartime sermons gave a blistering portrait of the kind of congregation that yearns for a pastor "who pleases the people." At the same time, under the inspiration of his own recent awakening to the sovereignty and glory of God, he did seek to inspire a reassuring hope in his parishioners. At times his preaching tone approximated the forward-looking, exuberant, sometimes lyrical tone of his forthcoming commentary on Romans. Barth's first edition *Römerbrief* was published in December 1918. With its appearance, twentieth-century theology began.[15]

PAULINISM AND THE WORLD OF THE KINGDOM

He reported at the outset that *Der Römerbrief* was written with a joyful sense of discovery. The trend in recent liberal scholarship had been to accentuate the differences between the religion of the historical Jesus and the religion of the "Christ myth" taught by Paul. Liberals like Wernle opposed various aspects of Paul's theology, especially his Christology, his idea of blood redemption, his typology of Christ and Adam, his disregard for the historical Jesus, his devotion to biblical authority, and his nonhistorical use of scripture. The eminent New Testament scholar at Marburg, Adolf Jülicher, represented a more moderate form of liberal revisionism. Jülicher granted greater legitimacy to the development of the Christ myth in early Christian history while agreeing that Paul could be salvaged for modern Christian teaching only by stripping away his theories of justification and blood atonement. The differences between Wernle-style historicism and Jülicher's more traditional liberalism were significant, but Barth increasingly regarded them as differences of degree, not kind. In both cases the liberal tendency was to eliminate various "contextual" aspects of Paul's theology that were said to be foreign to Jesus and which were certainly alien to the sensibilities of modern liberal scholars.

Barth knew this sensibility intimately. He had entered the ministry believing that Luther was superior to Paul and that Schleiermacher was superior to everyone. In his early career he had struggled mightily (and candidly) with the problem of how he should preach upon various Pauline texts that he found to be contrived or hopelessly mythological. The joyful discovery that fueled the writing of his Romans commentary was that Paul's mythical gospel of redemption and resurrection was the true gospel of Christ. Having discovered only recently that Paul was greater than Luther and Calvin, Barth presented Paul's religious message as a history-changing and history-transcending theology of salvation, grace, and glory. The core of this message was that through his redeeming death and resurrection, Christ has inaugurated a new world-embracing aeon of the Spirit that is the world's true salvation. A new creation begins with Jesus, Barth exulted. As the redeeming "hinge of history," Jesus has inaugurated a new aeon of real history that is different from the old unreal aeon of sin and death.[16] In the old aeon, God was hidden to the "old Adam" on account of the bondage of humankind to sin; but in the new aeon of Christ's triumph over sin, God's sovereign grace works upon all unbelief and sin (as well as upon all faith and righteousness) to bring about God's purpose.[17]

Paul believed that true history is made only through the inbreaking power of the Spirit. Barth contended that this is why the truth that Paul's message contains cannot be grasped by wielding the tools of modern historical criticism. The spiritual truth that Paul expressed cannot be appropriated by cutting Paul's theology to fit the worldview of modern academic culture. It can be known only by presenting Paul in all of his strangeness. In Barth's presentation, Paul was an apostle of the kingdom of God who speaks to all people of every age. The differences between Paul's age and the modern age were therefore purely trivial. Modern biblical criticism has a rightful place as a preparatory discipline, Barth allowed, but if it was necessary to choose between historiocriticism and the old doctrine of biblical inspiration, "I should without hesitation adopt the latter, which has a broader, deeper, more important justification." Biblical criticism, by itself, has little value, he implied, whereas the doctrine of inspiration is concerned with the apprehension of biblical meaning. This is the concern to which theology should be devoted primarily. Liberal theology was weak precisely because it historicized and psychologized the truth of the gospel. Barth's alternative was that theology should be "an endeavor to see through and beyond history into the spirit of the Bible, which is the Eternal Spirit."[18]

This proposal contained echoes from Plato's theory of forms and Kant's appeal to the thing-in-itself. For Barth, as for Plato and Paul, salvation was about the restoration of a broken existing ideal and the hunger for a new age. He spoke of this redeemed new age as "the truth of God written by the prophets of Israel, by Plato and their like." Like Plato and Kant, Barth thematized the notion of a "real reality" that lies beyond the world of appearances. An equally important influence on his presentation of this theme was modern expressionism. In rhetorical style and conceptual argument, his first edition *Römerbrief* was a form of expressionist theology.[19] Like the expressionist writers and painters he admired at the time, Barth distinguished between the surface appearances of the so-called "real world" and the "real reality" that lies beneath the world of appearances. He embraced the expressionist thesis that true reality can be glimpsed only by disrupting or breaking up the world of appearances that conventional historiography and other disciplines treat as "real." In his reading, this was precisely what Paul's message of salvation accomplished. Paul's letter to the Romans presented an idol-breaking critique of every merely human strategy of salvation.

To Barth, "so-called history" was the empirical subject of historical research, sociology, and similar disciplines. It was the phenomenal world history in which people find themselves and which they experience as past, present, and future.[20] "So-called history" is the history of the empirical world that lives under the judgment of sin and death. Paul did not believe that ordinary history contains no sign of God's better world, Barth cautioned. Paul believed that the presence of the Law within ordinary history contains the promise of a world in which sin and death do not prevail. For Paul, the presence of the Law was precisely "the highpoint of *so-called* history." But this Law can only judge and point, Barth explained; it cannot save, since it cannot generate the capacity within fallen human beings to fulfill its demands. Salvation comes only from the better world that the Law promises but cannot deliver. That is, salvation comes only from the world of God through the "real history" of God's saving action, where no complete repudiation has ever taken place. Barth urged that God's concern is always the entire world. God works through belief and unbelief alike to bring about his greater purpose, which is the salvation of the entire world.[21]

This was still a liberal Protestant appropriation of Reformationist teaching. Like his liberal teachers, Barth placed Moses, Plato, Kant, and Fichte in the same kingdom-bringing line as prophets of God's righteousness. His conception of salvation put him closer to the anti-imputationist revisionism of the Lutheran theologian and controversialist, Andreas Osiander, than to Luther or Calvin. In the mid-sixteenth century, Osiander opposed the theory of imputed righteousness that Luther deduced from the doctrine of justification by faith. With impassioned, sometimes violently polemical fire, Osiander countered that salvation effects a substantial transference of Christ's righteousness to the believer. In the first phase of his attempt to cast his thinking more in line with the Reformation than with recent theological liberalism, Barth took his key Reformationist bearings from Osiander. His conception of salvation as the disclosure of a transforming "true world" of God derived from a line of Protestant thinking that traced to Osiander, not to Luther or Calvin.[22]

Long after Barth renounced Osiander and resolved to become a good (neo)Calvinist, however, the notion of God's kingdom as the theater of "real history" remained crucial to his thinking. His first edition *Romans* cautioned repeatedly that the new world of the kingdom is not a second world standing apart from the existing "real" world. God's kingdom is rather this existing world made new through the inbreaking power of the Spirit. Barth soon relinquished the Christian Socialist conception of the gospel as a kingdom-bringing message of emancipation from the illusions and evil of the "real" world. His first edition *Romans* already lumped religious socialism with liberal theology, Pietism, and conventional church religion as faulty vehicles of salvation. He also stopped speaking of the kingdom as the "hidden motor" that drives "so-called history" through its own "real history." Barth discarded most of these liberalizing rhetorical motifs in the 1920s, while continuing to insist that the true meaning of what historians call "history" can be known only through the Spirit's penetration of history.[23] His turn away from liberal theology was first expressed as a joyful discovery of the supernatural nature of the kingdom, which breaks into human life as a world-transforming divine Word. His subsequent turn emphasized that the Word breaks into history not so much to transform the world as to shake it and throw it into crisis.

The rhetorical differences between Barth's first and second editions of *Romans* vividly conveyed this shift in religious consciousness. The key differences related to the book's tone, not to the rhetorical expressionism for which the second edition quickly became famous. Barth heightened the book's rhetorical expressionism in his second edition, but both editions featured heavy use of repetition, exaggeration, hyperbole, exclamation points and dashes, and other expressionist techniques. The crucial rhetorical difference was in tone. Barth's renowned second edition was angry, sharp-edged and prophetic, while the book's first edition was generally hopeful and exuberant. The first edition spoke in a warm and often lyrical voice that occasionally soared with forward-looking spiritual optimism. Among the relatively small group of readers it found, many were inspired by the book's spiritual passion and its torrential flow of metaphor. Barth was forced to caution some of the first Barthians that his commentary was meant to be an exercise in theological scholarship and not a source of religious enthusiasm. Nearly all of the book's academic reviewers made special note of its unusual rhetorical qualities. Philipp Bachmann remarked on Barth's "burning zeal" and described his work as a type of "'pneumatic-prophetic exegesis' redolent with an inexhaustible vividness." In a generally enthusiastic review, young Emil Brunner noted that the book's apparent naivete produced a first impression of astonishment and surprise. In a decidedly less favorable review, Adolf Jülicher allowed that Barth "knows how to speak penetratingly, at times charmingly, and always with colorful vividness."[24]

But did his theological perspective make sense? Was it a faithful and compelling expression of the gospel? Barth's blow against the theologians began to gain historical force as it acquired defenders on these points. The first stirrings of what became the "crisis theology" school took place in the postwar debates over "pneumatic-prophetic exegesis" that his book inspired. Jülicher's professorial defense of "scientific exegesis" pressed the key questions. It was appalling to Jülicher that Barth, a graduate of Marburg, explicitly privileged the doctrine of biblical inspiration over historical criticism. With evident sadness he noted that for people like Barth and Friedrich Gogarten, nothing was more certain "than that there is no more progress in history, that development is forever at an end, and that no optimism in the interest of culture moves us anymore."[25]

Jülicher judged that those who succumbed to such disillusionment made themselves unable to understand the past. In his reading, Gogarten no longer even tried to make sense of history, and Barth was only slightly less extreme. He noted that Barth dressed his book up with often-mistaken scholarly glosses on textual and exegetical problems. Barth at least recognized that the interpretation of a difficult text in a foreign language from ancient times requires a great deal of historiocritical expertise. But this knowledge was a source of immense conflict for him, Jülicher judged, because theologically Barth was committed to the claim that the true meaning of scripture is spiritual, not historical. He did not oppose historical understanding as such, but proposed to pass through it to the history-transcending spiritual world of the Bible.

There is a precise name for this kind of theology, Jülicher admonished. In the mid-second century, Marcion developed the very theological position that Barth was now advancing as original to himself via Paul's letter to the Romans. The Marcionite Gnostics—otherwise known to history as the Marcionite heretics—were precise forerunners of the antihistorical spiritualism that Barth was reading into Paul. They believed (like Barth supposedly believed) that those who came before themselves attained merely to a historical understanding, not a spiritual understanding. In theological argument, Jülicher observed, Marcion proceeded "with the same sovereign arbitrariness and assurance of victory, with the same one-sided dualistic approach of enmity to all that comes from the world, culture, or tradition, and never tired of tossing a few pet ideas in front of us." Marcion was not a pure Gnostic and neither was Barth, Jülicher judged; in his reading only Gogarten was taking the pure Gnostic flight from history. If Gogarten was a new Valentinus, stretching out his arms in writhing pain "toward the blessed pleroma above," Barth was a new Marcion, half-Gnostic, "with his radical dualism of all or nothing and his wrath against those who take only half."[26]

The first edition of *Romans* took a similar pounding from lesser-known scholars such as Karl Ludwig Schmidt (who also compared Barth to Marcion) and young Rudolf Bultmann, who dismissed the book as "enthusiastic revivalism" that reinterpreted history as myth. Though he welcomed Barth's critique of culture-religion, Bultmann reported that he could see in Barth's constructive position "little else than an arbitrary adaptation of the Pauline Christ myth." Barth tried at first to take this critical shower in stride. He told Thurneysen that Jülicher's critique seemed more like a "gentle evening rain" to him than a "fearful thunderstorm." He noted with interest that liberals like Jülicher and Harnack were already lumping him with Gogarten and other "outside friends." He further noted that they seemed especially eager to pin a heretic's hat on him. In the face of such criticism, he judged, it was advisable to avoid the spectacle of a youthful rebellion against an aging establishment: "In the presence of these scholars who know twenty-five times as much as we do we shall in the future lift our hats more respectfully, even though it seems to us quite idolatrous."[27]

THEOLOGY AND THE CRISIS OF LIBERALISM

The fact that the liberal establishment was taking the trouble to refute him gave encouragement to Barth that "the idol totters." His sensational address at the 1919 Tambach Conference on Religion and Social Relations gave notice that he was seeking to knock the idol off its pedestal. At Tambach he met Gogarten for the first time and also made a host of other new friends, including Günther Dehn and Hans Ehrenberg. With sweeping bravado Barth declared at Tambach that "we must win again the mighty sense of reality in which Paul is one with Plato and the prophets. Christ is the absolutely *new from above;* the way, the truth, and the life of *God* among men; the Son of Man, in whom humanity becomes aware of its *immediacy* to God." He gave a rousing farewell to every form of politicized religion, including religious socialism. The last thing that theology needed in the present postwar crisis, he urged, was to secularize Christ "for the sake of social democracy, or pacifism, or the youth movement, or something of the sort—as yesterday it would have been for the sake of liberal culture or our countries, Switzerland or Germany."[28]

The latter sentiment was appealing to many pastors and academics in the aftermath of the war. They were finished with Christian arguments for the support or renewal of German society, at least for the time being. Like Barth, some of them were repulsed by the spectacle of war experience theology. Like Barth, some of them were chastened enough by this spectacle to question the entire trend of the past generation toward an increasingly politicized culture-religion. The latter trend was epitomized by Friedrich Naumann, the eminent culture-theologian and longtime editor of *Die Hilfe.* Naumann was the spiritual leader of the German Democratic Party (a left-liberal party to the right of the Social Democrats) and a member of the Reichstag. He was also Martin Rade's brother-in-law. In his early career he had been a gospel-oriented liberal who worked in Hamburg's Inner Mission Movement. He had used his considerable influence to create a progressive Christian alternative to both secular Social Democracy and conservative Christian Socialism. Like the Berlin court preacher and Christian Social Party leader Adolf Stöcker, Naumann had tried to win workers away from the bitter anticlericalism of the Social Democrats. At the same time he strongly opposed the right-leaning nationalism of most German Christian leaders, which in Stöcker's case included a virulent anti-Semitism. Naumann's early career as a Christian leader was devoted to establishing the kind of social Christianity that was then taking root in Swiss Religious Socialism and the American social gospel movement.[29]

But in the mid-1890s Naumann had begun to move toward a new kind of nationalistic politics. Stöcker, an old-style monarchist and conservative socialist, wanted to bring the socialist-turning masses back to the church and the Kaiser. Naumann's nationalism was more current. He began to argue that what was needed was not a return to the old patriarchal state, but a forward-looking German imperialism. He reasoned that only a powerful German state could build a strong and healthy German economy. During the same period he made a chastening trip to Palestine which convinced him that Jesus couldn't possibly have intended to promote a social programme, since Palestine was too poor and desolate even to have decent roads. Later he judged that St. Francis of Assisi had nothing to teach people who rode express trains and used the telegraph. Naumann assured that modern people were right to judge St. Francis as, at best, a noble fool. St. Francis believed that a Christian's life should be wholly determined by Christianity. At the turn of the century Naumann attacked this illusion with vengeful persistence, renouncing what he called "complete Christianity," arguing that Christianity has no legitimate moral influence in the spheres of life that deal with human needs for self-preservation and social order. "Not all fulfillment of duty is Christian," he lectured, playing up the contrast between the pacifistic words of Jesus and the needs of "maintaining the State by a system of armed force."[30]

By 1905 Naumann was urging that a massive German military build-up was needed. He later exhorted the German Social Democrats to become good Germans by supporting the Kaiser's militarism. He came to epitomize the "serious" intellectual who cloaks his country's will to power with the armor of moral righteousness. In 1915, on the same day that Barth met with Blumhardt, he also had an angry argument with Naumann over Germany's responsibility for the war. As Barth later reflected, the fateful symbol of Naumann's later career was 4 August 1914, "the dark day on which the German Social Democrats betrayed socialism." Naumann had not only urged the Social Democrats to betray socialism for imperial Germany; he had also shrewdly predicted that they would do so. By then he was contending that Christianity was irrelevant to the serious concerns of the present age except as a source of support for nation-building and warfare. His politicization "led finally to setting up that new trinity of democracy, industry, and world power," Barth observed. What mattered in the real world was the attainment of national power, though always in the name of building a good and healthy social order. Barth noted that during the war Naumann kept up with church affairs "with a certain mild superiority, as one who has looked behind the scenes and no longer lets himself be taken in." It was his impression that Naumann looked back on his early career "with that sad smile with which one recalls the ideals and errors of his youth." In 1918 Naumann was still prominent enough to be considered for the presidency of the new government. Barth's reaction was, "All these things will I give thee, if thou wilt fall down and worship me."[31]

By 1920 many of the academics and pastors who came to places like Aarau and Tambach for religious edification were also looking for another kind of modern Christianity. Barth's show-stopping appearance at Tambach made him a figure to be reckoned with in German theology. The doors of various German universities and church groups opened to him. His emphasis on the non-religious worldliness of biblical piety was especially attractive to Gogarten, who soon became (next to Thurneysen) Barth's most important theological comrade. Gogarten's eagerness to play this role was first signalled by his sharp reply to Jülicher that neither he nor Barth deserved to wear the heretic's hat.

"Not even so learned and respectable a scholar as Jülicher has the right to charge us with egoism and lack of piety," he protested. Jülicher characterized the immediacy claimed by Barth and Gogarten to Paul as "holy egoism," but Gogarten countered that good theology appropriated God's revelation in history through two distinct methods. "A person will have one relation to history when he regards the whole span of its development as the proper revelation of God, and he will have another when he sees the proper revelation in God's original action which does not enter into its own effects and consequences and is not modified by and recognizable in them, but which must be grasped ever and again in its pure original nature beyond its historical effects and forms, however important these may be," he wrote. In other words, historiocriticism always has important work to do in seeking to establish the actual historical facts, but because historical research itself is always part of the historical process that it seeks to judge, the verdicts that it renders are never anything more than probable judgments. Historical knowledge is inescapably bound within the sphere of probability and unending approximation.[32]

The problem is that this is not the sphere to which God's revelatory action belongs, Gogarten argued. The goal of God's original deed does not lie in the sphere of historical approximation and probability, for revelation works upon faith, not upon historical reconstruction. If the apostles had waited to possess exact historical understanding of God's revelation in Christ before they chose to follow Christ, they would never have become Christians. In this crucial respect, Gogarten observed, those who walked with Christ thus had no advantage over later generations. They had to make a leap of faith in Christ, just as we do. To grasp hold of that which is eternal, the apostles had to "leap out of the endless mediacy of history," just as we do. Martin Luther put the matter succinctly when he declared that "time makes no difference to faith." He believed that Adam had the same faith in Christ that we possess. Luther took it for granted that Christians are required to push through the historical realm to the spirit of the Bible, since God is the object of faith.

This is not bad company for a Protestant theologian to seek, Gogarten taunted Jülicher. One of the chief themes of the Reformation had become so alien to liberal Protestantism that liberal theologians were dismissing Luther's true successors as gnostics. The spirit of the Bible is not the spirit of historical probability, Gogarten lectured. The spirit of the Bible is the Spirit of God, which cannot be subjected to historical control. Liberal theology took pride in its achievements; it spoke often of the work that theology must undertake in seeking to understand the Christian past and uphold a Christian-based culture. But Luther always denied that human work can accomplish anything for the kingdom, Gogarten observed. Luther taught that the kingdom advances only when God's Word is allowed to act alone. Gogarten urged that it was this spiritual truism that Barth had begun to recover for theology. Liberal scholars like Jülicher derided Barth's spiritual exegesis with "superior mockery," but the joke was on them for believing that their historical tools could lay hold of the content of Christian faith.[33]

For this reason, Gogarten announced elsewhere, "it is the destiny of our generation to stand between the times." The age of theological liberalism was over. The content of Christian theology is supposed to be God's Word, he observed, but liberal theology was not open to any word that could not be subjected to scientific control. "You left us empty," Gogarten charged. "You do not know how it tormented us that we could hear nothing more. . . . We received much that was scholarly, much that was interesting, but nothing that would have been worthy of this word." Liberal theology relativized everything that it touched, but now a postwar generation was announcing that liberal theology itself was a passing phenomenon. The value of theological liberalism was relative to the world of its time. "Today we are witnessing the demise of your world," he declared. "We recognize disintegration even in the most hidden recesses, where you do not yet see it."[34] In the crisis of this moment, Gogarten urged, the only response that sufficed was to become open to God's creative activity and endure the divine judgment.[35]

"Here is a dreadnought on our side and against our opponents," Barth enthused to Thurneysen. "I have great expectations concerning him." Barth admired Gogarten's intellectual energy and his zeal for battle against the theological establishment. He took great satisfaction in having attracted such a tenacious comrade. He gave little pause to the fact that both he and Gogarten were leaning heavily on the arguments about faith, history, and Luther that Barth first heard from Herrmann. While both of them blasted away at the capitulation of liberal theology to various secularizing modern concerns, both of them defended their positions with Herrmann-style arguments about the primacy and transhistorical character of faith.[36]

By 1920 Barth's speeches and writings were setting off alarms in the liberal establishment, especially in its Harnackian mainstream. At the Aarau Student Conference, Barth sharply dissociated himself from the "outside" historiocritical approach to religious studies. Theology must speak from "inside and not outside . . . the knowledge of God and of the last things," he urged. In his view the key to biblical piety was precisely its antipathy to religion and the religious idea of sacredness. Biblical piety holds fast to a peculiar kind of worldliness that refuses to regard anything as sacred, Barth explained. Only God is sacred, and in the scriptural witness God is holy, incomparable, and unattainable. God cannot be grasped or put to use; God is only to be served and can only be served in utter obedience: "He is not a thing among other things, but the *Wholly Other,* the infinite aggregate of all merely relative others. He is not the form of religious history but is the Lord of our life, the eternal Lord of the world."[37] Though he still described the Easter message in Herrmannian liberal terms, Barth ascribed an importance to it that was foreign to most liberal preaching. "The only real way to *name* the theme of the Bible, which is the Easter message, is to have it, to show it, to live it," he exhorted. "The Easter message becomes truth, movement, reality, as it is expressed—or it is not the Easter message which is expressed. Let us be satisfied that all Biblical questions, insights, and vistas focus upon this common theme."[38]

One bewildered listener in particular was far from satisfied. Harnack found the speech appalling. "The effect of Barth's lecture was just staggering," he confessed to a friend. "Not one word, not one sentence could I have said or thought. I saw the sincerity of Barth's speech, but its theology frightened me." He compared Barth's thinking to a meteor "rushing toward its disintegration" and judged that "this sort of religion is incapable of being translated into real life."[39] To Barth directly he allowed that perhaps the church needed to be shaken up "a bit," but he advised Barth to keep his religious worldview to himself and not make an "export article" of it. In Barth's telling of the encounter, "Finally I was branded a Calvinist and intellectualist and let go with the prophecy that according to all the experiences of church history I will found a sect and receive inspirations."[40]

Harnack believed that Barth's approach to theology was apocalyptic and self-negating. The very possibility of a critical scientific theology would be negated if this kind of thinking gained the ascendancy. The thought that Barth's kind of theology might gain the ascendancy was intolerable to him. From Harnack's perspective, the most offensive aspect of Barth's theology was its eschatological character, but it was precisely this quality that Barth soon heightened dramatically. In the same letter in which he hailed Gogarten for blasting away at the liberal opposition, Barth reported that he could not allow the first edition of his book on Romans to be reprinted, and that for several reasons the book was already alien to him, barely two years after its completion.[41] Barth had written the book in the fresh excitement of what amounted to a conversion experience, but his comprehension of Pauline thinking had subsequently deepened in the course of his further studies of Paul's letters, especially 1 and 2 Corinthians. He had also strengthened his understanding of Plato and Kant and had begun to study Kierkegaard, Dostoyevsky, and the Swiss anti-theologian Franz Overbeck. Moreover, some of the positive reviews that the book had received from theologians made him realize that he had not expressed his understanding of Paul with nearly enough prophetic bite.[42] Under the pressure of these influences, Barth discussed his rapidly shifting position with Gogarten and decided that the book had to be reformed "root and branch."[43]

RETHINKING THE PAULINE MESSAGE

The question of the relative weight that should be assigned to each of these factors has sustained an ample scholarly debate for many years. Numerous Barth scholars have maintained that Kierkegaard's dialectic of existence and his rhetorically powerful emphasis on the otherness of God provided the decisive influence on Barth's theological rethinking.[44] Others argue that Barth's adoption of a severely dialectical and eschatological outlook in his second edition *Romans* was influenced, above all, by his rather eccentric interpretation of Overbeck.[45] In an earlier book, I made a case for the view that both of these influences were important to Barth and that Overbeck was the stronger formative influence during the period when Barth rewrote his *Romans* commentary.[46]

One of the problems with assigning relative weight to these sources is that Barth was influenced by them in different ways. In a crucial sense, for example, the younger Blumhardt had a greater positive impact on Barth than any of Barth's theological or philosophical interrogators. Blumhardt's vibrant eschatological faith in the living reality of the resurrected Jesus was enormously significant to Barth during the ten-year period that he cast about for a new way of theological thinking and speaking. For the rest of his life, Barth remained close in spirit and affection to both Blumhardts. He recognized that he owed much to them, certainly more than he owed to Kierkegaard or the others.[47] The Blumhardts inspired Barth to hold fast to the reality of the kingdom-bringing Spirit of the resurrected Christ. In the early 1920s, they innoculated him from taking Overbeck more seriously than he did. But the Blumhardts were Christian witnesses, not academic theologians. They could not provide for him the concepts or method that he needed to express theologically the gospel faith that he heard from them. For this task, which began as an overhaul of his commentary on Romans, Barth drew upon various theological, philosophical, and literary sources, especially Overbeck and Kierkegaard.

The immediate problem was the problem of his governing schema. Barth's first edition *Romans* was dominated by a sacred history *(Heilsgeschichte)* schematism in which the stream of God's "real history" made episodic appearances in the history of Israel (especially the prophets) and in figures such as Socrates and Plato before it broke fully into the world in the fullness of time ("the new age") in Jesus Christ. It disturbed him greatly when sympathetic reviewers such as Emil Brunner interpreted this theological scheme as an endorsement of a liberal conception of divine indwelling, a "divine reservoir in us."[48] Barth's insistence at Aarau that God is not an object or process within or among other objects, but the "wholly other" Spirit of sovereign glory and grace, "the infinite aggregate of all merely relative others," was meant to dispel this kind of misunderstanding.[49] As Harnack perceived, Barth's address at Aarau was a declaration of independence from the liberal tradition. From that point onward, he sought to make clear that he was working out of a different tradition, a project that began with his wholesale rewriting of the *Romans* commentary. Under the influence of Kierkegaard's and Overbeck's attacks upon Christendom, he recognized that his first edition was overloaded with organic metaphors that made the gospel message seem like a progress report. Under Overbeck's influence especially, he resolved that he had to overhaul the entire age-of-Adam/age-of-Christ schematism that supported his conception of sacred history.

Overbeck was a strange figure whose theological legacy became even more strange after Barth drew attention to his work. He was an atheist who taught New Testament and early church history from 1870 to 1897 at Basel, where his closest friend was Friedrich Nietzsche. Overbeck did not share his friend's personal animosity for Christianity, but he did believe that the Christian religion was untrue and that it was fated to become extinct by "a gentle fading away." On the basis of what amounted to an early form of form critical analysis, he taught that genuine Christianity ended with the apostolic age. The earliest Christian communities were intensely eschatological and apocalyptic, he emphasized. Original Christianity was fundamentally characterized by its expectation of an immanent apocalyptic intervention from above. Overbeck invented the term *Urgeschichte* (primal history) to describe the relationship to historical process that this worldview presumed. The early Christians lived in history but were not part of it, he explained;

their world was a counter-world to ordinary history. They had no concept of "Christianity" as a new religion that would produce its own historical tradition. They hoped and expected to be delivered soon from history by a history-ending act of God.[50]

Overbeck allowed that it was necessary and inevitable that the postapostolic church relinquished the apocalyptic consciousness of original Christianity. He believed that Paul was a transition figure who belonged already to a second stage of adjusted "Christian" awareness while retaining some of the marks of apocalyptic super-history.[51] He found signs of the church's early adjustment in the book of Acts. With pointed insistence, he argued that institutionalized Christianity was not Christian at all. Genuine Christianity thrived on the super-historical expectation of Christ's imminent second coming, but with the loss of this expectation, Christianity lost its vitality and itself. The literature of patristic Christianity adopted the literary forms of the dominant profane culture. The apocalyptic consciousness that produced the unique literature of New Testament and apostolic Christianity was lost altogether. An oxymoron, "historical Christianity," replaced the gospel faith. The only kind of "Christianity" that could make its peace with history was the kind that turned a super-historical faith into a religion.[52]

Overbeck believed that he was witnessing the final stage of this degenerative process in the bourgeois culture-Protestantism of his time. Modern Christianity was totally corrupt. It sought nothing higher than to be of use to modern culture. It perpetuated the illusion of remaining within Christianity in order to keep its place at the cultural table. The perfect symbol of its degeneration was Bismarck, who had no interest in Christianity itself, but who greatly valued the therapeutic benefits of a domesticated culture-affirming Protestantism. Overbeck warned that those who defended "modern Christianity" theologically were kidding themselves about the long-term viability of their apologetics. They were also kidding themselves about their own relation to Christianity. In actuality they were twice removed from genuine Christianity, first by their historical religiosity and second by their modernism. Their actual religion was modernism, he judged, but rather than face up to the novelty of their outlook even within a compromised "Christian tradition," they insisted with pathetic determination to link themselves to Luther, Augustine, Paul, and Christ. In his later years, Overbeck sought to free modern people from this regressive attachment by playing up the contradictions between modern culture and genuine Christianity.[53]

In 1919 Overbeck's lecture notes and papers on these themes were published (fourteen years after his death) by one of his former students. The book was badly edited, but its blast against the very idea of "Christian religion" was intoxicating to Barth. It gave ballast to his attacks on all forms of Christian religiosity and historicism. Barth was also reading Kierkegaard at the time, and though he recognized that Overbeck did not press his critique (like Kierkegaard) in the name of true Christianity, he tended to read Overbeck in the light of Kierkegaard's earlier attack upon Christendom.[54] Both of them were allies in his struggle to "kick against these pricks" of Christendom. "We rejoice at this book," he declared. "We greet it gladly in the hope that it will raise up comrades for us in our loneliness."[55] Barth recognized that Overbeck made an unlikely comrade for a theologian, for Overbeck taught that "Christian theology" is a contradiction in terms. Just as Kierkegaard emphasized the qualitative break between time and eternity, Overbeck insisted that one must choose between Christianity and history. "Historical" means "subject to time," he explained, but only a thoroughly distorted "Christianity" could be subject to time. History is precisely the basis on which genuine Christianity cannot be established, for the religion of Christ himself never had any historical existence whatsoever under the name of Christianity.[56]

In 1910 Barth had listened to Troeltsch lecture at Aarau about the coming end of Christendom and the advent of a cultural ice age. This depressing experience confirmed his judgment that the historical approach was a dead end.[57] He resolved to go beyond even Herrmann's compromised antihistoricism. He found spiritual comrades for this project in Overbeck, Kierkegaard, Dostoyevsky, and Blumhardt. With Overbeck he affirmed that history is an abyss "into which Christianity has been thrown wholly against its will."[58] With Kierkegaard he affirmed that Christianity is about the invasion of the eternal into time in the moment. With Dostoyevsky he judged that the church prefers to give people what they want—mystery, authority, and miracle—rather than to preach freedom through Christ. With Blumhardt, Barth conceived Christianity as a kingdom faith that proclaims the transformation of the present from beyond.[59]

His appropriation of Overbeck was strange at best. He put considerable stock in Overbeck's remark that "theology can no longer be established through anything but audacity." Barth resolved that he would reestablish theology with appropriate audacity, brushing off the fact that, in the next sentence, Overbeck pronounced that even audacity would be useless "to a person who has already lost faith in theology as a result of studying early church history!" Eberhard Jüngel later observed that either Barth didn't notice the bitter irony of this remark or he consciously ignored it.[60] In either case, he was shielded from Overbeck's destructive edge by his knowledge that a thoroughly eschatological Christianity was still a possibility for modern Christians. The elder and younger Blumhardts had shown this to him. The Blumhardts were emphatic that only a thoroughly eschatological Christianity has anything to do with Christ. Their ministries were founded on the anticipation of a new outpouring of the Spirit of the risen Jesus. To Barth, Overbeck and the younger Blumhardt stood together, but faced in opposite directions: "Blumhardt stood as a forward-looking and hopeful Overbeck; Overbeck as a backward-looking, critical Blumhardt. Each was the witness to the mission of the other."[61]

Together these witnesses drove Barth to declare his categorical break from theological liberalism. He retained the Pauline dialectic of Adam and

Christ, but he stopped describing the new creation under Christ as a new world that becomes a "life process" in human history. The new world cannot be born until the old world has died, he judged. All human history stands under the sign of sin, death, and judgment, including all Christian history. Liberal theology taught that history has an inner capacity for renewal because God is an aspect of the temporal order, but Barth urged that this was precisely the domesticating religious ideology that had to be given up. History is not a "life process" brought to fulfillment by a divine indwelling, he argued. History is the life of the old world that exists under the judgment of death. History lives "between the times"—between the primal divine history that Overbeck called *Urgeschichte* and the Parousia that will bring history to an end.

Moreover, the "object" of theology is not an object at all, or a process within or among other objects. Theology is like trying to draw a bird in flight, Barth observed. Apart from the movement, theology has no standpoint or ground. That is, apart from the movement of the Spirit that transcends and penetrates human history, theology "is absolutely meaningless, incomprehensible, and impossible." What the theologian must avoid is the temptation to make the movement itself an objectified thing. Apart from God's history-shaking movement in history, he insisted, "a movement which has neither its origin nor its aim in space, in time, or in the contingency of things," theology is nothing but idolatry.[62]

Barth was not oblivious to the problem that his negative dialecticism created for theology. He stood in danger of losing any basis for making positive affirmations about God. Put differently, he stood in danger of becoming another Overbeck. He therefore proclaimed with the memory of Blumhardt's witness firmly in mind that "there *must still* be a way from there to here." Theology is possible only as "inner waiting" for and openness to God's revelation, he wrote: "However much the holy may frighten us back from its unattainable elevation, no less are we impelled to venture our lives upon it immediately and completely."[63] To be a faithful Christian is to live, like Blumhardt, in "the fullness of what is" while at the same time waiting inwardly "for that which seeks to be through the power from on high."[64]

For Barth, both aspects of "hurrying and waiting" were crucial. Blumhardt lived in the fullness of the present historical crisis. He had no use for compromised Socialism, compromised Christianity, or the kind of blended compromises promoted by the Christian Social Party. He did not try to lure the workers away from Social Democratic socialism, like Stöcker and Naumann. Neither did he accommodate the gospel faith to modern cultural sensibilities, like all of the liberal theologians. He joined the Social Democratic party outright and refused to trim either his Socialism or his Christianity. "No world war and no revolution could make him a liar," Barth observed. Though he lost his pastorate and most of his German followers in the process, Blumhardt was joyful in his anticipation of God's kingdom. In Barth's words, "The unique element, and I say it quite deliberately, the prophetic, in Blumhardt's message and mission consists in the way in which the hurrying and the waiting, the worldly and the divine, the present and the coming, again and again met, were united, supplemented one another, sought and found one another."[65]

Blumhardt's capacity to live in the fullness of the social crisis as a radical socialist was sustained by his Christian hope, but he never reduced the meaning of this hope to his politics. He saw the idol in most forms of Christian Socialism. In its negative function, Barth's theology also became absorbed in a critique of idolatry. He described all of the world's religions as monuments to the "no-God." He proclaimed that the only basis for a nonidolatrous affirmation of God and the world is "the possibility of a new order absolutely beyond human thought." Only a kingdom-oriented eschatological Christianity bears any true relation to Christ, he insisted. But for the kingdom to become an actual possibility to theology, "there must come a crisis that denies all human thought."[66]

CRISIS THEOLOGY AS KIERKEGAARDIAN DIALECTIC

Barth's second edition *Romans* announced that the present death rattle of Christendom presented such a possibility. He described the gospel message as "the fire alarm of a coming new world."[67] Leaning heavily on Kierkegaard's notion of the "moment" and his dialectic of time and eternity, Barth presented the apparent crisis of the moment as a permanent, universal condition that negates all human strategies of salvation. Human history stands under the crisis of judgment, he warned. This crisis was the presupposition of Paul's message. "In this world men find themselves to be imprisoned," Barth explained. "In fact the more profoundly we become aware of the limited character of the possibilities which are open to us here and now, the more clear it is that we are farther from God, that our desertion of Him is more complete, and the consequences of that desertion more vast than we had ever dreamed."[68]

God's power to save us from this imprisonment cannot be detected in the world of nature or in our souls, he insisted. God is unknown, "and precisely because He is unknown, He bestows life and breath and all things." God's power is completely different from the powers of observable forces: "It is the KRISIS of all power, that by which power is measured, and by which it is pronounced to be something and—nothing, nothing and—something." God is neither a power alongside other powers nor a "supernatural" power standing above other powers. Barth explained that God's power is rather "that which sets all these powers in motion and fashions their eternal rest. It is the Primal Origin by which they all are dissolved, the consummation by which they all are established." God's power is "pure and preeminent" and beyond all other powers.[69]

Luther taught that faith directs itself toward invisible realities. Only that which is hidden can provide an opportunity for faith. Barth emphasized that this is a Pauline theme. "The Gospel of salvation can only be believed in; it is a matter for faith only," he declared. "It demands choice. This is its seriousness." To those who cannot accept the inner contradiction of the gospel, he observed, the gospel message is a scandal; but to those who cannot escape the necessity of contradiction, the gospel becomes a matter of faith. "Faith is awe in the presence of the divine incognito; it is the love of God that is aware of the qualitative distinction between God and man and God and the world; it is the affirmation of resurrection as the turning-point of the world; and therefore it is the affirmation of the divine 'No' in Christ, of the shattering halt in the presence of God." The righteousness of God is manifested wherever God's faithfulness encounters human faithfulness. This is the theme of the Pauline gospel message, Barth contended.[70]

He appropriated virtually all of the key concepts of Kierkegaard's *Training in Christianity* in explicating this theme. It was Kierkegaard who gave Barth the language for speaking of faith as "awe in the presence of the divine incognito." The "divine incognito" was Kierkegaard's description of the incarnation. He emphasized the paradoxical character of the incarnation and the "infinite qualitative distinction" that separates God and humanity. In dialectical fashion he argued that direct communication with God is impossible. In response to the question of how one might become a true Christian despite the qualitative gulf that separates God and the world, Kierkegaard described the possibility of becoming "contemporaneous" with Christ.[71]

Barth took up all of these motifs, excepting Kierkegaard's concern with the problem of how one becomes a Christian. Like Kierkegaard, he referred to Christ as "the paradox" and "the divine incognito." With Kierkegaard he insisted that faith is "always a leap into the darkness of the unknown, a flight into empty air." Faith cannot be communicated to oneself or to one from another, he explained; it can only be revealed by the Father of Jesus. Because the revelation of the Father given by Christ is the revelation of God's righteousness, it is necessarily "the most complete veiling of His incomprehensibility." Through Christ, God is made known "as the Unknown, speaking in eternal silence." Barth played up the Kierkegaardian implications of this theme. Just as Kierkegaard argued that genuine Christianity is destroyed when it becomes a form of direct communication (and therefore loses its capacity to shock), Barth declared that in Jesus "the communication of God begins with a rebuff, with the exposure of a vast chasm, with the clear revelation of a great stumbling block." To have faith in Jesus is to call upon God in God's utter incomprehensibility and hiddenness. To live faithfully is not to seek rational stability or religious comfort, but to embrace "the absolute scandal of His death upon the cross."[72]

Luther claimed that Romans 3:22–24 is the kernel of all scripture: "For there is no distinction, since all have sinned and fall short of the glory of God; they are now justified by his grace as a gift, through the redemption that is in Christ Jesus." With Luther and Kierkegaard, Barth proclaimed that the righteousness of God is displayed by the absolute separation between God and humanity. Nothing can be known about God apart from this recognition. "The paradox must be maintained absolutely, in order that the scandal may not be obscured, and in order that Christianity may be disclosed in its true nature as 'a problem which is itself essentially a riddle, and which sets a question-mark against every human achievement in history,' " he declared, quoting Overbeck. "Nothing must be allowed to disturb this paradox; nothing must be retained of that illusion which permits a supposed religious or moral or intellectual experience to remove the only sure ground of salvation, which is the mercy of God." Religion never saved anyone, but because God is merciful and God has laid upon all people without distinction the command to have faith, the possibility exists "that all flesh may see His salvation."[73]

Barth emphasized that this message of salvation pays no respect to circumstance. Appropriating Kierkegaard's concept of "the Moment," he heightened his earlier claim that Paul veritably speaks to all people of every age. "We demand the subjection of all human being and having and doing under the divine judgement, precisely in order that it may always and everywhere await the divine justification, and because, seen from God and for God, nothing can ever be lost," he declared. Salvation is about the invasion of the eternal into time in the Moment, which is not a "moment" *in* time, but the eschatological Moment in which redeemed sinners are clothed with the righteousness of God. "We remove from the 'Moment' when the last trump sounds all likeness to the past and the future, and thereby proclaim the likeness of all times, of all past and future," Barth asserted. In God there is no past or future. The fact that Paul lived and taught long ago is therefore irrelevant to the truth of his message of salvation. If Paul was right, we lack any ground for boasting except hope, regardless of time or circumstance: "We are deprived of the possibility of projecting a temporal thing into infinity or of confining eternity within the sphere of time."[74]

The dialectic of time and eternity made paradox the essential language of faith. Barth's text abounded with the metaphors of disruption, cleavage, and annihilation. For him, as for Kierkegaard, God was an impossibility whose possibility cannot be avoided. "God is pure negation," Barth declared. "He is both 'here' and 'there.' He is the negation of the negation in which the other world contradicts this world and this world the other world. He is the death of our death and the non-existence of our non-existence."[75] The grace of God was likened to an explosion that blasts everything away without leaving a trace. Divine grace is not a religious possibility standing alongside sin, Barth cautioned. It is rather a "shattering disturbance, an assault which brings everything into question."[76] Then how does the new world of the Spirit make contact with the existing world of Adam? Barth replied that it touches the old world "as a tangent touches a circle, that is, without touching it." Because the new creation does not touch the old world, he explained, "it touches it as its frontier—as the new world."[77] Christianity is true only as eschatology.

Among other things, this eliminated the possibility of systematic theology: "If I have a system, it is limited to a recognition of what Kierkegaard called the 'infinite qualitative distinction' between time and eternity, and to my regarding this as possessing negative as well as positive significance: 'God is in heaven, and thou on earth.' "[78] Within time, the receiver of grace experiences eternity in the absolute moment of revelation and anticipates the complete overcoming of time by eternity. Did this mean that God is part of the dialectic of finite and infinite existence? Did the prohibition on "projecting a temporal thing into infinity" apply to the dialectic itself? Put differently, did Barth follow Kierkegaard in interpreting the divine-human relation from the standpoint of the reflective self? Kierkegaard sought to explain how an "existing individual" can appropriate revelation and thereby become a Christian. In opposition to Hegel's individual-absorbing dialectic of Spirit, he held out for the reality of the reflective individual self who finds unique, unsubstitutable truth in the process of seeking self-knowledge. His refutation of Hegel's idealistic philosophy of the Absolute emphasized the existential character of Christian truth. He interpreted the divine-human relation dialectically from the standpoint of the reflective self, contending that the necessary precondition for becoming a Christian "is to become unconditionally turned inward."[79]

Many of Barth's interpreters have read his crisis theology as being Kierkegaardian in precisely this sense. Jüngel is a prominent example. In his reading, Barth shared with his crisis theology comrades the Kierkegaardian dialectic of existence and its theory of religious truth as "existential encounter." What made crisis theology "dialectical," he argues, was its commitment to a theological approach that began with an analysis of the human predicament and which then appealed to revelation as the solution to a fallen human existence. Jüngel contends that Barth, like Brunner, Bultmann, Gogarten and others, assumed, with Kierkegaard, that the divine-human relation must be conceptualized on the basis of the best possible (dialectical) understanding of the structure of human existence.[80]

The conventional interpretation of Barth's theological development joins this reading of Barth's crisis theology to the claim that Barth later discarded dialectical thinking altogether. Hans Urs von Balthasar's highly influential interpretation of Barth established the ruling categories and chronology that support this schematism. According to von Balthasar, in the early 1930s Barth shifted from a predominantly dialectical mode of argument to a predominantly analogical mode. Under the pressure of his need to find a constructive ground for dogmatic statements, and under the influence of his study of Anselm's approach to theology as "faith seeking understanding," Barth developed a method that mediated between the theologies of exaggerated immanence (liberalism) and transcendence (crisis theology). Carefully presented as an alternative to the Roman Catholic analogy of being, Barth called his method the "analogy of faith."[81] In this reading, it was Barth's development of the analogy of faith and his repudiation of existential dialecticism that made it possible for him to construct his massive dogmatic system. On various occasions in his later career Barth endorsed the main outline of this reading.[82] For this reason, those who have ventured to dissent from von Balthasar's enormously influential account of Barth's theological trajectory have usually found themselves in the awkward position of having to claim that they understand Barth better than he understood himself.

This problem is not as disabling as Barth's conventional interpreters have traditionally presumed, however. Barth's recollections of his early career were often faulty and he had a lifelong tendency to exaggerate the degree of his various shifts of position. His later theology contained crucial dialectical elements, for example (especially the dialectic of divine veiling and unveiling), yet at the same time he claimed to have no interest in dialectical reasoning and lamented that he was "the originator of this unfortunate term."[83] These factors and others related to them have fueled a sizable scholarly debate about Barth's development in recent years. Barth interpreters such as McCormack, Michael Beintker, Ingrid Spieckermann, and even (to a lesser extent) Jüngel have corrected the exaggerated representation of a decisive break in his thought in the early 1930s. With occasional exaggeration on the revisionist side, and with some important disagreements among themselves, these interpeters have demonstrated a fundamental continuity between the Word-oriented "dialecticism" of Barth's crisis theology period and his later theology. While Barth's mode of argument clearly became more analogical and less overtly dialectical in the course of developing his later dogmatic project, his crisis theology writings had already made "Barthian" arguments against the yoking of any philosophy or worldview to the gospel faith.[84] His earliest lectures on dogmatics (in 1924) made extensive use of both negative and positive analogical arguments.[85] In fact, virtually all of the chief distinctive components of Barth's later theology were contained in his first lectures on dogmatics.

Without rehearsing the wide range of arguments that the debate over these points has raised, the question of Barth's commitment to a thoroughgoing existentialism in the early 1920s is pertinent to the present discussion. Is Jüngel correct in affirming the traditional view that Barth's early appropriation of Kierkegaard's dialectic of existence committed him to an anthropocentric starting point? Here it appears to me that the revisionist reading (which Jüngel shares in other respects) is more correct on the crucial point. Barth did not convert to Kierkegaardianism in 1920. His second edition *Romans* contained only a few (though important) references to Kierkegaard and these references soon disappeared altogether from his writings. For all of the conceptual tools that Barth appropriated from Kierkegaard (especially the method of indirect communication), Kierkegaard's existentialism was still a form of anthropocentric theology. It structured affirmations about divine reality and the divine-human relation on the model of a philosophical account of human existence.

But the very point of Barth's theological turn during the Great War was to focus on God as the subject of revelation. McCormack rightly observes that by 1920 Barth was clear that the question of God "can only be raised where

God makes Himself known."[86] As Barth explained in the lecture that horrified Harnack, "the Bible has only *one* theological interest and that is not speculative: interest in God himself." This is what he meant by saying that scripture is unhistorical. The Bible has no interest in religious experience or the sacred at all, he contended; the single interest of scripture is God's holy presence and rule.[87] His second edition *Romans* made it clear that this claim was, at least, an accurate piece of self-description. Kierkegaard's preoccupation with establishing the integrity of individual human existence was brushed aside. "There is only life under His judgement and under His promise; there is only life characterized by death but qualified, through the death of Christ, as the hope of life eternal," Barth declared. "The Lord alone is the assurance of promise."[88]

The crucial difference between Barth and most of his allies was there at the outset of the crisis theology movement. Barth was not always clear or consistent in expressing it. For several years he shied away from pressing the difference with Bultmann and Gogarten, partly because he wasn't sure that he could defend his position from their objections. In 1921 he began his academic career as Honorary Professor of Reformed Theology at Göttingen, a position for which he felt grossly unqualified. He had no doctorate, he did not own a copy of the Reformed confessions nor had he ever read them, "quite apart from other horrendous gaps in my knowledge."[89]

DIALECTICS AND DOGMATICS

Barth scrambled for several years to fill the gaps, immersing himself in the history of Christian dogmatics. His ignorance of premodern theology and his alienation from what he called "the good society of contemporary theology" drove him to reeducate himself theologically. "All day long I am reading pell-mell hundreds and hundreds of pages: Heim, Thomas Aquinas, Fr. Strauss, Alex. Schweizer, Herrmann," he told Thurneysen.[90] He despaired that he found himself "so to speak without a teacher, all alone in the vast field." He accepted that the Bible "had to be the master in Protestant dogmatics" and that he needed to struggle anew with the Reformers, but how was he to carry out this project, he wondered, "if no one instructs me?" It was in this state of mind that Barth first read Heinrich Heppe's *Reformed Dogmatics,* a collection of texts on all of the loci of dogmatics by Reformed theologians between the sixteenth and eighteenth centuries. He also read Heinrich Schmid's parallel compendium of Lutheran texts. He later recalled that he approached "the old churchmen" with apprehension and soon found, as he expected, that they were "out of date, dusty, unattractive, almost like a table of logarithms, dreary to read, stiff and eccentric on almost every page I opened."[91]

But the old dogmatists also impressed Barth deeply with their theological rigor and their devotion to the church. Their seriousness was chastening to him. Having assumed responsibility for teaching Reformed theology to the church's next generation of leaders, Barth allowed himself to be taught by the old churchmen. It was a formative experience. Though much of their writing brought to mind Herrmann's cutting remarks against "the old orthodoxy," Barth later recalled that he found in the old orthodoxy an impressive display of learning, academic rigor, and church-centered spiritual discipline. It struck him especially that the old dogmatists didn't gerrymander like most liberals, but gave rigorous attention to all of the major themes of scripture. He told Thurneysen that "after much head shaking and astonishment," he found himself agreeing with the old Reformed and Lutheran churchmen on almost every point and heard himself saying things in class that he could never have dreamed of during his pastoral career.[92] His theology and rhetoric both became more chastened, realistic, and dogmatic as a result. Barth became not only a teacher of the Reformed tradition of Christian dogmatics, but a dogmatist within this tradition.[93] The expressivist metaphors and word plays that filled his early crisis theology writings gradually disappeared from his work. He later recalled that in the mid-1920s he began to learn "along with a great centralization of what was material, to move and express myself again in simple thoughts and words."[94] His language became more representational and mimetic as a function of his resolve to serve the church as a dogmatic theologian.

The irony of Barth's career is that he began to lose followers nearly from the outset of the crisis theology movement and then remained a rather isolated figure long after he was widely recognized as the major theologian of the twentieth century. His attack on theological liberalism set him against all of his teachers and most of the theological establishment. He later recalled that during his early years at Göttingen he realized increasingly that he was alienated "from almost the whole of modern theology." He launched a new theological movement in reaction, but his insistence that Christian theology must live by God's self-authenticating Word alone eventually set him apart from nearly all of his major allies, especially Bultmann, Gogarten, Brunner, and Tillich. In the early 1930s he went to considerable lengths to accentuate the gap between himself and these figures. Moreover, Barth's earlier shift to the dogmatic rhetorical form alienated various others who preferred his "crisis theology" attacks on theology as a discipline. While working on his first lecture cycle of dogmatics, he confessed to Thurneysen that he often sighed "under the awareness of the complete isolation of the whole undertaking."[95] In 1925 a telling, if extreme, sign of this isolation was rendered by Hermann Kutter.

Kutter had barely tolerated Barth's early crisis theology writings. Then in 1923 Barth founded (with Gogarten, Thurneysen, and Georg Merz) a theological journal titled *Zwischen den Zeiten (Between the Times).* Crisis theology became not only a lecture circuit fad, but a theological movement. It attracted some of the most promising theologians of the postwar generation, including Bultmann, Brunner, Günther Dehn, Erik Peterson, and Heinrich Schlier. To Barth's surprise, Bultmann was greatly impressed by the second edition *Romans;* his long and generally favorable review of the book was published in *Die Christliche Welt.*[96] This review drew Barth and Bultmann into a friendship and, for a few years, a movement-oriented partnership. With bold self-assurance, Barth and his comrades (especially Gogarten) presented their movement as the harbinger of a new theological era. They stood between the end of theological liberalism and the postliberal age to come.

But to Kutter the very concept of a theological movement, "Barthian" or otherwise, was disheartening. Having thought for a time that Barth was some kind of disciple, he was deeply disappointed when Barth turned into some kind of dogmatic theologian. In 1925 he informed Thurneysen that with deep regret he could no longer sustain a spiritual fellowship with Barth. "I can do no other than recognize in the Barthian theology, however interesting and healthy it may be for the rest of theology, a straying away from that which—imperfectly enough!—burns in my heart and soul," he announced. The gospel mission is to proclaim the reality and coming of God, he observed, but the Barthian movement was turning this kingdom-bringing faith into a theology. Even worse, it was turning the gospel mission into "a theological controversy—a ready meal for the theological eagles who are delighted that in disputing about the *concept* of God they may forget the striving after *God himself* and stake everything on the fact that the question of God is a theological uproar from which they can take their profit."[97]

Kutter did not dispute that what he called "the Barthian crisis" was doing much good in the field of theology. Later that year, upon his retirement as Zurich city pastor, he still held Barth in high enough regard to recommend him as his successor.[98] But he could no longer speak to him directly. For all of the good that Barth's writing was doing in theology, he lamented, it was still merely theology, "and all theology is a talking about God with a bad conscience." There is only one true way to speak about God, Kutter insisted, and that is to speak in God's own Word and Spirit. "There is a very great difference between proclaiming God himself once more to a society that has fallen away from him and distinguishing between a true and a false concept of God," he admonished. "The first was once our common task but it is now torn apart into two parallel developments." Though theology has its own necessary work to do, he allowed, it serves a lesser purpose than the work they once shared. "No theology is of any account when we have to do with God himself," Kutter insisted. "Only God's coming mattered to me, however little I am in a position to give a fitting expression to this great concern."[99]

Thurneysen protested in reply that Barth was doing theology precisely in Kutter's spirit. "He makes clear that no one can attain to God with his concepts, that when God speaks he can do it only in his own Word," he observed. The whole point of Barthian "crisis theology" was to make theology relinquish its concepts in order to bear witness to God himself. "Our whole intention is no other than to draw forth as clearly as possible from this preparatory witness of theology the actual witness that must follow in the preaching," Thurneysen explained. He told Kutter that it was through his witness that he and Barth had come to recognize that bearing witness to God himself must be their central concern. Was it really necessary to assume that theology can never bear witness to God truly? "Should it not be possible also that *God* can and will acknowledge this way as one way that we may go and ought to go?" he asked. More personally, "Are you really going to turn away from us as though we had already failed?" Thurneysen allowed that his and Barth's recent theological turn posed the "frightful danger" of betraying their common spiritual concern, but he pleaded that they did not deserve to be treated as though they had already hopelessly betrayed it.[100]

Many years later, at the end of their careers, Emil Brunner made a blistering attack on Barth that repeated Kutter's charge that Barth's theology betrayed the kingdom-seeking spirit of his earlier thinking and preaching. Brunner traced the point of betrayal to Barth's dogmatizing turn in 1924.[101] From Kutter's standpoint, the fateful turn occurred even earlier, with the rise of crisis theology as a movement. In both cases Barth was quick to shake the dust from his feet. He told Thurneysen that he could not have matched Thurneysen's civility if he had been forced to reply to Kutter. He grasped that Kutter was consigning him to "the same pit with Ragaz." He was prepared to accept this consignment if only Kutter recognized "that he, too, with his GOD is in it." As it was, he had no patience for a debate with Kutter about who served God or merely a concept of God. In his reading, the heart of the difference between them was that he was developing a deep appreciation for theology as a work of the existing church. The religious socialists regarded themselves as advocates of a new church or as prophets within the churches, but Barth's cram sessions with the old churchmen were giving him a deeper sense of connection to the present life and premodern history of the existing church. He emphasized that his earlier attacks on the church had been offered as inside criticism, not as attacks from a sectarian or outside position. He reflected that his pilgrimage out of theological liberalism led first "to the *Bible,* and then logically again to *dogma,* and at least to the insight that the proceedings concerning the *sacramental* concept are not yet closed." This pilgrimage had evidently carried him far from Kutter, whose posture now seemed "so reactionary, so irrelevant" to him. Not for the last time, Barth moved on without looking back.[102]

The old churchmen deepened his sense of connection to the premodern church and also drove him to define his freedom from it. In the course of preparing his first lecture cycle of dogmatics, Barth became a student not only of Protestant orthodoxy, but also of the early church fathers and medieval scholasticists, especially Thomas Aquinas. In form and content, his developing theology increasingly followed the example of what he called the "masters of the old theological school."[103] He generally followed the order of loci of Reformed orthodoxy (beginning with revelation) and also developed a new appreciation for the doctrine of the divine trinity, which he described as "the problem of the inalienable subjectivity of God in his revelation."[104] Many of his friends in the crisis theology movement shook their heads in disbelief as he increasingly adopted the thought forms of the older dogmatists.

But Barth's appropriation of the old orthodoxy was emphatically something new. He refashioned not only "the old doctrines," but also a cluster of defining liberal themes that he took from Herrmann and Kutter. He apologized for needing to develop a theological prolegomenon and then proceeded to develop a prolegomenon that recast the entire basis and structure of Protestant orthodoxy. With originality and persistence Barth applied Kutter's test to the work of dogmatics. He made the work of preaching God's Word the focal point of dogmatics. Put differently, he developed a new kind of revelational theology that placed extraordinary emphasis on the Word-disclosing role of the preacher as Christian witness. Barth explained that the Word of God is disclosed in three forms as revelation, as scripture, and as preaching. In language as plain and direct as Herrmann's on this point, he asserted that scripture is not revelation; rather, scripture comes from revelation. Neither is preaching to be equated with either revelation or scripture, he cautioned, though preaching comes from both revelation and scripture. "Revelation is from God alone, scripture is from revelation alone, and preaching is from revelation and scripture," he argued. Barth was emphatic about what this did not mean. It did not mean that revelation is the Word of God more than scripture, or that scripture is the Word of God more than preaching. "There is no first or last, no greater or less," he taught. "The first, the second, and the third are all God's Word in the same glory, unity in trinity and trinity in unity."[105]

The old dogmatists identified scripture as revelation and usually developed their doctrine of scripture before dealing with the Trinity, the incarnation, or the work of the Holy Spirit.[106] Barth's doctrine of the threefold Word broke the equation of scripture with revelation and placed the doctrine of scripture after the doctrines of the Trinity, the incarnation, and the work of the Holy Spirit. Though he apologized for needing a prolegomenon (only modern theologians need to explain their concepts and method, he noted; Aquinas and Calvin plunged directly into real theology), his own prolegomenal reformulation of his dogmatic assumptions breathed new life into the discipline of dogmatic theology. "We are not allowed to imagine that we are at another point in history," he cautioned. "We adjust under protest, but we still adjust." He allowed that it was too late to repeal the scholasticist turn in Protestant theology that occurred in the seventeenth century or the turn to liberal religious consciousness that occurred in the nineteenth century. Barth believed that both of these movements distorted and retreated from the great themes of the Reformation, but he also accepted that his alternative could not credibly strive to repristinate Calvin or Luther. The only worthy alternative would be a new Reformation theology. In the modern age dogmatics had to be modern: "It must be part of a conversation; it must be open to discussion." Among other things, this meant that instead of drawing straight from the subject of dogmatics, it was necessary to speak also about the subject.[107]

Much of what Barth said *about* the subject consisted of variations on Herrmann. Virtually all of the Reformed dogmatists ascribed great importance to the doctrine of natural revelation, he noted, "but for my part, although I am Reformed, I want no part of it." Like Herrmann, he wanted no part of a support system strategy that appealed to apologetic proofs. Unlike Herrmann, he pressed the point that appealing solely to revelation also excludes looking for traces of the divine presence in conscience, consciousness, the religious sense, or the like. "Either God speaks, or he does not," Barth maintained. "But he does not speak more or less, or partially, or in pieces, here a bit and there a bit. This is a contradiction in terms, an anthropomorphism, a basic naturalizing of revelation which fits Schleiermacher very well, but which ought not to have found any place among the older Reformed." The old dogmatists built a case for natural revelation from the confession that all truth is of God, but Barth countered that this confession is rightly understood as referring to the totality of truth. "Truth that really goes back to God cannot be a particle of truth," he explained. "It is either the whole truth or it does not go back to God and is not revelation at all."[108]

Zwingli taught that only God can make us certain of God's grace. Barth insisted that the implication of this principle for the doctrine of scripture is that scripture *is* God's Word because it is *God's* Word. Luther and Zwingli understood that no human proof can prove or disprove that scripture is God's Word, but the guardians of Protestant orthodoxy were not able to uphold this principle for long. Barth invoked Calvin as a mostly-sympathetic witness on this point, though he allowed that Calvin gave some marginal space to apologetic and natural revelationist arguments. In the case of Calvin, he reasoned, it is at least possible to judge that the apologetics game was played to the glory of God, since Calvin invested no real importance in his apologetic arguments. The real problem in the Reformed tradition is that many Calvinists afterward invested enormous importance in apologetic arguments. By the time that the Westminster Divines wrote the Westminster Confession in 1647, Barth noted, most Reformed dogmatists identified Reformed orthodoxy with a pile of apologetic proofs concerning the heavenly contents of the Bible and the divine majesty of biblical prose. The scholastic turn in Reformed orthodoxy was especially strong among continental theologians. Instead of trusting in the self-authenticating sufficiency of God's Word, Protestant scholasticism defended Christian belief with a load of probabilistic arguments, some of which were very dubious.[109]

On similar grounds, Barth took for granted Herrmann's rejection of orthodox propositionalism. He argued that the old dogmatists took refuge in the doctrine of the verbal inspiration of scripture because they could not abide the paradox of confessing that scripture is the Word of God in human words. "They could no longer bear to stand on the knife-edge between faith and unbelief in face of this purely historical entity," he observed. "They could no longer bear to read the Bible as a human word, to read the texts exactly as they are with all that they imply when read historically." In the face of challenges from early forms of biblical criticism, the Protestant scholastics reduced Christian doctrine to a system of formulas. They reduced holy scripture to a book of propositions and obscured the paradox of the hiddenness of God's revelation in scripture. In effect, Barth contended, the orthodox dogmatists rejected revelation itself by refusing to recognize that God's presence in scripture is veiled by the historical character of scripture.

"They did not have too much faith but too little," he judged. "They did not see in the growing seriousness of the historical approach a challenge to balance the scales the other way, to undertake the venture of faith and obedience more boldly." By turning revelation into direct revelation, the old dogmatists set revelation aside. They created a paper pope "from which we are to get oracles as we get shoes from a shoemaker." The irony of Protestant orthodoxy was not only that Protestantism produced its own form of papal machinery, however. To Barth the deeper irony was that the orthodox theologians inadvertently historicized revelation by reducing revelation to the words of the Bible. In the seventeenth century, theologians such as Francis Turretin (Reformed) and Johann Gerhard (Lutheran) undoubtedly had a different purpose in mind when they divinized the biblical text virtually without remainder. Nonetheless, Barth observed, by refusing to recognize the paradox of God's hiddenness in scripture, the old dogmatists launched the fatal historical process by which revelation was subjected to historicizing human control. "I need not describe the disaster which then followed on the other side," he remarked, referring to secular Enlightenment historicism. "Marching, not without cause, under the banner of truth and credibility, historicism would never have taken on the openly anti-Christian significance that it did had Christianity itself, and especially Christian theology, ventured to insist on its own truth and credibility, and to maintain the *indirect* identity of the Bible with revelation." This is the project that must be taken up at the end of the liberal era, Barth urged, "and it will be a very painful process."[110]

In both cases the logic was Herrmannian, but where Herrmann appealed to the autonomy of faith as a revelatory experience, Barth appealed to the totalizing sufficiency of God's revelation in the Word. Revelation is its own basis, he contended. It has no need of supporting arguments or proofs and it lacks nothing as the proper basis for theological affirmations. It followed for him that Christian dogmatics must be precisely "scientific reflection on the Word of God which is spoken by God in revelation, which is recorded in the holy scripture of the prophets and apostles, and which now both is and should be proclaimed and heard in Christian preaching."[111] This formula distinguished three addresses within the single Word of God: in revelation God alone speaks, in scripture the biblical writers speak, and in preaching the number of possible speakers is theoretically unlimited. But in all three cases, the Word of God is one, Barth cautioned. The Word of God is always God's speaking.

From the outset of his rethinking of Christian dogmatics he emphasized what he called the "qualified temporal element" of this assertion. The Word of God is never a thing, but always an event, a turning from past to present. It is God's ongoing speech. The extraordinary importance that Barth's creative new blend of Reformationist, orthodox, and liberal theologies gave to preaching is fully disclosed in this connection. The point is often missed by those who play up the importance of Barth's traditional-sounding appeal to the Word of God as the single proper authority for Christian theology, but in Barth's reformulation of the doctrine of the Word, it is only as preaching that the Word of God bears an ongoing character. In the strict sense of the term, he explained, the Word of God is not ongoing as revelation, for the Word as revelation "never took place as such." The statement "God revealed himself" does not have the same meaning as the statement "revelation took place." "Revelation is what it is in time, but as the frontier of time remote from us as heaven is from earth," Barth contended. "Nor is God's Word ongoing as holy scripture. It is in time as such. It took place as the witness given to revelation. But in itself it is a self-enclosed part of history which is as far from us as everything historical and past."[112]

We do not live in a historical context that is continuous with the experiences of the apostles. Barth's often-misunderstood endeavor to see "through and beyond history into the spirit of the Bible" did not presume otherwise. He noted that even if one of Paul's missing letters to Corinth were to be found and added to the New Testament canon, this would not constitute an ongoing continuation of the Word as scripture. It would represent merely an extension of the concept of scripture. It would still belong to the past. There is no conceivable extension of scripture that could belong to the present, Barth observed. This is why the movement of the Word as preaching was so crucial to his interpretation of the Word as threefold event. By the logic of his doctrine of the Word, it was only as Christian preaching that the Word remains ongoing. The Word becomes present as preaching in the same way that the Holy Spirit makes God present to us. That is, just as the Holy Spirit proceeds from the Father and the Son, the Word as preaching proceeds from revelation and scripture. Barth's point was not that the revelatory and scriptural forms of the Word cannot be made present. Rather, just as the Father and Son are made present only through the movement of the Spirit, the Word as revelation and scripture are made present "in, with, and under" preaching and only through preaching.

By "preaching" Barth meant more than Sunday sermonizing or even the general ministerial work of pastors. Preaching included all forms of genuine Christian witness, including "whatever we all 'preach' to ourselves in the quiet of our own rooms." It included even the work of theologians, insofar as they understood and practiced theology as a service rendered to God's Word. Genuine Christian theology is a ministry of the Word of God and therefore a form of preaching, he argued.[113] In 1923 Harnack countered that the task of theology "is at one with the task of science in general." If Barth's understanding of theology should gain the ascendancy, he warned, it would lead to the obliteration of theology as an academic discipline. "On the basis of the whole course of Church-history I predict that this undertaking will not lead to edification but to dissolution," he announced. More precisely, he warned that if Barth's method should prevail in theology, it would not replace liberal theology for long, since Barth's approach was self-negating. No one would bother to teach it. The triumph of the Barthian movement would deliver theology instead, he predicted, "over into the hands of devotional preachers who freely create their own understanding of the Bible and who set up their own dominion."[114]

Barth noted in reply that by Harnack's criterion, Luther and Calvin failed to qualify as theologians, as well as the apostle Paul.[115] Harnack later confirmed the point, explaining that from the standpoint of a scientific theology, those who expressed their Christianity as witnesses were properly regarded as objects of theology, not subjects. He judged that the list of religious witnesses who therefore did not qualify as real theologians included Paul, Luther, and Barth.[116] Barth countered that Luther, Calvin, and Paul were better theological models than any liberal theologian. It was liberal theology that obliterated the content of theology, he charged. The content of Harnack's theology was the "simple gospel" that Harnack found beyond the scriptural text and apart from the Holy Spirit by the use of historical criticism. In liberal theology, Barth noted, this meagre human concoction was given the place that the Reformers gave to the correlation of scripture and Spirit. That is, scientific theology displaced the Word of God with a liberal academic impression of it. For all of the obvious tactical and practical differences that obtained between the practice of doing theology in an academic setting and preaching the gospel in a Christian pulpit, Barth contended, it was inconceivable to him that the theme of Christian theology should be some "second truth" that stands next to the theme that Christian preachers are obliged to express.[117]

Whether it is expressed inwardly or outwardly, the Word becomes present as speaking. Preaching is the Word made present. In Barth's words, the Word preached is a "mediated addressing and hearing of the Word of God from revelation and scripture." It followed for him that the purpose of dogmatics was to aid the preacher's reflective understanding of God's Word and the role of preaching in making the Word present. Dogmatics is the "methodical execution" of the movement from preaching to its underlying basis in revelation and scripture, he proposed. It is through the study of dogmatics that the witness comes to understand the Bible as holy scripture. That is, it is through the study of dogmatic theology that the witness should expect to struggle with the totality of the prophetic and apostolic witness. Negatively, dogmatics is the criticism of preaching. Positively, it is reflection on that which is given—God's Word—which we hear as "the wonderful song of praise of the Christian church" whenever the gospel is faithfully proclaimed.[118] Barth observed that it is easy to speak about God if one dispenses with the biblical witness to God's speaking. It is always easier to talk about something that you have experienced nonparadoxically as your own possession. But the task of dogmatics, he urged, is to remind the witness that preaching is meant to make God's Word present. The Word is made present not by describing the preacher's psychological experiences or her ideas about the "national soul," but by preaching scriptural teaching in the fullness of its witness, where God the Holy Spirit bears witness to himself.[119]

On the basis of these themes, the Barthian/dialectical movement effected as dramatic a transformation of the theological landscape as Christian history has ever witnessed. Crucial to the movement's success was the fact that Barth-style and even Brunner-style "neoorthodoxy" were more novel theologically than they acknowledged. Barth restored to theology the orthodox theme of the primacy of revelation, but he conceived revelation in a way that extinguished a host of problems endemic to orthodoxy. Repeatedly he pressed the theme that the content of revelation is God alone, wholly God, God made known in the three persons of a single divine essence. This formulation allowed Barthian theologians to uphold the indirect identity of scripture with revelation without having to deny that the Bible contains internal contradictions, myth, legend, and the like. Barth and Brunner made much of the fact that both Luther and Calvin practiced forms of biblical criticism that were later prohibited in Protestant orthodoxy.[120] They rarely noted the fact that both Luther and Calvin did not share their abhorrence for the idea of propositional revelation. For Barth especially, nothing was more crucial for theology (negatively) than its faithful willingness to clear the field of all concepts of revelation.

Repeatedly he cautioned that that which becomes sacralized as sacred text or sacred image or sacred history is never the true holy. The "true holy" is always spirit and never thing: "The *Deus Dixit* is revelation, not revealedness."[121] To believe the gospel on the basis of its Spirit-illuminated Word is not to look for proofs or historical evidences or other revelations. Neither is it to ground Christian teaching on appeals to religious experience or moral value. Neither is it to establish an idea of revelation on a principle that might be announced in advance of God's revelatory action, which Barth later accused Luther of doing. Neither is it even to look for analogies or similitudes, for revelation has no analogy. "Revelation is not the peak of the particular on the mountain of the usual and the universal," Barth proclaimed. "It is the heaven above all that is distinctive or general."[122] On the strength of this theme, Barth became a towering figure in modern theology, but with tellingly few followers.

3

SELF-AUTHENTICATING?

The Break-Up of Dialectical Theology

In 1928 Paul Schempp aptly noted that for all of his enormous success in redirecting the field of theology, Barth stood "just as much alone today as he was ten years ago."[1] At the time Barth was Professor of Dogmatics and New Testament Exegesis at the University of Münster (Westphalia) and author of the first half-volume of a projected three volume dogmatics, *Die christliche Dogmatik im Entwurf.*[2] By then the most powerful current in theology was something usually called "the Barthian movement," though as Schempp implied, none of Barth's major followers appeared to accept his insistence that theology must be based upon the Word of God alone.

Ten years later Barth made the same observation, during the very period when religious thinkers were beginning to call him the most important theologian of the past hundred years. In 1930, he had become Professor of Systematic Theology at the University of Bonn, where his courses attracted large crowds of students from numerous countries. In 1932, the prolegomenal first half-volume of his *Church Dogmatics* was published. The following year, after Adolf Hitler and the National Socialists seized power in Berlin, he had become the chief theological voice of a dissident church movement that resisted a state-supported campaign to blend Christianity with German fascism. In this capacity, as a leader of what came to be called the Confessing Church movement, Barth authored the historic Barmen Declaration of 1934. The following year he was dismissed from his position at Bonn for refusing to sign the required oath of loyalty to Hitler.[3] He returned to Switzerland in 1935 to become Professor of Systematic Theology at the University of Basel, where he remained until his retirement in 1962. By the time he began his teaching career at Basel, Barth's theological preeminence was acknowledged even by his sharpest critics. The publication of his massive second half-volume of dogmatics in 1938 confirmed that he was set upon a mind-boggling scale for his definitive theological project.

Yet, he noted the same year that he was still very much alone among theologians. For all of the apparent world-shaking influence of the Barthian school, it seemed to him that no "Barthian school" existed at all. In one sense this was fine with him. Barth often claimed that he was not a

"Barthian" either and that he wanted no responsibility for supervising or defending a theological school. In a more serious sense, however, he did recognize that his theological position was more isolated than he should have wanted or expected it to be, given his towering stature over the field. "My lifework seems to be wanting in a certain accumulative power—even more, that a certain explosive, or in any case centrifugal, effect seems to inhere in it," he confessed.[4]

The structure and substance of his mature theological position had taken shape over the preceding decade. In the course of debating with Bultmann, Gogarten, Emil Brunner, and others about the role that philosophy (of any kind) should be allowed to play in Christian theology, Barth had developed an understanding of the dogmatic enterprise that left him remarkably isolated from his ostensible theological allies. In the early 1930s he made a fresh beginning on his dogmatic project, repeating his earlier experience of rewriting a major work. This time he was motivated partly by his determination to accentuate the gulf that separated him from his former comrades. From his standpoint, virtually all of his major associates (except Thurneysen) had shown themselves to be unwilling to break free from the controlling influence and security of philosophical speculation. Having debated the matter with most of them for the past decade, Barth resolved to declare his independence from them and purge his own theology of its remaining existentialist elements. He proposed, in 1932, "to say the same thing over again, but the same thing over again in quite a different way."[5]

Thus did his earlier "Christian" dogmatics, which could still be understood as the dogmatic self-understanding of a "dialectical theology movement," give way to Barth's *Church Dogmatics,* in which the notion of dogmatics as a free science was explicitly renounced. The only genuinely Christian dogmatics is one that is "bound to the sphere of the Church," he declared.[6] With that statement and a fair amount of accompanying polemics, Barth made a virtue of his theological isolation. He sought to develop a dogmatic self-understanding for a modern Word-oriented Protestant church that barely existed anywhere. The following year, after Hitler came to power, he watched with horror as many of his former students and purported friends, notably Gogarten, made their peace with so-called "German Christianity." Barth later recalled that he "saw my dear German people beginning to worship a false God."

For him there was never any doubt that the church must not promote Nazi ideology or otherwise become assimilated into the National Socialist state: "Here I acted instinctively. I did not even have to think about rejecting all this."[7] Some of Barth's dialectical theology friends were equally opposed to German Christianity, including some who did not share Barth's theological position. Tillich was forced to flee Germany, for example, and (to Barth's surprise) Bultmann joined the Confessing Church. The fact that so many of his friends sought a religious accommodation with fascism, however, confirmed Barth's judgment that the crisis theology movement had been compromised all along by its openness to various paganizing ideologies, philosophical support systems, and apologetic strategies. With unrelenting and sometimes rhetorically blistering insistence, he proclaimed in the early 1930s that the church must say good riddance to all that.

He was slow to arrive at this point. In the 1920s Barth wanted the crisis theology movement and its journal to succeed. For this reason he was inclined to play down his differences with Bultmann, Gogarten, Brunner, and others in public. There was a deeper reason why his parting of ways theologically did not occur until the early 1930s, however. Though Barth's first lectures on dogmatics contained nearly all of the elements of his mature theology, including his Herrmannian rejection of apologetics, he was not completely certain during the early and mid-1920s that his strictures against philosophical support systems were theologically necessary. The question dominated much of his interaction with theologians in the *Zwischen den Zeiten* circle. Nearly from the outset of the crisis theology movement, he expressed misgivings about the commitments of Gogarten, Bultmann, and Tillich to various philosophical programs. He questioned why Tillich insisted on playing "hide-and-seek with the frosty monster 'the unconditioned.' " He charged that Tillich's philosophically-constructed God seemed closer to the God of Schleiermacher and Hegel than to the God of Luther and Kierkegaard.[8]

Barth was more circumspect in dealing with his closer allies. He worried about Gogarten's movement-oriented militancy and his commitment to an existential "philosophy of life," but for the most part he expressed these concerns only to Thurneysen, Georg Merz, and a few others. He later recalled that he "always smelled something about Gogarten which I did not quite like."[9] In 1922 Barth was already biting his tongue with Gogarten in public to avoid giving comfort to their enemies. "The Christological problem is dealt with and solved by him with the help of a speculative I-Thou philosophy," he told Thurneysen. "Heaven only knows where that will yet lead."[10] Barth opposed Gogarten's "unbearably pretentious" proposal to name their journal *The Word.* "It would be better to call it *The Ship of Fools* than burden it with this sacred millstone," he judged.[11] Later he complained that Gogarten "would like in general to see us occupy only the *front*-line trenches where mines are bursting constantly, but that is not the way to carry on a war."[12] In 1925 Barth concluded shrewdly that on the crucial issue that divided the *Zwischen den Zeiten* theologians from each other, Gogarten was much closer to Bultmann than to himself.[13]

But, at the time, he was not completely certain that this meant that Gogarten and Bultmann were wrong. In the mid-1920s, Bultmann's rising stature as the leader (with Martin Dibelius) of form critical interpretation made Barth especially wary of expressing his misgivings about Bultmann's commitment to existential philosophy. He exulted in Bultmann's unexpected support and friendship. He and Bultmann had first met during Barth's student days at Marburg in 1908, but their friendship began only after Bultmann published his lengthy review of Barth's second edition

Romans. Even that generally favorable review raised issues that later opened a deep gulf between them. Bultmann praised Barth for recovering the deepest meaning of Paul's teaching about faith and grace, but he objected that Barth still made arbitrary appeals to the Pauline Christ myth. He further protested that Barth gave no consideration at all to such important questions as the degree of Paul's dependence on Jewish theology or his dependence on Hellenistic sacramental beliefs or the like.[14]

SPIRIT OF THE WHOLE OR CRITICISM OF SPIRITS?

To Bultmann these were crucial problems that compromised Barth's claim to deal with the subject-matter of Paul's letter. Bultmann was a product of the history of religions school at Marburg, where his *Doktorvater,* Johannes Weiss, taught him to understand early Christianity in its context among the religions of the eastern Mediterranean during the Hellenistic age. His early writings distinguished strongly between the noncultic Jesus of Palestinian Christianity and the mythical Christ of cultic Hellenistic Christianity.[15] In 1921 he published a colossal pioneering work in form criticism, *The History of the Synoptic Tradition,* which established the probable community origins of the sayings and narrative units of the synoptic gospels. This epochal work maintained that the synoptic narratives provide relatively little historical information about Jesus.[16] It also immediately established Bultmann as a major figure in New Testament studies.

To be praised by such a figure in *Die Christliche Welt* was deeply gratifying for Barth, especially after Bultmann panned his first edition *Romans.* He welcomed Bultmann's expression of support while defending his procedure from Bultmann's historiocritical objections. For Barth, the heart of the matter was that the Spirit of Christ must not be placed alongside any other spirits that historical criticism may identify in scripture. He did not deny that scripture contains the kinds of historical influences that Bultmann described. What Barth disputed was Bultmann's assumption that the spirit of Hellenistic sacramentalism or the spirit of rabbinical theologizing were part of the genuine subject-matter of Paul's teaching. "It seems to me impossible to set the Spirit of Christ—the veritable subject-matter of the Epistle—over against other spirits, in such a manner as to deal out praise to some passages, and to depreciate others where Paul is not controlled by his true subject-matter," he explained. "Rather, it is for us to perceive and to make clear that the whole is placed under the KRISIS of the Spirit of Christ." Scripture contains the whole, he allowed. The voices of other influences are surely part of the whole. "The problem is whether the whole must not be understood in relation to the true subject-matter which is—The Spirit of Christ."[17]

To Barth, the work of the faithful interpreter was precisely to screen out the voices of other spirits in order to make present the Spirit of Christ. It was to speak *with* Paul rather than merely compose an outside commentary *about* Paul. When the faithful interpreter carries out his or her work in this

Spirit, he contended, it becomes possible for the interpreter to see the fragments of the whole in the context of the true subject matter. That is, "all the other spirits are seen in some way or other to serve the Spirit of Christ."[18]

Bultmann praised Barth's recovery of the radical Pauline understanding of faith. He granted that this recovery was made possible by Barth's remarkable capacity to think and speak *with* Paul. At the same time, he protested that speaking *with* is not enough in serious scholarship. Barth simply ignored much of what needed to be understood about the historical influences on Paul if Paul's teaching was to be understood. Barth replied that this seemingly reasonable position was not only illegitimate, but an offense against literary taste. "He asks me to think and write WITH Paul, to follow him into the vast unfamiliarity of his Jewish, Popular-Christian, Hellenistic conceptions; and then suddenly, when the whole becomes too hopelessly bizarre, I am to turn around and write 'critically' ABOUT him and against him—as though, when all is strange, this or that is to be regarded as especially outrageous."[19]

Crucial to Barth's perspective was his sense that modern biblical scholarship routinely committed this offense against literary taste. Paul was strange and Spirit-filled, but modern scholars like Jülicher invariably drained all of the life and strangeness out of Paul. They tried to make Paul reasonable by appropriating only those aspects of Pauline teaching that fit into their worldview. For the most part, their commentaries focused on word studies and historical influences while bracketing out—in the name of academic sophistication—the actual subject-matter of Paul's teaching. Barth reminded them that Paulinism "has stood always on the brink of heresy." He chided the biblical scholars that their books on Paul were "utterly harmless" and domesticated by comparison.[20]

Bultmann ventured a careful balancing act in response. He sought to affirm Barth's theological purpose while defending the procedures of contemporary biblical scholarship. In the latter vein he asked Barth with apparent incredulity whether his manner of interpreting Paul's subject-matter did not bear some affinity to the old doctrine of verbal inspiration.[21] In effect, Barth replied that he certainly hoped so. Calvin's doctrine of inspiration engendered a better tradition of biblical interpretation than modern theology, he judged. Whatever their other faults, at least Reformers and the old churchmen apprehended the spiritual subject-matter of scripture.

This was not simply a case of special-pleading for biblical teaching, Barth cautioned. Scripture bears a unique status on account of its character as a revelatory witness, but the canons of good literary sense apply to all literature. The way that modern Bible scholars carried out their work was wrong not only for biblical interpretation, he insisted, but wrong for any piece of literature. "Is there any way of penetrating the heart of a document—of any document!—except on the assumption that its spirit will speak to our spirit through the actual written words?" Barth demanded. This assumption was the key to the possibility of any genuine apprehension of meaning. It did not require the faithful interpreter to be slavishly devoted to the words of the text, he contended. Criticism of the letter by the spirit is part of the work of faithful interpretation. Such criticism was practiced "in masterly fashion" by Calvin "without the slightest disregard for the discipline by which alone liberty is justified."[22]

Barth explained that this was the kind of exegesis to which he aspired. "The Spirit of Christ is not a vantage-point from which a ceaseless correction of Paul—or of anyone else—may be exercised schoolmaster-wise," he declared. "We must be content if, despite other spirits, we are not wholly bereft of the Spirit; content if, standing by Paul's side, we are able to learn and to teach; content with a readiness to discern in spiritual fashion what is spiritually intended; and satisfied also to recognize that the voice with which we proclaim what we have received is primarily nothing but the voice of those other spirits."[23] The latter point was crucial. Barth was not disputing what Bultmann called "the relativity of the word."[24] No human word is absolute truth, he allowed, including any word of Paul's. But we cannot see through Paul and beyond him, he urged, if we do not first endeavor to penetrate his meaning "with utter loyalty and with a desperate earnestness." This is what he missed in modern biblical criticism, including books like *The History of the Synoptic Tradition.*

In different ways over a series of related issues, Barth and Bultmann replayed this disagreement for the next forty years. Bultmann emphasized the historical discontinuity between early and modern Christianity, the mythical character of early Christian teaching, and the need for a demythologized theology that embraces a modern worldview. Barth countered that historical discontinuity is theologically insignificant, that mythical speech is intrinsic to the gospel, and that Christian theology has no business endorsing worldviews of any kind.[25] By the early 1940s when Bultmann became best known as the leading advocate of theological demythologization, the chasm between him and Barth was so great that it was hard to comprehend how they ever could have been allies. The signs of the differences between them were already evident in the early 1920s. Moreover, both figures remained essentially committed to their established positions for the rest of their careers. In the early years of the crisis theology movement, however, Barth and Bultmann held enough in common to oppose a tottering liberal establishment. As a critical scholar Bultmann was unfailingly a product of Johannes Weiss's myth-deconstructing school of *Religionsgeschichtliche* criticism, but as a constructive theologian he was also the protege of his theological mentor, Wilhelm Herrmann.

He was quick to discern and appreciate the Herrmannian elements in Barth's thinking.[26] Like Barth, Bultmann shared Herrmann's radical emphasis on faith, his rejection of doctrinal propositionalism, and his cleavage between faith and history. To a considerable degree, Bultmann's theology was shielded from the destructive aspects of his own radical biblical criticism by his Herrmannian insistence that genuine faith has no historical basis.[27]

"To speak of the faith of men is to accept the full paradox of asserting something which is completely unverifiable as a spiritual situation and which must never be identified with any such situation," he contended. As long as one regards faith as a state of consciousness, it cannot be true faith at all. In 1924, this was Bultmann's description of Barth's position, but it was also his own. He explained that in practice "faith always happens as an act of God; and seen from the human point of view it is the abandonment of every position." This was Herrmann's "faith without weapons" in dialectical form. Bultmann embraced Barth's thesis that theology speaks out of faith alone and that the subject of theology is God.[28]

HEIDEGGER AND THE QUESTION OF PHILOSOPHICAL PREUNDERSTANDING

But these assertions were always qualified by an anthropocentric wedge that made Barth uneasy. The subject of theology is God, Bultmann affirmed, but it speaks of God "because it speaks of man as he stands before God."[29] He explained elsewhere that the believer has reason to speak of God as the Lord of reality only when the believer "knows himself in his own existence to be claimed by God."[30] In the mid-1920s Barth puzzled over the logic of these statements while observing, very warily, the increasing influence of Martin Heidegger over Bultmann's thinking.

Heidegger and Bultmann were colleagues at Marburg during the period when Heidegger wrote his early major work, *Being and Time.* Heidegger argued that human beings are a special type of being on account of their unique capacity to inquire about the primordial ground that allows all that is to come into existence. In his language, human beings are the unique type of being through whom Being (the primordial ground) presents itself to be known. Though he later distinguished himself forcefully from an ascending "existential philosophy" movement, Heidegger's early work blended existential analysis with the phenomenological method of his teacher, Edmund Husserl. He emphasized the difference between the individual being of a self *(Existenz)* and the being of objects in nature *(Vorhandenheit),* attributing (in his early work) greater significance to individual being. His description of the structures of existence contained vivid accounts of the "thrown" character of human "being-there" *(Dasein)* and the perils that attend the self's coming-to-awareness of its arbitrarily given ("thrown") existence. In his description, the "undifferentiated" self lives in infantile unawareness of its thrown condition, but as a self becomes aware of its determined situation, it faces a choice between two possibilities, which Heidegger called "inauthentic" and "authentic" existence. The inauthentic self falls into anxiety, or it replaces the first totalized form of life with another one, or it gives up caring ("fallenness"). By contrast, the authentic self faces up to one's nothingness and becomes a caretaking "being-toward-death" who changes the form of one's totalized givenness through one's death-accepting moral courage and care for the world.[31]

Heidegger was an atheist, but his rhetorically powerful description of the conditions of existence impressed Bultmann deeply as a philosophical redescription of the New Testament view of the human predicament. Bultmann was struck especially by the analogies between Heidegger's account of human "thrownness" and authenticity and the New Testament drama of sin, confession of sin, and redemption. He increasingly read the New Testament through a Heideggerian lens, arguing that Paul, for example, conceptualized the world "in an existential sense, as the way in which an actual existing individual lives as such." Thus the Pauline idea of the "world" was not to be understood as an object, he urged, but in Heidegger's sense as a manner of individual existence.[32] In this way Bultmann maintained that Heideggerian existentialism offered not only a significant apologetic tool for modern Christian theology, but also a means to better understand early Christianity. Just as the church fathers Christianized neo-Platonism and Thomas Aquinas Christianized Aristotelian philosophy, modern theologians were obliged to translate the meaning of the Word into the best philosophical account of reality that was available to them. It is not an option for theologians to disregard philosophy, he warned. Any theology that fails to provide an explicit account of its philosophical underpinnings will inevitably presuppose some account of knowledge and understanding (perhaps a bad one) that tacitly controls everything that is affirmed theologically.

In the mid-1920s Bultmann pressed this argument with particular urgency upon Barth. He warned that Barth stood in danger of implicitly presupposing a bad philosophy and that Barth's dogmatic affirmations had no "clean concepts" to work with. Barth resisted this critical warning without rejecting it outright. He countered that Bultmann's theology was "too anthropological-Kierkegaardian-Lutheran (+Gogartenian)." He worried that Bultmann's focus on "speaking of man" was creating a new form of theological anthropocentrism, this time with Kierkegaard and Heidegger as its architects. Barth appreciated why Lutherans like Bultmann, Gogarten, and Tillich were attracted to existentialism. In their own ways, Kierkegaard and Heidegger focused on the same problems of sin-consciousness and anxiety that preoccupied Luther. It seemed to Barth, however, that under the influence of this anthropocentric preoccupation Bultmann interpreted the Bible "with a shocking eclecticism"—just like Luther. Bultmann approached the Bible with a predetermined theory of understanding and existence, and then found support for this set of ideas in scattered biblical texts. Moreover, Bultmann's decision to write a book on the historical Jesus reinforced Barth's impression that he had "not yet got free of the historical eggshells." Like his liberal historicist mentors, Bultmann still seemed to approach the New Testament as a source of historical material.[33]

These points of difference hardened into battle lines in later years, but in the mid-1920s Barth was not ready to draw battle lines against his ostensible comrades. He allowed that there was "really something to be said" in favor of the argument about clean concepts. He worried that Bultmann was right that every theology implicitly or explicitly presupposes some philosophical account of understanding. Though his mind was clearer on the "historical Jesus" question, even here he tried for a time to put off an open debate with Bultmann. Bultmann's *Jesus and the Word* was published in 1926. The following year, after Bultmann heard that Barth was sharply critical of the book, he pressed for a debate on their disagreements, but Barth protested that he wasn't ready "to advance any stupid questions or objections."[34]

Barth was keenly disappointed that Bultmann still apparently sought to establish a (minimal) picture of the historical Jesus behind the concrete picture given in the gospel narratives. It disturbed him that instead of treating the New Testament as a witness, Bultmann was still approaching the text in the liberal manner as a source for critical judgments about the historical figure of Jesus.[35] But Barth was also keenly aware that his own thinking and, especially, his readiness to defend it were still in a formative stage. He doubted that an open debate with Bultmann would be fruitful. He even doubted that a real encounter between them was possible at the time. Barth noted that most of his differences with Bultmann and the others were rooted in "the old controversies between the Lutherans and the Reformed, which were never settled," especially those pertaining to the relation of law and gospel. He worried that "a great explosion" was brewing within the *Zwischen den Zeiten* circle over these differences. "But for the moment, apart from all the tactical reasons which may make sense, I feel a need to work as theoretically as possible and to give you and Gogarten time to develop more clearly what you are after," he explained. "Later will be the time for debates if they are unavoidable."[36]

But conflict became unavoidable later that year, after Barth published his *Christliche Dogmatik*. His Göttingen lectures on dogmatics had already conceptualized the threefold Word of God as the center of his theology, but Barth never published the Göttingen lectures. It was his 1927 "outline" of dogmatics, "a beginner's attempt in this area," that disclosed the decisive shape that his thinking had taken.[37] He argued that the *diastasis* between God and humanity that his Romans commentary had featured was actually *itself* God's Word, properly understood. The relationship between God and humanity does not become God's Word through human speech, he explained. It is, rather, God's Word from the beginning.[38] Though Barth continued to relate dogmatics to preaching, as in his Göttingen lectures, his *Christliche Dogmatik* was more emphatic in understanding dogmatics as reflection on the *Word of God* proclaimed in preaching. His prolegomenon was elaborated as a doctrine of the Word.

In 1927, it still retained some existential elements. Barth began with a phenomenological analysis of Christian proclamation that underscored the objectivity of the revelation to which scripture gives witness, but he correlated these arguments with an existential method that presented the Word in its subjective character from the standpoint of the hearing subject. He reasoned that as a hearer of the Word, the receiving human subject must be included in the concept of the Word of God. On that basis, Barth still allowed that existential analysis can be a basis for sound statements about the Word of God.

The force of his total argument moved overwhelmingly, however, in the direction of a disclosure-model theological realism. *Christliche Dogmatik* made a blistering case against theological overdependence on philosophy. Barth insisted that to commit Christian theology to any philosophical system is to prevent the Word from being able to express itself. His own modest enterprise, by contrast, was merely to make "a preliminary leap into the subject-matter itself."[39] With Kutter's warning in mind, as well as Georg Merz's recent lament that he was apparently becoming a scholastic, he sought to avoid the appearance of making a theology out of the Word of God. Barth confessed that as a fallible human subject he had only a doctrine of the Word at his disposal and not the Word itself, which is not a thing to be possessed. The Word of God will either speak for itself or not, he declared.[40] The work of the theologian is to be open to the movement of the Word and not to throw human constructs in the way.

To Bultmann, this meant the debate was on. He chided Barth for refusing to debate his friends, especially Gogarten (and implicitly, himself). Then he turned to the main business. "You have a sovereign scorn for modern work in philosophy, especially phenomenology," he observed with regret. Heidegger's *Being and Time* had finally been published the previous spring, but Barth seemed to have no idea of Heidegger's importance for theology. "What you say (and often only *want* to say) is beyond your terminology, and a lack of clarity and sobriety is frequently the result," Bultmann judged. What was the point of allowing that philosophy has a legitimate role to play in theology if Barth never actually used philosophy seriously? "It seems to me that you are guided by a concern that theology should achieve emancipation from philosophy," Bultmann observed. "You try to achieve this by ignoring philosophy. The price you pay for this is that of falling prey to an outdated philosophy."[41]

He surmised that, having refused to think about it, Barth was stuck in the outdated ontology of patristic and scholastic dogmatics. But this is impossibly wrongheaded, Bultmann scolded. "Your planned ignoring of philosophy is only apparent." The problem of philosophy cannot be solved by remaining in the clutches of an unacknowledged and discredited ontology, he urged: "If dogmatics is to be a science, it cannot avoid the question of appropriate concepts." The choice was not between using philosophy or not, since every theology is guided by implicit or explicit philosophical understandings about knowledge, the knowing process, and reality. The choice was between using philosophy intelligently or not. Bultmann noted that theologians who use philosophy intelligently can limit the degree of their theological dependence on philosophy, but those who ignore the philosophical problem inevitably allow an assumed philosophy to control their theological thinking. His own theology used Heidegger's phenomenology of existence to illuminate the New Testament message and to limit the dependence of theology on philosophy. Because faith is always the faith of a believing, existent person, he contended, "dogmatics can speak only in existential-ontological terms." So-called theological "anthropocentrism" is unavoidable. But the concepts that are required for such speaking can only be worked out by an appropriately critical philosophical analysis, Bultmann urged. The alternative was the bad option that Barth was taking, which was to remain in bondage to the discredited ontology of Protestant scholasticism.[42]

Barth's first response was irenic and diplomatic. He still wanted to avoid a public debate. He confessed that perhaps it was simply not in him to debate with Gogarten. A genuinely critical exchange between them would probably get ugly, he reasoned, and he doubted that it would produce anything worthwhile. He was grateful for Gogarten's role in their movement, but he preferred to leave their disagreements alone: "I would find it hard to deny that he is not congenial to me *kata sarka,* since he plans his essays and books in a way that would be intolerable to me, and above all I find in and behind him everything that is abhorrent to me in Luther."

As for the business about his philosophical limitations, Barth conceded that perhaps someone else with the same devotion to the primacy of the Word could "do better in achieving a sober terminology" than he had managed. Bultmann's description of the choice at issue made enough sense to him that he wasn't prepared to defend, in principle, his lack of a philosophical orientation. He used philosophical concepts in an eclectic fashion whenever they helped him explicate his theological meaning. He had never meant to deny that theologians should use philosophical analysis in this way. "But the fact is that no philosophy influences me in the way that Heidegger's obviously does you," Barth noted. Moreover, he believed that it wasn't healthy for theologians to commit themselves wholeheartedly to any particular philosophical system. "I have come to abhor profoundly the spectacle of theology constantly trying above all to adjust to the philosophy of its age, thereby neglecting its own theme," he declared. Theology needed to have its own work to do.

Barth recognized that his eclectic use of philosophy opened him to the charge of "a terrible dilettantism." At the time, he was willing to live with the charge. He did not accept the judgment that his concepts were hopelessly inadequate, nor was he convinced that classical orthodoxy had been badly served by its Platonism and Aristotelianism. Harnack had never persuaded him on the latter point. "My own concern is to hear at any rate the voice of the church and the Bible, and to let this voice be heard, even if in so doing, for want of anything better, I have to think somewhat in Aristotelian terms," he explained. He was still pleading to be left alone to express his understanding of the Word as the Word expressed itself to him. He understood that Bultmann did not approve of the way that he was carrying out this project, but he asked only that he not be required to understand "the craft that with such admiration I see you practicing." At the time Bultmann must have taken from this statement the assurance that Barth was not charging him with accommodating the gospel to an alien philosophy.[43]

But that is exactly the verdict that Barth reached over the following two years. In 1929 his programmatic lecture on the problem of religious philosophy laid the groundwork for his break from the dialectical theologians. In "Fate and Idea in Theology" he declared that "the great temptation and danger" for the theologian is always that he "will actually become what he seems to be—a philosopher." Because the philosopher is always in a position to say everything "so much better, more freely, more universally," Barth explained, the temptation to betray theology to philosophy is never-ending for the theologian. Philosophy at its best is eloquent and rational, but the theologian who pays heed to God's Word "has to speak in such a crabbed, constricted, and paradoxical way." For this reason the theologian is always tempted to take refuge in a better-sounding philosophy. "Theology stands under the insufferable pressure of a situation where it can speak only humanly and where this occurs so much better in philosophy," he observed. "Indeed philosophy manages to speak profoundly in human language without hearing the Word, without the troublesome connection to Bible and church, and without the recurrent counter-question that constantly casts doubt upon the idea of a divine miracle confirming a human word."[44]

Church history is therefore littered with examples of theologians who did not bother to listen to what the Lord of reality says to us in God's Word about reality. So-called Christian theology has often spoken not on the basis of the Spirit-illuminated Word, Barth observed, but on the basis of some thinker's impressive-sounding substitute for it. To him, this was the fatal problem of Catholic and Protestant scholasticism, as well as liberal Protestantism. He would soon claim that it was also the problem with the dialectical theology movement.

MEDIATING REALISM AND IDEALISM

In "Fate and Idea in Theology," Barth made a case for a Word-expressing alternative without claiming that theology can escape the fundamental problem of philosophy. Though he emphasized that theology must have its own work to do within this context, Barth allowed that theology operates in the same context as philosophy. "Theology too must come to terms with the two boundaries of human thought."[45] That is, the problem of realism and idealism is unavoidable. Even the most Word-oriented theologian cannot avoid the necessity of assuming some position with regard to the philosophical questions of reality and truth. Barth observed that realism is oriented to the question of reality while idealism is oriented to the question of truth. Realists assert the objective existence of the external world prior to and apart from human awareness of the world, while idealists variously describe mental activity or the movement of spirit as the key to the nature of reality.

Barth granted that the differences between these positions bear considerable implications for theology. Theological realists assert not only that the world is real apart from our awareness of it, but also that God is real apart from our awareness of God. By upholding the objective existence of God, theological realism stands against any suggestion that theological knowledge belongs to some special framework apart from philosophical knowledge. One cannot say "God is" without affirming (in the language of realism) that God takes part in being. In its classical form which, Barth noted, is the form set forth by Thomas Aquinas, theological realism logically derives a third proposition from these claims, to the effect that everything that exists as such participates in God. "Everything that is exists as mere creature in greatest dissimilarity to the Creator, yet by having being it exists in greatest similarity to the Creator," Barth explained. This was the core idea of the Catholic doctrine of *analogia entis* (analogy of being), according to which there is something in the being of human beings that is analogous to the being of God. In a formulation that was decisively influenced by dialogues with Jesuit theologian Erich Przywara, Barth explained that "*analogia entis* means the dissimilarity and similarity to God which I myself have as knower and the thing outside me has as the known." Human knowledge of God is possible on account of the similarity that exists in being between Creator and creation. For the realist, Barth emphasized, the affirmation that God and the world are real bears a crucial implication for the question concerning how God can be known. Theological realism moves from its knowledge of a directly-experienced real world to knowledge of God. As Barth observed, the realist "confidently supposes that in what is given he is able to encounter something similar to God, and this confidence gives definition to his teaching." Knowledge of God is properly read off from that which is given and not from any other source or means.[46]

But, Barth objected, the God that is simply read off from the given world is something less that the Wholly Other God of grace and glory who has power over the world. The God of God's Word comes always as light into darkness, announcing something new, but the God derived from the analogy of being is merely a hidden feature of the world. Barth contended that pure theological realism thus reduces God to fate. It makes revelation and grace superfluous. "Does revelation really do no more than confirm and reinforce supernaturally a naively presupposed human capacity and necessity apparently somehow given with our existence?" he asked. In his judgment, it was this conception of revelation and its accompanying notion of grace as the fulfillment of nature that disastrously reinforced the paganizing tendencies of Catholic spirituality. Catholic theology makes God's reality accessible apart from God himself as the giver of his Word, Barth claimed, but the effect of abstracting God's reality from the event of grace was the loss of God's actual presence. "For grace is the event in which God comes to us in his Word, an event over which God has sole control, and which is strictly momentary," he admonished. "Otherwise God could not be distinguished from a hidden feature of reality as such. He could not be distinguished from fate." The possibility of experiencing God is open to us not because it is fated by God's presence, but because God chooses to come to us.[47]

Barth gave idealism a softer work-over. He observed that the idealist tradition in philosophy is distinguished by its emphasis on critical reflection. From Plato to Decartes, Kant, and Hegel, the idealists always press the question of the nature of truth. "Idealism means the self-reflection of the spirit over against nature," he noted approvingly. "It discovers a correlation between thinking and truth." In its various forms, philosophical idealism always finds in the creative logos the source through which the dualism of subject and object can be overcome. Idealist thinking exalts reason or self-reflected spirit over the power of fate and thereby obtains mastery over the limitations that fate imposes on human life.[48]

In its essential character, idealism therefore has a deeper affinity with theology than realism, Barth acknowledged. This was a telling judgment, coming from the modern champion of doing theology as exegesis of an outside Word. Barth's insistence on the given reality of God and the necessity of beginning with God's revealed Word made his theology fundamentally realist, yet he allowed that "even realist theology cannot be theology without drawing heavily on idealism." Even the realist emphasis on the given reality of God must deal with the problem of the non-given truth of God's reality, he cautioned. All theology is required to deal with the divine given in light of the immanent reality that remains hidden to thought and experience. Thus even Aquinas developed a negative theology. Barth observed that the great strength of the idealist tradition in theology is that it emphasizes God's nonobjectivity. At its best, as in Augustine and Calvin, idealistic theology always strenuously reminds us that all thinking and speaking about God is inadequate. It protects the divine mystery from being identified with other objects. "It directs us to the God who is God only in genuine transcendence." Without the corrective antidote of critical idealism, Barth warned, theology inevitably degenerates into "pagan monstrosity."[49]

It is precisely because idealism is closer to the truth than realism, however, that it poses a greater danger to theology than realism. Barth explained that idealism is prone to fall into a peculiar and destructive pride. Where the realist asserts that "God is reality," the idealist asserts that "God is truth." The idealist emphasis on the transparency of reality enables theological idealism to give witness to the divine truth that shines within, behind, and beyond the "real," but it also tends to brush aside the chastening realist focus on the accidental and particular truths of history. This is a fatal weakness, Barth cautioned. A proud theology is always a monstrosity. Even the most critical theology is demonic if it trusts in the power of its rationality. "If theology is to remain grounded in God's revelation, then the idealist is going to have to dampen his ardor for a generally accessible truth, and to join forces with the realist," he argued. "He is going to have to grant that 'accessibility' here can only mean the possibility of God's access to us, not of our access to

God." More pointedly, the idealist must accept that God's truth makes its way to us definitively in the singular revelatory event of Christ. In this case, Barth contended, the idealist theologian must give up the idealistic tendency to regard revelation as a general human possibility. The possibility of distinguishing truth from reality so cherished by idealism is itself made possible only by revelation, which is a possibility specific to God alone.[50]

He gave short shrift to liberal idealistic theologies that linked the self-transcendence of created spirit to God's transcendent Spirit. God cannot be reached with a humanly-constructed ladder of consciousness, Barth warned: "Theology is certainly intellectual work, but its object of inquiry is neither spirit nor nature, and therefore strictly speaking it belongs just as little to the humanities as to the sciences." The object of theology is "the Word dwelling in inapproachable light," which theology neither produces nor articulates, but to which it bears witness. Moreover, the knowledge of God to which theology bears witness is substantiated by God's action alone and not by God's action along with ours. Faith is a possibility given by God through the Word. It is not in any constitutive sense a human work. In a regulative sense, Barth allowed, the knowledge of God given to faith is always mediated by human language and experience—since the only thought available to us is human thought—but this condition does not make faith itself dependent on human effort. "There can be no question of reciprocity between God's action and our own," he maintained. "It is strictly a matter of the command in which we know our obedience to be grounded." True theology wields no weapons. It does not try to prove that the divine command exists. It only bears witness that God's command is spoken through the Word.[51]

"Fate and Idea in Theology" was a curious piece of throat-clearing. In effect, it was a harbinger of movement-shattering polemics disguised as irenic description. It implicitly criticized the Thomist and liberal Protestant traditions without noting the implications of its argument for Barth's own circle of theological comrades. It made a call for a Word-obedient dialectic that avoided what Barth called the dangers of "pure realism and pure idealism," but it made no precise judgment on whether Augustine, Calvin, or even Aquinas had averted these dangers. It treated the Catholic *analogia entis* as a product of the Thomist realist tradition without acknowledging that this doctrine has deeper roots in Augustine's ontological idealism.

The latter feature of Barth's argument was especially curious in light of the fact that his thinking about the problem of the *analogia entis* had been stimulated chiefly by Przywara, whose conception of the analogy of being was based on Augustinian grounds. Augustine argued that while a God who was wholly dissimilar to creation could not be known at all, the true God who has made himself known has made himself known as greatly dissimilar. In the same spirit, Przywara developed his doctrine of the analogy of being, conforming closely to the language of *similitudo Dei* and *major dissimilitudo* decreed by the Fourth Lateran Council (1215). With Augustine and the Fourth Lateran Council, he emphasized the dissimilarity between God and creature, describing the analogy of being as "greater dissimilarity in great likeness."[52]

Various interpreters later criticized Barth for misrepresenting Przywara in this respect. Hans Urs von Balthasar maintained that Przywara's version of the analogy of being was an abstract formulation of a radically Christocentric position that was actually closely related to Barth's.[53] Eberhard Jüngel concurs that Barth's early notion of the analogy of being as a presumptuous grasping after God was a "horrible phantom" that Barth later relinquished (without explicit acknowledgment) after he adopted a type of analogical method (the analogy of faith) as the necessary precondition for Christian speech about God.[54] Without denying that Barth's later condemnation of the analogy of being was excessive, Bruce McCormack defends Barth's early argument with Przywara. He suggests that the main purpose of "Fate and Idea in Theology" was to show Przywara that his doctrine of analogy belonged more deeply to the Thomist tradition than to Augustine's idealism. "Barth was asking Przywara if he did not see that the transcendence of God is something different from the self-transcendence of created and finite spirits which expresses itself in concepts like the Unconditioned," McCormack argues. The very phrase "analogy of being" smacked of natural theology to Barth. It suggested that Przywara was committed to the natural theology project of conceiving God and human beings as exemplifications of a higher concept, namely, "being."[55] In this reading, Barth was pressing Przywara to see that his "Augustinian" orthodoxy was less critical and more deeply akin to Thomism and Hegelianized liberal Protestantism than he supposed.

Barth's muted tone and his imprecise judgments left ample room for competing interpretations of his theological claims. "Fate and Idea in Theology" was intentionally vague and slippery on key points. This essay bears a singular importance for the interpretation of Barth's development, however, because it marked the beginning of the end of his period of personal and movement-protective evasion. Whatever one makes of his attempts to criticize or influence Przywara's position, it is clear, and crucially important, that Barth took a decisive first step, with this essay, into a many-sided debate over issues that he had previously sought to avoid. "Fate and Idea in Theology" committed Barth to a realist-leaning mediating position in the unavoidable debate between epistemological realism and idealism. Shortly afterward, he brought an end to various puzzlements that Bultmann, Merz, Gogarten, and others were expressing about him.

BREAKING RANKS: THE SUFFICIENCY OF REVELATION

Barth's further studies in Augustine and Luther and his belated reading of Przywara's 1926 volume on the philosophy of religion deepened his conviction that the entire Augustinian theology of being had to be overturned.[56] In September 1929, he told the Lutheran theologian Paul Althaus that "as long as we do not root Augustinianism completely out of the doctrine of grace, we will never have a Protestant theology."[57] The following month he denounced the Augustinian notion that the divine-human relation contains an element of continuity. Przywara had spoken of the human creature as being "open upwards" to God on the basis of a continuity in being between God and creation, but Barth sharply denied that the human creature stands in a place "from which he can establish and survey . . . his relation to God."[58] Every variation of the Augustinian attempt to understand the divine-human relation on a model of similarity and dissimilarity in being amounts to a denial of revelation and grace, he insisted. Human beings find continuity with God only in the miracle of God's love that comes from without as a gift. Knowledge of God is possible, therefore, not on account of any inherent capacity or endowment of being that human creatures possess, but only because God comes to us in inexplicable grace.[59]

Barth admitted to Althaus that his anger at the situation in theology and his animus against Catholicism were rising in tandem. This confluence of feelings later received memorable expression in the opening pages of the *Church Dogmatics* in 1932.[60] The following year Barth found himself pitted against Althaus as well, who warmly applauded the rise of the Hitler regime.[61] In the closing weeks of 1929, however, the chief cause of Barth's rising anger lay closer to home. Theologically he felt more isolated than ever. He no longer belonged to any movement or circle that he could defend. In his perception, all of his major dialectical theology comrades had forsaken their ostensible commitment to the primacy of the Word. In January 1930 Barth gave a lecture at Marburg and, after hurrying home a day early, sent to Bultmann the verdict that he could not give him in person. From his standpoint, all of them were embarked upon "a large scale return to the fleshpots of Egypt," he reported. Gogarten was developing a new "states of life" theophilosophy, Brunner was defending an "eristic" theology of natural revelation, Bultmann was baptizing Heideggerian existential phenomenology, and various lesser figures were otherwise accommodating the gospel to modern philosophy and culture. Barth recognized that his former comrades were not exactly recapitulating nineteenth-century liberalism, but the effect was the same, he judged, since all of them were recommitting the liberal mistake of conceptualizing faith as a human possibility.[62]

He was prepared to admit that perhaps he had been wrong about Bultmann all along. Perhaps Bultmann had been committed all along to an up-to-date blend of Herrmann, philosophical existentialism, and the history of religions school. Perhaps he had never actually shared Barth's concern with the Word of God. In any case, Barth was no longer shielding himself from the realization that they were not allies. Neither did he judge that he was significantly closer to Gogarten or Brunner. "Where people play around with a natural theology and are so eager to pursue theology within the framework of a preunderstanding that has not been attained theologically, the inevitable result is they end up in rigidities and reactionary corners which are no better than the liberalisms of others," he declared. He wanted no part of a movement that put various culture-accommodating dialectical spins on the mistakes of nineteenth-century liberalism. In his judgment, old-fashioned Religious Socialism had far more integrity than the increasingly paganized and conservative theologies that the dialectical theology movement was producing.[63]

To his credit, Bultmann took this declaration not as the termination of his alliance with Barth, but as the beginning of a genuine discussion between them. He asked Barth to speak on natural theology at an upcoming conference at Marburg to which Gogarten and Brunner would also be invited. Barth reluctantly accepted this invitation while noting that he dreaded the prospect of being interrogated by Bultmann's students.[64] Several months later, however, not long before the conference took place, Barth backed out from attending, mostly on the pretext that he couldn't spare the time. Bultmann pleaded with him to reconsider and was offended when Barth refused.[65] In the testy exchanges that followed, Barth told Bultmann that for years he had noticed certain "remnants of liberalism" in his position but had declined to take them seriously. Now that he realized how serious was the breach between himself and Bultmann/Gogarten/Brunner, he reported, "something decisive has been lost between us which can hardly be discussed."[66] Bultmann objected that "you left us in the lurch in Marburg." Barth was wrong to back out and wrong to suspect the Marburgers of bad will, he protested: "I do not know how we aroused this mistrust, as though we wished to 'examine' you, and I find it unfriendly that you should describe in this way our desire to engage in serious discussion with you. Do you not think that I seriously want to hear finally what you really have against my work?"[67]

Barth replied that he carried no bad feelings toward Bultmann personally, though he disliked the "policelike acuteness" with which Bultmann's students were known to interrogate their visitors. "I have always felt at home with you, but I cannot abide the mixture of the fatherly and the policelike in your students," he explained. As for Bultmann's wanting to know what Barth really held against his work, Barth replied that by attaching himself to Heideggerian philosophy, "you have done something that one ought not to do as an evangelical theologian." If Bultmann asked, why not? Barth could only reply "not with an argument, but with a recitation of the creed." That would never go down in Marburg, he observed. The break between them was finally exposed, but he could still see no point in debating with Bultmann. "Let us allow a few years to pass, and above all let us allow time for some good personal talks," he proposed.[68]

By then Barth was having second thoughts about the adequacy of his *Christliche Dogmatik.* The book was due for a revised second edition in 1931, but in the midst of his breakup with the dialectical theologians and his ongoing research on Anselm's theological method, Barth resolved that his dogmatic project required a new beginning. The existential elements in *Christliche Dogmatik* were glaring, even embarrassing to him against the background of his conflict with Bultmann and Gogarten, and he was also chastened by the book's relative lack of clarity about his theological method. His work on Anselm helped him conceptualize and express more clearly the method of "faith seeking understanding" that his theology already used. Barth later reported that he wrote this book with a singular satisfaction.[69]

FAITH KNOWLEDGE: *FIDES QUAERENS INTELLECTUM*

In *Die christliche Dogmatik,* Barth had argued that the Word of God rests entirely in itself. In nature and history, he observed, the reality of any given object is knowable only in the correlation of the object and a knowing subject, but the Word of God is never enmeshed in the polarity of subject and object. Though it is true that all of the vehicles through which the Word gives itself are caught in this polarity, the Word itself does not belong to the world of objects. Barth cautioned that the Word therefore cannot be known in the same way that ordinary objects are known. If the Word is to be known, it can be known only on its own basis. The possibility of knowledge of the Word rests entirely in the Word itself. It followed for Barth that if I know God, "then *this* 'I know' must be distinguished most emphatically" from every other use of the phrase "I know."[70]

But if one has no control at all over the event through which the Word may be known, how does one come into knowledge of it? Barth's *Christliche Dogmatik* already invoked Anselm for the answer. Anselm argued that the search for religious understanding is immanent in faith itself. It is only on the basis of faith expressed through prayer that God can be understood, he contended.[71] Faith is a spiritual gift from God that gives birth to a desire for understanding, which cannot question its own basis. Barth's eccentric, exegetical, seminar-based study of Anselm, *Fides Quaerens Intellectum,* pursued the technical aspects of Anselm's formulation of this argument.

In his rendering, Anselm conceived theology as "thinking-after" faith. The nature of faith itself summons the believer to understanding, and true theology is based upon and seeks to understand the gift of faith. "It is the presupposition of all theological inquiry that faith as such remains undisturbed by the vagaries of the theological 'yes' and 'no,' " Barth remarked. The faithful person never achieves exact understanding of God's truth, but this does not detract from his or her reverence for it: "In place of the joy of knowing there remains reverence before Truth itself, which is no less Truth because this is so."[72] Faith inherently desires knowledge that is never entirely available to understanding, but faith draws the believer to comprehend all that can be understood about the revered Revealer.

"Every theological statement is an inadequate expression of its object," Barth asserted, expositing Anselm. Though the actual Word of Christ itself is never inadequate, every understanding of it is: "Strictly speaking, it is only God himself who has a conception of God. All that we have are conceptions of objects, none of which is identical with God." Though it should be humbling for the theologian to comprehend that "God shatters every syllogism," he observed, this truism does not make theology pointless. It only reminds the faithful seeker of understanding that God's grace can make inadequate concepts relatively adequate for their purpose: "Just as everything which is not God could not exist apart from God and is something only because of God, so it is possible for expressions which are really appropriate to objects that are not identical with God, to be true expressions."[73]

Fides Quaerens Intellectum was a study of Anselm's approach to theology, not an explication of Barth's theological method. Much of the book sought to demonstrate that Anselm's "ontological proof" for the existence of God was not an outside attempt to rationally deduce the necessity of divine reality from the idea of God, as commonly interpreted.[74] Anselm already believed on the basis of revelation that God exists, Barth observed. His argument in the *Proslogion* was content to show the impossibility of God's nonexistence and the meaning of God's existence confessed by the church's creed.[75] On various occasions afterward Barth expressed his disappointment that his book on Anselm attracted little attention. The fact that it stood at the entry-way to his *Church Dogmatics* should have clued more observers to its importance, he complained.[76]

The book's literal closeness to Anselm's texts and its lack of clarity about its implications for Barth's position made it minimally illuminating for most of his audience. For some observers, the book's scholastic armature and its strained (implicit) attempt to claim Anselm for evangelical Protestantism confirmed that Barth was retreating to the age of Protestant scholasticism, if not further back. Though Anselm tended to treat the church's *Credo* and scripture as revelation (what Barth called "revealed-ness"), Barth defended Anselm's theology from the charge of outright positivism without explaining how his own understanding of the *diastasis* between revelation and scripture differed from Anselm's.[77] The precise "analogy of faith" that Barth developed from his earlier doctrine of the Word and his analysis of Anselm were only developed later, in the *Church Dogmatics.* With the inauguration of this massive project in 1932, Barth ended various in-house debates about whether his thinking was ultimately a theology of the Word or existence. In the spirit of Anselm, he also established more clearly that dogmatics is not a free science of inquiry, "but one bound to the sphere of the Church, where and where alone it is possible and sensible."[78]

RESISTING GERMAN CHRISTIANITY

The historical situation in which this enterprise was launched was crucial to its character. Barth was slow to take seriously the threat from an ascending Nazi movement, as he later admitted ruefully. In the later 1920s he dismissed as ridiculous any suggestion that the German people were ripe for fascism. He thought that the National Socialists were too vulgar, stupid, and violent to be taken seriously as a political force.[79] Barth voted for the Social Democrats in the 1928 election with no apparent foreboding that the existence of the Weimar Republic was in danger.[80] Two years later, after the American stock market crash of 1929, the ascendancy of a new Catholic

Centre government in Germany, and the government's adoption of emergency-powers measures in a crisis situation, the Nazis made dramatic gains in a special parliamentary election, winning 112 seats to become the nation's second strongest party. In effect, the Republic came to an end as the Nazis turned parliament into a shambles and the Heinrich Brüning government governed entirely by presidential decree.

These circumstances drove Barth to join the German Social Democratic Party in May 1931. His former colleague, Emanuel Hirsch, opined that Barth's alliance with the democratic socialists proved that he was not really German "from boot to bonnet," but Barth protested that he was really both German and Swiss. He loved both of his countries. In both of them, during moments of national crisis, he joined the Social Democratic party because he wanted to stand with those who understood the "requirements of a healthy politics."[81] The following year he explained to Hans Asmussen that he had imposed a ten-year "political interlude" upon himself after moving to Germany in 1921. Upon recognizing that Nazi thuggery was gaining the upper hand, however, "I thought it right to make it clear with whom I would like to be imprisoned and hanged."[82]

In the same spirit he defended his friend Günther Dehn from a right-wing student uprising in 1931 and exhorted his theological colleagues to join him. Three years earlier, Dehn had made a mildly critical statement about Germany's responsibility for the Great War in a lecture given in Magdeburg. This remark ignited a student firestorm against him after he was appointed Professor of Practical Theology at Halle in 1931. The German Students' Union at Halle expressed their "fierce hatred and profound contempt" for Dehn and threatened to transfer to Jena or Leipzig if his appointment was not rescinded. To Barth these were fighting words. He published a statement of solidarity for Dehn's person and views in *Theologische Blätter* and appealed for support from numerous theologians, including Gogarten and Bultmann.[83]

Gogarten declined to sign the declaration and Bultmann hedged, pleading for a less sweeping indictment. He agreed with Barth that the students were wrong to politicize Dehn's appointment and also wrong to threaten the university, but he believed that Dehn was theologically unsuitable for this appointment in the first place. He asked Barth to draft another statement that made a narrower appeal to Dehn's right to academic freedom. He later signed a statement to this effect that was drafted by Otto Schmitz and Wilhelm Stählin of Münster, but he refused to sign Barth's unamended protest. In the prolonged controversy that followed, Hirsch became a leading supporter of the student opposition and Barth called for a "passionate, but scholarly" war for position. "Why not wage war all along the line?" he exhorted. "Why not take on the whole of 'dialectical theology' standing behind Dehn?" By then his alienation from the dialectical theology movement and his contempt for an ascending German fascism were explicit. Barth warned in December 1931 that the Nazi movement was essentially a bad religion with "deep-rooted dogmatic ideas about one thing, national reality" and a politics of sheer force.[84]

The spectacle of the "German Christian" nazification of the church after Hitler rose to power in 1933 repelled Barth from the outset. Though it was only now that he bothered to read Hitler's *Mein Kampf,* he grasped from the beginning that the National Socialists were committed to the obliteration of Christianity in Germany. He further understood that the Nazis would move toward this goal step by step "and in a variety of guises." On the day after Hitler seized power, Barth discussed with Albert Lempp (the owner of Christian Kaiser Verlag and publisher of *Zwischen den Zeiten)* whether the time had come to terminate their journal. Barth felt compromised by his implicit association with Gogarten. This feeling deepened to revulsion later that year after Gogarten spoke at gatherings of the Young Reformation Movement and, for a time, even the German Christians. Lempp convinced him to keep the journal going, but also agreed to remove from its masthead the names of the three editors. This compromise kept the journal afloat for another nine months, until Barth resigned with an angry farewell statement that condemned German Christianity and Gogarten's flirtation with it. "I cannot see anything in German Christianity but the last, fullest and worst monstrosity of Neo-Protestantism," he declared. Thus ended the dialectical theology episode.[85]

Barth was disgusted but barely surprised when Gogarten sought to accommodate fascism. It surprised him even less when Hirsch, Heidegger, and Althaus became outright Nazi apologists. What did surprise him was that Bultmann joined the Confessing Church. The Confessing Church grew out of the Pastors' Emergency League founded by Barth's friend Martin Nie-möller in 1933. Though it remained, for the most part, a deeply conservative and patriotic association of German pastors (with a smattering of academics), it took a stand against the outright takeover and nazification of the church that began shortly after Hitler's rise to power. The Confessing movement set up its own church government (called "Councils of Brethren") in areas that fell under the official administration of German Christian leaders, and it took its name from its confessional resolve to worship Jesus Christ alone as Lord.[86]

Theologically its chief voice was Barth, despite his vigorously Reformed identity, his dual citizenship, and his social democratic politics. In 1933 he launched a pamphlet series, *Theologische Existenz heute,* that sought to inspire the formation of what became the Confessing Church. Barth's first issue called for a Nazi-resisting church movement that proclaimed the gospel *in* the Third Reich, "but not *under* it nor in *its* spirit." He proclaimed that German Christianity was outright heresy. The church has no right under any circumstance to determine its membership on the basis of blood or race, he declared. With pointed insistence he denied that there was any legitimate third way between German Christianity and the "clear and radical opposition" movement that was needed. Barth explained that this meant saying "no" to the Young Reformation Movement led by Karl Heim and Walter

Künneth, which called for the preservation of ecclesiastical independence while also proclaiming a "joyful yes to the new German state."

Barth's uncompromising denunciation of the Young Reformers was offensive to many of his colleagues and church associates. His most quoted and notorious statement was less explicitly political, however. With characteristic bravado and exaggeration he declared that at this moment in German history it was important to do "theology and only theology"—"as though nothing had happened." Nothing could be more prophetic or liberating at this moment than for the church to produce faithful theology, he implied. Political resistance alone was futile if the German church sold its Christian soul to the Third Reich. More to the point, for Barth the question of the church's "theological existence" was an infallible indicator of its faithfulness and vitality. He reasoned that the very existence of vigorous theological thinking in the current context would be a crucial sign that serious Christianity still existed in Germany. His manifesto on this theme had a galvanizing effect. For the next year, Christian Kaiser Verlag struggled to keep up with the demand for Barth's inaugural pamphlet, selling thirty-seven thousand copies before it was banned by the government in July 1934.[87]

The Confessing Church movement was thus to a considerable degree Barth's creation. He worked with Niemöller and others to organize it and inspired pastors and academics to join it. He had to overcome his often-sharp disapproval of German Lutheranism and his lack of confidence in the Confessing Church leaders (especially Niemöller) even to believe that such an enterprise was possible.[88] To Barth's surprise, however, Niemöller became a strong and effective leader of a church resistance movement that included Bultmann. In July 1933, Bultmann assured Barth that despite their theological differences, he was prepared to support the work that Barth had commenced in *Theologische Existenz heute.* The following November, Barth confessed to Bultmann that he had expected him to join the German Christians. Barth had assumed that Bultmann's commitment to Heideggerian philosophy would lead him straight into cross-and-swastika religion. This belated confession was hurtful and disturbing to Bultmann, who grieved for months afterward over its implications. He observed that it proved that Barth had never really understood him.[89]

Barth conceded the obvious in reply, while noting that in most cases his suspicions about culture-accommodating "natural theologians" were being confirmed. He accepted Bultmann's proposal to "bury the hatchet" between them while cautioning that Bultmann needed to explain why he had not joined his otherwise like-minded brethren in their embrace or accommodation of German Christianity. "You will need to explain to me how far the possibility did *not* reside in *your* fundamental theology," he wrote.[90] On this point, mutual understanding was never achieved. Bultmann complained that Barth's scriptural exegesis was virtually always controlled by his dogmatic scheme. "After a few sentences one knows all that will be said and simply asks occasionally how it will be produced out of the words of the text that follow," he charged. Bultmann offered to improve the exegetical quality of *Theologische Existenz heute* by writing for the journal. He wanted very much to be identified with the inner circle of Barth's Confessing movement. He pleaded that he and Barth were "fighting together for the same cause" in the struggle against German Christianity. Though he promised not to take it personally if Barth turned him down, he fretted that Barth mistrusted him and he made it clear that his request for inclusion in Barth's circle was a test of their comradeship.[91]

But Barth replied that he could not afford to mislead uninitiated readers about the gulf between them. He judged that Bultmann's sermons were tedious and subjective, "something that ought not to happen in a 'good' sermon." He lectured that Christ is not truly proclaimed in Heideggerian talk about human anxiety and possibility. "Mistrust is not really a good word for what I experience in relation to you," he confided. With all of Bultmann's circling around the existence of believers, Barth explained, "I do not see how far, when the smoke has cleared, you have really broken through the scheme of eighteenth- and nineteenth-century theology." There were also significant political differences between them. Bultmann was politically cautious and reserved, while Barth despaired over the cautious and politically conservative character of the Confessing Church. Though he stifled his Social Democratic opposition to National Socialism as such, Barth refused to begin his lectures with the Hitler salute and he continually pressed the Confessing Church movement not to surrender its evangelical principles. Though his opposition to German fascism was grievously limited in certain crucial respects, his strident opposition to the Nazification of the church made him odious to governmental officials and many colleagues alike, costing him his position at Bonn in 1935. Later that year, he expressed his discomfort that Bultmann quietly took the Hitler oath.[92] For all of these reasons Barth declined to count Bultmann as a comrade. They made little contact with each other for many years afterward. Both of them grew accustomed to telling their students that the differences between them were not to be bridged, but presented a choice.

THE WORD ALONE: BARTH OR BULTMANN?

This parting of ways was rooted in serious long-standing theological differences. Is the Spirit of Christ the sole subject of the scriptural witness, or are the Bible's other spirits also part of the defining subject matter of scripture? Barth's early refusal to link the Spirit of Christ and the Bible's other sociohistorical spirits reappeared in all of his later debates with Bultmann. In various ways he persistently denied that the Bible's other spirits deserved to be linked by a compromising "and" to the Spirit of Christ. He countered that the fundamental axiom of true theology is the commandment against idolatry, which cannot be upheld by linking revelation with rational proofs or historical evidences or cultural apologetics. Barth explained that as an axiom, the first commandment is a statement that cannot be proven by other statements. At the same time, however, as a statement that forbids idolatry, the first commandment is not the kind of axiom that can serve as a point of contact for dialogue with other disciplines. In Barth's judgment, Bultmann and virtually all of the dialectical theologians were moving in bad directions because they refused to pay heed to this truism. Like all manner of scholastic and liberal theologians before them, the dialectical theologians were being lured into violating the fundamental axiom of Word-faithful theology by "that little but so weighty word 'and.' "[93]

Eighteenth-century rationalist theologies made a case for revelation *and* reason. Schleiermacher argued for revelation *and* religious consciousness. The Ritschlians advocated revelation *and* culture. The Troeltschians held out for revelation *and* critical religious history. As Barth understood it, dialectical theology was supposed to represent a break from all of these strategies. It was supposed to restore the unchallenged primacy of revelation as the self-authenticating basis of theology. In the early 1930s, however, Barth ruefully judged that the language of dialectic was itself part of the problem with the theological movement that he had named and which his thinking had inspired. Dialectic speaks of this *and* that, God *and* the world, thought *and* being, Word *and* existence. In the theologies of his former comrades, some of whom were flirting with German Christianity, it was currently producing new variations on the old mistaken polarities of revelation *and* reason, kerygma *and* human existence, law *and* gospel, commandments *and* the orders of creation.[94]

Barth countered that this way of thinking was tragically misguided. In 1934 he exhorted a student conference in La Chataigneraie, Switzerland, that the church is supposed to be the church of God, not the church of God and (hu)mankind. When the church begins to think of itself in the latter terms, he warned, it becomes no longer the church of God but, at best, "the Church of the pious man, the Church of the good man, the Church of the moral man, but, at any rate, the Church of *man*." This is exactly what the church has become in Catholicism, Protestant liberalism, and Pietism, he declared. Barth knew his audience. He was known to complain that all English theologians were Pelagians. Most of the students at La Chataigneraie were British or American. One after another, they fervently protested that his position was one-sided. Barth replied that he understood and even empathized with the charge: "I, too, have traveled the road which you indicate to me," he related. "I have tried about everything in this field. But there came a day when fear struck my heart. For I found something else in the Bible, something altogether different from the world's godlessness, but no less different from the godlessness of the Church and Christianity."[95]

The spectacle of German Christianity was a warning to the entire church, he admonished. "My dear friends from England and America, I am from Germany," he reminded them. "There we have reached the end of the road at whose beginning you are standing." He pleaded with them not to deceive themselves that the apostasy of the German church to nationalism was a peculiarly German problem. "If you begin to take the pious *man* serious, if you do not care to be one-sided, you will reach the same end before which the official German Church stands today," he warned. The road to paganism and nationalistic idolatry begins with anthropocentric idolatry. "Let me assure you that there are many sincere and very lovely people among the German Christians," Barth cautioned. "But it did not save them from falling a prey to this error. Let me warn you now. If you make a start with 'God *and* . . . ' you are opening the doors to every demon." The only way to keep the demons out, he exhorted, was to be relentlessly one-sided.[96]

MAINTAINING *SOLA GRATIA:* BARTH AND BRUNNER

Barth's notorious polemic against Brunner during this period is comprehensible only against this background. By the mid-1930s Barth judged that Bultmann had apparently always regarded theology and anthropology as interchangeable concepts. He reasoned that it was probably inevitable that his former friend Georg Merz "should work out his own salvation in a half-patriarchal half-pastoral combination, with a bit of Luther, a bit of Hitler, and a bit of Blumhardt." He was resigned to the fact that something as odious as Christian fascism was able to attract such able and respectable proponents as Althaus, Hirsch, and the eminent New Testament scholar Gerhard Kittel, who charged that Barth rejected German Christianity on account of his "ecclesiastical docetism." Barth claimed to accept that "it had to be that Friedrich Gogarten should develop into a sinister-looking new German state theologian." The fact that so many of his earlier fellowships had dissolved "like the morning mist" proved to him that he had never had many true fellowships with theologians in the first place.[97]

This verdict was rendered with particular finality with regard to his friendships with Gogarten and Brunner. In the mid-1930s Barth noted ruefully that Brunner had turned "to a new apologetic of his own invention" and thrown himself into the arms of a pietistic fellowship called the "Buchman Group movement." He judged that Brunner treated "God" as merely another word for "neighbor" and that he reduced revelation "to something subordinate, a mere shadow" by distinguishing between special and natural revelation.[98] The latter distinction drew Barth's furious denunciation, "No!" in October 1934, five months after he wrote the Barmen Declaration. Within the circle of major dialectical theologians, Brunner's position was closest to Barth's. This very proximity and his politics made him a candidate for Barth's most withering protest when Brunner looked for an "and" within revelation.

He was a special case from the outset of the dialectical theology movement. Brunner came into the movement from the same Religious Socialist background as Barth, but he never became part of Barth's inner circle. His father was a Swiss schoolteacher from Winterthur (near Zurich) and both of his parents were active Religious Socialists. Brunner therefore knew Christoph Blumhardt, Hermann Kutter, and Leonhard Ragaz as family friends.[99] He earned his doctorate in theology in 1913 from the University of Zurich, where Ragaz was one of his teachers. The following year he published his first book, *Das Symbolische in der religiösen Erkenntnis,* an interpretation of the role of symbolism in religious knowledge that reflected the influence of Kantian epistemology and Husserlian phenomenology upon his early thinking.[100] Brunner's later thinking owed more to Kant than any other philosopher, but he recalled with pride that Edmund Husserl praised his first book for its rare comprehension of phenomenological methodology.[101]

One of the factors that complicated his relationship with Barth from the outset was his friendship with Barth's brother, Heinrich Barth. Brunner and Heinrich Barth sustained a close friendship throughout their entire adult lives. In its early years, this friendship was fueled by their shared admiration for Platonism and Kantian epistemology. In his later life, when he was closer to Heinrich Barth than the two Barths were to each other, Brunner pointedly observed that he owed much of his Kantianism to Heinrich Barth, "with whom I have always had more intimate contact than with his more famous brother, Karl." A further complicating factor in Brunner's uneasy relationship with Barth was that they shared the same early mentor, Hermann Kutter, but only Brunner remained close to him afterward.

Brunner unfailingly acknowledged and expressed his appreciation for the sizable spiritual debt he owed to Kutter. In later life he lauded Kutter as the greatest figure he had ever known. In 1915, after completing his year in the Swiss border defense, Brunner joined his long-time family friend as a vicar in Kutter's congregation. He shared Kutter's love of the preaching vocation. He was also greatly impressed by Kutter's blend of biblical realism and neo-Platonist idealism. Though Kutter railed against the distorting influence of theology on the church's preaching mission, he was equally at home with the Bible, Plato, the neo-Platonists, and the Greek and Latin church fathers. He read Plato every day and his favorite writer was the ninth-century Irish neo-Platonist theologian John Scotus Erigena. His preaching contained heavy traces of the panentheism and dialecticism that he imbibed from Erigena, Augustine, and Pseudo-Dionysius.[102]

Brunner was too influenced by Kantian criticism to simply blend together the spiritual imagery of neo-Platonism and the Bible in the manner of his mentor. At the same time, in the early years of the first World War, he played down his Kantian misgivings about Kutter's neo-Platonism. He admired the emotive power and spiritual effect of Kutter's religious worldview. He shared Kutter's passion for preaching "God himself." He identified with Kutter's prophetic Christian socialism. It was only after the war dragged on, against his expectation, that Brunner began to have serious second thoughts about Kutter's worldview. The colossal evil of the war gradually made Kutter's philosophical idealism and Socialism unreal to him. He studied Kierkegaard for the first time and also turned to Luther with a new appreciation and intensity. Like Barth, Brunner began to question whether Kutter's religious worldview was actually consistent with the scriptural witness to reality.

The war shattered his faith in social progress. He later recalled that the horrendous killing and destruction of the war made his Religious Socialism "look suspiciously like a beautiful illusion."[103] Brunner married Kutter's niece and accepted a pastoral call to a small mountain congregation (Obstalden) in the canton of Glarus, where he found plenty of time to immerse himself in Luther and Kierkegaard. Together they tore apart the elements of religious and political idealism that undergirded his inherited worldview. He was thus perfectly suited to recognize and appreciate the spiritual sensibility that reverberated through Barth's first edition *Romans.* Brunner was the first reviewer to praise the book as potentially epochal in its importance. He hailed Barth's recovery of the "timeless, supra-psychological, 'absolute' nature of faith" and lauded his refusal to psychologize the experience of faith.[104] Though Barth soon judged that this review misunderstood the book in ways that revealed the book's inadequacies, he welcomed Brunner as a kindred spirit.

Except for his friendship with Eduard Thurneysen, however, Brunner never became part of the crisis theology inner circle. During the period when Barth gave his sensational address at Tambach (September 1919) and acquired a core of theological supporters, Brunner accepted a fellowship to study and teach at Union Theological Seminary in New York. He disliked the liberal Ritschlianism that prevailed at Union, but he made contacts with numerous American academics and clergy. Some of these personal contacts made his later American fame possible. Brunner returned to his Glaronese congregation in 1920, "deeply filled with impressions, new insights, and questions." With an interesting lapse of memory he later explained that he never became part of Barth's *Zwischen den Zeiten* group because he was in America when this group launched its journal.[105] In fact, the Barth-circle was just beginning to form when Brunner returned in 1920 and the journal was not launched until 1923. Brunner came closer to the mark in reflecting that from the beginning of the crisis theology movement, he sought more consciously than other "Barthians" to develop a position that was independent of Barth. More importantly, in the movement's early years, Barth was wary of Brunner for reasons that, at first, had more to do with differences in personality and style than with substantive theological disagreements.

Brunner's style of expression was often aggressive and always clear, self-confident, and direct. These qualities gave him significant advantages over other dialectical theologians after crisis theology became a major movement. For many years he was easily the movement's most influential proponent among English-speaking readers. Nearly from the beginning of their acquaintance with each other, however, Barth was put off by Brunner's air of self-assuredness and his claims to theological certainty. He worried that Brunner was too cocksure to be a good theologian. He kept a careful distance from Brunner and cautioned Thurneysen against allowing him to become part of their inner circle.[106] At the same time Barth maintained reasonably friendly relations with Brunner and supported his ongoing work. In the same year that Barth's group founded *Zwischen den Zeiten,* Brunner sent to Barth the manuscript of his major work on Schleiermacher, *Die Mystik und das Wort,* which condemned Schleiermacher's regrounding of theology in religious experience. Brunner charged that the effect of Schleiermacher's methodological revisionism was to betray Protestant theology to a form of mysticism that blended Pietist and romanticist themes.[107]

Barth's second edition *Romans* made its own judgment to this effect, declaring that Schleiermacher betrayed Christ through his attempt to make a religion out of the gospel.[108] In most of his public remarks on Brunner's book, Barth was careful to endorse Brunner's critical judgments. He praised Brunner's basic theological position and his demolition of Schleiermacher's experiential revisionism. He told one of his classes that his purpose in teaching Schleiermacher to them was merely to make it possible for them to understand Brunner's book.[109] Near the end of his mostly favorable review of the book, however, Barth expressed his unease with Brunner's categorical judgments and sweeping forms of expression. He hinted that "mysticism" might not be exactly the right term of abuse to apply to Schleiermacher. He suggested that good theology should not express with such certainty its claim to possess the key that unlocks all theological doors. In Brunner's case, the key was something called "the biblical-Reformation faith."[110]

Barth later recalled that he found Brunner unapproachable on this subject. Barth often attacked Schleiermacher violently, but he also greatly admired Schleiermacher. He told his students that it was crucially important for them to understand why Schleiermacher was the greatest theologian of the modern era. On various occasions he praised Schleiermacher's love of the church, his commitment to the vocation of preaching, and his deep sense of the importance and beauty of theology.[111] Shortly after Brunner's book on Schleiermacher was published, Barth asked Brunner if they could get together to study various issues pertaining to Schleiermacher more closely. Brunner replied that this would not be possible, since he had already burned his papers on Schleiermacher. Barth was horrified. Recalling the incident many years later to Terrence Tice, he could still be moved to sorrow and rage at the memory of Brunner's attitude. "He was done with him!" Barth exclaimed with disgust. "Imagine! For me, Schleiermacher is present, within the church, my comrade, the finest of them all!" To Barth, Schleiermacher was the greatest theologian of the modern period because he appreciated the beauty of theology with singular profundity.[112]

In the mid-1920s, while they were allies in an establishment-challenging movement, Barth and Brunner kept their various disagreements about how theology should be asserted and defended to themselves. The question of the relation of law and gospel was a key example. Brunner believed that a "dialectic" of law and gospel was needed as a propaedeutic to dogmatic theology. He argued in *Die Mystik und das Wort* that knowledge of God's law is possible without revelation. The kind of knowledge of God that comes from recognizing the law is not saving knowledge, he reasoned, but it is a form of genuine knowledge of God. It requires no understanding or even exposure to God's Word, since the possibility of knowing God through the law is innate in human rationality. In effect, natural knowledge of God's law is the kind of knowledge that prepares a sinner to hear the saving Word of God. Brunner judged that the person who recognizes the law necessarily recognizes his or her placement under judgment. This is the place in which sinners hear and take to heart the saving knowledge of God made known through grace. Saving grace is not a result of the crisis of judgment made known through the sinner's recognition of the law, he cautioned, but it does break into a sinner's life and become known only under the crisis of judgment.[113]

This was the kernel of the very argument that ignited a theological firestorm a decade later. In 1934, at the outset of his furious denunciation of Brunner's argument for "natural revelation," Barth expressed sharp disappointment that it was Emil Brunner who had crossed his path, in the church's darkest moment of apostasy, as an exponent of paganizing natural theology.[114] The bitterness of Barth's polemic against Brunner was surprising to a theological audience that had grown accustomed to speaking of "Barth and Brunner" as a single entity. But in fact, Barth and Brunner had been debating this issue for ten years before their disagreement sparked a public controversy. In 1924, Barth protested to Brunner that his "law and gospel" dialectic was pure Lutheranism. This judgment was briefly chastening to Brunner, but a few weeks later, after brushing up on Calvin, he countered that it was not only Luther among the Reformers who believed that knowledge of the law is innate in human rationality. Calvin made the same argument. Brunner allowed that there was a significant difference between Luther and Calvin over the relation of the Old and New Testaments, but in this case, he contended, Luther's emphasis on the supercession of the gospel over the law was correct. Luther understood that only Jesus Christ was univocally God's Word, he explained, but Calvinism paved the way to the orthodox equation of the Word of God with the words of the Bible.[115]

The seeds of a full-scale theological blowout were thus already sown in the mid-1920s. Because it presented itself as a recovery of the Reformation faith in modern forms of thinking and expression, the dialectical theology movement had a great deal at stake in the question of how Luther and Calvin should be interpreted with regard to the questions of natural revelation and natural theology. The fact that Luther and Calvin never addressed these questions in a systematic way made it difficult, however, for Barth and his colleagues to get their bearings in this critical area. In the mid-1920s Barth therefore backed away from attacking Brunner for the same reasons that he averted public disputes with Gogarten, Bultmann, and the others. He feared that public disputes would hurt the movement and that his own thinking was not sufficiently developed to afford an inner-movement controversy. To Thurneysen, he fretted that Brunner was "rushing headlong into destruction" with his dialectic of law and gospel. To Barth, "destruction" meant adopting the conservative Lutheranism of Althaus and Karl Holl.[116]

Having argued that what Protestant theology needed most was to develop its own theme, however, he devoted himself to working out his own understanding of theology as Word-faithful exegesis.

BRUNNER AND GOGARTEN: BARTHIANISM AS A MOVEMENT

Meanwhile Brunner became a leading voice of what was usually called the "Barthian" or "dialectical theology" movement. In England and the United States, he was the movement's leading voice. In 1924 he accepted the Chair of Systematic and Practical Theology at the University of Zurich. Three years later his *Religionsphilosophie protestantischer Theologie* introduced the chief ideas of the crisis theology movement to a wide audience.[117] The following year he made a triumphal lecture tour in the United States, speaking at seven theological seminaries that included Union (New York), Harvard, Princeton, and Hartford. These lectures, published as *The Theology of Crisis,* became a second influential guide to the "new Reformation" theology.[118] Both volumes displayed Brunner's movement-oriented knack for presenting the new theology as a distinctive alternative to Protestant orthodoxy and liberalism. During the same period Brunner published a massive systematic work on Christology titled *The Mediator* (1927).[119] Though he later disavowed this work on account of its docetic tendencies, *The Mediator* showed the seriousness of the Barthian movement. Its six-hundred-page treatment of a single dogmatic theme showed that dialectical theology, by whatever name, would not be a passing fad.[120]

With distinctive self-certainty, Brunner assured that Barth/Brunner theology was the true heir to Luther and Calvin. Like Barth, he emphasized the diastasis between revelation and scriptural word without acknowledging that his disbelief in the divine verbal inspiration of scripture put him at odds with Luther and Calvin. Like Barth, he conceptualized revelation as divine *self*-disclosure without acknowledging that this idea derived from Hegel and the right-Hegelian Philipp Marheineke, not from any sixteenth-century Reformer. "There is no such thing as revelation-in-itself, because revelation consists always of the fact that something is revealed to *me,*" he insisted, in a way that aroused Barth's early suspicion. "Revelation is not a thing, but an act of God, an event involving two parties; it is a personal address."[121] Though Brunner never did own up to the Hegelian aspects of his theory of revelation, he forthrightly identified with Kierkegaard's emphasis on revelation as existential address. He sustained and even heightened his commitment to Kierkegaard's dialectic of existence after Barth cut his ties to it.

He specialized in a form of dialectical apologetics that was designed to provoke and draw lines. To those who knew him personally, Brunner was noted for his warm-hearted friendliness and his fervent neo-Calvinist piety, but his writings, while bearing these qualities, were also distinguished by their aggressive spirit. Brunner routinely attacked his opponents, especially fundamentalists, evangelicals, old-style confessionalists, and liberal modernists. He repeatedly blasted conservatives and fundamentalists for turning the Bible into “a holy object, a fetish.” With an apparent relish that often offended evangelicals, he declared that scripture abounds with “thousands of contradictions and human characteristics.” The Bible is “full of errors, contradictions, and misleading views of various circumstances relating to man, nature, and history,” he asserted. “It contains many contradictions in its report of the life of Jesus; it is over-grown with legend, even in the New Testament. Some parts of it are written in very helpless, colloquial, and even faulty language, while others again rise to the level of the greatest works of literature.”[122]

Brunner cautioned that the parts of scripture that are well written are no more or less God’s Word than the parts that are badly written. He appealed to Luther as a kindred spirit, because Luther grasped that there is a paradoxical unity between the word of scripture and the Word of the Spirit. In his reading, however, the Protestant movement after Luther quickly developed fundamentalist tendencies. Beginning with Melanchthon, Brunner explained, the Protestant movement increasingly deduced the divine truth of scripture from its effects. Protestant orthodoxy took the fatal step of regarding scripture as revelation in itself, which inevitably led to the conclusion that every detail of the Bible must be revelation. The Protestant dogmatists became incapable of understanding how Luther could regard scripture as “the cradle in which Christ lies.” Brunner was fond of recalling that Luther found numerous errors in the prophetic and historical books of scripture. Luther called the book of James “an epistle of straw” and the Chronicles “no more than a Jewish calendar.” He declared that “if our opponents allege Scripture against Christ, we allege Christ against Scripture.”[123]

This is the free-speaking, Christ-centered faith that needs to be recovered, Brunner urged: “Christianity is either faith in the revelation of God in Jesus Christ or it is nothing.”[124] So-called “crisis theology” was merely a modern recovery of the genuine voice and spirit of the Reformation. It was a protest against the backwardness and idolatry of orthodoxy and the sheer apostasy of theological liberalism. Brunner blasted his liberal teachers with the same dismissive finality that he applied to conservatives. He noted that virtually all of the theologians of his generation had begun as Ritschlians. Most of them embraced some form of idealistic immanence-faith that pretended to be Christian. But by the turn of the century, he recalled, the self-deception that the liberal theologians were still Christians became very difficult to sustain. The fate of the liberal tradition and the crucial clue to its true identity were disclosed by the ascendancy of *Religionsgeschichtliche* relativism. Theological liberalism led inevitably to Troeltsch. Brunner judged that this was the fate that liberal theology deserved. Liberal theology descended into the utter bankruptcy of Troeltsch’s relativistic historicism because liberal Christianity “has nothing in common with Christianity except a few words.”[125]

If Jesus was merely a teacher or moral exemplar, Brunner countered, “then it does not matter whether he lived or not, whether the world remembers or forgets him.” We get no further with this Jesus than we might get with no Jesus at all. Christianity is pointless if Jesus is not accepted as God's living Word. Like Barth, however, Brunner's pursuit of this theme developed a form of neo-Calvinist fideism that owed more than a little to liberal theology. He warned that an outsider's question "can never be answered unless he ceases to be an outsider." To ask how one might know that Jesus is the Word is to make an inquiry from the standpoint of a spectator, he observed. Brunner countered with Herrmann's question: "Would a revelation which is capable of proof still be a revelation?" What sort of revelation would it be that is subordinate to scientific or historical proof? "Revelation means that what is said here is truth recognized as being true only by him who permits it to be told to him," Brunner asserted. "It is truth carrying its trustworthiness within itself, just as all rational truth carries its trustworthiness in itself."[126]

Calvin taught that the truth of God's revelation is "autopistic," or self-authenticating. Because scripture is self-authenticating, he asserted, "it is not right to subject it to proof and reasoning." And the certainty that scripture deserves with us "it attains by the testimony of the Spirit." Calvin explained that scripture does not seek to impress us with its majesty or intellectual power. It affects us seriously "only when it is sealed upon our hearts through the Spirit."[127] This was the Reformed principle later obscured by apologetics-oriented Reformed scholastics that Brunner and Barth defended with Herrmannian arguments. "If God speaks to me, I can hear him only by letting him speak to me," Brunner explained. "Every theoretical understanding is in its very inception a misunderstanding." Faith of any kind is always a venture by which one trusts in the truth of a word. Brunner noted that no faithful suitor would hire a detective to spy on his beloved after asking for her hand in marriage. In the case of Christ, he insisted, one does not trust in faith on account of one's courage or willpower, but because one cannot do otherwise under the Spirit-illuminated power of the Word.[128]

Dialectical theology recovered traditional biblical ways of speaking without becoming entangled in modern historiocritical debates about the historical foundations of Christian belief. This was a crucial key to its appeal. Though he rarely made use of historiocritical techniques in his own exegesis, Barth repeatedly identified himself as a proponent of radical biblical criticism. To him (at least in theory), radical historiocriticism liberated the true subject matter of scripture—the Spirit of Christ—from the control of historical reason. For the same reason Brunner also called himself "an adherent of a rather radical school of Biblical criticism." Brunner was careful to establish that biblical criticism had certain limits. He assured his readers that scholars of scripture would never be able to disprove that Jesus considered himself the Messiah or that the early church revered Jesus as the risen Lord. Beyond these baseline assurances, however, he argued (following Kierkegaard) that anyone who argues for or against the doctrine of the deity of Christ on rational grounds has missed the point. The doctrine of the incarnation means that God became "really man," he observed. That is, God was veiled so completely in the man Jesus that God can be recognized in Jesus only by faith.

The question of Christ's deity therefore cannot be decided by history. The historian sees only the human incognito of the Christ, Brunner explained, but the "real Christ" is visible only to the spiritual eye of the believer.[129]

Brunner's vigorous presentation of these themes made him the movement "battleship" that Barth had expected Gogarten to become. In 1925 Adolf Keller, one of the movement's most perceptive interpreters, observed that the Barthian circle was developing a distinctive style of exegesis, philosophy, and systematic theology. Keller judged that Barth was the movement's chief exegete, Gogarten was its philosopher, and Brunner was its systematic theologian. This judgment was a telling assessment of Brunner's early role in the movement.[130] Though Brunner's ideas about revelation, history, theological method, the orders of creation, and the relation of law and gospel were actually very close to Gogarten's, he expressed these beliefs with a sharper theological focus and clarity. His writings were more lucid and theologically systematic than Gogarten's. They also exuded a more attractive spirit than Gogarten's.

Gogarten was a creative, interesting, and tremendously prolific thinker. He was the first theologian to adopt Ferdinand Ebner's existential I-Thou concept, which gained a long-running vogue in theology after Gogarten and, especially, Martin Buber developed its theological implications in the early 1920s.[131] In the early 1930s Brunner made the I-Thou relation the centerpiece of his own theological program.[132] Gogarten later became a prominent advocate of Bultmann's demythologizing strategy and a leading interpreter of the implications of secularization for Christian belief.[133] His writings on demythologization and secularization greatly influenced Gerhard Ebeling, Ernst Fuchs, and other "post-Bultmannian" liberal theologians in the generation following the Second World War.[134] Perhaps more than any thinker aside from Dietrich Bonhoeffer, Gogarten helped two generations of theologians think about what it means to be a Christian in a sociocultural context that has been desacralized by modern science, technology, philosophy, and economics.

But he was not well suited to build the movement that changed the course of modern theology. Gogarten's style was turgid, argumentative, and often arrogant. His books were organized in a way that frequently made it difficult to discern the point or even the drift of his argument. His reputation was damaged by his nationalistic fixations and his brief flirtation with outright fascism. Throughout the early and mid-1920s, Barth groused privately about Gogarten's nationalistic complex, his philosophical preoccupations, and his Lutheranism. These long-nurtured misgivings came to a head after Gogarten criticized his *Christliche Dogmatik* for its lack of an anthropological foundation. Like Bultmann, Gogarten argued that all theological concepts inevitably contain some implicit understanding of humanity on account of their worldly and historical nature. He contended that good theology must at least explicate its implied understandings in a theory of the self or human nature.[135]

Barth's opening volume of the *Church Dogmatics* replied that God's Word does not speak to human beings on their own ground. Faith is not an anthropological datum or ontic element to be explained by or fitted into some ontological theory, he asserted. Faith is the divine gift of God's freedom. Barth acknowledged that the problem of "unpurified concepts" that Gogarten and Bultmann pressed upon him was a serious one for any genuine theology of the Word, but he countered that it was better to work theologically with the ambiguity of unpurified ideas than to work with ideas that had already been "cleansed" by a controlling philosophy.[136]

In the early 1930s, Gogarten's drift toward fascism made an appalling and powerfully-instructive impression on Barth. Among other things, it confirmed his predisposition against all forms of philosophical preunderstanding. In the year before Hitler ascended to power, Gogarten's *Politische Ethik* used the I-Thou concept to explicate the meaning of the Lutheran doctrine of the orders of creation for contemporary political life. He celebrated the necessity and grandeur of state power, claiming that God has given "no greater gift" to humanity than the authority of the state.[137] The following year, after the German Christians began to take over the churches, Gogarten proclaimed that God's law is identical with the law of the German people. He supported Ludwig Müller's appointment as Reich Bishop of the Evangelical Church, and, for a brief period (during the summer of 1933), he joined the German Christian movement outright.

For Barth, these events marked the end of any possible relationship between himself and the dialectical theology movement. He could no longer stand to be associated with Gogarten or numerous lesser-known figures like him in any way. His blistering "farewell" to dialectical theology judged that Gogarten had been headed all along toward an "increasingly massive dogma of orders." Since the *Zwischen den Zeiten* circle was now producing people who were supporting the "monstrosity" of German Christianity, he observed, he could only conclude that the entire founding and history of this venture had taken place on the basis of a misunderstanding. Therefore Barth made a clean break with it. In effect, he abolished *Zwischen den Zeiten* and set himself against all of his major theological colleagues.[138]

This was the highly-charged religious and political context in which Brunner produced a pamphlet titled "Nature and Grace: A Contribution to the Discussion with Karl Barth." Brunner was stunned by what he called Barth's "great purge, in which the valuable periodical *Zwischen den Zeiten* was eliminated." He reported that even before Barth "disowned" virtually "all other theologians" in his farewell to dialectical theology, numerous colleagues had exhorted him to give Barth the polemical pasting he deserved. Many of them resented Barth's posture of righteousness. They were offended that Barth was casting aspersions on their faithfulness to the gospel. They urged Brunner to return fire. Their reasons for preferring Brunner for this task were straightforward: Brunner was the major theologian whose position was perceived to be closest to Barth, he had an obvious taste for polemic, and in recent years Barth had repeatedly represented him (in Brunner's words) as "a thoroughly unreliable theologian who showed treacherous inclinations both towards Thomism and towards Neo-Protestantism."[139]

BRUNNER ON NATURE AND GRACE

For ten years Barth had shaken his head at Brunner's determination to rehabilitate the doctrine of natural revelation and the practice of apologetics for dialectical theology. In 1929, Brunner made a case for a type of polemical apologetics that he called "eristics." Kierkegaard was his ideal of the theologian as eristiker; Gogarten was his contemporary exemplar. In addition to its dogmatic task of explicating the Word of God, Brunner asserted that theology also bears responsibility for making people open to the Word, or at least for preparing people to hear it. The proper task of eristic theology was to work upon the "point of contact" in all people that makes them capable of hearing the Word. Brunner had earlier described this "point of contact" as the knowledge of the law that people possess apart from revelation. This time he construed it as the autonomous knowledge of God that resides in every person by virtue of having been created in the image of God. The upshot was the same in either formulation. Without a "point of contact," he urged, it would not be possible for any person to respond to God's gift of grace in the Word. The Word preached and revealed does not address a self who knows nothing of God. But because there is an autonomous point of contact in every person that theology can address apart from special revelation, theology must speak to it as preparation for the hearing of God's saving Word.[140]

To Barth, this argument sadly confirmed that Brunner was basically no different from Gogarten or Bultmann. Brunner felt that he had already been excommunicated when he wrote "Nature and Grace." "Now I belong to the unpleasant category of neutrals who are neither hot or cold, who say neither entirely Yes nor entirely No," he ruefully remarked. He protested that this judgment on his standing was grossly unfair, but he also claimed not to be angry with Barth for maligning him. Barth was his friend, he insisted. He admired Barth above all others. "The credit of having given back to Protestant theology its proper theme and subject-matter is due, without qualification and, if I may use the expression, without competition, to Karl Barth," he acknowledged. "Within the space of a few years he completely changed the Protestant theological situation." Because of Barth, theologians no longer spoke about religion, but about the Word of God. It was Barth who ended the reign of liberal theology and brought the scriptural Word back into the church. "We others who have assisted Barth in this struggle have all of us first had our eyes opened by him," Brunner professed. Therefore he could not be angry with Barth or set out to attack him. To him, Barth was like a loyal soldier on night-time sentry duty "who shoots everyone who does not give him the password as he has been commanded, and who therefore from time to time also annihilates a good friend whose password he does not hear or misunderstands in his eagerness." "Nature and Grace" was presented as a comradely attempt to clear up a misunderstanding that had occurred not because of anybody's bad faith or ill will, but "because of Barth's one-sidedness."[141]

Brunner denied at the outset that the root of their disagreement was the dialectical "and." He agreed with Barth about the seductive and fatally compromising character of the "and" as a form of coordination. The only difference between them on this issue was that Barth claimed there was a difference between them, he asserted. Like Barth, Brunner spoke of issues in dialectical pairs to identify the existence of a problem, such as the problem of the relation of law and gospel, or reason and revelation, or church and culture, or grace and nature. Because he believed in *sola gratia* and *sola scriptura* as much as Barth, he protested, he believed no less than Barth that scriptural authority must not be paired with the authority of reason, or grace with moral effort, or the like.

The problem was that Barth drew a series of one-sided conclusions from the doctrine of *sola gratia.* In Brunner's rendering, Barth taught that the image of God in which human beings were created was obliterated entirely (without remnant) by sin. In Brunner's rendering, Barth further taught that every attempt to discern a general revelation of God in nature, conscience, and history was mistaken. He denied that there was any legitimate basis for distinguishing between general and special revelation, claiming that scripture knows only the single complete revelation in Christ. It followed from Barth's confession of Christ as the sole saving grace of God that no trace of God's grace is available to us from God's creation or preservation of the world. Otherwise the church would have to teach that there are two or three kinds of grace. Barth therefore concluded that neither the doctrine of divine orders of creation or the notion of a "point of contact" for the saving action of God have any legitimate basis, since both of these ideas violate the principle of *sola gratia.* His theology thus had no room for any notion of the new creation as a perfection of the old creation. To Barth, the new creation came into being exclusively by destruction and replacement.[142]

Brunner allowed that these theses had to be inferred from Barth's arguments, since he never actually presented a systematic formulation of his position. Without pausing to consider that Barth might have had a serious reason for failing to provide such an account, however, Brunner plunged into "my counter-theses and their proof." He did not deny that the original image of God in humanity has been destroyed by sin. In his reading, what was missing in the present debate over natural revelation was the distinction between formal and material images. In the formal sense, he proposed, human beings are distinguished qualitatively from the rest of creation by the presence of God's image within them, both "before" and "after" the Fall. Scripture assumes that, even as sinners, human beings remain distinctive subjects. That is, human agents are rational creatures endowed with the God-given capacity for self-conscious speech and the burden of being morally responsible for their actions. Whether sinful or not, the human creature is always a derived and morally responsible subject whose formal *imago* is not diminished by sin in any way. What *has* been lost utterly is the material image of God in the self, Brunner argued. There is nothing *in* the human creature that has not been defiled by sin. Formally the human creature remains a person (a derived subject), but materially the sinful creature is "not a personal person but an anti-personal person." Personal existence is communion with God in love, but the sinful creature is alienated from God and is therefore defiled in every material faculty of being.

A similar logic justified his distinction between natural and special revelation. Brunner straightforwardly affirmed that there are, indeed, two kinds of revelation. Scripture testifies not only to the revelation given in Jesus Christ, but also to the revelation given in creation. It assumes that God's action always leaves an imprint of the divine nature upon creation and history and it repeatedly asserts or implies that genuine knowledge of God is attainable through knowledge of the law. Brunner appealed to another distinction to explain why natural revelation is truly revelatory but not saving. The word "natural" in this connection must be broken into its "objective-divine" and "subjective-human-sinful" senses, he contended. Creation always bears the objective imprint of its maker, but it is not possible for the sinful "natural" self to apprehend this knowledge truly apart from Christ. Put differently, God is objectively revealed in creation, but true natural knowledge of God is possible only for those who stand within the revelation of Christ.

Brunner's distinction between the grace of Christ and God's general or "preserving" grace followed from these distinctions, especially the double-nature concept. He proposed that God is present to fallen creatures through God's preserving grace, which abolishes the "worst consequences" of sin without abolishing sin itself. It is through God's preserving grace that the state acquires its divine authority to block the worst ravages of sin, he contended. Though general grace is not saving, it makes possible "the whole sphere of natural life and its goods." General grace is the grace by which people live before they come to know Christ. It is also the grace that establishes the various orders of creation recognized by scripture and Christian doctrine, especially monogamous marriage.

All of these notions presume "that there is such a thing as a point of contact" between God and sinful creatures, Brunner urged. More precisely, the point of contact that makes human subjects able to receive God's Word is the *formal* image of God within all creatures that even the worst sinner retains simply by virtue of being a human creature. "Not even sin has done away with the fact that man is receptive of words, that he and he alone is receptive of the Word of God," Brunner observed. The saving receptivity that human creatures retain is a purely formal possibility, he cautioned; because of sin it holds no material basis whatsoever. But this receptive capacity remains nevertheless the crucial precondition of every person's ability to hear the Word of God. Brunner allowed that the creature's capacity to *believe* the Word is created by the Word under the power of the Holy Spirit, but he insisted that the prior capacity to *hear* the Word is necessarily constitutive to the self as a human subject. "The Word of God could not reach a man who had lost his consciousness of God entirely," he reasoned. It would be pointless to say "repent and believe the gospel" to a person who has no conscience in the first place. The natural person's natural knowledge of God may be grossly confused and distorted, but it remains "the necessary, indispensable point of contact for divine grace."

The last counter-thesis disputed Barth's purported eliminativism. Scripture never claims that the old self is entirely obliterated in Christ, Brunner lectured. Though Paul exclaims, "It is no longer I who live, but it is Christ who lives in me" (Gal. 2:20), this cannot be taken to mean that the sinner's *formal* personality is obliterated when the "Old Adam" within him or her is negated by Christ's Spirit. For Paul affirms that Christ now lives *in me,* Brunner observed. Moreover, while scripture does invariably call faith the work and gift of the Holy Spirit, it never says that the Spirit within me has faith. Scripture always says that *I believe* through the power of God's Spirit. It always testifies that a personal God meets us personally through the Spirit's action, restoring to a "new creation" that which has been lost. This was the second crucial point. If it was not possible to hear the Word without possessing some formal capacity to be addressed, neither was it possible "to repair what no longer exists." What *is* possible, Brunner concluded, is to repair something "in such a way that one has to say: this has become quite new."[143]

"Nature and Grace" appealed to Calvin for support. Brunner argued that the concept of the *imago Dei* was fundamental to Calvin's anthropology and that Calvin's ethical thinking was "simply unthinkable without the concept of the ordinances of creation." Everything that Calvin taught about the ethics of sexuality, the authority of the state, and similar problems rested upon his belief in the existence of a God-given order of nature. Though Calvin always treated the problem of natural theology as a side-issue, Brunner allowed (because for Christians natural theology is inadequate and unnecessary), he nonetheless took the legitimacy of natural theology for granted as a correlate of natural revelation. Calvin showed how to base a Christian account of the moral life upon the orders of creation without lapsing into Catholicism.

Brunner's description of the difference was remarkably unfair to Catholic teaching. He explained that while Catholic doctrine does recognize the existence of sin, it does not acknowledge that the image of God in the human subject has been negated by sin. The Catholic church therefore teaches that natural reason is capable of developing a self-sufficient system of theological knowledge apart from revelation, he claimed. That is, because Catholicism denies that the *imago Dei* has been defiled by sin, it insists that natural theology can be derived from reason alone and that it provides a sure foundation for church teaching. "Sin has, as it were, nothing to do with this question," Brunner explained. "This means that there is an *unrefracted theologia naturalis.*" In Catholic doctrine, the divine order of creation "is entirely accessible and adequately intelligible to reason." Catholic teaching draws a "neat horizontal line" between nature and grace. Though faith is needed to deal with supernatural matters that bear upon redemption, natural reason is perfectly sufficient to deal with nature.

Brunner allowed that the Reformers did not pay much attention to the problem of natural theology, but, he contended, to the extent that they did they replaced this unrefracted Catholic approach with a dialectical natural theology that placed natural knowledge of God where it belonged. Where it belonged was in the twilight. Calvin and Luther recognized that natural theology has its own legitimate work to do, especially in the ethical arena, but they obliterated the paganizing Catholic dualism of nature and supernature. They accepted the biblical teaching that the image of God in humankind has been negated by sin. They recognized that reason is therefore deficient in dealing with anything, including the divine order of creation. To them, any statement about nature that did not take Christ into account could not be correct.[144]

The Reformers rejected the undialectical Catholic demarcation between reason and revelation, Brunner explained, but they never repudiated natural theology altogether. Only Karl Barth imposed this stricture upon true Protestantism. If one asked why Barth "should so violently and brusquely deny a doctrine which is obviously in accordance with the Scriptures and the Reformation," Brunner mused, the only plausible explanation was that he could not see his way beyond a one-sided concept of revelation. "Barth refuses to recognize that where revelation and faith are concerned, there can be anything permanent, fixed, and, as it were, natural," he observed. "He acknowledges only the act, the event of revelation, but never anything revealed, or, as he says, the fact of revelation."[145]

Brunner allowed that this vigorous assertion of the actual was the great strength of Barth's theology. On the other hand, he charged that Barth's exclusively one-sided focus upon the actual made his theology unreal. In Brunner's reading, Barth's one-sided actualism drove him to ignore, if not deny, the fact that God speaks to us presently because God *has* spoken in the past. Barth relentlessly emphasized that the scriptures become God's Word for the believer only through the movement of God's Spirit.[146] This principle is correct, Brunner conceded. The problem with it was that Barth did not pay heed to the reason why the Bible alone is the vehicle of God's Word to us. The scriptures can become God's Word to us because they already *are* God's Word, Brunner urged: "They became it through *that, which* is written, the solid body of words, sentences and books, something objective and available for everyone." He compared the relation of revelation and scripture to the sound of music that is heard from the engravings on a phonograph recording. Scripture is a similar kind of record, Brunner observed; it is "an action become substance." Scripture is a substantiated event, "a piece of world at anyone's disposal, even though the fact of its being a revelation is not at anyone's disposal." God speaks God's uncontrollable personal Word to us through substantial things. With tart disapproval, Brunner lectured that any person who grasped this teaching should be able to comprehend that God also speaks to us through God's work in nature "in the wide sense of the old usage."[147]

The sarcasm could not have been lost on Barth. Brunner was explicating (though not really amplifying, as it appeared) Barth's own distinctive doctrine of scripture, half of which had recently been published in a volume running nearly six hundred pages. Brunner had two further shots to make against him, however. He noted that Barth was the first theologian in history to claim that the Catholic "principle of analogy" was the crucial point of difference between Catholicism and Protestantism.[148] "For Barth holds the strange doctrine that there is no creature which has in itself any likeness to God," he remarked. Barth claimed that creatures are only raised to the status of likeness by revelation and the Spirit.[149] Brunner judged that by comparison to this piece of nominalism, Occam's appeared harmless.

There was also the question of a certain hardness of heart or spirit, he suggested. The spirit of Barth's theology was severe, unyielding, and, yes, "one-sided." It seemed to have no regard whatsoever for the problem of the "how" that is faced by every pastor. How does one acquire faith? How can one be certain of God's loving care? Brunner allowed that the "what" of Christian witness is always a holy matter, as Barth insisted, but he argued that the "how" is equally holy. Every pastor deals with situations in which the "how" is at least as important as the "what." It is possible to be right about the "what" but still "go to hell on account of the How," Brunner remarked. This set up his most cutting judgment: "To despise the question of the How is a sign, not of theological seriousness but of theological intellectualism," he declared. "The What is, as it were, guarded by faith, but the How has to be guarded by love. But where the How and therefore love is lacking, there faith must be lacking also."[150]

NO! *AUTOPISTIA* AS POLEMICS

This was a stunning conclusion to a statement that began with professions of love and admiration. For decades afterward commentators routinely highlighted the fury of Barth's response to Brunner without noting that, in its own way, Brunner's statement was at least equally demeaning and judgmental. Though most observers overlooked the rather ugly implications of Brunner's closing indictment, Barth took them to heart. He was enraged not only by Brunner's position, but especially by the combination of sweet-talk and personal aggression in which it was packaged. He thus began his reply with one of the most inadvertently hilarious lines in modern theology: "I am by nature a gentle being and entirely averse to all unnecessary disputes."

Barth restrained his rage for a few impression-managing sentences. He declared that he had long admired Brunner for his "extraordinary abilities" and "determined will-power." He lamented that Brunner had crossed his path so provocatively. He acknowledged that Brunner was much closer to him theologically than a German Christian like Hirsch, but for that very reason it seemed to him that Brunner was "much more dangerous" at the present time than someone like Hirsch. Barth explained that he had heard the applause that immediately greeted Brunner's essay. Otto Weber, Paul Althaus "and all the other half- or three-quarter German Christians" had loudly thanked Brunner for setting the matter straight. "His essay is an alarm signal. I wish it had not been written," Barth declared. What it confirmed, to him, was that the greatest danger to the church was coming not from the Nazi bootlickers, but from those who gave comfort to the half-German Christians.[151]

This included Brunner, who was aligned politically with one of the groups that was trying to split the differences between German Christianity and the Confessional movement. In "Nature and Grace," Brunner proposed to his friends on both sides of the current theological divide that it was the task of their theological generation "to find the way back to a true *theologia naturalis.*" Barth was incredulous. To him this statement was a mockery of everything that the dialectical theology movement was supposed to have been about. He replied that if this was what Brunner really thought, "how can he think that, in spite of this opinion, he has a right to be mentioned 'in one breath' with—of all people—me, to be my 'ally,' my 'good friend,' and that I have merely failed to understand him and therefore have in error shot at him by night?" Whatever confusions he may have suffered in the early and mid-1920s, he observed, "my soul is innocent of ever even having dreamt" that it was their common task to rehabilitate natural theology.

Perhaps they had never actually been allies, he reflected. Barth (mistakenly) recalled that it was only in 1929 that Brunner had begun to talk openly about a "point of contact" and related notions. He also recalled that he had warned Brunner strenuously against moving in this direction. He sought to dissuade Brunner from his lurch into natural theology because he thought that a genuine basis of unity existed between them and because he also thought that Brunner "was still curable." But these impressions now belonged to the distant past, he announced: "I am 'angry' with Brunner because on top of all this he did not refrain from showering me with love and praise and from maintaining that the matters in which I differ from him are mere 'false conclusions.' " If Brunner needed to stage a public debate with him, "he might have lent it dignity and status by addressing me from that distance which does as a matter of fact exist between us." As it was, the experience gave him new feelings of affinity with Luther. Barth explained that he felt manipulated in a way that eerily resembled the way that "another man at Zurich provoked someone out there in Germany" during the Reformation.[152]

Personal matters aside, Barth found Brunner's argument unforgivable, at least for the moment. It was not enough for Brunner "to stab me in the back" while making himself look righteous, he explained. What was worse was that Brunner had played for the applause of the German Christians and half-German Christians with arguments that portrayed Barth as a foolish-looking systematizer and Calvin as a paganizer. Brunner's formulation of Barth's purported system of "theses" made his critique of Barth's position look reasonable. Barth countered that there was a serious reason why he had never systematized his opposition to natural theology into a series of abstract formulations. To commit himself to an abstract foundational system of any kind would violate his actual commitment to do theology as exegesis of the Word, he explained. Brunner assigned a systematized anti-natural theology argument to him, but this still amounted to a type of natural theology. For this reason, Barth explained, Brunner's first mistake was to treat Karl Barth "as one of his kind." The very point of Barth's Word-faithful rejection of natural theology was that natural theology does *not exist* within the subject-matter of genuinely Christian theology, even as something to be opposed. The enterprise of speculative theology is always mistaken from a Christian standpoint, Barth insisted, even as a form of anti-speculative speculation.

"If you really reject natural theology you do not stare at the serpent, with the result that it stares back at you, hypnotizes you, and is ultimately certain to bite you, but you hit it and kill it as soon as you see it!" Barth exclaimed. "Real rejection of natural theology can come about only in the fear of God and hence only by a complete *lack* of interest in this matter." For years, Barth had found Brunner to be too cocksure and dogmatic in his theological statements. In his reading, the first problem with their present debate was that Brunner was making Barth sound like a reverse-image of Brunner. "Brunner makes me much too straightforward and doctrinaire, too confident and lacking in reserve," he remarked. This explained his verdict that Brunner was actually incurable. Because he trusted so much in his own power of rational persuasion, Brunner was incapable of recognizing that natural theology is both terrible and ineffective.[153]

Barth gave equally short shrift to Brunner's series of distinctions. He questioned what it could possibly mean to affirm the sovereign and freely-electing grace of God if human beings possessed a "capacity for revelation" apart from grace that is merely supported by grace. "What is the relevance of the 'capacity for revelation' to the fact that man is man?" he asked. Barth did not deny that people are different from turtles or that the image of God in human beings (in the formal sense defined by Brunner) has not been destroyed. It can be taken as given that human beings are human beings, he agreed. But, if grace is taken seriously, what relevance could any supposed "capacity for revelation" bear for the fact that human beings are human? If a person is saved from drowning by a competent swimmer, Barth analogized, "would it not be very unsuitable if he proclaimed the fact that he was a man and not a lump of lead as his 'capacity for being saved?' " Unless the point was that, as a man, he was able to help himself by swimming a few strokes, what was the point of proclaiming that his humanity was an enabling condition of his salvation?

Barth suspected that he knew the answer, but he did not press it. It was enough for him to insist that Brunner's distinction was either meaningless or heretical. If the remaining "purely formal" image of God in human beings is actually purely formal, he reasoned, it adds nothing to the self-evident truism that human beings are human. Neither does it conflict with the Reformationist/Pauline teaching that we are saved entirely by grace alone. But this also makes the "capacity for revelation" meaningless. If Brunner's insistence on the pure formality of the remaining image of God in human beings is to be taken seriously, Barth contended, then nothing can be said about it beyond that which was obvious without it. In that case, the formal/material distinction doesn't actually do any work for theology and it doesn't deserve to be taken seriously. Human beings have no "capacity for revelation" that *means* anything.[154]

The debate on this point was somewhat marred by a lack of mutual understanding about the nature of the distinctive capacity that Brunner was actually attributing to human beings. Barth took Brunner's term *Wortmächtigkeit* (literally, "capacity for words") to mean *Offenbarungsmächtigkeit* ("capacity for revelation"). Since "Word" functioned as a near-synonym for "revelation" in both of their theologies, Barth undoubtedly reasoned that the two compound terms had identical meanings. Brunner protested later that *Offenbarungsmächtigkeit* was a misleading rendering of his argument, since it carried the connotation of active control. The only capacity that he claimed for human beings, he explained, was the purely passive capacity to be reached by revelation and hear the Word when it was spoken.[155] Barth's persistent rendering of *Wortmächtigkeit* as "capacity for revelation" wrongly suggested that Brunner attributed to the human recipient of revelation some role in the act of revealing.

This objection helped to clarify Brunner's meaning and also corrected Barth's connotatively slippery use of the term *Offenbarungsmächtigkeit.* It did not answer Barth's main argument, however. Barth questioned the significance that Brunner attributed to the distinctively human capacity to be reached by revelation. He noted that Brunner usually spoke of this attribute as the capacity to *recognize* revelation. If this reference to human cognition means anything, Barth contended, it surely means that "something very material" has been added to what was supposedly a purely formal category. It implies that human beings possess some capacity of their own to know God. He observed that this purported knowledge inevitably has some relevance to salvation. The implication of Brunner's claim that the true God can be known through creation apart from the revelation of Christ was that human beings can swim a little on their own, after all.

Brunner invoked the distinction between preserving and saving grace as protection from this charge, but Barth denied that Christian scripture supports any such distinction. Nothing that Brunner sought to construe as grace under either category can be saved "unless the one revelation of Christ in the Old and New Testaments is taken into account," Barth lectured. In effect, Brunner's dichotomy between preserving grace and the redeeming grace of Christ severed the connection between creation and reconciliation that is presupposed throughout scripture. "Does not the Bible relate all that

Brunner calls a special 'preserving grace' to prophesy and fulfilment, to law and gospel, to the covenant and the Messiah, to Israel and to the Church, to the children of God and their future redemption?" Barth asked. "Where did Brunner read of another abstract preserving grace?" While emphasizing that Brunner never found this theme in the Bible, Barth noted that he could have come upon it elsewhere, especially in Roman Catholicism, in various forms of Pietism and enthusiasm, and, lately, in German Christianity.

The same problems and dubious company came with Brunner's doctrine of the orders of creation. In this case Barth moved quickly to the main point, taking only a brief pass at his moral and political objections. He argued that if human beings can know and fulfill the law "to some extent" without Christ, as Brunner asserted, then it was ridiculous for Brunner to maintain the fiction that his posited capacity for receiving revelation was purely formal. *This* human subject is already on quite good terms with God apart from Christ, Barth observed. If it is really possible for a man or woman to know and fulfill some measure of God's law without Christ, "if he can swim enough to help his deliverer by making a few good strokes," then it was pointless to continue to speak of *sola gratia.*[156]

All of Brunner's distinctions were drawn to support his theory of a point of contact. He argued that humankind possesses a distinctive point of contact with God by virtue of a uniquely human capacity to receive revelation. Though he emphasized that this capacity comes alive only through revelation, the point of contact was nonetheless necessarily anterior to revelation. Barth noted that even the claim to a purely formal and unique point of contact was problematic on its own terms, however. Brunner took his stand on the claim of unique human receptivity, but this left the angels out of account. His theory implicitly presumed that the only beings in existence are human beings. His emphasis on receptivity also left out all human beings who possess no capacity for language, including infants and the mentally impaired. Barth pressed the point that Christ died for these people too. In his desire to link all people to God apart from Christ, Brunner subordinated the meaning of *sola gratia* to a theory of existential "encounter" that actually excluded vast numbers of human beings.

Barth's judgment on this outcome was severe: "Brunner has been unable to adhere to *sola fide-sola gratia.* He has entered upon the downward path." Brunner claimed that 1 Corinthians 2 and Galatians 2 supported his position, but Barth demanded to know which of the sixteen verses in 1 Corinthians 2 held out for the existence of another knowledge of God before and beside "Jesus Christ, and him crucified" (v. 2), before and beside the "demonstration of the Spirit and of power" (v. 4), before and beside "God's wisdom, secret and hidden" (v. 7), or before and beside that which "God has revealed to us through the spirit" (v. 10). In Galatians 2:15–21, Paul declares that because he is now crucified with Christ and dead to the law, he now lives only in the faith of Christ given for him. This statement does contain the suggestion of an abiding formal personality, Barth allowed, but Paul never claims that true knowledge of God is possible on the basis of this formal personality apart from the grace of Christ.[157]

The limitations of theological debate as polemic were amply displayed on both sides. Both thinkers made tellingly unimpressive attempts to claim Calvin for their position. Brunner compiled a list of proof texts that seemed to demonstrate Calvin's belief in the existence of true natural knowledge of God. Barth disputed some of Brunner's weaker citations, appealed to a forthcoming essay on this subject by his brother Peter Barth (a Calvin specialist), and blasted Brunner for leaving out "the very important brackets within which Calvin always speaks of the natural knowledge of God." These brackets were the expression *si integer stetisset Adam,* which recognized natural knowledge of God only as a *hypothetical* possibility, and Calvin's strict insistence that true theology can be done only *within* Christ's church and *under* the sign of grace. Barth charged that Brunner turned Calvin into a natural theologian only by sweeping aside these fundamental assumptions and then treating Calvin's exegesis of difficult texts (such as Rom. 1:20–21) from the standpoint of theology as free speculation.

This was the only context in which Barth himself faced up to the problem of Romans 1:20–21. Though he shredded some of Brunner's scripture citations, Barth carefully bypassed Romans 1:20–21 until his discussion of Calvin's exegesis made avoidance impossible. Brunner noted that Barth *always* avoided this text in his writings because he didn't agree with it.[158] Paul taught that God's eternal power and nature have been understood and seen since the creation of the world "through the things he has made." The pagans are therefore "without excuse," he contended, "for though they knew God, they did not honor him as God or give thanks to him, but they became futile in their thinking, and their senseless minds were darkened." Barth explained that Calvin took this passage to presume the theoretical *possibility* of a natural knowledge of God. Implicitly, this was also his own tack. "The fact that God is revealed in all his works is God's scriptural testimony to us against the ignorance of man," Barth reasoned, explicating Calvin. Paul believed that the revelation of God in nature justified God's wrath and judgment upon humanity. To Calvin, this scriptural assurance established that men and women are morally responsible for their inability to know God, but it did not serve to credit any positive attribute to human nature. There is nothing that we can make of it that contributes to our salvation.

The sticky point came next. Paul and Calvin did believe that human beings possess the ability to recognize evil apart from Christ. They explicitly argued that human beings are convicted of their guilt by their ability to distinguish good from evil.[159] Barth granted the point on both counts. What he disputed was the seemingly-logical deduction by Brunner and others that Paul and Calvin therefore recognized that human beings possess a natural knowledge of God's law apart from Christ. Barth countered that neither Paul nor Calvin drew this systematic conclusion. Neither of them taught that human beings possess a natural knowledge of God's law or that such "knowledge" should be put to a positive theological use either antecedently or in faith. On the contrary, Barth insisted, Calvin "plainly denied that knowledge of the ethical good is gained by means of an ability *(facultas)* of man."[160] Calvin taught that "whatever our nature conceives, instigates, undertakes, and attempts is always evil."[161] He therefore insisted that any knowledge of the good possessed by anyone (including the regenerate) must be a daily-renewed benefit of the Holy Spirit.[162] Barth scolded that it did not require "any special exegetical virtuosity" to recognize that that this theology of Word and Spirit was a world removed from Brunner's self-helping "point of contact."

Various related points were passed over quickly, some of which returned in later years with greater urgency. One was Brunner's caricature of Catholic teaching. Barth's acquaintance with Pryzwara and other Catholic theologians helped him correct Brunner's misrepresentation of Catholic thinking on grace and nature. In effect, he charged that Brunner's rendering of Catholic doctrine was a fictional Protestant conceit that obscured the deep connection between Brunner-style "eristics" and actual Catholic teaching. Aquinas taught that "grace does not destroy nature, but perfects it." By the time that Brunner wrote "Nature and Grace," this statement had become a favorite proof text of German Christians who sought to justify their bonding of Christianity to blood-and-soil German nationalism. Though his title and his argument bore unmistakably Thomist associations, Brunner obscured these connections by claiming that Roman Catholicism separates grace and nature by a "neat horizontal line."

Barth replied that this was utter nonsense. The Catholic approach actually coordinates grace and nature, he observed. In its own more sophisticated way, Catholic teaching achieves an effect that came quite close to Brunner's position. Barth explained that in all Catholic theology that derives from the Augustinian-Thomist school, true knowledge of God is never attainable from reason and nature apart from prevenient and preparatory grace. Catholic doctrine follows Aquinas (and Augustine) in teaching that nature presupposes grace and grace presupposes nature.

Far from drawing a "neat horizontal line" between them, the Catholic church views grace and nature as inherently intertwined. Far from basing much of its case for Christianity on natural reason alone, Catholic theology teaches that supernatural revelation is always the only appropriate sphere and ground for theological claims. Aquinas taught that reason is incurably sick without the illumination of grace. This is the key to the genuinely Catholic conception of the relation between reason and faith, Barth observed. Roman Catholicism maintains that reason can produce true statements about God and the world only after it has been illumined "or at least provisionally shone upon" by Spirit-inspired faith. In Catholic doctrine, these statements are regarded as truths of reason, but they are also articles of revelation. Barth suggested more than once that since Brunner and others like him were headed in this direction anyway, they were well-advised to become better acquainted with Catholic theology. Catholic teaching coordinates grace and nature with greater profundity and often with better distinctions, he judged, than "many imprudent people on our side."[163]

LEGACY OF A THEOLOGICAL BLOWOUT

This debate was replayed several times in subsequent decades, especially by Calvin scholars, who often noted that the questions of natural theology and natural law were minor issues during the Reformation. Barth and Brunner invested far greater significance in their positions on these questions than the Reformer whose position they claimed to uphold. Though Calvin occasionally identified the natural law with the Decalogue, he never gave a clear account of his view of the capacity of reason to know it. Though he clearly asserted the existence of natural law, he also argued that human beings are too sinful to make effective use of it or (perhaps) even to know it.[164] In the 1930s, Peter Barth and Peter Brunner argued that Barth was the better Calvinist, while Günter Gloede supported Brunner's position.[165] In 1952, the debate was reignited by the publication of Edward Dowey's *The Knowledge of God in Calvin's Theology,* which supported Brunner's view, and T. H. L. Parker's *Calvin's Doctrine of the Knowledge of God,* which supported Barth.[166]

By then the specific theological differences between Barth and Brunner had narrowed significantly. Barth developed his doctrines of creation and reconciliation in a decisively different historical and political context. Though he began this enterprise with considerably less confidence than he brought into his earlier work on the doctrines of God and the Word of God, his later volumes of the *Church Dogmatics* contained a richer, less exclusive and, in a sense, more "humanistic" account of the human condition than his earlier work presented.[167] Without relinquishing the essential difference in principle that sparked his confrontation with Brunner, his later volumes argued that all human beings are "Covenant-partners of God" and that all humanity is "fellow humanity." He affirmed especially the "common bond" between the Christian church and Greek culture and the "common humanity" between Christians and non-Christians.[168] He contended that because the Word of God speaks in all directions and because all things in creation are subject to Christ, it must be assumed that Christ's Word is also spoken in certain "secular parables of truth" outside the sphere of the church. "We cannot possibly think that He cannot speak, and His speech cannot be attested, outside this sphere," Barth asserted. Though he refrained (unlike Zwingli) from giving any examples of such Word-illuminating outside parables (Barth counselled that this was a matter for the church to discern, usually with the benefit of hindsight), he emphasized the importance of affirming that Christ's sovereignty over the entire world is surely attested through extrabiblical parables that "illumine, accentuate, or explain the biblical witness."[169] In pointed contrast to his early dialectical wholly otherism, which set the human creature—

"this miserable wretch"—against an impersonal transcendent deity, he also urged that a truly biblical theology must emphasize the personal, creature-relating humanity of God.[170]

With typical exaggeration, Brunner claimed that these arguments amounted to a wholesale concession that "made almost meaningless our disagreement during the thirties." It offended him that Barth explicitly changed his position on the common ground between Christans and non-Christians but "never explicitly retracted the anathemas."[171] He glossed over the fact that Barth conceived the "secular parables" in thoroughly Christocentric terms and that he still vehemently condemned all natural theology. Though his divisive confrontation with Barth won considerable sympathy for Brunner from European and American theologians, and though most theologians clearly favored his side of the argument, Brunner never put the harsh words of 1934 behind him. He protested that Barth's unjust polemic tarnished his name and diminished his stature in the field of theology. He charged that Barth's one-sided extremism "injured the legitimate claims of Biblical theology."[172] The words of 1934 made it very difficult for either theologian to listen to any further word from the other. Their personal relationship ended and was never restored, aside from occasional brief encounters. Though Brunner occasionally praised Barth's intellectual energy and his towering stature in the history of theology, his references to Barth nearly always left a whiff of resentment as well. He complained that, because of Barth's attack on him, his theological importance "almost disappeared" to a succeeding theological generation.[173]

Barth was characteristically less inclined to look back or feel regret. Though he continued to acknowledge that Brunner was closer to him than Bultmann or Gogarten, in his view they all remained on the wrong side of a categorical divide. Had Brunner kept quiet in 1934, some significant relationship between them might have been possible afterward. The memory that Brunner, instead, gave comfort to German Christianity made Barth uninterested in making amends with him afterward. In 1934 Barth warned a wavering Dietrich Bonhoeffer that "the German church is on fire." He bitterly observed at the same time that Brunner had chosen that historical moment to dress up a distorted version of Thomism as "the very latest thing" and the way of the future. Politically Brunner aligned himself with the fascist-accommodating "middle grounders" whom Barth regarded as "the most undesirable figures" of the time.

Worst of all from Barth's perspective was the fact that Brunner described his paganizing religious worldview as Calvinist theology. This was the offense that made him write Brunner off. Barth countered that Calvin knew no "other task" of theology. For Calvin, he declared, God's revelation in God's Spirit-illumined Word was everything. The only genuine religious knowledge that Calvin might have granted to natural reason was the knowledge of our condemnation. To do theology in Calvin's spirit is to accept that "where God speaks, man has to listen, where God gives, man has to receive;

where God acts, man has to be present *without* considering his own importance." These were the themes of Calvin's opening chapters in the *Institutes.* The task of theology in our time is not to find the way to a new natural theology, Barth lectured, but to rewrite Calvin's opening chapters, "this time in such a way that no Pryzwara and no Althaus can find in it material for their fatal ends."[174] This was why Barth aspired to "do theology and only theology," with or without any notable followers, while the German church burned.

4

OTHERWORLDLY POSITIVISM?

Modern Theology against Barth

As the preeminent theologian of his century, Karl Barth was the single figure that all other twentieth-century theologians had to deal with, if not define themselves against. By the time that he dissociated himself from the dialectical theology movement, Barth had given all of his former comrades much to define themselves against. Nearly all of them charged that his later theology betrayed the anti-dogmatic spirit of crisis theology. In the early 1930s Barth noted ruefully that this charge was levelled at him "in every possible key from friendly regret to blazing outbursts of anger."[1] Even his friends shook their heads at his engagements with Aquinas, Anselm, and the church fathers. Barth observed that most of his friends believed that good theology began in 1517. Virtually all of them believed that good theology took nothing from the seventeenth century. The dialectical theologians appealed to the authority of the Word of God, but they wasted little time with vain speculation about the doctrine of the divine trinity or the virgin birth of Christ. For the rest of his theological career, long after dialectical theology ended as a movement, Barth's preoccupation with establishing correct biblical doctrine on such matters and his methodological insistence on doing theology as exegesis of the Word alone drove one major theologian after another to consign him to the backwaters of scholastic dogmatism or otherworldly irrelevance or both.

The same essential verdict was rendered by theologians who shared little with him, such as Paul Tillich and Reinhold Niebuhr, and by those who were closer to him, such as Emil Brunner and Rudolf Bultmann. Some of the sharpest forms of this critique were delivered by younger theologians whose thinking was heavily indebted to Barth, notably Dietrich Bonhoeffer and Helmut Thielicke. A generation later, theologians such as Wolfhart Pannenberg, Langdon Gilkey, and John B. Cobb, Jr., similarly judged that Barth led modern theology into a ghettoizing revelational positivism. The earliest notable form of this critique was delivered by Tillich in 1923.

TILLICH AND THIELICKE: THE LIMITS OF OTHERWORLDLINESS

Tillich's central judgment was that Barthianism was a sophisticated form of supernaturalism. Though Tillich praised Barth's withering assaults on idolatry, he charged that Barth's "destruction of idols" was insufficiently dialectical. In his reading, Barth fought against the "unparadoxical claim of religion to be absolute" with a one-sided dialectic of transcendence. Under the guise of an unyielding polemic against religion, he explained, Barth offered the God of Pauline supernaturalism as an answer to modern religious needs. Tillich allowed that Barth's reversion to the old faith undoubtedly spoke with considerable power to many disillusioned modern people, but he judged that it amounted, nonetheless, to a one-sided supernaturalism that was neither credible nor even cognizant of its religious elements. Barth's religion of faith was still religion, Tillich protested. Barthianism presupposed creation and grace, but these religious realities can be spoken of truly only by speaking of them dialectically. That is, they are knowable only as realities made known paradoxically *everywhere,* "in nature and spirit, in culture and religion."[2] Tillich urged that theologians are therefore obliged to be not only theologians, but also philosophers of culture.[3]

From Tillich's standpoint, the later Barth simply heightened everything that was wrong with his crisis theology. In 1936, he charged that Barth's theology was merely paradoxical and not dialectical, because he did nothing to bring its "yes" and "no" together.[4] Nearly thirty years later this remained his chief objection to Barthianism. "Dialectic involves an inner progress from one state to another by an inner dynamics," Tillich explained, but Barth eliminated the possibility of genuine dialectic by negating every point of identity between God and humankind. Tillich judged that this reactionary move produced "a number of other antiliberal doctrines," including the impossible notions that theology should begin with revelation and that it should proceed without confronting the problems of historical criticism. Barth tried to silence the problems of historical criticism, especially the question of the historical Jesus, Tillich observed, "but problems cannot be silenced."[5]

A similar judgment on Barth's ostensible "otherworldliness" was rendered in the early 1930s by one of his students at Bonn, Helmut Thielicke. Thielicke later recalled that Barth was an enthralling teacher whose irony-filled polemics "darted like tongues of fire from the precipitous towers of his theological system." Like most of his students, Thielicke enjoyed Barth's combination of profundity and cheekiness. But he never accepted Barth's assurance that the Word possesses a power of its own that must be allowed to create its own audience. Bultmann and Gogarten made more sense to him in this regard. From Thielicke's neoorthodox Lutheran standpoint, Barth replaced the dialectic of law and gospel with a magical concept of the Word "which robbed the Gospel of its concreteness and brought back the old heresy of docetism in a new and extreme form." In effect, Thielicke judged, Barth's method simply ignored the crucial question of how outsiders should be prepared to hear the Word. It eliminated the possibility of establishing common ground with outsiders and thus negated much of the necessary groundwork of Christian ethics. Thielicke's verdict that Barth "left the human being with no theological guidance in life" provided the key to his reading of Barth's entire dogmatic enterprise. Instead of developing the ethic that dialectical theology sorely lacked, he explained, Barth "transferred his doctrinal endeavors to remote metaphysical spheres, expending his intellectual energy in speculation on the Holy Trinity and other 'heavenly' themes."[6]

Tillich and Thielicke charged that Barth's otherworldly supernaturalism made his theology grievously deficient in the realm of social and political ethics. Tillich often lamented that Barth's opposition to fascism was too late and too narrow. In essence, he argued that Barth failed to speak out against a rising fascist movement in the name of Christianity in the early 1930s, "although there were many occasions for doing so," and that later he shared the key limitations of the Confessing Church movement. Tillich recalled that the churches kept quiet when the first Nazi assaults on Jewish life and property began in April 1933. It was only after their own rights were infringed that Barth and others created the Confessing movement, he noted: "This is one of the great shortcomings of the German churches, but also of Karl Barth."[7] Moreover, Tillich often noted ruefully that the Confessing movement never moved beyond a narrowly nonpolitical form of religious resistance. The Confessing Church resisted the Nazification of the German churches, but it carefully steered clear of any action that could be construed as political opposition to Hitler's regime.

Tillich acknowledged that Barth's famous 1941 letter to British Christians (which exhorted them to remain steadfast in their country's war against Hitler) marked a crucial breakpoint in his approach to the politics of Christian resistance to fascism, but even here, it disturbed him greatly that Barth issued his appeal entirely on Christian grounds. "It was not the common fight of people of all religions and creeds against the National-Socialist distortion of humanity that interested him, but the defense of the church as the finger pointing only to heaven and not to earth," Tillich explained. "He, like all pessimistic supranaturalists, is not interested in history as such nor in a social transformation for the sake of humanity." In his *Systematic Theology,* Tillich noted that Barth derived the duty of making war against Hitler from the resurrection of Christ. This kind of theological reasoning deserved to be called "neoorthodox," he judged. As a political refugee from Nazi Germany, Tillich gave credit to Barth for rallying Christian opposition to the Nazi attack on Christianity, but he protested that Barth was too detached from history to oppose fascist evil more broadly.[8]

Based on his experience of Barth as a teacher, Thielicke judged that the problem, more precisely, was the infinite qualitative wedge that Barth drove between the proper subject matter of theology and all things pertaining to mere politics. Barth's problem was not that he had no interest in history as such, but that his theology did not support any such interest beyond the unavoidable affairs of the church. Thielicke later recalled, "When we asked him on the eve of the Third Reich to say something about Christianity and National Socialism just for once, he refused to do so with his usual argument that current political problems were 'not a subject for theology.' He did, of course, have a personal opinion on all of these matters and was, he said, very happy to disclose them to us privately in individual tutorials."

Barth struggled to keep the infinite qualitative dichotomy between theology and politics in place even after he rallied the Confessing movement into existence. Thieliecke noted that he thus reinforced the movement's ghettoized preoccupation with its own existence and creed. "For the Confessing Church the issue was almost exclusively one of preserving church identity," he recalled. With bitter irony he noted that many Confessing Church leaders would have allowed themselves to be burned at the stake if Hitler had impugned the Augsburg Confession or the Heidelberg Catechism. As it was, however, the Nazi bosses had no inkling "that such venerable documents existed." Thielicke acknowledged that, by 1937, Barth tried to push the Confessing movement into more explicitly political forms of resistance. The Nazi oppression of the Jews compelled him to bridge the chasm between Christianity and politics. Barth and other Confessing Church leaders finally began to face up to the need "to look beyond their own borders." But the Confessing movement never did overcome its fundamental self-imposed handicap. As Thielicke explained, it never did find a way to resist Hitler's seizure of power in those areas that constituted the church's "worldly surroundings." Thielicke pinned a sizable portion of the blame for this failure on the otherworldly theology that the Confessing movement received from Karl Barth.[9]

REINHOLD NIEBUHR: OTHERWORLDLINESS AS DISTORTED POLITICS

In the years that followed the Second World War, the political shortcomings of Barth's "otherworldliness" were similarly blasted by Reinhold Niebuhr, Emil Brunner, and numerous others, especially after Barth made it clear that he did not support the West's cold war against communism. In 1948 Barth gave the opening lecture at the inaugural assembly of the World Council of Churches (W. C. C.) in Amsterdam. The theme of the conference was "The Disorder of the World and God's Design," but Barth protested immediately that this order was backward. He urged the World Council of Churches not to begin by speaking of the world's disorder, nor by speaking of whatever social or even religious measures it hoped would solve the world's problems. The place from which Christian speech about the world must begin is God's kingdom, he countered, "which has already come, is already victorious, and is already set up in all its majesty." Put differently, the world's churches needed to begin "with our Lord Jesus Christ, who has already robbed sin and death, the devil and hell of their power."

Much of the Council's literature was secular and politicized by comparison. Barth reported that the advance materials for the conference gave him "the same strange impression as garments of deep mourning." He called the newborn World Council of Churches to come out of its mourning. Christians are called to be God's witnesses, he urged; they are not called to be God's lawyers or managers or engineers. The conference literature was long on Christian plans to rebuild and reform the postwar world, but Barth countered that "God's design" is not "something like a Christian Marshall plan." It is not the business of the church to straighten out the world, he exhorted: "Burdened with this thought we should straighten out nothing; we should only increase disorder in church and world still more." The churches must begin instead, he countered, by confessing and remaining mindful that the world belongs to God. The church is not the world's caretaker. It is rather the body of God's children who are called to trust in God and proclaim God's victory over sin and live according to God's way.[10]

To Barth's surprise, Reinhold Niebuhr took strong exception to this prescription. In the United States it was commonplace to link Barth and Niebuhr together as proponents of a "neoorthodox" alternative to theological liberalism. Though Barth hated the label, he presumed that he and Niebuhr shared essentially the same critique of the moralistic reformism that informed most of the W. C. C.'s preparatory documents.[11] For all of his scorn for liberal Christian pacifism and moralism, however, Niebuhr was still essentially a product of the American social gospel tradition. He still believed that the church is called to use its power and persuasive force to promote world order, freedom, and social justice. His Christian realism rejected the idealistic moralism that most social gospelers took for granted, but he took for granted the social gospel assumption that the church is called to care about and help bring about the right ordering of the world.[12]

Niebuhr was therefore appalled by Barth's assertion that Christians have no business accommodating the gospel faith to the axioms of modern secular thought. Barth urged that the only standpoint from which Christians should speak to the modern world is its confession of faith in Christ crucified and risen. Niebuhr countered that by this logic the apostle Paul was wrong to reason with the Athenians about the meaning of their tribute to "an unknown God." He noted that in modern times the Athenians included anti-Christians like Julian Huxley. Modern theologians are obliged to answer Huxley with something besides a mere recitation of the creed, he argued. Barth's otherworldly evangelicalism negated the church's capacity to defend Christian belief from its modern critics. Niebuhr added that it also made Barth's ethical thinking seriously deficient.

He conceded that Barth gave "a very powerful witness to Christ" in the hour of the German church's crisis with fascism. Barth's prophetic evangelicalism inspired an ethic of "heroic heedlessness" within much of the Confessing resistance movement. "But perhaps this theology is constructed too much for the great crises of history," Niebuhr mused. "It seems to have no guidance for a Christian statesman for our day. It can fight the devil if he shows both horns and both cloven feet. But it refuses to make discriminating judgments about good and evil if the devil shows only one horn or the half of a cloven foot." After two centuries of liberal Christianity, it went nearly without saying for Niebuhr that Christian faith "can easily degenerate into a too simple moralism." He and Barth agreed about that. But Niebuhr warned that Christianity can also degenerate "into a too simple determinism and irresponsibility when the divine grace is regarded as a way of escape from, rather than a source of engagement with, the anxieties, perplexities, sins and pretensions of human existence." This was the grave error that Barth was indulging, he charged. For Niebuhr it was axiomatic that "the Christian must explore every promise and every limit of the cultural enterprise."[13] For Barth it was axiomatic that the church has no business seeking to fulfill or accommodate any of the promises of the cultural enterprise.

This debate had a cold war subtext. By 1948 Barth had made it clear that he did not endorse the West's cold war against communism in the name of Christianity. In pointed opposition to Brunner, who urged that the Christian church was obliged in principle to oppose communist totalitarianism with the same militant fervor that it previously aroused against Nazi totalitarianism, Barth insisted that the two cases were dissimilar from a Christian standpoint.[14] From the standpoint of a *Christian* ethic, he argued, it was not pertinent whether communist totalitarianism was structurally similar to fascist totalitarianism. There is no such thing as a Christian political system, he explained. The church does not rightly sacralize or condemn political systems as such. It does not properly concern itself with ideologies, and therefore it does not speak "on principle" about the legitimacy or illegitimacy of political systems as such. "The Church never thinks, speaks or acts 'on principle'," Barth asserted. "Rather it judges spiritually and by individual cases." At least, he cautioned, that is how the church is supposed to act, regardless of how many times it has violated its spiritual nature in the past. The church had no business anathematizing the Communist political system as such because it has no business making principled judgments that identify Christ with or that sever Christ from any political ideology.[15]

Brunner objected that Barth passionately condemned the Hitler regime in the name of Christ and called for its overthrow, but Barth replied that it was not on the basis of any political principle that he did so. As much as he despised National Socialism, he did not condemn it in the name of Christ on account of its noxious political ideology. From a Christian standpoint, he explained, what made Nazism different was its power to overwhelm and corrupt Christian souls. Nazism was an evil religion that subverted the soul of the German church. "We were hypnotized by it as a rabbit by a giant snake," Barth recalled. "We were in danger of bringing, first incense, and then the complete sacrifice to it as to a false god." For that reason the Confessing Church struggle against fascism was much more than a struggle against a monstrous ideology, he explained. "It was a matter of life and death, of resistance against a godlessness which was in fact attacking body and soul, and was therefore effectively masked to many thousands of Christian eyes." For that reason he dared to invoke Christ's name against the Hitler regime, nor could he forgive the collaborators, "least of all those among them who were cultured, decent and well-meaning."[16]

Barth did not deny that Communism was abhorrent from the political standpoint of justice and freedom. He granted that President Truman was justified in condemning Communist totalitarianism as a dreadful thing. What he disputed was the existence of any spiritual parallel for the church between anti-nazism and anticommunism. The German church nearly lost its soul to nazism, he reasoned, but where was the spiritual threat that Communism posed to American or Western European churches? That is, in the countries where church leaders were presently calling for "Christian" crusades against Communism, where was the spiritual threat to the church that the truth of an anticommunist crusade might extinguish? "Are they not already sure enough of the justice of their cause against Russia without this truth and our Christian support?" Barth asked. He left the implication between the lines. In the context of America's affluence and political might, he implied, the existence of a militantly "Christian anticommunism" was not a spiritually healthy phenomenon.[17]

Niebuhr accepted the thrust of Barth's insinuation that Americans always presumed that God was on their side. He welcomed Barth's continuing effort to extricate Western Christianity "from the idolatries of our day." But he protested that opposition to idolatry should not prevent Western theologians from recognizing the anti-Christian evil of Communism *as theologians.* Niebuhr noted disapprovingly that Barth seemed to regard the differences between the Communist and democratic nations "as insignificant when viewed from the ultimate Christian standpoint." He recalled that in the early months of the Third Reich, "before nazism was revealed in its full demonic dimensions," most of Barth's followers saw little difference between fascism and other forms of political evil. Now Barth was repeating the terrible mistakes of Gogarten and Merz, he implied.[18]

From 1948 to 1958 Barth's theological output was staggering. He published the last three volumes of his theology of creation and the first two volumes of his theology of reconciliation in addition to numerous occasional writings that included a poignant reconsideration of the humanity of God and a sharp critique of Bultmann's demythologizing program.[19] When he reflected on the significance of this period in his theological career, however, his impassioned opposition to anticommunism as a *Christian* cause eclipsed everything else. His debate with Bultmann earned only a paragraph, while he carried on at length against the "madness" and "absurdity" of the cold war. Barth noted that in Switzerland, "where, remarkably enough, there are many small McCarthys, I have fared badly." His patriotism and even his humanity were repeatedly impugned by Swiss anticommunists. Barth spurned few opportunities to provoke them, just as he infuriated Niebuhr and many others by declaring in 1958: "I regard anticommunism as a matter of principle an evil even greater than communism itself."[20]

The following year, after an East German pastor asked Barth if he should pray for the abolition of the Communist government in East Germany, Barth cautioned the pastor to beware that such a prayer "might be awfully answered, so that some morning you would wake up among those 'Egyptian fleshpots,' as one obligated to the 'American way of life.' " Barth advised the pastor that it would be better for him to pray for the East German government rather than against it. He cautioned the pastor that from a Christian standpoint, the ascendance of a dreadful Communist government in East Germany had to be regarded in some sense as the rod of divine punishment. "This power would not have overwhelmed you if leaders and people, in society, state and church, had not sinned so grievously in the past," he scolded. Barth's various writings on this subject always emphasized that historically, Communism was an unwelcome but natural product of Western developments. He believed that the Western nations had only begun to pay the full price for Western imperialism and war. As he explained to the anonymous East German pastor, "Certainly your part of the world is undergoing a painful purgation, such as the West, sooner or later and in one form or another, will likewise be subjected to (perhaps at the hands of Asia or Africa)."[21]

In the meantime, and at all times, Barth urged, the pertinent question is the question of who sits in the seat of judgment. It is not those who wield the tool of God's judgment, he counseled, but God alone who sits in the judgment seat. The only judge that should be taken seriously is the gracious and merciful God who wills that all people—"Christians and the whole of mankind"—should be saved and come to the knowledge of God's truth. "God above all things!" Barth repeatedly exclaimed. Because God is surely above all things, he counseled, God is certainly above "the legalistic totalitarianism of your state." This was Barth's basis for exhorting the pastor not to fear the East German government. Communism is totalitarian "in a godless and inhuman fashion," he observed. As a system of political rule, Communism was limited precisely by its godlessness and inhumanity. "One day its officeholders will halt at those limits, or else they will be destroyed," Barth predicted. He noted that in its distorted way, Communist totalitarianism was a reverse-image of the totalitarian character of grace: "But of course grace is 'totalitarian' by its free and freeing action, not by law. It is all-embracing, 'totalitarian,' in a sense precisely the opposite of the totalitarianism that sets up a cunning snare of theses and antitheses, that employs every device of coercion and pressure to have them recognized and realized, that overwhelms and crushes opposition wherever it appears."[22]

It followed for Barth that, as a system of totalitarian godlessness, Communism was not sustainable and not worth the spiritual price of committing the church to anticommunism. The church is not called to resistance "in the name and for the honor of any kind of principles," he insisted. The church is not called to aim or force anyone to accept any particular political system in theory or practice: "She can only follow Jesus; that is, she cannot but keep her sights constantly fixed on the merciful God and on man who is to receive

God's mercy and be set free." Barth asked rhetorically if the church was not busy enough giving joyful and wholehearted witness to the good news of God's kingdom. Put differently, he concluded: "My advice would be the same I once gave the German Christians: do not orient yourselves, neither positively nor negatively, by what some do or don't do, but set your eyes straight toward Jerusalem!"[23]

Niebuhr took Barth's "Egyptian fleshpot" crack about the American way of life as a sneering cheap shot. He took Barth's Christian neutralism as a provocation. He shot back that the East Germans surely had been no more sinful than their West German kin. If the East Germans were suffering for their sins, how was one to account for the immunity of West Germany? Niebuhr judged that for the most part Barth did adhere to "the strategy of approximating the divine impartiality" to which he aspired. He recalled that in the days of the Nazis, Barth dared to make "hazardous detailed judgments" on a regular basis, but now it was only on a rare occasion that his "robust humanity" so betrayed him. Now he desperately aspired merely to be impartial, like God. "The price of this desperation is of course moral irrelevance," Niebuhr declared. Barth's pursuit of prophetic purity was necessarily a pursuit of moral irrelevance. Niebuhr did not grant, however, that Barth had actually attained pure impartiality in his moral judgments. He judged that Barth's arguments were still loaded with "merely human political" sentiments, such as, most notably, his animus against America. He also believed that Barth needed to realize "that he is not the only prophet of the Lord." These points built up to a vintage Niebuhr verdict: "Barth is a man of talent to the point of genius. But even a genius cannot escape the dilemma that the price of absolute purity is irrelevance and that the price of relevance is the possible betrayal of capricious human loves and hates even in the heart of a man of God."[24]

With impressive regularity, the major theologians of the Barthian era charged that Barth was otherworldly, antihistorical, overly dogmatic, irresponsible, and irrelevant. Though Niebuhr conceded that Barth's revelationism marked an improvement over "the older dogmatisms of orthodox religion," he charged that the value of Barth's dogmatic enterprise was vitiated by his failure to validate Christianity "in experience against competition with other religions."[25] Sophisticated dogmatism is still dogmatism, he chided. The truth and moral relevance of the faith must be demonstrated. Niebuhr's conviction that Barth pushed modern theology into a wrong direction belatedly drove him to reconsider his own relation to theological liberalism. Near the end of a long career that was fueled mainly by his polemical blasts against liberal theology, Niebuhr made it clear that he identified with the liberal tradition and not with any Barthian-shaped neoorthodox corrective to it. "When I find neo-orthodoxy turning into sterile orthodoxy or a new Scholasticism, I find that I am a liberal at heart, and that many of my broadsides against liberalism were indiscriminate," he reported. "On the whole I regret the polemical animus of my theological and political activities."[26]

BRUNNER: THE PROBLEM OF DOGMATISM

The crowning verdict of this kind was rendered by Emil Brunner near the end of his career. In 1938, Brunner wrote a popular guide to the I-Thou "encounter" model of understanding titled *Wahrheit als Begegnung* ("truth as encounter"). In effect, this book explained and defended his wholesale adoption of the Gogarten/Martin Buber model of existential epistemology. The book was especially popular in the United States, where it was published in 1943 as *The Divine-Human Encounter.*[27] Brunner's first edition made little attempt to distinguish his position from other dialectical or existential theologies. Without describing his relation to Barth or Bultmann, it offered a straightforward case for existential encounter theory as the best model for understanding the truth claims of scripture.

Brunner's revised edition of this book took an instructively different tack, however. Near the end of his career, thirty years after Barth blasted his "point of contact" apologetic, Brunner rewrote the book with an eye toward his place in the history of theology. He described his own theology as the genuinely biblical alternative to Barth's dogmatism and Bultmann's paganizing subjectivism. Brunner explained that his theological lifework remained distinctively faithful to the original program and spirit of the dialectical theology movement. In his account, he continued to explicate the movement's gospel basis after Barth lapsed into dogmatic objectivism and Bultmann lapsed the other way into pure subjectivism. Barth betrayed the genuinely biblical spirit of the dialectical theology movement by overly objectivizing the gospel as dogma, he argued, while Bultmann turned the gospel into a merely subjectivist illustration of Heideggerian themes.[28]

He was equally rough on his former comrades. Brunner judged that Bultmann "lost touch with the historical revelation" altogether and that he tried to compensate for this loss by reducing Christian faith to Heidegger's theory of self-understanding. The fact that Heidegger became an outright Nazi did not speak well for Bultmann's judgment, he noted: "Bultmann tremendously underestimated the potency of Heidegger's philosophy, and failed to recognize its incompatibility with what the Bible understands as faith." Brunner recalled that his own early warnings to this effect were ignored by Bultmann. Theology must always be ready to learn from philosophy, he allowed, but theology must always draw its sustenance and inspiration from the interaction of Word and biblical history: "What resulted from Bultmann's connection with Heidegger was a mutilation, not an interpretation, of the New Testament witness to Jesus Christ."[29]

This tart assessment sharply distinguished Brunner from Bultmann, but his score-settling account of the legacy of dialectical theology was more concerned to set Barth in his place. Brunner allowed that it was "an event of the greatest significance" when Barth summoned the courage to take the biblical message seriously again in the years following the First World War. He recalled that the faith of the Reformers had nearly been extinguished in modern Protestantism. It was Barth who recovered the biblical dialectic of Word and Spirit for a desiccated modern Protestantism. Barth recovered the radical Pauline perception that faith rests upon the movement of God's Spirit in the Word rather than doctrine. With the help of Kierkegaard and the two Blumhardts, Barth taught the church to pray for a new outpouring of the Holy Spirit. With Kierkegaard he spoke of theology as a "little pinch of cinnamon" and repudiated the very thought of a theological system.[30]

But then Barth began to aspire to a system, Brunner recalled. He read Heppe's *Reformed Dogmatics* and began to think of himself as a kind of modern successor to the old Scholastics. A subtle change of emphasis soon appeared in his conception of faith. Brunner argued that the first sign of this change occurred when Barth embraced "the ancient Catholic doctrine" *natus ex Maria Virgine.* The Barth who wrote *The Epistle to the Romans* would not have defended the myth of the virgin birth as an indispensable Christian doctrine, Brunner suggested, but the system-aspiring Barth did bring himself to defend the early church's confusion about how Christ must have been conceived. Brunner countered that the virginal conception story told by Luke and Matthew was based on a substantialist misunderstanding of the gospel message. Luke and Matthew presumed that Jesus could only have been the Son of God if he was literally God's son. This crudely literalistic mentality was alien to Paul and John and other apostolic writers, Brunner contended. The gospel truth pertaining to the incarnation is that God encounters human beings in Christ. It has nothing to do with a substantialist notion of a Son of God begotten in a supernatural manner.[31]

Brunner implied that Barth understood all of this well enough before he became an aspiring dogmatist. By the time that Barth began lecturing on dogmatics at Göttingen, however, he began to replace the gospel truth that authenticates itself in our conscience with supernatural *facts* that compel assent on the strength of their dogmatic authority. This is precisely the logic that produced the church's dogmas of the triune God and the two natures in Christ, Brunner observed. From 1924 onward, Barth the dogmatist treated these doctrines as subjects of belief. He wrote books that "continually swelled in bulk" as a consequence of his ever-deepening Scholastic-like fixation with intellectual distinctions. The early dialectical Barth hoped for a new outpouring of the Holy Spirit and the consummation of God's reign, but Brunner judged that "there is hardly a trace of this hope left in Karl Barth."[32]

In Brunner's estimation, the later Barth fit his resented label precisely: he was a neoorthodox dogmatist. A chief symptom of this regression was Barth's later tendency to speak of something called "theological existence." Brunner recalled that the Barth who launched the crisis theology movement understood (via Kierkegaard) that *faith* is an existence. The fact that the later Barth made an "absurd connection" between existence and *theology* perfectly symbolized his regression into the theologism of the old Scholastics, Brunner charged. "There is indeed such a thing as believing, or Christian existence, but no such thing as theological existence," he lectured.[33] In

1934, the scholasticist-turning Barth accused Brunner of entering "the downward path" into Catholicism, but Brunner countered belatedly that it was Barth who betrayed the faith of the Reformers.

Luther and Calvin taught that subject and object are identical in faith, but the later Barth taught that faith is merely "the subjective realization of an objective *res*." Barth explained that faith "only finds what is already there both for the believing and the unbelieving man." Brunner countered that this objectivization of faith betrayed the apostolic faith recovered by the Reformers. The normative theme of apostolic and Reformationist preaching was the theme of 1 Corinthians 13, he explained. This is the teaching that hope and love are bound together in a unity with faith. In the New Testament, Brunner observed, faith, hope, and love are all equally important and all-important, but in Barthian theology, an intellectualist preoccupation with the object of faith overwhelmed everything else. Barth devoted hundreds of pages to the dogma of the Trinity with no apparent regard for the fact that his fascination with this *objectum fidei* was not shared by scripture, Luther, or Calvin.[34]

Luther and Calvin grasped that all discourse about God is the discourse of faith. They insisted that true knowledge of God comes to us only by faith. They unfailingly correlated the truth of revelation and the truth of faith. But Barth relegated his discussion of faith to the end of the *Church Dogmatics,* Brunner observed. More importantly, his references to faith throughout the *Church Dogmatics* clearly subordinated faith to revelation. This observation set up Brunner's most slashing judgment. He allowed that Barth's enterprise produced a dogmatic alternative to Schleiermacher's system, but in its own way, he contended, Barthian scholasticism departed as sharply from the biblical witness as Schleiermacher's outright distortion of it. The biblical witness is always a witness of faith, Brunner explained, but Barth "shattered" the biblical correlation of revelation and faith and replaced it with metaphysical speculation about God's inner-trinitarian being.[35]

BARTHIAN THEOLOGY AND BARTHIAN POLITICS

In all of these cases, Barth's deficiencies were measured against the defining contrary positions of his critics. Barth was a highly useful foil for Tillich's opposition to supernaturalism and his advocacy of a religious philosophy of culture. Barth's opposition to natural theology and to the Lutheran schematism of law and gospel made him a similarly useful foil for Brunner's apologetical eristics and for Thielicke's ethic of orders. Some of the criticism heaped upon him by these figures was plainly unfair. Tillich repeated the same points against Barth's otherworldly dialecticism and his reliance on paradox for decades after Barth extensively developed analogical ways of speaking about God. Tillich and Niebuhr also blasted Barth's supposed disregard for politics and history, but this charge was equally misleading for, in his own way, Barth remained deeply engaged in sociopolitical affairs throughout his career.

Besides his theological leadership of the Confessing Church movement,

Barth refused to begin his classes with the customary Nazi salute, he refused to take the obligatory oath of obedience to Hitler, and he gave personal assistance to a stream of Jewish and political refugees. He was apparently the last official member of the Social Democratic Party during the Third Reich, a peculiarity that resulted from his agreement with the Minister of Education not to use his professorial position as a forum for anti-government propaganda.[36] Barth thus kept his politics out of the classroom, more or less, but he also made it clear, as he put it, with whom he wanted to be hanged.

In one crucial respect, as Tillich rightly emphasized, Barth's activism during the Nazi period was grievously deficient. He was appalled by the refusal of the Confessing Church movement to speak out against Nazi persecution of the Jews, but, in the face of this opposition, he backed away from pressing the issue at the Barmen Confessing Synod in 1934. Thus, the Synod failed even to debate whether the Barmen Declaration should condemn Hitler's oppression of Jews. Barth confessed later that he was wrong not to have forced the Barmen Synod to at least "go through the motions of fighting." He noted elsewhere that, as a Swiss citizen, he felt "somewhat reluctant to involve myself in German affairs," and that, in hindsight, he realized that he should have done more to force the issue in public settings.[37] On the other hand, Barth did argue with Confessing Church leaders about the need to combat their movement's insularity, political accommodationism, and anti-Semitism.[38] In 1935, he protested to one of his closer associates among the Confessing Church leaders, Hermann Albert Hesse, that the Confessing movement "still has no heart for the millions who suffer unjustly. It still has nothing to say on the simplest questions of public honesty. When it speaks, it speaks only about its own affairs."[39] Barth expressed this conviction publicly in the later 1930s after he recognized that the Confessing movement had erred by refusing to oppose Hitler's regime politically. Shortly after the war began he appealed to his Swiss compatriots to abandon their neutrality, and in 1941 he exhorted British Christians to continue their support for England's war against Hitler.[40]

Near the end of the war he appealed publicly for a policy of reconciliation with the Germans. Barth urged that the Germans needed friends, not teachers.[41] After the war he campaigned against German rearmament and especially against German possession of nuclear weapons. He also opposed the restoration of the pre-Nazi traditional state church system. Barth's vigorous opposition to the West's cold war against Communism during this period may not have been admirable from Niebuhr's perspective, but it certainly qualified as a form of political activism. With ample justification he complained that Niebuhr falsely portrayed him as "a sort of super-Lutheran fleeing from all responsibility." Far from making a secure home out of Noah's ark, he observed, "I have for ten years been rebuked from Germany for bringing the gospel and the law, faith and politics, the church and democracy, into too close connection with one another."[42] In 1956 he urged an interviewer, "Don't forget to say that I have always been interested in politics, and consider that it belongs to the life of a theologian."[43] Barth held no lack of political opinions about freedom and democracy, but at the heart of his persistent campaigning against anticommunism was the Christian conviction that the human solidarity of East and West under God was more important than the conflict between Communism and liberal democracy. He could not confess allegiance to "the so-called 'Christian West,' " he explained, because "I think that the locus of Christianity is to be sought above today's conflict between East and West."[44]

Throughout his career, Barth brushed off most attacks on his person and thinking as protests from advocates of other ways. He did not expect to find meaningful agreements with people who did not share his fundamental presuppositions or method. Though he was surprised to learn how little he held in common with Niebuhr, he generally took criticism from other theologians in stride. In 1960 he effected a personal reconciliation of sorts with Brunner, but three years later, after Brunner blasted his dogmatism, Barth plaintively asked Brunner's son, a Zurich pastor, if he could not prevail upon his father to stop embarrassing all of them. "Your father cannot stop provoking me," he noted sadly. Barth took none of Brunner's criticisms seriously. "I had thought he and I could end our days in a kind of truce," he lamented, but Brunner persisted in caricaturing his theology, "every statement a wild distortion." Barth declined to address Brunner directly—"which might have excited him unnecessarily"—and he chose not to make any public reaction to Brunner's polemical blast in the hope that Brunner's "ancient anger" might be defused.[45]

THE ORTHODOX DIFFERENCE: BARTH'S DOGMATIC TURN

In one significant respect, however, Brunner's assessment of Barth's career deserved to be taken much more seriously. To Brunner, it was crucially important to pinpoint exactly when and how Barth's theology degenerated into a "neoorthodox dogmatism." His case for his own significance in modern theology rested heavily upon his claim to have stayed true to the biblical/existential point of departure that Barth abandoned. In the conventional account of Barth's development established by Hans Urs von Balthasar, the major turn in Barth's thinking occurred only in 1931, as a by-product of Barth's teaching and writing on Anselm's theological method. Von Balthasar contended that it was only after Barth replaced his reliance on dialectic with his appropriation of Anselm's analogy of faith that the mature dogmatic phase of his career began. In this reading, the key to Barth's later theology was his belated recognition that theological reason is based upon and seeks to understand the gift of faith. Barth interpreted the Anselmian description of God as "that than which nothing greater can be conceived" not as a definition of God's being, but as a way of naming God in the form of a noetic rule. The meaning of "God" cannot be known except by "thinking-after" *(nachdenken)* God's self-giving in the meaning of these ordinary words, he argued. It followed for Barth that the search for theological understanding is immanent in faith itself, which spontaneously and necessarily gives birth to a desire for understanding and which cannot question its own basis.[46]

On various occasions Barth confirmed that his study of Anselm's argument was crucially important for his theological development. The analogy of faith that he derived from Anselm enabled him to overcome his aversion to ontological language and his merely-dialectical way of describing divine presence. He explained that his earlier emphasis on the momentary and paradoxical nature of divine presence gave way to the more stable and objective rhetoric of dogmatics. Brunner was clearly less impressed by this ostensible turning point than by the import of Barth's earlier dogmatic turn, however. The notion that theology is necessarily and only a product of self-authenticating faith is a theme that Barth first appropriated from Herrmann. Brunner may have regarded most of Barth's "faith seeking understanding" model as the common possession of Herrmann's crisis theology successors. He may have recalled, in addition, that in the mid-1920s Barth already employed a battery of negative and positive analogical models. In his Göttingen lectures (which von Balthasar never read), Barth already drew various analogies between human and divine action, as well as between the relationships of the threefold Word and the communion of persons in the divine Trinity. Barth's Göttingen lectures contained most of the key elements of his later theology, including his conviction that the doctrine of a Trinity of being was the key to making the rest of his theology "come out right."[47]

Brunner may or may not have borne these matters in mind when he put forth his account of Barth's theological development. What is certain is that he perceived a fundamental continuity in Barth's thought from 1924 onward on account of Barth's reversion to a doctrine-based objectivism. From this standpoint, the crucial issue was not how Barth smoothed out his objectivism, but his earlier decision to treat theology as the explication of doctrine. Brunner recalled that, during his crisis theology period, Barth understood that faith and revelation are indissolubly intertwined. But from 1924 onward, he observed, Barth objectified the content of faith and subordinated faith to revelation. This was the crucial turn in his career. Barth the dogmatist defended the doctrine of the virgin birth as constitutive and necessary to the gospel. He thus committed himself to an objectivizing procedure that established even historically-incredible "events" on positive grounds—that is, on grounds posited by dogma. Barth emphasized, of course, that this dogma was based on scriptural narrative, but Brunner objected that the issue was Barth's reversion to an objectivist way of establishing biblical truths. Having lurched all the way to the virgin birth, he implied, it was a short step afterward for Barth to make the Trinity the dogmatic key to everything else.[48]

THE VIRGIN BIRTH IN THE LOGIC OF LOGOS CHRISTOLOGY

The crucial turn took place in Barth's Göttingen lectures on the incarnation. At the outset of his career as a dogmatic theologian, Barth committed himself to an Alexandrian-type Christology that conceived the unity of Christ's divine and human natures as a unity of divine Subject. He called this "a special Reformed doctrine" by virtue of its ostensible endorsement by the Heidelberg Catechism (Qu. 48). The Christian doctrine of the incarnation does not affirm the indwelling of a human subject by a divine Subject, Barth maintained. Aligning himself with the Christological tradition of Cyril of Alexandria and select Reformed fathers, he explained that the doctrine of the incarnation properly affirms the union of Christ's human and divine natures in a single divine Subject, the divine person of the Logos. Christ is the Logos of God "beyond his union with humanity, just as the Trinity is more than the incarnation," Barth reasoned. "As the Father is not just the Creator, so the Logos is what he is even apart from Jesus Christ."

One implication of Logos Christology so conceived is that Christ's human nature had no personhood of its own: "It is *anhypostatos*—the formula in which the description culminates," Barth contended. "Or, more positively, it is *enhypostatos.* It has personhood, subsistence, reality, only in its union with the Logos of God." Citing various Reformed and Lutheran dogmatists for support, he taught that Mary is rightly called the Mother of God *(theotokos)* because the one whom she bore was *nothing apart* from being God's Son. "He was in human nature, but this human nature was real only in the person of God's Son." It followed that human nature itself has subsistence only in and through the Logos. Christians must not reverse this Christological truism, Barth warned. It is not correct to say that the Logos subsists only in the human nature of Christ. The proper Reformed view was summarized by Maresius: The Logos unites the human nature to Himself to the point of completely indwelling it, but the Logos is also "totally transcendent and infinite outside it." Lutheran scholasticism dubbed the latter affirmation "the Calvinist *extra,*" but to Barth, the Calvinist insistence on the transcendence of the Logos did not weaken the Christian affirmation that God is wholly present in God's revelation, as the Lutherans feared. The Logos in Christ's flesh and the Logos outside Christ's flesh are the same totality, Barth countered. The God revealed in Christ on earth also resides in heaven. In its dialectic of the Logos as "totally in and totally outside," Barth urged that Reformed orthodoxy wisely preserved a "valuable safeguard of the mystery, of the indirectness of revelation."[49]

This was the doctrinal context in which Barth defended the truth and necessity of the virginal conception of Jesus. He observed that the doctrine of the virgin birth expresses "the absolutely miraculous character of revelation" in a way that is paralleled only by the doctrine that Christ rose from the dead. The two doctrines are intimately joined, he taught: "God is in the flesh, in time, in the world of contradiction, himself human, pilgrim man, a man like any other, yet God, so that the time is fulfilled, and a limit is set for the contradiction." In the gospel narrative Christ is flesh of Adam's flesh and born like all others, yet he is also God himself born of the Virgin Mary and conceived by the Holy Spirit. It is pointless and spiritually wrong to rationalize any part of this divine mystery, Barth contended. The doctrine of Christ's conception by the Spirit is an account of a miracle, which, like any miracle, can only be rejected or believed. To make this teaching plausible by referring to examples of parthogenesis in plants or animals "makes no more sense than to defend the resurrection with the help of occultism and spiritism."[50]

Barth acknowledged that the doctrine of Christ's virginal conception is weak on biblical attestation. It is not mentioned by Paul or the earliest canonical Gospel, Mark, and it receives mention only in two later Gospels, Luke and Matthew. For Barth this was no reason to regard the virginal conception story as dispensable, however. He noted that the early church could have opted for the story that Jesus was the son of a chosen married couple who enjoyed the blessing of heaven. Instead, the church clearly opted for "born of the Virgin," as attested by Luke and Matthew. Why would the church jeopardize the credibility of the gospel narrative by commiting itself to this story?

Marcion's answer was that the church wanted to discredit sexuality as such. Barth countered that the virginal conception story told (differently) in Luke and Matthew is not about sexuality as such, but about the church's need to get the male sexual agent out of the picture. The church had to break Christ's connection to Adam. The doctrine of the incarnation does not teach that the Logos was united with a human person, Barth repeated. Christianity rightly asserts the union of the Logos and human nature. The Logos is the Son of God himself who "wills to be the person of the God-man." But in this case the "person" must be absent, for in history the person is always a human agent who attains his or her name, status, and rights through the father. "World history is not for nothing male history," Barth remarked. The history of the world is soaked with male privilege. Barth reasoned that it was this inheritance of Adam that had to be broken if the world was to be saved and renewed: "*He* was created in God's image, through *him* sin came into the world, *he* must be renewed in God's image."[51]

But "he" can only be saved and renewed by a new Adam, and a new Adam cannot be born if the old Adam is not displaced. This is the spiritual necessity of the virgin birth, Barth contended. With the Virgin Mary, "a reversal takes place in favor of the female." Because Adam is the bearer of original sin, he must stand aside while God brings salvation to the world through Mary. Joseph is marginal to the gospel story because, as the son of Adam, he can only beget sinners. Man as creator is the creator of sin. "God must take his place," Barth asserted. "That is the point. The person of the Son must be conceived by the person of the Spirit in order that a new humanity may arise." The Logos is bonded not to the old Adam, but to human nature as such. It is humankind as creature, not as will-to-powering creator, to which Christ is bonded in the incarnation. By necessity, the bearer of human creatureliness is female.[52]

Barth cautioned that the female creature is also fallen and in need of redemption. The daughters of Eve are alienated from God no less than Adam. The difference is that the human creature does not need to be replaced, he argued. Though women share the fallenness of men, they are "not incapable of being justified and sanctified by the miracle of God." This miracle takes place as revelation in concealment. Human nature as such becomes "the dwelling of the Logos" through divine action that Mary facilitates. A new history begins, though it remains concealed until Christ's resurrection. The mortal creatureliness of Mary is the organ by which God turns human mortality and corruption into immortality and incorruptibility (1 Cor. 15:54). "This is why we have 'born of the Virgin Mary,' " Barth contended.[53]

He acknowledged that this kind of language and reasoning had become foreign to Protestant theology. To Barth, this was the crucial clue to the weakness and superficiality of modern Protestantism. Serious dogmatic teaching requires solid concepts that give appropriate expression to the dignity of biblical themes, he argued. For this reason, "whether we like it or not we shall have to tread the paths that were taken by the early church doctrine." He judged that recent Protestant theologies were useless as aids to this venture in understanding because, "to put it mildly, they rest upon a much less profound and serious knowledge of the matter." The church fathers and Protestant dogmatists made many mistakes, Barth allowed, but at least they took the themes of scripture seriously. They did not always find the best concepts to express scriptural teaching, but at least they knew what they were talking about. Barth exhorted that "this is what we have to learn again in some way or other."[54]

His dogmatic project was not merely to restore certain themes to theology or even to restore the authority of the Spirit-illuminated scriptural Word to theology. It was also to recreate a theological discourse that, by his estimation, had not been spoken in Protestant theology for the past two hundred years. "To take it up again is not so easy," he conceded. Barth proposed to begin by seeking to discern and follow the sense of early Christian doctrine. He was convinced that Christianity could not give up the Trinity and the virgin birth without losing its soul. The history of modern Protestantism was his proof. In the course of giving up the Trinity and the virgin birth, he observed, modern Protestantism lost the "entire third dimension" of life, the spiritual dimension of mystery. Having sold its soul to modernity, modern Protestantism was reduced to a desiccated intellectualized religiousness that no longer spoke the language of mystery at all. Barth's *Church Dogmatics* began with a blistering denunciation of the spiritual ravages of this loss. He assailed the "constantly increasing barbarism, tedium, and insignificance of modern Protestantism." He recalled that modern theology began by throwing out the Trinity and the virgin birth, "only to be punished with every possible worthless substitute" afterward. These substitutes included high church ecclesiasticism, religious socialism, "and similar miserable cliques and sects." A final stage of degeneration was presently displayed by the German Christian movement, he observed, in which modern Germans were finding religious insight "in the intoxication of their Nordic blood and in their political *Führer*."[55]

Against this background Barth insisted that theology must explicate the sacred mysteries of the church's scripture and dogmatic tradition. He defended the doctrine of the virgin birth and became a chief celebrant of the triune mystery of God. Though he pointedly dissociated himself from all of his former theological comrades except Eduard Thurneysen, he accumulated a sizable new core of spiritual brethren among pastors and theologians. His circle of theological comrades included Ernst Wolf, Hermann Diem, Karl Steinbauer, Hans Joachim Iwand, Oscar Cullmann, and Günther Dehn. A younger circle of Barthian students included Georg Eichholz, Walter Fürst, Helmut Gollwitzer, Heinz Kloppenburg, Walter Kreck, Lili Simon, Karl Gerhard Steck, and Hellmut Traub. After he returned to Switzerland the student Barthians included Gollwitzer, Kreck, Walter Sigrist, Eduard Schweizer, Thomas F. Torrance, and Hans Heinrich Wolf, while his cluster of theological colleagues included Thurneysen, Wilhelm Vischer, and Walter Lüthi. Barth prized his friendships with like-minded Confessing Church pastors, especially those to whom he dedicated his book *Credo,* "in memory of all who stood, stand and will stand: Hans Asmussen, Hermann [Albert] Hesse, Karl Immer, Martin Niemöller, and Heinrich Vogel."[56] He also forged treasured friendships with the ecumenical leader Willem Adolf Visser 't Hooft and French pastor Pierre Maury, the latter of whom became a contributor to the new pamphlet series *Theologische Studien* that Barth launched after *Theologische Existenz heute* was banned by the Nazis.[57]

These friendships were crucially inspiriting to Barth during the years that marked the end of the dialectical theology movement and the beginning of his definitive theological enterprise. Several of his friends became important theologians in their own right, especially Cullmann and Torrance. For many years Torrance spearheaded a remarkable Edinburgh-based group effort that made the *Church Dogmatics* available to English readers. Many of these friends remained close to Barth for the rest of his life. Among all of Barth's numerous friendships with theologians and pastors, however, there was one that belonged to a category of its own on account of its theological and, ultimately, historical significance.

BONHOEFFER: SECULARITY AND REVELATIONAL POSITIVISM

Dietrich Bonhoeffer was Barth's Confessing Church collaborator and most creative theological follower. He became a young Barthian during the very period (1924) when Barth made the turn to dogmatics, though his personal relationship with Barth did not begin until 1931—the same year that his second book sharply criticized Barth's theory of revelation. Bonhoeffer was uncomfortable with young Barthians, whom he found sycophantic and more than a bit arrogant. He explained that, in their presence, "No Negro is allowed to pass for white; his finger-nails and the soles of his feet are carefully scrutinized."[58] At the same time, he found that Barth himself managed to combine an intense concentration of intellectual energy with a remarkably direct and engaging spirit that was open to criticism. He enthused to a friend that Barth "is even better than his books."[59]

Barth found a kindred Christian spirit in Bonhoeffer and a trusted colleague. When Bonhoeffer fled to England in 1933, mainly out of confusion and anger with the accommodating spirit of the Confessing Church, Barth presumed on their friendship. He chastized Bonhoeffer for leaving and told him to get on the next ship for Berlin, or at least the one after that. Barth sharply reminded Bonhoeffer that he was German, not English, and that the German church was on fire. Bonhoeffer failed to return until 1935, but he admitted to Barth that it was very difficult for him to bear the knowledge that Barth was personally disappointed in him.[60] Bonhoeffer sounded a similar note several years later, after he became, secretly, a political conspirator against Hitler. In 1942, Barth pointedly questioned how it was possible that Bonhoeffer possessed an official passport to travel outside Germany. Bonhoeffer pleaded in response that "it would be unbearably painful for me" if Barth did not trust him in this matter. Until the end of his life, Bonhoeffer looked to Barth for theological and ethical guidance, and for personal approval.[61]

This did not stop him from criticizing some of Barth's fundamental theological positions. In this respect, Bonhoeffer was always more like Barth than the Barthians. His early works, *Sanctorum Communio* (1927) and *Act and Being* (1931) combined a sympathetic appropriation of Barth's theology with his own concern to mediate between a Barthian-style actualism and various philosophical theologies of being.[62] The latter work criticized Barth directly in its attempt to mediate the theological problem of "being in the truth." Barth repeatedly asserted in *Der christliche Dogmatik* that God's being is pure act and not a substance analogous to created being. Bonhoeffer replied that this radical actualist theme undercut Barth's capacity to say anything about any presumed continuities within or between the being of God and human beings.[63] If God's being is purely being in act, Bonhoeffer observed, it is difficult to see how God is or can "be" continuous with himself or his relation to the world. Barth's emphatically negative dialecticism compounded the problem, he noted, for in Barth's case even the existence of continuities within the human self and between human beings was thrown into question.[64]

Bonhoeffer appreciated that it was Barth's radical actualism that enabled him to make soaring assertions about God's unconditional freedom from everything that is conditional. For Barth, he observed, God is always coming and never existent: "God remains always the master, always the subject, so that if any man should think he has God as an object, it is no longer *God* whom he has." Bonhoeffer appreciated that this formal understanding of God's activity as radically contingent was the root idea of Barth's dialectic. Barth insisted that every God-statement must include a "not-God" disclaimer and every "believing-I" statement must include a "not-I" disclaimer in order to guard against the petrification of theological concepts into fixed ontological abstractions. He used dialectic to give appropriate witness to the destabilizing act-character of God's being, which is always subject and never an object of cognition. God is the divine subject who creates the world through God's own knowing. In the Barthian dialectic, Bonhoeffer observed, God is bound by nothing whatsoever, "not even by the manipulable 'entity' of his 'historical' Word." God enters time and history without becoming part of either time or history.[65]

Bonhoeffer recognized that this strategy was fundamental to Barth's attempt to get around the Kantian dictum that God cannot be an object of knowledge. Barth turned the tables on Kant by making God the knowing subject itself. Bonhoeffer also allowed that Barth's radical actualism gave admirable witness to the themes of God's sovereignty and prevenience in grace. Barthianism was nothing if not a rhetoric of divine holy mystery. The problem was that Barth secured these gains by negating the central claim and concern of Christian revelation. Bonhoeffer countered that the central concern of the gospel revelation is not the question of God's freedom from the world. The gospel message is not primarily concerned to establish the truth of God's eternal isolation and aseity. Rather, the driving concern of the gospel is to proclaim God's "forth-proceeding, his *given* Word, his bond in which he has bound himself."[66]

The strongest attestation of divine freedom is that God has freely bound himself in Christ to humanity. This is the gospel message, Bonhoeffer urged. Christianity is liberating because it proclaims that God has given himself freely to us in Christ, the Word of his freedom. Because God has "placed himself at man's disposal," there is a Christian way to speak intelligibly about the continuity of God's revelation: "God *is there,* which is to say: not in eternal non-objectivity but . . . 'haveable,' graspable in his Word within the Church." God's being becomes knowable to us in the coming of Jesus Christ. On the other hand, Bonhoeffer observed, to give primacy to a theory of revelation as pure act is to undermine the Christian capacity to speak intelligibly about God's inner continuity in being, or the continuity of God's revelation, or the possibility of continuities within and among human beings. Even the distinction between profane and theological thought breaks down if theology is restricted to paradoxical utterances about God's eternal nonobjectivity.[67]

This critique of Barth's dialectical actualism anticipated Barth's own. In the mid-1920s, Barth increasingly perceived that his actualism was too thin and one-dimensional to provide a sufficient account of God's relation to the world. On various occasions he remarked that his thinking needed, above all, to become more deeply trinitarian. In the Göttingen lectures he argued that the doctrine of the Trinity is the "true center" of the concept of revelation and that the question of the nature of revelation is the crucial issue for trinitarian theology. Properly understood, he asserted, the ontic and noetic basis of revelation are identical. Revelation has no analogy, despite the elaborate trinitarian analogizing of Augustine, Gregory of Nazianzus, Hegel, and a host of others.[68] In the early 1930s, however, during the period when his former colleagues began to blast him for reverting to trinitarian speculation, Barth judged that his thinking was still insufficiently trinitarian. While there is no material evidence that this judgment was influenced by Bonhoeffer's criticism, Barth's thinking took a more deeply trinitarian turn that, inadvertently or not, addressed the heart of Bonhoeffer's critique. In the postprolegomenal volumes of the *Church Dogmatics,* he took the very plunge that his former comrades warned against. He developed a massive account of God's inner-triune self-relation that accounted for continuities within and between God and created being.

This dogmatic description began with a crucial distinction between God's primary and secondary objectivity. Because God surely knows himself first of all, Barth reasoned, God is firstly objective to himself. "In his triune life as such, objectivity, and with it knowledge, is divine reality before creaturely objectivity and knowledge exist." Barth distinguished this primary objectivity of God from God's secondary objectivity, which is the objectivity that God has for us in God's revelation, "in which He gives Himself to be known by us as He knows Himself." God's secondary objectivity is distinguished not by any lesser revelatory truthfulness or objectivity, he cautioned; it is distinguished only by the form that it takes in order to be suitable for creaturely appropriation. To himself, God is immediatedly objective: the Father, Son, and Spirit are all object to each other without mediation. But to us, the same triune God is objectively mediate: revelation occurs only under the sign and veil of objects that are different from God.[69]

Barth's elaborate description of God as the triune mystery whose being is act and whose being is mediated objectively by the action of Jesus Christ put an end to various protests that his theology was merely a dialectical rhetoric of difference, disruption, and discontinuity. With particular force he insisted that in the veiled but nonetheless objective event of Jesus Christ, "God is who He is." God is the objective triune mystery who is subject, predicate, and object in the event of Jesus Christ, he taught. As Father, Son, and Holy Spirit, God is the revealer, the act of revelation, and the revealed all at once: "We are dealing with the being of God: but with regard to the being of God, the word 'event' or 'act' is *final,* and cannot be surpassed or compromised. To its very deepest depths God's Godhead consists in the fact that it is an event—not any event, not events in general, but the event of His action, in which we have a share in God's revelation."[70]

Charles Marsh argues that Bonhoeffer's later theological work is best understood as a project that works within Barth's trinitarian framework. Against the common tendency to view Bonhoeffer primarily as a "christomorphic" or "christocratic" theologian, he proposes that Bonhoeffer's preoccupation with the continuities between Christ, the Christian community, and the world should be understood against the background of Barth's theology of trinitarian self-relation.[71] More precisely, Bonhoeffer's various reflections on the continuities between Christ, church, and world sought to explore certain implications of Barth's theory of the primary objectivity of

God's triune self-relation and the secondary objectivity of God's revelation in Jesus Christ.[72]

This proposal sets Bonhoeffer's thinking in an appropriatedly deeper and richer theological framework than the Christological framework favored by most liberal Protestant interpreters. It also helps to account for the special sense of kinship that Bonhoeffer felt for Barth despite their often sharp disagreements and the fact that their friendship, while deeply respectful, was never close. For his part, Barth's references to Bonhoeffer in the *Church Dogmatics* were rare, but nearly always appreciative. He praised Bonhoeffer's biblical excursus on the question of how God is able to see, recognize, and discover himself in his creative work.[73] He compared Brunner unfavorably to Bonhoeffer in addressing the question of how the constancy of the divine moral command and human action should be understood. Though he criticized Bonhoeffer's doctrine of divine "mandates" for its arbitrary character and its vestiges of "North German patriarchalism," Barth allowed that at least Bonhoeffer attempted to acquire his ethic entirely from the scriptural Word.[74] Elsewhere his defense of "dear grace" invoked Bonhoeffer's warnings against "cheap grace" in *The Cost of Discipleship.*[75] Barth's later discussion of discipleship judged that Bonhoeffer's book was "easily the best that has been written on this subject." He confessed that he was tempted simply to insert entire sections of Bonhoeffer's book into his own. "For I cannot hope to say anything better on the subject than what is said here by a man who, having written on discipleship, was ready to achieve it in his own life, and did in his own way achieve it even to the point of death," he wrote. "In following my own course, I am happy that on this occasion I can lean as heavily as I do upon another."[76]

For all of the affection and intellectual respect that Barth and Bonhoeffer held for each other, however, it was Bonhoeffer who delivered, among all of the attacks on Barth's theology by fellow theologians, the one that pierced most deeply. During his imprisonment Bonhoeffer mused repeatedly on the future of Christianity and the possibility of a Christian church that dispensed altogether with religious trappings and dogma. He judged that the strategy of appealing to the "spiritual needs" or religious experiences of people no longer worked in a "world come of age" in which modern educated people seemed to get along perfectly well without religion. Liberal Christianity tried to cope with this problem by ceding to the modern world the right to determine Christ's place in the world, he observed: "In the conflict between the church and the world it accepted the comparatively easy terms of peace that the world dictated."[77]

Liberal theology thus piled surrender on top of defeat. In the wake of the First World War, Bonhoeffer recalled, a smattering of theologians tried to revoke the surrender of their liberal teachers. Karl Heim tried to revive heart-religion pietism. Paul Althaus tried to salvage a bit of space for Lutheranism "and otherwise left the world to its own devices." Paul Tillich proposed that all culture is fundamentally religious. "That was very brave of him, but the world unseated him and went on by itself," Bonhoeffer judged. Tillich sought to understand the modern world better than it understood itself, "but it felt that it was completely misunderstood, and rejected the imputation."[78]

These strategies were losers. All of them tried to find a job for religion in a world that no longer found religion necessary. It was Barth who comprehended that theology needed to give up the liberal project of trying to save a role for religion, Bonhoeffer observed. Barth's second edition *Epistle to the Romans* set the gospel of Christ against all religion, *pneuma* against *sarx*. Bonhoeffer judged that this table-turning move remained Barth's "greatest service" to modern theology. Barth admonished the church's theologians that religion never saved anyone. In principle, Bonhoeffer reflected, the crucial distinction between religion and saving grace was preserved in Barth's later dogmatics. The problem with Barth was not that he lost his prophetic sense of religion as idolatry. In Bonhoeffer's judgment, the problem was not even (as so many claimed) that Barth failed to provide adequate ethical guidance. The problem with Barth's later thought was that he lost any capacity to formulate non-religious interpretations of his theological concepts after he became a dogmatic theologian. Put differently, Bonhoeffer explained, instead of pursuing the difficult work of interpreting theological concepts in a critical non-religious fashion that did not make religion a precondition of faith, Barth simply lapsed into revelational positivism. He contented himself with dogmas imposed from above.[79]

"Barth was the first theologian to begin the criticism of religion, and that remains his really great merit," Bonhoeffer allowed. "But he put in its place a positivist doctrine of revelation which says, in effect, 'Like it or lump it': virgin birth, Trinity, or anything else; each is an equally significant and necessary part of the whole, which must simply be swallowed as a whole or not at all."[80] Bonhoeffer did not dispute that Barth derived his dogmatic themes from scripture. What he did dispute was that "like it or lump it" *("Friss Vogel, oder stirb")* is a biblical way of thinking. "There are degrees of knowledge and degrees of significance," he objected. Against Bultmann, Bonhoeffer recognized that Christianity contains mysteries of faith that must be protected from demythologizing criticism and other forms of profanation. The New Testament does not clothe a universal truth in mythological garb, he reasoned. In Christianity, the dying-and-rising God myth is the thing itself. On the other hand, against Barth, he protested that scripture never identifies faith with any system or structure of doctrinal themes. "The positivism of revelation makes it too easy for itself, by setting up, as it does in the last analysis, a law of faith," he judged. By making marginal themes like the virgin birth necessary to the whole of Christian faith, Barth "mutilated" the gift-character of faith. Having rejected the orthodox doctrine of biblical inspiration, he presumed that he was not a positivist; but Bonhoeffer protested that the logic of "like it or lump it" was no less authoritarian.[81]

Not all of Bonhoeffer's prison reflections were this vivid or penetrating. Bonhoeffer vaguely suggested that Barth's understanding of revelation as history was overly vertical, but he confused the point by asserting that in Barth's theology, "the world is in some degree made to depend on itself and left to its own devices."[82] If he meant to criticize Barth's insufficiently horizontal conception of revelation or his tendency to collapse world history into salvation history (as, for example, viewing the fascist threat almost exclusively through the prism of the church struggle), this was a strangely convoluted way of making the argument. Some of Bonhoeffer's statements on other subjects were equally puzzling, a fact that Barth played up after Bonhoeffer's letters were published in 1953.

But his chief arguments pertaining to revelational positivism and "non-religious interpretation" were significantly more intelligible than Barth acknowledged. Following Barth's own earlier practice, Bonhoeffer often set Jesus Christ against "religious" words and institutions. To him, all religious concepts were always problematic, but not Jesus Christ. In his *Ethics,* Bonhoeffer characteristically asserted that "what matters in the church is not religion, but the form of Christ and its taking form amidst a band of men."[83] Bonhoeffer unfailingly regarded faith as participation in the existence of Christ. Even his most despairing prison letters reasserted his faith in Christ as he called for a "non-religious interpretation" of Christianity. By emphasizing that Christ is the true ground and subject of faith, he made it clear enough that for him "non-religious interpretation" meant Christological interpretation. By emphasizing the sheer meaninglessness of religious language to modern people, he also sought to establish that Christological reinterpretation must be existential.

Bonhoeffer rejected Bultmann's demythologizing program as a constructive response to the modern problem of religious language, but he accepted Bultmann's dictum that theologians are obliged to translate the gospel message into forms of expression that speak to the experience of modern people. In 1942, he praised the "intellectual honesty" of Bultmann's biblical scholarship, including Bultmann's work on demythologizing. He reported that he welcomed every opportunity "to expose myself to the breath of fresh air which comes from him." Bonhoeffer noted later that he found it more difficult to breathe the air of Barthianism. While taking care to distinguish Barth's position from the older-style orthodox positivism of many Confessing Church leaders, he complained that in both cases a certain refusal to struggle with critical problems was plainly evident. In his judgment, Barthian theology was long on the reformulation of traditional dogmas and very short on dealing seriously with the reasons that modern people questioned Christian teaching. "Karl Barth and the Confessing Church have encouraged us to entrench ourselves persistently behind the 'faith of the church,' and evade the honest question as to what we ourselves really believe," he charged. "That is why the air is not quite fresh, even in the Confessing Church."[84]

The point of this critique was clear enough to many others in the generation that followed the Second World War, but Barth repeatedly insisted that it made no sense either on its own terms or, especially, coming from Bonhoeffer. He described Bonhoeffer's critical statements as "impenetrable" and "enigmatic."[85] He questioned whether Bonhoeffer's memory was justly served by their publication.[86] For the rest of his life Barth disputed that the tag of "revelational positivism" applied to him. He protested that he never simply threw doctrines at people in a "take it or leave it" fashion.[87] He mused that real positivists like the Holland hyper-Calvinists must have found it rather perplexing to find him consigned to their group. The only sense that he could make of Bonhoeffer's criticism, he claimed, was to recall that Bonhoeffer was "an impulsive, visionary thinker who was suddenly seized by an idea which he gave lively form, and then after a time he called a halt (one never knew whether it was final or temporary) with some provisional last point or other." Barth surmised that Bonhoeffer's recollection of the *Church Dogmatics* must have become rather hazy in prison, and thus produced his bizarre aphorisms about Barthian positivism.[88]

Despite his insistence that the label was nonsense, the "revelational positivist" label stuck to Barth for the rest of his life, as he ruefully recognized. Near the end of his career he caustically described himself as "the poor neo-orthodox theologian, the supernaturalist, the revelational positivist, as I had to hear from so many quarters on both sides of the Atlantic."[89] Bonhoeffer's iconic stature as a modern matryr gave extra weight to his restatement of a long-running critique of Barth's approach to theology. In his last years, Barth disclosed that he had never realized his importance to Bonhoeffer. After reading Eberhard Bethge's massive biography of Bonhoeffer, he told Bethge that "until now I have always thought of myself as one of the pawns, not the knights or castles, on his chessboard." He further revealed that he had never recognized that Bonhoeffer was the first and nearly only churchman "to face and tackle the Jewish question so centrally and energetically." Barth repeated earlier confessions that his own resistance to anti-Semitism was very late and ineffectual by comparison.[90]

But he conceded nothing with regard to his purported dogmatism. "Non-religious interpretation" made no sense at all, he judged, and as applied to himself, neither did "positivism of revelation." Without pressing the point too vigorously, Barth questioned Bonhoeffer's competence as a theologian. He judged that even Bonhoeffer's *Ethics* was deficient as a systematic work.[91] With greater warrant he protested against the rise of various Bonhoeffer-quoting theological fads of the 1960s, while suggesting that Bonhoeffer's fate in being linked to them was his own fault. John A. T. Robinson lauded Bonhoeffer, Tillich, and Bultmann as prophets of a new secularizing "honest to God" theological liberalism; Harvey Cox described Bonhoeffer as the visionary of a world come-of-age "secular city"; William Hamilton claimed Bonhoeffer as a forerunner of "death of God" theology.[92] Various theologians in the Bultmann school, notably Gerhard Ebeling, Ernst Fuchs, and Schubert Ogden, contended that some form of Bultmannian demythologizing offered the best way to take Bonhoeffer's statements seriously and move forward in theology.[93]

Barth reported that in his good moods he called all of these strategies "flat tire theologies" *(Plattfusstheologie).* Though he was personally fond of Fuchs, he regarded all of the secularizing existentialist theologians as lacking in *pneuma.* When the air goes out of an automobile tire, he explained, the car either goes out of control or doesn't go anywhere. In other moods he considered the existential/secularizing trend in theology, especially the Bultmann school, as the second coming of the company of Korah: "You remember the story in Numbers 16," he told John Godsey. "Korah led the rebellion of the Levite priests against Moses and Aaron, and he and his whole company were swallowed up by the ground!" Barth warned that it was impossible to mediate the differences between himself and Bultmann. Some of Bonhoeffer's followers, notably Heinrich Ott, pointed to Bonhoeffer as an exemplary model of how to negotiate the differences between Barth and Bultmann, but Barth protested that these differences presented a fundamental choice, not a series of negotiable arguing points.[94] Overall he grieved that it became Bonhoeffer's legacy to have aided and even inspired a downward trend in theology. He speculated that Bonhoeffer might have recovered his better judgment had he survived the war. "Might he not later have simply dropped all those catchy phrases?" Barth wondered. "Even when he uttered them, did he himself really know what he meant by them?"[95]

OPEN TO DIALOGUE OR CRITICISM?

Barth claimed that he didn't understand the point of Bonhoeffer's criticism, and he strongly implied that Bonhoeffer didn't know what he was talking about, either, but to many others in the postwar generation, the problem with Barthianism that Bonhoeffer described was clear enough. Many theologians and biblical scholars who were otherwise reasonably close to Barth's position shared much of Bonhoeffer's opinion. In the 1940s and 1950s, a Barthian-influenced Biblical Theology movement dominated the field of biblical studies in England and the United States, but virtually all of the movement's proponents used historiocritical methods more aggressively and consistently than Barth. Biblical theologians such as Alan Richardson, H. H. Rowley, and G. E. Wright maintained against Barth that Christian truth claims must be dissected and defended on historical grounds and even defended on philosophical grounds.[96]

Among theologians, Barth's successor at Basel, Heinrich Ott, spoke for many in contending that Barthian positivism was problematic not because it proclaimed Christian dogma, but because it did so in a way that was not open to criticism or open-ended discussion. In a word, Ott contended, the style of Barthian theology was monological, but what was needed in theology was a spirit of openness to the multivocality of the biblical Word in its interaction with variously situated modern readers. Ott judged that in this crucial respect, Barth's dogmatics compared unfavorably with Aquinas's *Summa Theologica.* Aquinas's system sustained a genuinely dialogical conversation, he explained; Aquinas invited criticism from all quarters and did not rule out objections on *a priori* grounds.[97]

Ott lamented that, by contrast, the spirit and style of Barthian theology were overwhelmingly declaratory. Barth conceived theology as a form of preaching in a single commanding voice. He disregarded critical challenges to Christian belief on the ground that Christian truth cannot be subjected to any criterion of truth different from itself. In his protest against the stifling irrelevance and unreality of revelational positivism, Ott observed, Bonhoeffer opposed the kind of preaching that simply proclaimed the gospel message as a Word from outside the world of the hearer. But this was exactly how Barth conceived preaching and theology. With some allowance for polemical intent, Ott concluded, Bonhoeffer's broadside against Barth's approach to theology was thus exactly right. Barthianism amounted to a new kind of dogmatic positivism and thus, despite Barth's protests, a neoorthodoxy.[98]

Consigned to this category, Barth's theology was driven to the margin. In the early 1940s it was possible to question whether Barthianism was already losing its dominating theological influence. A decade later, while Barth produced his extraordinary four-volume doctrine of reconciliation, the sharp decline of his influence was clear. Later he witnessed the fragmentation and radical pluralization of his field with mounting dismay. He judged that a variety of paganizing neo-Protestantisms had seized control of the field and he worried that Catholic theologians like Karl Rahner were taking modern Catholicism down the same road. Except for a late-life fragment on the doctrine of baptism, he stopped work on the *Church Dogmatics* after retiring from Basel in 1962.[99] When people asked him if he intended to complete his thirteenth volume of dogmatics, Barth sometimes asked if they had read the first twelve. Many medieval cathedrals and most medieval *Summae* were left unfinished, he noted, not to mention Mozart's *Requiem.*[100]

In darker moods he confessed that he couldn't see any point in trying to finish his dogmatics. The current theological situation made it pointless to try. "In the face of the thrust of our theological existentialists, the more I go on the more I can only feel disgust and abhorrence," he told his friend and theological ally, Helmut Gollwitzer. "Does it make any sense for me to write a thirteenth or fourteenth volume, if the twelve volumes I have written so far have not been able to prevent the outburst of this flood?" Barth worried that in his later life people only paid attention to him out of respect for his historical stature "without really listening." He told C. H. Ratschow that he delighted in the fact that his works were still read "by a considerable number of pastors, a good collection of non-theologians—and Roman Catholics." It was his impression that some Protestant theologians still read them also, but he realized only too well that very few of them were Barthians. For all of his protests about not being a Barthian, Barth was keenly disappointed to find, in his closing years, that so few theologians adopted his approach to theology. He urged that instead of looking for some standpoint between or beyond himself and Bultmann, it made greater sense "to follow either the one or the other consistently along his way and to pursue it to the end."[101]

The Bultmannian option was attracting more than its share of able proponents, he lamented, while on his side, though he knew an assortment of Barthians, he judged that no one was carrying his dogmatic project forward. In 1964 Barth confided to young Jürgen Moltmann that he had viewed him for a time as the best candidate. "I have been looking for decades—I was looking even in the twenties—for the child of peace and promise, namely, the man of the next generation who would not just accept or reject what I intended and did in theology but who would go beyond it positively in an independent conception, improving it at every point in a renewed form," he reported. Barth was intrigued that Moltmann's *Theology of Hope* took up the very subject that the *Church Dogmatics* left untreated, the doctrine of eschatology. Moltmann proposed to reinterpret Christianity from the standpoint of eschatological expectation. With hopeful anticipation that Moltmann might be the creative, independent, forward-looking Barthian that he had been looking for, Barth read the *Theology of Hope*— but judged that Moltmann didn't come close to treating his subject adequately.

He recognized the kinship between Moltmann's futurism and his own early appropriation of the Blumhardts and Franz Overbeck, and he appreciated that *Theology of Hope* was filled with mostly-favorable references to his writings. Barth protested, however, that Moltmann's argument for theology as eschatology merely baptized Ernst Bloch's philosophy of hope. In his reading, Moltmann subsumed the riches of Christian faith to an eschatological principle. Moltmann's one-sided futurism reduced the "eternally rich God" of the Bible to "rather a pauper." Barth asked him plaintively if he had really learned so little from the discussions of threefold time and the threefold parousia of Jesus Christ developed in the *Church Dogmatics.* Without giving up the hope that Moltmann might outgrow his "inspired onesidedness," Barth therefore pronounced that "very definitely, then, I cannot see in you that child of peace and promise."[102] The further-developed Barthianism that was needed would amplify Barth's later sense of the trinitarian richness of Christianity, not his earlier celebrations of wholly otherness and, especially, one-sidedness.

In later life Barth insisted that he was content to give the *Church Dogmatics* to later generations who might rediscover the riches of Christianity within them. He refused to weep "even the smallest tear" over the situation in which Protestant theology currently found itself. He judged that his dogmatic project offered "the opening of a new conversation" about how theology should proceed. If contemporary theologians were not interested in pursuing the approach to theology that he pioneered, he reasoned, the *Church Dogmatics* would "have to wait their time."[103] Having dominated his field for decades with singular redirecting force, Barth lived long enough (until 1968) to see his theology taken seriously only by a handful of thinkers who disappointed him, like Moltmann and Ott, and by an assortment of epigones who didn't mind the neoorthodox label.

BARTHIAN NEOORTHODOXY AS SCIENCE: T. F. TORRANCE

For most of the past generation Barth has belonged to the Barthians. His theology has been claimed mostly by thinkers who see no reason not to identify with Barth's ostensible objectivism or revelational positivism. Theologians such as Eberhard Jüngel, T. H. L. Parker, Robert Jenson, and the dean of the Barthian school, Thomas F. Torrance, have made enduring contributions to theology that share the neoorthodox-Barthian emphasis on the objectivity of revelation.[104] Though all differ from each other in significant ways, all of them have contributed to the project of carrying Barth's legacy forward along objectivistic neoorthodox lines. Torrance's landmark attempt to carry forward the heart of Barth's theological enterprise is especially significant. He contends that Barth's theology is chiefly distinguished by its presentation of the ontology and objectivity of the divine Word and by Barth's accompanying emphasis on the scientific nature of dogmatics. These are the closely-related qualities that first attracted him to Barth in 1935, Torrance recalls. They remain the key to the superiority of the Barthian approach to theology. The key to Barth's theological achievement is that he rehabilitated theology as a scientific discipline.

Torrance explains that science does not indulge in free thinking. Scientists are bound by the nature of the object they investigate in their particular fields of inquiry. Because science is inescapably bound by whatever object it investigates, he observes, scientists are necessarily committed to a constellation of assumptions about the objective reality and intrinsic rationality of their discipline. In this precise sense of the term, Torrance contends, theology is practiced truly only as a science: "Far from thinking in some free, detached, or dispassionate way, we think as we are compelled to think by the evidential grounds, and we develop explanatory theories or laws strictly in accordance with the nature of things and their inherent rational order as they are brought to light in the course of scientific inquiry."[105]

It was Barth who rehabilitated the possibility of doing theology in this way, he contends. Far from making theology impervious to modern knowledge, Barth reestablished the conception of theology as a basic form of rationality governed by its proper object. All knowing is dependent upon our allowance of the reality of an object to shine through to us, Torrance observes. In Barth's work, this scientific truism was regained for theology. If God is to be known, our knowledge must rest upon the reality and grace of God. "Barth rightly insists that in the knowledge of God we cannot raise questions as to its reality from some position outside of it," Torrance remarks.[106] By doing theology as exegesis of the Word in accordance with a "consistent and rigorous scientific method," Barth revolutionized theology in precisely the manner that Einstein revolutionized modern physics. Torrance explains that just as Einstein questioned the validity of schematizing physics according to the framework of an antecedent conceptual system (Euclidean geometry), Barth questioned the antecedent conceptual systems of all putatively "natural" theologies. Just as Einstein dismantled much of the confining Newtonian superstructure of mathematical time and space and established that physics must incorporate geometry into the structure of physical knowledge itself, Barth insisted that natural knowledge must be incorporated into our actual knowledge of God "where it is indissolubly bound up with its epistemological structure and serves its scientific articulation and formulation."[107]

Torrance allows that Barth did not fully comprehend the fact or implications of his Einstein-like reconceptualization of theological rationality. Barth therefore underestimated the gains for theology that can be made by exploring the basic interconnections between theological and modern scientific concepts. Because God makes God's self known to us through the very spatio-temporal structures and intelligibilities of the universe that science investigates, Torrance argues, theologians are obliged to make use of the theologically-relevant knowledge that science brings to light. Rightly understood, this project does not require any displacement of the divine Word as the starting point and object of theology. It amounts, rather, to a deepening and extension of Barth's conception of theology as a form of scientific rationality governed by its proper object. "In theology we have to do with a divine Object that demands and creates reciprocity so that our knowledge of God involves right from the start a union and not a disjunction between subject and object." In Torrance's language, God is the divine Object who makes human knowledge of Himself possible through His union with human subjects, but God joins Himself to human subjects in a way that does not entangle Him in human subjectivity. Because God distinguishes Himself from us we are capable of knowing God in His divine being and Objectivity without mixing up God with our own subjective being.[108]

The Word-oriented theologian is properly drawn out from his or her isolation by "the attack of a masterful, concrete objectivity." As a scientist, Torrance explains, the theologian is compelled to submit to the forms and conditions of knowledge that are dictated by the proper Object of one's investigation. In this crucial sense, pure theology and pure physics are both forms of dogmatics. Both disciplines are bound to their proper object and both are obliged to conceive that object in accordance with its nature. As a form of science, good theology is both positive and dogmatic, just like physics, but it is not authoritarian. Barth sometimes remarked that even though he taught and expounded dogmatics, he was not a dogmatic person. Torrance proposes that the crucial distinction is between being dogmatic and dogmatical. Good theology is dogmatic in its devotion to the facts and their inner logic, he explains, but this humble submission to reality is the opposite of being dogmatical or authoritarian. Like the church itself, church dogmatics "stands or falls with sheer respect for the Majesty and Freedom of God in His Word and for the transcendence of His Truth over all our statements about it."[109]

This emphasis on the objectivist nature of Barthian theology is surely a plausible way to conceptualize Barth's dogmatic project and keep it alive. Aside from Torrance's glosses on Einstein and his own constructive theorizing about the interconnections between theology and natural science, which he allows that Barth did not pursue, he adheres closely to a cluster of formulations that Barth developed in the mid-1920s and elaborated in his early volumes of the *Church Dogmatics.* He correctly notes that Barth's commitment to the primacy and objectivity of the Word was already firmly established by the mid-1920s. It was aggressively expounded in Barth's *Christliche Dogmatik.* It was fully developed in the prolegomenal volumes of *Church Dogmatics,* where Barth emphasized not merely the act of God in the Word, but the *being* of God in God's act in the Word. For Torrance, all of Barth's other motifs and later developments pale in comparison to this one. "It is all-important to realise that for Barth the Word of God refers to the most completely objective reality there is, for it is the Word of *God* backed with God's own ultimate Being," he explains. For Barth, as for Torrance, the content that God directs to us in his Word is his own Being, "the downright actuality of God, the ultimate objectivity."[110]

Torrance allows that his insistence on a unitary realist epistemology takes a Barthian argument further than Barth dared to go. Barth never relinquished his early insistence that theology must not exclusively embrace either epistemological idealism or realism, but Torrance presses for the necessity of a critical realist theory of knowledge. He reasons that Barth never completely overcame the imprint of his early metaphysical dualism. Though Barth adopted an essentially realist epistemology in making the transition to a Word-centered dogmatic theology, he explains, Barth never completely expunged the vestiges of "Wholly Other" dialecticism from his mature thinking. Torrance urges that for those who seek to take Barthian theology forward, this is the frontier.[111] The kinds of natural theology that Barth attacked all deserved to be condemned, but a genuine partnership between theology and science is now possible on the basis of Barth's rehabilitation of theology as a science.

Torrance therefore shares the emphasis of this present work in reading Barthianism primarily as a theology of the Spirit-illuminated Word, but he reformulates this theology as a straightforward science of revelational objectivism. In his reading, Barthianism has a material essence and a formal essence, and both are grounded in Barth's objectivist doctrine of the Word. Put differently, Barth's position is controlled by a single motif that constitutes both the essential content of his theology and its essential structure. The utter domination of this motif in Torrance's interpretation of Barth makes Torrance's Barthianism a highly rationalistic affair. His smooth and assuring rhetoric of objective truth heightens the scholastic tone of Barth's dogmatizing. "Rationality" and "objectivity" take on the qualities of virtual

God-terms. Barth's emphasis on the *diastasis* between the words of the text and the Word of the Spirit is recognized, but downplayed. Barth's actualist understandings of biblical inspiration, the incarnation, and the analogy of faith are formally affirmed, but subordinated to a dominating assurance that God is objectively knowable. Barth's continued use of dialectical rhetoric in his later theology is virtually ignored. His continued emphasis on rupture and discontinuity gives way, in Torrance's neoorthodoxy, to an overwhelming emphasis on the rationality of Christian truth. Barth insisted that Christian theologians must never get into the business of endorsing any kind of philosophical worldview, but Torrance plainly endorses critical scientific realism in the name of Barthian objectivism.

Torrance holds out for the "inseparability of empirical and theoretical components in knowledge," but Barth warned against the kind of realism that expunges all or even most idealistic elements from theology. "Idealism is the antidote to all demonology passing itself off as theology," he contended. "By stressing God's non-objectivity it reminds us that all human thinking and speaking about God is inadequate." Torrance maintains that the way forward in Barthian theology is to affirm "the indissoluble unity of being and form," but Barth aptly warned that this is precisely the move that eventually confuses the proper Object of theology with other objects. Christian theology needs a strong reserve of idealistic elements in order to direct us to the God "who is God only in genuine transcendence," Barth argued. "Theology needs this antidote and this modesty."[112]

Torrance's Barthianism is not completely purged of idealistic elements (he conceptualizes the uniqueness of Christ partly upon Christ's uniquely perfect unity of form and being), but it is very short on epistemological modesty. It all but negates Barth's antidotal emphasis that God is hidden, holy, and mysterious, the ineffable source of revelation and grace who dwells in "unapproachable light" (1 Tim. 6:16). George Hunsinger aptly notes that Torrance's theological project is permeated by the atmosphere of the physics lab. It is possible to appropriate much of the content of Barthian theology by playing up its clinical aspects, Hunsinger allows, but Torrance loses much of Barth's spirit in the process.[113] One way to defend Barth against the charge of neoorthodox positivism is to defend neoorthodox positivism, but there are other ways to appropriate Barth's theology for a later generation.

COUNTERMELODIES: REREADING BARTH

In recent years a wide assortment of postliberal, evangelical, dialectical and other theologians have sparked a revival of discussion about Barth's theology. Some of them share Torrance's commitment to making scientific claims for theology; some evangelicals appeal to Barth as the exemplar of a truly postfundamentalist evangelicalism; others defend more conventional versions of a once-dominant neoorthodoxy.[114] The very notion that Barth should be read as a neoorthodox positivist has come under attack by a sizable number and variety of interpreters, however. Because the view of

Barth's development established by von Balthasar and Torrance is often assumed by those who identify Barth as an objectivizing, dogmatic positivist, much of the literature that disputes this identification dissects the problems with von Balthasar's "dialectic to analogy" interpretive schematism. In the 1970s and 1980s, Barth interpreters such as Eberhard Mechels, Ingrid Spieckermann, and Michael Beintker variously emphasized the coexistence of dialectical and analogical modes of argument in Barth's dogmatic work from 1924 onward.[115] In 1972, Friedrich-Wilhelm Marquardt sparked a more heated controversy by emphasizing (and exaggerating) the role of Barth's lifelong commitment to democratic socialism as a factor (Marquardt claimed it was the key factor) in the development of Barth's theology.[116] During the same period, Trutz Rendtorff proposed that Barth should be read as an innovator within the tradition of theological liberalism who shared much of the Enlightenment critique of traditional authorities. Though Barth clearly rejected most of the Enlightenment project of theological liberalism from Schleiermacher onward, Rendtorff allowed, his theology was nonetheless a product of this tradition. Instead of seeking to secure the freedom and autonomy of human agents from all overarching authorities, Barth pursued a modernist Enlightenment project from the radically opposite standpoint of seeking to secure the freedom and autonomy of God from all merely-human ideas and institutions.[117]

These interpretive proposals have fueled a many-sided renewal of debate about the character and legacy of Barth's theology. Building on the genetic arguments of Spieckermann and Beintker, Bruce McCormack maintains that Barth remained a dialectical theologian with an epistemological commitment to critical realism for his entire career as a dogmatic theologian. Like Rendtorff, he proposes that Barth is best viewed as the proponent of a new kind of theology that turned Enlightenment anthropocentrism on its head even while remaining, in its peculiar way, within the liberal tradition. More cautiously than Marquardt, McCormack also emphasizes that Barth's theology sought to address the sociopolitical circumstances of his time and that he rejected the notion that theologians should strive for timelessness in their dogmatic formulations.[118]

Various others go further than McCormack in seeking to dissociate Barth from the tradition of modern neoorthodoxy. An assortment of Yale-school "postliberal" theologians influenced by Hans W. Frei and George A. Lindbeck read Barth as the precursor of nonfoundationalist narrative theology, in which the biblical story is viewed as the meaning of doctrine rather than the other way around. Most notably among this group, George Hunsinger argues that all essentialist readings of Barth are mistaken because Barth employed a variety of actualist, particularist, objectivist, personalist, realist, and rationalist modes of thought.[119] Others such as Walter Lowe, William Stacy Johnson, and Graham Ward highlight the postmodern or even deconstructionist aspects of Barth's thought. Johnson emphasizes the Barthian theme of God's hiddenness and mystery, contending that "the last thing

Barth wished to do" was to repristinate or otherwise rehabilitate a bygone orthodoxy.[120]

In all of these cases we are far removed from the atmosphere of Torrance's science-claiming neoorthodox objectivism. The fact that Barthian theology has given rise to such a contradictory profusion of readings must count as some kind of evidence for the postmodern thesis of the instability of meaning. Barth's thinking purposely defied categorization. He employed multiple modes of thought and drew freely from various theological and philosophical traditions, including some that he vigorously denounced, in order to explicate his always-provisional understanding of the meaning of the Word. He unfailingly insisted that theology can be healthy and free only if it remains open to a multiplicity of philosophies, worldviews, and forms of language. Barth opted for a pluralistic and eclectic approach to philosophy precisely in order to save theology from the bondage of a closed system, including the system of conventional neoorthodoxy.

The notion that Barth never belonged to the theological movement that his work inspired, however, is historically implausible and overly defensive of Barth's reputation. McCormack ties the "myth of the neo-orthodox Barth" to the influence of von Balthasar's account of Barth's development. Building on the interpretive work of Spieckermann, Beintker, Jüngel, and others, he makes a generally compelling critique of the "dialectic to analogy" schematism propounded by von Balthasar and Torrance.[121] The problem for his argument about why Barth has been misinterpreted as a neoorthodox dogmatist, however, is that the prevailing image of Barth to this effect actually owes little to the influence of von Balthasar's schematism.

As we have seen in the past two chapters, nearly all of the major theologians of the Barthian era blasted Barth's dogmatic positivism long before von Balthasar's book was published in 1951. For Tillich, Brunner, Bultmann, Thielicke, Bonhoeffer, Niebuhr, and numerous others, the problem with Barthianism was precisely Barth's insistence on rehabilitating a bygone orthodoxy. Though most of them perceived the countermelody of divine hiddenness and mystery that McCormack and Johnson (differently) accentuate in their interpetations of Barth, all of them protested that Barth's dogmatics resounded with the overpowering harmony of positive revelational content. Theological liberalism had at least begun to treat other world religions as possible vehicles of divine grace, but Barth's overwhelming Christocentrism excluded interreligious dialogue from the proper business of theology. He gave only slightly more consideration to historical criticism and he dismissed, sometimes rudely, the possibility of feminist theology.

His early clashes with Henriette Visser 't Hooft and other feminist Christians probably saved him from taking a disastrously chauvinist position on the ethics of gender in the *Church Dogmatics.* Henriette Visser 't Hooft was the wife of Barth's friend, ecumenical leader W. A. Visser 't Hooft. In 1934, she published an article that protested against the domination-and-submission motif of 1 Cor. 11:5–9 and related scriptural passages. Against the apparent Pauline implication that women exist for the sake of men, she argued for an egalitarian Christian ethic of mutual interest, mutual trust, and mutual responsibility. Barth replied that she simply misunderstood the spiritual necessity of patriarchy. In a private letter he explained that there were crucial reasons why the New Testament shared the patriarchal outlook of the Old Testament. The New Testament assumes everywhere that Christ belongs to the people of Israel, he observed; it further assumes that as a man, Christ confirmed Adam's superiority. More importantly, if Paul had assumed an ethic of mutuality between men and women, he would not have been able to express the superiority of God over humanity. This was the heart of the issue for Barth. "It is just so," he lectured, that man is superior to woman just as God is superior to humanity. It was "just so" that the Bible assumed an ethic of father rule, not mutuality.[122]

Fourteen years later, at the World Council of Churches assembly in Amsterdam, a handful of women dared to assert that good ecumenical Christianity should recognize the equal rights of women in church and society. Barth lectured them disapprovingly that Galatians 3:28 was not the only pertinent text on gender relations. The scene was painfully embarrassing to W. A. Visser 't Hooft, who basically agreed with Barth, but who lived with Henriette Visser 't Hooft. He later recalled that unfortunately, Barth "made fun of such women who, in his eyes, appeared to 'rush to equality.' " Upon reading Barth's dismissive remarks on the rights on women, Henriette Visser 't Hooft told him that she was deeply saddened by his sarcasm and chauvinism, especially in light of the fact that his contribution to the assembly was otherwise so constructive. Barth's definitive discussion of the theology and ethics of gender appeared three years later, in *Church Dogmatics* III:4. Fortunately, Henriette Visser 't Hooft must have given him second thoughts about his male chauvinism. The patronizing rhetoric of "it is just so" gave way to a torturous grappling with the problem of gender relations from a scriptural perspective. Though his English translators mistakenly represented him as denying any "false superiority" of men over women, Barth's German text did not speak of "true" or "false" superiority. He affirmed that men are not superior to women in any way. At the same time, he admonished that the church is obliged to adhere to the teaching and implications of the biblical doctrine that women are "second in sequence" to men. As sons of Adam, he asserted, men bear a "primacy of service" before God in the divine order revealed by scripture: "We cannot avoid the fact that it is real subordination." Moreover, though women were "entitled to complain" about any disrespectful or discriminatory treatment that they received, Barth opined that they were not entitled to complain about their "second place" spiritual status as daughters of Eve. Like it or lump it.[123]

For all of his insistence on the freedom of the Word, Barth's insistence on correct doctrine and his exclusivist reading of biblical teaching thus established the "myth of the neo-orthodox Barth" long before von Balthasar schematized his road to it. If some of his followers exaggerated his objectivism, the *Church Dogmatics* nonetheless contained ample basis for Torrance-style "Barthianism." With an assurance that derived from close personal acquaintance, the dialectical theologians perceived that the crucial turns in Barth's thinking occurred early. From 1924 onward Barth subordinated faith to revelation, and he treated doctrines as subjects of belief. Though "neo-Reformationist" would have been a more accurate signifier for his theological purpose, he therefore earned the description "neoorthodox" at least as fully as Brunner and his mid-century American followers. Barth associated the term "neoorthodoxy" with the stuffy Erlangen-style confessionalism that he despised. He rightly protested that his thinking was truer to the Reformation and more deeply modern than that. The kind of theology that he inspired and developed is rightly called "neoorthodox" only if one emphasizes the modern "neo" elements that are fundamentally constitutive to it. Put differently, Barthian theology took shape as a revolt against the liberal tradition while remaining importantly shaped by one of its main offshoots.

Barth left Herrmann behind as a theological interlocutor in the 1920s, but his thinking thereafter took crucial elements of Herrmann's theology for granted. Some of these elements he creatively reinterpreted. Like Herrmann, Barth wrote theology with unfailing mindfulness of the restrictions placed on theological reasoning by Kant. Like Herrmann, he judged that these restrictions and the integrity of the inscripturated subject matter required that history had to be kept in its proper place. Like Herrmann, he insisted that the revelatory basis of faith is its own basis and must not be supported or defended with outside arguments. Barth's intentional vagueness about epistemology opened the door to endless debates about his realism or critical realism or postmodern antifoundationalism. There is one aspect of the slippery question of religious epistemology about which Barth continually struggled to gain as much clarity as possible, however. This is the question of the relation of Christian resurrection faith to history, which McCormack, Johnson, Torrance, and other recent interpreters have treated as secondary at most. Barth's thinking contained too many patterns to be reducible to any single doctrine or principle, and his unusual blend of motifs ultimately defied precise categorization, but there is a single cluster of questions that distinctively reveals the character of his theology. The peculiar mixture of subjectivist and objectivist motifs that characterized his mature perspective is best illustrated by the twists and turns of his struggle to get clear about the historical basis of the gospel message.

5

THEOLOGY WITHOUT WEAPONS

History and the Open Word

In February 1925 Karl Barth remarked to Eduard Thurneysen that his lecturing on dogmatics was introducing him to "a lot of remarkable things, long assigned to the lumber room." In nearly every case he found that there was something "worth saying again" in various old doctrines that his liberal teachers had discarded. At the same time, in the same letter, he noted that Wilhelm Herrmann's recently-published *Dogmatik* had recently arrived in the mail. His reaction to it contained suggestions of self-recognition and misgiving. "Yes, I see in it, certainly in a respectable form, as though through a reversed telescope, the place from which we have come," he acknowledged. "Should we not perhaps have remained there?"[1]

Barth did not really doubt that he had made the right choice in revolting against his teachers. His occasional suggestions to the contrary reflected his envy of certain well-stationed Herrmannian acquaintances, not any serious misgivings about his theological direction. It is likely, however, that his comments on his relation to Herrmann contained the suggestion of another kind of misgiving. For all of his new-found appreciation for angelology and the doctrine of the virgin birth, Barth was still his teacher's disciple in crucial respects. In his ungenerous moods he could dismiss Schleiermacher's theology as "just one gigantic swindle," but the line of continuity between Herrmann's thinking and his own was too strong to permit a similarly sweeping condemnation of Herrmann's liberalism.[2] The publication of Herrmann's lectures on dogmatics undoubtedly reminded him that much of his own theological position still derived from these lectures. Most likely this was an unnerving reminder for him. In the decades that followed it was not only the Barthians and numerous anti-Barthians, but Barth himself who exaggerated the extent of his break from Marburg liberalism.

Herrmann was in the last stage of his prolonged movement away from the historicist and apologetic aspects of the Ritschlian school during the period (1907) when Barth was his student. He had never been a pure Ritschlian, even as the founder of the Ritschlian school. In the 1890s his successive editions of *Der Verkehr des Christen mit Gott* moved increasingly in Schleiermacher's direction; in 1906 his *Christlich-protestantische Dogmatik* gave an almost purely Schleiermacherian account of Christian faith while barely mentioning Ritschl. Herrmann's writings and lectures during this period blasted all attempts to prove the truth of revelation, but not without marginal equivocations. He still made Ritschlian appeals to the "historical facts" of Christianity and he still left a bit of room on the side for three kinds of apologetic arguments. Herrmann allowed that theologians were obliged to defend the integrity of religious truth claims against those who dismissed all religious claims as illusory. He also allowed that Christian theology needed to establish the possible relation between religion and ethics and that theology should defend religion as the only possible ground of a unifying conception of reality.[3]

These marginal apologetic claims cut against the spirit and logic of his position, however. They compromised his fervently-expressed commitment to do theology without weapons. Herrmann increasingly recognized that they also compromised his capacity to defend a clear alternative to the consistent historicism of an ascending history of religions school. Over the course of a twenty-year period, he therefore gradually relinquished the Ritschlian notion of a critically established historical core of Christian faith. His later editions of *Der Verkehr des Christen mit Gott* heightened the book's polemic against all forms of historical foundationalism. He continued to speak of the "historical fact" of Jesus, but he dropped his Ritschlian assurances that historical criticism always yields the Christ of faith. By the time that Barth studied at Marburg, Herrmann clearly represented the possibility of a gospel-claiming liberal alternative to the compromised historicism of the Ritschlian school and the more thoroughgoing historicism of its *Religionsgeschichtliche Schule* offshoot. A few years later, having pondered Ernst Troeltsch's repeated critical attacks upon him, he dropped his last apologetic equivocations.[4]

Herrmann completed his prolonged process of relinquishment in the years just before the outbreak of World War I. He discarded his remaining apologetic crutches and concessions. He eliminated the apologetic sections from his lectures on dogmatics and embraced what Troeltsch, not unfairly, called "the agnostic theory about the nature of religious knowledge." Troeltsch cautioned that Herrmann's deepening anti-historicism was an instructive example of the "subjective mysticism" that came from the "abandonment of firm and adequate knowledge."[5] Less charitably he pronounced, in 1911, that Herrmann's religious claims were "obscure and mystical," if not "violently" willful, and that Herrmann's refusal to ground his religious claims in the verdicts of historical criticism was "almost incomprehensible to people who think historically and critically." Herrmann's appeal to a mystical inner Christ preserved the orthodox claim to a religious absolute, he judged, but it completely failed the test of historical credibility.[6]

The latter shrewdly-aimed shot against Herrmann's purportedly orthodox yearnings was offensive to Herrmann. Having parried respectfully with Troeltsch for years, he countered sharply in 1912 that it was Troeltsch who clung to an orthodox security blanket. In Troeltsch's case, the security object was a science-claiming historicism that presumed its own certainty *and* its right to serve as the ground of religious faith. Herrmann replied that faith is not a form of scientific knowledge. By confusing religion and science, he observed, Troeltsch's historicism distorted the experiential character of religious truth. It reduced the genuine truth of Christianity, which is the experience of Christ, to a mere idea.[7] Herrmann's theological system made a clean break with all such confusions and all of his earlier concessions to them. Without giving up the assurance that Christianity possesses a factual grounding in history, he categorically denounced the notion that theology should seek or even desire to establish its historical basis on historiocritical grounds. With no apologetic asides he insisted that all religious statements about God, creation, morality, and everything else are lifeless and groundless apart from their source in religion itself.[8]

HERRMANN ON REVELATION AND TRUE RELIGION

Herrmann urged his students to see the Kantian revolution all the way through. As his student, Barth took this admonition to heart and, in his own way, remained true to it. Kant liberated religion from its distorting connection to scientific reason, Herrmann taught, but he failed to recognize that religion possesses an independent and underivable essence. The early Schleiermacher corrected Kant's identification of religion with the ethical will, but Schleiermacher's later system lost the Kantian recognition that religion belongs only to a particular kind of individual experience. Schleiermacher's dogmatic system deduced religious reality from the unity of human self-consciousness. Herrmann allowed that this account may have described the condition of the possibility of religion, but he protested that it obscured, through its ostensible universality, that which constitutes true religion itself.[9] True religion is an historical phenomenon that exists only in the life of particular individuals.

It followed that true religion can be understood only by those who live in it. Herrmann did not deny that it was possible to show people of good moral will the *way* to religion. Because religion belongs to history and not to nature, he reasoned, religion inevitably bears an historical character. But true religion can never be created or experienced as a product of moral will or historical reason or any other kind of human initiative. Human beings can be saved only by that which is given to them in revelation as their most compelling experience. The content of this experience is more than a person's consciousness of absolute dependence, he insisted; it also contains the simultaneous experience of inward independence or freedom. "We can only have an idea of this fundamental religious experience which we call revelation if we are able to recall a time when we knew a moment of utter dependence which was also an act of free will," Herrmann argued. "We could not imagine such an experience, but we can recognize it when it is really there."[10]

What we need, we must be given. A person can become a truly live self (*das etwas für sich selbst sein will*) only by experiencing a reality that one cannot produce from within oneself. "We seek God when we long for such a reality," Herrmann taught. "When we encounter such a reality, God reveals himself to us."[11] True religion is the simultaneously liberating and submissive response to revelation, and revelation is the experience of a spiritual Power "which acts on us as the manifestation of pure goodness." To experience the working of this Power is to settle, or have settled for us, the question whether God is a reality: "It simply depends on whether we remain loyal to the truth, that is, whether we are prepared to treat the fact of such a Power as what it really is for us. The moment we desire dependence upon it, and submit ourselves to it in reverence and trust, this spiritual Power is really our soul's Lord." Only the Spirit gives life. The Spirit often works through the moral will, but it is never merely a product or function of morality. True religion is an awakening to the revelation of God's Spirit in all of the life-giving movements of one's inner life.[12]

As a nineteenth-century liberal, Herrmann resisted the shift in early twentieth-century biblical interpetation toward an apocalyptic understanding of Jesus and the kingdom of God. Though he emphasized that the "worldview of Jesus" question was irrelevant in any case to the question of faith and true religion, he tended to describe the character and presence of the kingdom in a manner that fit his account of true religion.[13] To him the kingdom of God was, above all, the rule of God in the hearts of Christ-following individuals. It was never precisely described or pictured in the teaching of Jesus because Jesus sought to describe, not the nature of a supreme good, but the nature of genuine inner righteousness. At the same time, for all of his typically liberal proclivity to reduce the kingdom to individual spiritual experience, Herrmann unfailingly cautioned that the kingdom comes only by God's initiative and that it is knowable only through revelatory experience. "The Kingdom of God comes from the other world," he asserted. "It is not the result of human activity, but a gift of God." It does not matter that Jesus and the early church believed many things that we do not believe, for what links us to Jesus is the revelatory experience of God as righteous, providential, and loving.[14]

Through such experiences we come to know the inner life of Jesus. Herrmann explained that the person of Jesus "becomes to us a real Power rooted in history, not through historical proofs, but through the experience produced in us by the picture of his spiritual life which we can find for ourselves in the pages of the New Testament." This saving picture is available to us nowhere else. We gain access to Christ only through the New Testament and the revelatory movement of God's Spirit. We possess our knowledge of Christ only from our own experience and only for ourselves. "We cannot receive religious knowledge by having it proved to us, nor can we thus impart it to others," Herrmann urged. "It must arise in each man afresh and individually; and by virtue of it he is then born into a new life."[15]

Revelation is its own basis. It cannot be subordinated to a doctrine of scriptural authority or subjected to tests of right reason without violation.

Herrmann insisted that religion finds its true origin without remainder "in revelation understood as a unique personal experience" (*als ein eigenes Erlbenis erfasster Offenbarung*). In 1909, at the height of his position-clarifying debates with Troeltsch and the Marburg neo-Kantian philosophers Paul Natorp and Hermann Cohen, he remarked that his entire career had been devoted to showing that the only true ground of religious teaching is "that experience which is its revelation."[16] Understood correctly, he explained elsewhere, theology is rightly pursued only as explication of a revealed Word of God without resort to supporting arguments or proofs. "If a Christian has come to recognize the constraining power which comes upon him from the Person of Jesus as a revelation of God, he can take as a word of God only that which is in some way recognizable as an expression of this fact," Herrmann argued. Revelatory experience does not disclose propositional doctrines about God or religion. What it does disclose is the life-giving presence and Power of the Revealer: "Christian faith is that renewal of the inner life which men experience in contact with Jesus as he becomes for them that revelation of God which is the foundation of God's rule in their hearts." It followed for Herrmann that the Christian church is the community of those who know Christ as the revealed spiritual power of their lives. The true unity of the Christian community, the only unity that is worth having, is the one that derives from sharing this experience in common.[17]

Faith is a spiritual gift of God's Spirit. To defend the Spirit's gift with reasons is to reveal that one is secretly ashamed of it, Herrmann taught. Genuinely Christian theology therefore has no place at all for apologetics. He pointedly cautioned that the gospel message pertaining to Easter faith and history admits no exceptions to this stricture. It is one thing to recognize that Christianity would not have survived if Jesus had not appeared to his disciples after his death, he allowed. Calvary became a redemptive event in the eyes of the disciples only after Jesus reappeared to them. But Christianity is not fundamentally a belief about the resurrection of Jesus, nor is the Easter message provable by historical demonstration.

Herrmann explained that the disciples experienced Jesus as their redeemer before he was crucified. Calvary nearly shattered this faith, but the disciples regained their faith in its life-giving power through the impression of Christ's Easter appearances. Because the disciples' faith was regenerated by the Easter appearances, the early church's testimony to the teaching and ministry of Jesus was preserved for later generations. In this way, Herrmann acknowledged, the Easter message is inextricably bound up with the possibility of our salvation. We would not have received the effective means of our salvation—the gospel picture of Jesus—without the resurrection appearances.

It is in this respect and this respect only, he taught, that the Easter message comprises part of the assured content of Christian faith. Though Herrmann cautioned that the structure of certainties on which Christianity is based cannot be established or confirmed by any outside means, he insisted on calling it "the fact on which our faith is based." To the extent that the Easter message is inextricably bound up with our experience of Christ as redeemer, he reasoned, it must be considered part of the certainly-established core of Christian faith. For this is the aspect of the Easter message that comprises part of our own experience. Because we know from direct experience that Christ is our redeemer, the Easter message is part of our faith experience.[18]

What is not available to us is the experience of the original disciples. Herrmann cautioned that we cannot know for certain what the disciples experienced in the events that gave rise to the Easter message and that we gain little insight from outside historical investigation. "In Christian preaching, therefore, the Scripture story of Easter can only be used in such a way as to point the congregation to that which alone can create faith in its members," he instructed. "Christian preaching must confine itself strictly to that which is presented to it as an indubitable fact." The resurrection narratives are contradictory and obscure; to read them for their purported evidentiary value is to misuse them. What matters is that those who constructed the gospel pictures of these events were helped by these pictures to live in the power of the person of Jesus. If we keep this truism in mind, Herrmann advised, it will cease to trouble us that "what happened at that time remains by God's will veiled from us."[19]

HERRMANNIANISM AND HISTORICISM: BARTH, BULTMANN, FUCHS, AND EBELING

By 1925, Herrmann's piety and assurances were like echoes from a lost world to Barth. He readily assembled a list of Herrmannian themes that seemed hopelessly wrong to him. Chief among these were Herrmann's emphasis on individual experience, his self-contradictory claim to universality, his inadequate account of how people actually come to faith, his appeal to the "inner life" of Jesus, his Monophysite Christology, his strained (if rare) appeals to scripture, his strained (and too frequent) appeals to Luther, his relegation of the Trinity to three paragraphs at the end of his dogmatics, and his disregard for the authority of scripture and church tradition.[20] Herrmann eschewed Schleiermacher's universalistic theorizing about the nature of (religious) consciousness, but this did not stop him from claiming universal validity for his account of the "way to religion." He rightly resolved to do theology without weapons, Barth observed, but he substituted individual religious experience for the weaponlessness of the divine Word. He rejected orthodox Christology as mythical and replaced it with the emaciated Monophysite assurance that God works upon us through "the Power of the man Jesus."

These were terrible trades, Barth judged. Having stumbled only recently upon the Alexandrian/arguably-Reformed doctrine of the union of the Logos and human nature in Christ, Barth lectured that "orthodox Christology is a glacial torrent rushing straight down from a height of three thousand metres; it makes accomplishment possible." By comparison, he judged, Herrmann's Christology presented a "hopeless attempt to raise a stagnant pool to that same height by means of a hand pump; nothing can be accomplished with it."[21] This withering judgment was the key to Barth's dogmatic turn and his dismissal of liberal theology. He charged that liberal theology was literally weak, shriveled, and deflated. It replaced the great doctrines of scripture and Christian tradition with its own domesticated pieties and cultural prejudices, some of which were no longer up-to-date. Herrmann's Christology reduced Christ to an inspiring religious leader. He got nothing more out of the doctrine of the Trinity than the reminder that God is an unsearchable mystery.[22] By 1925, Barth had begun to glimpse the staggering difference that orthodox Christology and the orthodox theme of the inalienable subjectivity of God's triune self-relation could make for his own dogmatic theology.

"It is scarcely enlightening to say of the Bible and dogma (in specific relation to the impossible theory of the 'power of the man Jesus') that they are expressions of human faith, 'religious ideas of other men,' and therefore they are not binding upon us," he admonished. If the Bible and the church's dogma are *nothing but* the religious thoughts of opinionated writers, "then they have *no* authority; neither can they gain it." Barth countered that Christian theologians cannot establish scriptural authority or the authority of counciliar dogma as an afterthought. Experience cannot establish genuine authority, he explained: "An authority is either there or not there. What is not authority from the beginning cannot become such."[23] The Bible has no authority at all for faith if it is not treated from the outset as the church's unique authoritative witness to revelation. On every issue, Barth judged, Herrmann's creative and often inspiring spirit needed the corrective discipline of the divine Word. The church fathers and reformers spoke a deeper, richer, and ultimately more liberating language of faith because they experienced the freedom that derives from submitting to the sovereignty of the open Word.

These bruising judgments were delivered in a tone that said, "good-bye to all that." Though he repeatedly interrogated Schleiermacher's writings afterward and wrote long essays on Schleiermacher's legacy, Barth never dealt again with Herrmann. Aside from a few scattered references in the later volumes of the *Church Dogmatics* and a dismissive half-paragraph in the first volume, Herrmann disappeared from his theological horizon, even as a cautionary example.[24] Barth's later work took for granted the themes that he took from Herrmann. He did not bother to deal with Herrmann when he reformulated these themes and he completely lost interest in debating the kind of liberal Protestantism that Herrmann represented. Even his debates with Rudolf Bultmann largely ignored Herrmann's influence over both of them, despite the fact that Barth's disagreements with Bultmann were explicable as conflicting interpretations of Herrmannian themes.[25]

Despite his reticence on this point, however, it was Barth's reworking of themes and positions that he took from Herrmann that "made accomplishment possible" in all of his later work. Though he replaced Herrmann's anthropocentric hand pump with the giant waterfall of the biblical Word and orthodox dogma, it was precisely the Herrmannian elements in Barth's theology that saved it from degenerating into a sterile orthodox dogmatism. Chief among these were his interpretation of revelation as self-revelation and his insistence that revelation is self-authenticating. Barth eventually appealed to the authority of Calvin to support the latter argument, but the former position, having derived from Hegel and subsequent nineteenth-century German idealism, was too modern for any such appeal to orthodox tradition. Like Herrmann, Barth aggressively pressed the negative implications of conceiving revelation as self-revealing and self-authenticating: Revelation is not doctrine, faith is not assent to doctrine, revelation is not any "thing" at all, faith is not the outcome of an argument, apologetics is not a legitimate theological enterprise, Christian faith is not a worldview, and critically established history is not the basis of faith. All of these arguments were significantly reshaped in Barth's thinking by his commitment to the priority and authority of the divine Word. Herrmann maintained that it was enough for faith to apprehend the inner life of Jesus. Barth countered that it was enough only for faith to live by the inscripturated Word of Christ in all of its Spirit-illuminated realism and sovereignty.

In both cases the existence of a radically autonomous theological ground was affirmed. Barth was no less emphatic than Herrmann in affirming the importance of Kant's liberation of theology from scientific reason.[26] More importantly, in their generational context, Barth remained a Herrmannian in his insistence that Christian truth, while belonging to history, is independent from the canons of historiocriticism. The path that Barth followed in working out his alternative to an ascending history of religions school historicism was the gospel-claiming path that Herrmann cleared.

The *Religionsgeschichtliche Schule* was strongly essentialist and structure-oriented in its interpretation of Christianity and other religions. It contended that every living religious tradition is fueled principally by cult and liturgy, not theology, and that biblical religion is primarily mythical and eschatological in its character, not theological or moral.[27] Troeltsch explained that Yahweh-religion must be understood primarily in its relation to the history of Arabian nomadic religions. "The same may be said of the further development of Yahweh-religion into prophetism, into legalism and priestly religion, into messianism, and into apocalypticism," he asserted. It followed that Christianity can be understood only on the basis of its critically-established historical background and development. In 1913 Troeltsch noted that the superiority of the history of religions approach was becoming so widely recognized that it was losing its identity as the property of a school. History of religions historicism was simply the *method* that all serious scholarship had to employ.[28]

Barth did not dispute the plausibility or integrity of the history of religions approach on its own terms. Herrmann had taught him that while historical criticism should never be viewed as a constitutive element or form of theology, historiocritical interpretation is valuable as a means of attaining intellectual freedom from Christian dogma and tradition.[29] In this outside or even prolegomenal function, Barth asserted, Christian theologians should welcome the most radical historical criticism imaginable, even if, as in his case, they rarely actually used it. In any case, he insisted, the crucial point was that in its own sphere, Christian theology is obliged to listen to scripture in a different way, seeking to hear the Word of God.

This appeal to a Self-revealing Word acquired greater security and theological substance than Herrmann's resort to the inner life of Jesus. Herrmann appealed to biblical passages pertaining to the messianic consciousness of Jesus that later biblical scholarship, notably Bultmann's *History of the Synoptic Tradition,* attributed to the church.[30] Though he sought to make clear that it was the power of Jesus himself (mediated by the gospel records) to which he appealed, and not to the factuality of Jesus as attested by the gospels or even historical criticism, Herrmann's subsequent followers were left to struggle with the perplexing question of how the "inner life" of Jesus could be ascertainable if all of the biblical testimony about it belongs to the period of second generation Christian reflection.[31]

In the 1950s and 1960s, proponents of the "new hermeneutics" movement sought to rehabilitate Herrmann's picture of Jesus as the ground of faith. Ernst Fuchs, Gerhard Ebeling, and others proposed that instead of focusing on the Bultmannian question of how Jesus became the object of faith, it was more fruitful to return to Herrmann's question of how Christ's witness of faith became the basis of Christian faith. The later Heidegger's theory of language as the primal speaking voice of being provided crucial support for their challenge to Bultmannian existentialism. Bultmann embraced the early Heidegger's phenomenological account of the nothingness-pervaded "thrownness" of human existence, including its view that language is objectivizing and secondary to existence. This philosophical description undergirded his claim that the aim of good biblical scholarship is to recover the understanding of existence that underlies the language of the scriptural text. Heidegger's later philosophy turned away from the existentialist view of language as secondary and objectivizing that he propounded in *Being and Time.* In *Holzwege,* he described language as "that event in which for the first time being as being is disclosed to man." His often-cited 1950 lecture, "Die Sprache," declared at the outset that language "belongs to the closest neighborhood of man's being." This conception of language as the speaking voice of being was taken up by Fuchs and Ebeling to assert, against Bultmann, that history is the history of language spoken as a response to the call of being. Following the later Heidegger's emphasis on the creative primal character of language, they proposed to rethink the significance of Jesus as the "language event" (Fuchs, *Sprachereignis)* or "word event" (Ebeling, *Wortgeschehen)* of faith. Fuchs and Ebeling sought to recover the "language event" behind the theological formulations of early Christian preaching, a project that required, as they affirmed, a new generational quest for the historical Jesus.[32]

Bultmann opposed this historical quest for basically the same reasons he opposed its predecessors. Though all of the players in this debate quoted

Herrmann for support, Bultmann suggested that his own combination of historical criticism and existential interpretation saved the core of Herrmann's message in its most credible form. He objected that those who invested theological significance in the "inner life" of Jesus or the "language event" behind the early church's kerygma unavoidably based Christian faith on some purported historical fact about Jesus. Against Herrmann's deeper purpose, he objected, the latter-day Herrmannians thus launched another ill-advised quest for the historical Jesus and exposed "Christian faith" to the possibility of historical refutation. They tried to rescue Herrmann's "inner life of Jesus" motif by clothing it with a new form of its supposed objective content. The "new hermeneutics" movement thereby lost the Herrmannian insight that faith *is* an existence. Bultmann protested that this was what came from treating faith, falsely, as the acceptance of some particular historical fact.[33]

Herrmann's appeal to the saving power of Christ's inner life was thus inextricably fraught with the very kind of historical complications that his argument tried to avoid. In his later career Barth shook his head at the outbreak of a theological controversy over Herrmann's legacy on this subject. To him it was as though theology had returned to the sandbox. The gains of his own return to the revealing-Word were being swept away even by theologians that he respected, such as Fuchs and Ebeling. All of Barth's work from *The Epistle to the Romans* onward sought to listen for the Word of God that disrupts and transcends all historical categories. There *is* a genuinely Christian self-authenticating alternative to history of religions historicism, he urged, but its basis is the revealed Word that eludes human control. To read the Bible with the presuppositions of *Religionsgeschichtliche* criticism in mind is to close off the possibility that the Word will be heard. To read the biblical creation stories as examples of religious myth analogous to the myths of other religions, for example, is to understand scripture according to the presuppositions of a colonizing academic discipline. By this procedure the biblical witness is discarded at the outset.

MYTH AND HISTORY

Barth did not deny that there are myths and even outright fairy tales in the materials out of which some of the biblical narratives were constructed. What he did strenuously dispute was the modernist assumption that a biblical narrative must be historical in order to be a true witness of God's Word. In this respect his theology differed sharply from the theologies of many of his neoorthodox followers in the Biblical Theology movement. Barth insisted that to hear scriptural narrative as God's Word has nothing necessarily to do with defending its historical character or some putative historical element within it. To the contrary, the notion that biblical narratives must be historical in some sense in order to convey God's truth is a disastrous inheritance of both theological liberalism and orthodoxy: "Both Liberalism and orthodoxy are children of the same insipid spirit, and it is useless to follow them," he asserted. There is no good reason "why the Bible as the true witness of the Word of God should always have to speak 'historically' and not be allowed also to speak in the form of saga."[34]

Herrmann vigorously asserted the right of theologians to speak of Christianity as "historical" apart from any claim to historiocritical demonstration. Barth embraced this claim and expanded upon it. He defended the right and necessity of affirming the historicity of New Testament events that do not submit to historiocritical control. In a similar spirit he invented the phrase "non-historical history" to provide a category for biblical accounts that he believed should not be categorized as mythical. The biblical creation stories offer pure examples of what he called the Word spoken through "non-historical history." Barth emphasized that the creation stories are narratives about the history of creation. They do not present timeless mythical truths or a philosophy of creation; they present narrative accounts of once-for-all words and acts. As accounts of particular events, Barth reasoned, the creation stories do describe a kind of history, but it is a non-historical history in which God is the only content. In the modern critical sense of the term, there can be no "history" of an event that has no creaturely element. These accounts nonetheless take the narrative form because they do mean to witness to historical reality, albeit a reality that does not submit to any of the tests of critical history.

Barth appreciated that the notion of non-historical history exemplified by scriptural narrative is puzzling (at best) to the modern Western mind. He noted that modern readers are inclined to interpret Genesis as "a more or less explicit myth, in the poor light of which the historical, what is supposed to be the only genuine history, can only seem to be an ocean of tedious inconsequence and therefore demoniac chaos." He countered that this seemingly obvious reading is not an option for genuinely Christian theology, however, because it is alien to biblical faith: "We must not on any account take this course. In no way is it necessary or obligatory to maintain this rigid attitude to the 'non-historical' reality, conception and description of history. On the contrary, it is necessary and obligatory to realise the fact and manner that in genuine history the 'historical' and 'non-historical' accompany each other and belong together." Modern Christians assume that Genesis is either myth or (bad) history because the modern Western mind has a chronic lack of imagination, he observed: "It acts as if only 'historical' history were genuine history, and 'non-historical' false. The obvious result is to banish from the portrayal and understanding of history all immediacy of history to God on the pretext of its non-historicity, dissolving it into a bare idea!" For Barth it was precisely this "ridiculous and middle-class habit of the modern Western mind" that had to be given up if the Word in the biblical witness was to be heard.[35]

What kind of literature is non-historical history? Barth proposed the term *saga,* "an intuitive and poetic picture of a pre-historical reality of history which is enacted once and for all within the confines of time and space." In his assessment the biblical creation stories are pure sagas, since they are both non-historical and prehistorical in a distinctively pure sense. Barth judged that scripture otherwise contains few examples of either pure saga or pure (historical) history. Most of the Bible not only mixes saga and history but blends these literary forms so thoroughly together that it is impossible to definitely distinguish one from another.

As the true witness of God's Word, scripture is obliged to speak in the form of saga "precisely because its object and origin are what they are, i.e., not just 'historical' but also frankly 'non-historical.'" Just as the Word is never contained or exhausted by history, the medium of God's Word is never merely historical, either. The Bible would not be scripture if it did not absorb the non-historical element into its witness, "and if it did not usually do it by mingling the two elements." One does not look for revelation only in the historical element that may or may not be possible to disentangle from a particular narrative, he insisted: "The decision about its nature as revelation, the confirmation of its reality as the Word of God, is reached by the fact that in its 'historical' parts and also particularly and precisely in its 'non-historical' (or sagas)—though always in connexion with the former—it attests the history of the great acts of God as genuine history, and that this witness is received and accepted through the power of the Holy Spirit."[36]

Barth invested considerable importance in the distinction between myth and saga because he viewed biblical faith as fundamentally myth-negating. Though he recognized that numerous biblical accounts contain mythical elements, he argued that the biblical witness is never merely mythical in the genuine sense of the term because "genuine myth never means a genuinely pre-historical emergence, a beginning of the reality of man and his cosmos in encounter with distinct divine reality." In a word, genuine myth is always monistic. It knows only the single reality of a sacred cosmos that includes humanity. It may speak of God or gods, but it always understands the divine as a mere agent or agents within the economy of a single consuming reality: "It speaks of creators and creations, but it understands the process of emergence with which it is concerned only as an element in this one reality."

For this reason it is always a mistake to speak of "creation myths," Barth contended, for genuine myth never makes creation its theme or object. "It only appears to tell of creation, but in reality it speaks of a particular view or solution of the enigma of the world; of a combination of real or supposed world-elements by which a man or an era think that they can explain the existence of these elements in their cyclical aspects." It was a telling truism for Barth that human reason and desire find themselves most at home in the world of myth: "On the remarkable road of myth, away from the reality of an everyday view of things, he ascends to the heights of a significant world of images, returning to the final depth of a vision of reality, of the One in All, which is to be seen in the contemplation of that world of images, but only as in a well-polished mirror, while in reality it is a third thing which belongs neither to this world, nor to the reality of an everyday view."[37]

The mythical imagination easily finds a home in its hall of mirrors, but at the expense of having no history. It has no creation, but rests in itself, seeking at-one-ment with a world of its own devising. Since there is no such thing as a genuine creation myth, Barth argued, it is doubly mistaken to describe the biblical creation stories as myths, for the message of these stories is deeply myth-negating. Genesis repudiates the mythic view of humanity and its cosmos as self-moved and self-resting. In the biblical witness God is a sovereign Creator who is distinct from the creature and who acts in history. Scripture does not only *use* narrative, as myth does; scripture is *itself* narrative through and through. It does not teach a philosophical worldview, like philosophy or myth, for what it says can be said only as narrative. "Putting it this way, and only in this way, it really speaks of God's creation and it really speaks pre-historically, attesting that the reality of man and of his cosmos is not infinite, that it is not the One and All of reality, but that it has a genuine horizon which cannot be transcended and which cannot be absorbed in the immanence of that reality," Barth observed.[38] This horizon is the ever-gracious will and activity of the divine Creator, through whom human history bears a transcendent meaning.

By restricting myth to monistic pictures of the One and All, Barth sought to establish that biblical faith is not mythical even when it incorporates mythical elements. He reduced all religious myth to only one kind of myth, taking no account of exceptions to his schematism nor to the problems posed by dying-god mythologies such as Mithraism that closely resemble Christianity. By referring to the mythical aspects of scripture as saga, he denied that biblical faith begins with a spiritual sense of dependence or relation to the whole. Biblical religion begins rather with God's gracious approach to humanity in Christ, the pre-existent Word foreshadowed in Hebrew faith and history. In his resolve to uphold the priority of a revealing myth-negating Word, Barth thus promoted a rather contrived and reductionist theory of myth. He acknowledged only reluctantly that the scriptural witness makes important spiritual use of mythical language. He probably would not have conceded even this much if Bultmann's aggressive pursuit of "demythologization" had not forced him to defend the mythical aspects of the church's testimony to Christ.[39] To him the crucial point was always the Herrmannian theme that Christ himself is the future and ground of all redemptive possibility.

THE WORD WITHOUT CRUTCHES

The eschatological Word is enough. It is never an object of perception or cognition, but can only be believed. The Word is different from all other objects because it gives itself. Barth echoed his liberal teacher's admonition that the crucial choice is between living faithfully by the ever-renewing Spirit of Christ or resorting to sickly substitutes. His list of poor substitutes was considerably longer than Herrmann's. Herrmann opposed apologetics, but he nearly always spoke of religion in positive terms. Barth's list of faith-negating substitutes included every form of natural theology, religious symbolism, and ritual practice. It included even the sacramental notion that the

Word is expressed or made visible through such symbols employed in scripture as the cross or the dove. "We do not believe in symbols," he admonished. Symbolism is a philosophical means of communication, but Christian theology testifies to what God has done. Theology proclaims and repeats the spoken Word offered to the church. "We are *told* to testify by our lives, to live within the community of the Church, to take part in the work of proclamation," he explained. "But who is told to light candles?" Barth allowed that if Paul visited today's churches, he would undoubtedly find most worship services uninspiring and barren, "but he would not suggest that we light candles!" What the church needs instead is an outpouring of the Spirit of Christ, he urged. To prescribe pictures and symbols in this situation is like recommending that an ailing hospital patient change his bed.[40]

Barth was oblivious to the presence of the Spirit of Christ in the images, music, and practices of sacramental religion. Though he employed an exemplary pluralism of views and rhetorical forms within the range of means by which he found the Spirit of Christ to be mediated, his conception of Word-mediation was severely Protestant. Despite his deep affection for Mozart's music, his theology had no room for it as a vehicle of divine expression.[41] When pressed on the point, he did allow that God is free to use any means that God may desire to speak to his church. He even professed to be ready "to be open to God's Word as in fact it may be spoken to me also in nature, history, art, and who knows, even my own heart and conscience." But as a member of the church that God has already called into being, he explained, he was obliged to respect the single means by which God has clearly chosen to speak to his church. We meet Christ only through scripture and scripturally-based preaching. The question of other means must be left to God's omnipotence, as the Second Helvetic Confession asserts.[42] Barth occasionally acknowledged that the liturgical traditions tend to nurture and sustain a deeper spiritual resonance than the non-liturgical Protestant traditions. His friendships with numerous Catholic theologians were inspired partly by his respect for the spiritual depth and beauty of Catholicism. But his commitment to the Reformation principle of *sola Scriptura* precluded any recognition of the Word's movement outside the reading and preaching of scripture. For similar reasons he rejected all appeals to confirming evidence as alien to the Spirit-given circle of faith.

For him the problem of apologetics was like the problem of candles. With Herrmannian conviction Barth urged that it is always a mistake for Christians to try to convince unbelievers that Christianity is rational, reasonable, or historically credible, because every attempt to defend Christianity inevitably takes place upon some standpoint outside faith. The truth of the gospel is then evaluated by a pagan criterion of rationality or meaning. Christian faith neither needs nor is aided by any supporting outside evidence that might be cited, he insisted. Faith is sustained by the movement of the Word only, not by arguments for God's existence or the resurrection of Jesus. To appeal to any outside apologetic is to impede oneself (or the church) from living a Spirit-filled life of faith. In effect, it is to deny revelation. "We cannot believe and yet at the same time not believe but want to know [on independent grounds]," Barth insisted. "This is not to believe at all."[43] If one could prove the resurrection of Jesus historically, it would not *be* the resurrection, for revelation is its own basis. History as a category is too poor and laden with scientific conditions to contain the transhistorical conquest of death that God has accomplished and revealed through Christ.

BARTH AND BULTMANN: HISTORY AND EASTER FAITH

Then how should the historical character of the resurrection be conceived? Was Bultmann right to classify the resurrection of Jesus as a "nature miracle" or "miraculous proof" that must be demythologized? Does it not falsely objectify the Christian understanding of existence to assert that the resurrection of Jesus must have an objective historical character of some kind? If the New Testament writers conceptualized the claims of Easter faith in the language of a mythical worldview that modern science has discredited, what should modern theologians say about the nature of the Easter event? Bultmann argued that the Easter event is not about something that happened to Jesus; Easter is about the rise of faith in Jesus that the first disciples experienced. In a demythologized theology, he explained, the resurrection is not regarded as a nature miracle or proof of Christ's divinity. The resurrection of Christ is properly understood to be an aspect of the church's eschatological kerygmatic message, the supratemporal meaning of which is open only to faith.[44]

Barth was deeply concerned to distinguish his position from this one, not only because he regretted Bultmann's enormous influence in theology, but also because he shared much of Bultmann's theological outlook. In the period of their theological comradeship, both of them took key Herrmannian assumptions for granted, both were strongly influenced by existentialism, both accepted the Weiss-Schweitzer picture of early Christianity as thoroughly eschatological, and both appealed to the authority of a non-objectified revelatory Word as the salvation of modern theology. During his crisis theology period, Barth described the resurrection in terms that were barely distinguishable from Bultmann's. His second edition *Epistle to the Romans* characterized the resurrection as a "non-historical happening" that has meaning only in its eschatological character. "The raising of Jesus from the dead is not an event in history elongated so as still to remain an event in the midst of other events," Barth asserted. "The resurrection is the non-historical relating of the whole historical life of Jesus to its origin in God."[45]

Aside from the assumption that the resurrection took place in history somewhere outside the gates of Jerusalem, he explained, nothing about its "when" or "where" is important to faith. In 1924, Barth's *Die Auferstehung der Toten* similarly assured that "time and place are a matter of perfect indifference" to Easter faith.[46] With his customary attention to scholarly detail, Bultmann lamented that this commentary on 1 Corinthians 15 was somewhat lacking in exegetical clarity and precision. He also protested against Barth's refusal to pursue a critical analysis of Paul's sources and arguments. But Bultmann recognized a kindred spirit in Barth's theological characterization of the resurrection faith. Like Herrmann, both of them still used the terms "faith" and "life" interchangeably. For Barth he explained, as for himself, the resurrection faith was not to be understood in any way as something objective: "It is between time and eternity. In the judgment *of God* we are the justified, and the 'final possibility' that this may become a reality in our temporal life is 'love.' "[47]

To all appearances, for all of their differences on lesser issues, Barth and Bultmann seemed to believe essentially the same thing about Easter faith during their dialectical-movement period. It was on this point of similarity, in particular, that Barth struggled to reposition himself in his later debates with Bultmann. The fact that his later "objectivizing" turn with regard to Easter faith has often been used to support a mistaken reading of his theological development should not be allowed to obscure the fact that he did later distinguish his position from Bultmann's on the question of the historical "happenedness" of the Easter appearances. The conventional reading of Barth's development exaggerates his objectivizing turn in the 1930s and his relinquishment of dialectical modes of argument. As we have seen, Barth's dogmatic turn was already established in 1924, he employed a considerable array of analogical models from the outset, and his later theology continued to emphasize the dialectical movement of God in self-revelation and the dialectic of presence and hiddenness in Christian existence.

These latter elements falsify the image of Barth as the dogmatist of an objectivist neoorthodoxy. He unfailingly emphasized that the dialectic of presence and hiddenness cannot be broken in either direction without betraying the living truth of revelation. To break the dialectic in the direction of presence is to falsely objectify the gospel, he warned; but to overemphasize God's hiddenness or "wholly otherness" is to betray the truth of God's revelation in Christ. All of Barth's theology from the second edition *Epistle to the Romans* onward was permeated with the conviction that true knowledge of God begins with the knowledge of God's hiddenness *and* that the hidden God is apprehended *indirectly* in Christ. In Christ the hidden God is apprehended, he explained, "not to sight, but to faith. Not in His being, but in sign. Not, then, by the dissolution of His hiddenness—but apprehensibly."[48] The Word made flesh is the definitive sign of all signs, but the Word is made known to us only after the flesh, under the veil of human limitations, through the movement of the Spirit.

Nothing that Barth's dogmatic theology affirmed about God's revelation in Christ is comprehensible apart from his stringent insistence that Christ is made known only in sign. The dialectical strictures against objectivism that filled his *Epistle to the Romans* remained crucial to his thinking afterward. His massive volumes on the doctrine of God were pervaded by the dialectic of divine veiling and unveiling. He cautioned repeatedly that God is hidden to us apart from the grace of God's revelation in Christ. We cannot speak even of Christ "without the veil, and therefore without the reservation of His hiddenness."[49]

At the same time Barth's dogmatic thinking did emphasize that God makes his revelatory presence in Christ known to us by the revelatory action of the Spirit. His later thinking added objectivizing elements to his position that sharply distinguished his theology from Bultmann's. In the *Church Dogmatics* Barth affirmed that genuine knowledge of God is always an event "enclosed in the bosom of the divine Trinity." Though it is true that theology works with the disadvantage of attending to a hidden object, and though it is true that theology is therefore restricted to mere approximations in carrying out its work, he explained, theology also has one surpassing advantage over all other disciplines. This advantage is that the revelatory ground of theology is the ground of all truth: "Theology is on firm ground for its undertaking—indeed, on disproportionately firmer ground than all other sciences," Barth contended. It followed for him that the work of theology is properly carried out only in a strong and confident voice. We cannot believe that God raised Jesus from the dead and still want to prove it to ourselves or others, he insisted. God's Spirit is the guarantee that the presence of God in Christ that we indirectly apprehend is sealed in truth. "We know Him in truth, and this knowing may and must be a confident knowing," Barth exhorted. Crisis theology abounded in images of "infinite qualitative distinctions" and of futile attempts to paint birds in flight, but Barth's later dialectics emphasized that real presence *is* one of the poles of genuine Christian existence.[50]

The most significant example of this objectivizing turn in Barth's later theology was his emphasis on the objective character of Christ's resurrection. Against Bultmann, who folded a demythologized existential resurrection into his account of the experience of being crucified with Christ, Barth affirmed that Easter faith is the heart of Christian belief. Against various neoorthodox thinkers who consigned Christ's resurrection appearances to a noumenal realm of divine extrahistory analogous to Kant's noumenal space and time, the later Barth countered that the crucified Christ was raised from the dead in historical space and time. In *Church Dogmatics* IV:2 he described the resurrection as an event that "actually happened among men like other events, and was experienced and later attested by them."[51] Christ's appearances were seen with human eyes and heard with human ears, he affirmed, "in space and time, by the lake and in the cities of Galilee, in Jerusalem, and on the way to it, in the circumstances of specific individuals."[52] Barth heightened the emphatic specificity of this language after a host of Bultmannians, liberals, evangelicals, and even a few Barthians questioned him about it. In *Church Dogmatics* IV:3 he asserted that Christ's resurrection "did not take place in a heavenly or supra-heavenly realm, or as part of an intra-divine movement or a divine conversation, but before the gates of

Jerusalem in the days of Tiberius Caesar and therefore in the place and time which are also ours, in our sphere."[53] Salvation history *(Geschichte)* took place in our sphere, not in some Kantian noumenal world or Platonic heaven beyond the world of ordinary historical experience.

Barth persistently cautioned that the historical concreteness of the resurrection appearances does not make these appearances credible as outside evidences or proofs. The resurrection of Jesus was not a public event open to anyone regardless of faith, he explained. Jesus never appeared to Pontius Pilate or to his Jewish opponents or to the Roman senate or to anyone else who might impress a secular historian. Barth strongly affirmed the modern historiographical principle that an event can be deemed to be historical (factual *Historie*) only if the "how" of its outline can be known independently of the standpoint of the observer and within its general and specific contexts. Moreover, the event in question must have such a character as to be comparable to other historical events. But in the case of the resurrection, he observed, there is no such thing as an outside or impartial witness; moreover, the "what" that is claimed is not analogous to any known historical event. Even the later Barth thus assumed that the resurrection narratives contain only what he called a "tiny margin" of historical material.[54]

Barth assumed with Bultmann that historical knowledge is inherently too ambiguous and relative to serve as the basis of faith. The bewildering variety of historical Jesuses offered up by the past two centuries of biblical scholarship confirmed for both of them the futility of basing one's faith upon any particular historical argument about Jesus. Both of them would have given short shrift to the current wave of historical questers who variously portray the "historical Jesus" as a spiritual visionary, a subversive sage, a marginal non-eschatological moralist, or a parable-spouting cynic.[55] To Barth and Bultmann, the ongoing enterprise of producing even more "historical Jesuses," each of them presented as the "real" figure behind the gospel narratives, was self-refuting. Their refusal to base Christian faith on historical arguments was sealed by their acceptance of the modern historiocritical principle that *Historie* must be assumed to be a closed chain of cause and effect. Barth plainly accepted this principle as reasonable and necessary on its own terms. He acknowledged that the critical historian must look for the sufficient causes of historical events within history. To explain any historical event as caused by divine intervention is to move outside the realm of historical explanation. For this reason, especially, the resurrection narratives cannot be regarded as historical in the modern critical sense of the term.

Barth allowed that Bultmann was right this far. The kinds of events that the gospel narratives describe pertaining to Christ's resurrection are inherently unverifiable from a critical historical standpoint. Critical history knows no miracles. To Barth, the problem with Bultmann's account of the resurrection was the religious conclusion that he drew from this historiocritical standpoint. It is one thing to recognize that the kinds of events portrayed in the resurrection narratives do not submit to historical control, Barth allowed. It is another matter entirely to conclude that these events, therefore, must not have occurred. Bultmann jumped to the latter conclusion. His theology of the resurrection began with the only fragment of the Easter story (besides the crucifixion) that he regarded as historical, which was the rise of faith in Jesus by the first disciples. He dismissed the rest as dispensable myth and apologetics.[56]

Barth countered that this strategy was wrong on both counts. Just because an event cannot be shown on account of its nature to be historical does not mean that it did not or could not have occurred, he insisted. "We may well accept as history that which good taste prevents us from calling 'historical' fact, and which the modern historian will call 'saga' or 'legend' on the ground that it is beyond the reach of his methods, to say nothing of his unavowed assumptions," he explained. "It belongs to the nature of the biblical material that although it forms a consecutive historical narrative it is full of this kind of history and contains comparatively little 'history' in Bultmann's sense."[57] The difference between saga and legend was, to Barth, a matter of degree. Just as the fairy tale is a degenerate form of myth, legend is a degenerate form of saga that depicts an individual personality in the form of saga.[58] In either case, the crucial point for him was that scripture is filled with accounts that mix saga or saga/legend with history, and in most cases, the aspects of biblical narrative that submit to historical control are very small. Yet it would be absurd to assume that none of the events portrayed in biblical saga actually occurred, he observed: "It is is sheer superstition to suppose that only things which are open to 'historical' verification can have happened in time. There may have been events which happened far more really in time than the kind of things Bultmann's scientific historian can prove," such as the resurrection of Jesus.[59]

If Bultmann's first mistake was to dismiss the objectivity of the resurrection on account of its lack of critical historicity, his second mistake was to claim that nothing important is at stake in this negation. Barth countered that belief in the resurrection as something that happened to Jesus is the key to the very existence of Christianity: "It is not peripheral to the New Testament, but central; not inessential or dispensable, but essential and indispensable." Every word of the New Testament presupposes that Jesus was raised from the dead. The Easter event is the starting point for everything that the New Testament says about Jesus and everything else. There is no other Jesus to base a Christology upon and no other basis for Christian existence. "Either we believe with the New Testament in the risen Jesus Christ, or we do not believe in Him at all," Barth declared.[60]

By this standard Bultmann had to be counted among the unbelievers. Bultmann claimed that faith in Christ's resurrection is "nothing other than faith in the cross as the salvation event."[61] He reduced the meaning of the resurrection to an aspect of believing in the cross and reduced the meaning of the cross to the experience of being crucified with Christ. He allowed nothing to be said about the risen Christ as such. For Barth, the resurrection was something that happened first to Jesus and then to the disciples, but, for

Bultmann, the resurrection was a dispensable explanation of the early church's faith. It had the secondary status of what Herrmann called a "thought of faith." Barth replied that one might have hoped that at least with regard to the resurrection, Bultmann would have recognized that some objective referent was necessary to establish a basis for Christian proclamation. But in Bultmann's account, the disciples beheld the glory of the resurrected Christ only after his Lordship was proclaimed and the church's early kerygmatic message was formulated. "He seems to think that in the kerygma Jesus Christ is on his way to rising in us. And that is just why I cannot understand him," Barth concluded. "I am sorry to have to say this."[62]

WORLDVIEWS AND THE WORD OF CHRIST

Bultmann tried to evade Barth's either/or by changing the question. He claimed that the crucial either/or for modern theology is whether it adapts Christianity to a modern worldview. The worldview of the biblical writers was thoroughly mythical, he observed. The biblical writers pictured the world as a three-story structure in which supernatural agents based in heaven (above) and hell (below) waged spiritual warfare for control of human minds and, ultimately, the destiny of earth (the middle ground) itself. Earth was conceived as a theater in which God and his angels and Satan and his demons fought continuously to determine the outcome of history. This mythical world picture pervades every page of the New Testament, Bultmann cautioned. The New Testament picture of salvation derives from it. Christian scripture teaches that a preexistent divine being appeared on earth as a man, atoned for the sin of the world with his death, abolished humanity's sentence of death through his resurrection, vanquished the powers of Satan, ascended to heaven to sit at God's right hand, and is due to return on the clouds at any moment to bring an end to history.[63]

In the manner of his teacher Wilhelm Herrmann, Bultmann played up the absurdity of equating Christian faith with the acceptance of any aspect of this outdated worldview. It is not possible to use a radio and still believe in the New Testament world of demons and spirits, he insisted. We cannot repristinate the mythical worldview of the biblical writers, nor should we wish that we could do so.[64] Herrmann repeatedly cautioned that to make the acceptance of an outdated mythology a demand of faith is to reduce faith to a work. Bultmann urged that theology was therefore obliged to translate the meaning of a demythologized Christian faith into the concepts of a credible modern worldview. He judged that early-Heideggerian existential phenomenology offered the best available vehicle for modernized myth translation.

Barth did not doubt that Herrmann was right about the importance of not equating Christian faith with an ancient worldview. What he did dispute was Bultmann's sacralization of a modern worldview. In Bultmann's case, he observed, theology acquired its modernist seal of approval by accepting the "anthropological straight-jacket" of Herrmann and Schleiermacher. Barth protested that the modernist worldview deserved nothing like this degree of authority in Christian theology. "Is this modern view so binding as to determine in advance and unconditionally our acceptance or rejection of the biblical message?" he asked. "What if modern thought is not so uniform as our Marburg Kantians would have us believe?" Bultmann's "world of fact" was a closed system; he talked about "modern science" and the "world known to modern science" in Newtonian terms. Barth was not interested in pursuing the problems that quantum mechanics posed for Bultmann's mechanistic Newtonian worldview, however, since he had no theological interest in replacing one scientific world-picture with another. His concern cut deeper. What Barth disputed was the basic modernist assumption that theologians are obliged to adapt Christianity to the regnant or best available worldview. "Is it true that we are compelled to reject a statement simply because this statement, or something like it, was compatible with the mythical worldview of the past?" he asked.[65]

His answer was that theology should not be in the business of endorsing worldviews of any kind: "After all, is it our job as Christians to accept or reject world-views? Have not Christians always been eclectic in their worldviews—and this for very good reasons?" Rather than commit itself to any particular worldview, he proposed, theology should use or appropriate as many worldviews and forms of language as are necessary to explicate the truth of the Word. Just as theology should not privilege literal meaning over the language of paradox, irony, and dialectic, neither should theology commit itself to the enervating task of adopting and then discarding one worldview after another. A healthy pluralism in philosophy and rhetorical forms is needed if theology is to be free to do its work of locating the event of correspondence between human word and divine truth.[66]

If this debate had broken out during their crisis theology period, Barth undoubtedly would have pressed the problem of idolatry. He could have argued that the biblical sanction against idolatry applies to worldviews. To invest spiritual significance in the credibility of an up-to-date worldview is to sacralize an idol that will someday be discredited. Any theology that ties itself too closely to the physics or popular science of its time is guaranteed to become obsolete before long.[67] By the time that Barth's conflict with Bultmann was fully aired in the late 1940s and early 1950s, however, Barth was less disposed to press this kind of argument against his theological opponents. His somewhat-softened attitude toward religion made him less inclined to see "idolatry" in every mistaken theology.

He argued instead that Bultmann's modernist chauvinism caused him to unfairly demean the worldview of the biblical writers. "We ought not to overlook the fact that this particular world-view contained a number of features which the primitive community used cautiously but quite rightly in its witness to Jesus Christ," Barth observed. He urged that it was precisely because modern people do not speak of demons and spirits that contemporary theology found itself in the position of needing to recover these lost features of the biblical message. Contemporary theology needed, above all, to recover the dimension of spiritual mystery that two centuries of modernizing theological liberalism had drained away. "Consequently we have every reason to make use of 'mythical' language in certain connexions," Barth insisted. "And there is no need for us to have a guilty conscience about it, for if we went to extremes in demythologising, it would be quite impossible to bear witness to Jesus Christ at all." Faced with Bultmann's enormously influential deconstruction of Christian myth, Barth was driven to the very un-Barthian resort of defending the mythical character of Christian speech, defending myth as an indispensable vehicle of the revealing-Word. Bultmann dismissed the biblical connection between sin and death and spurned the mythical way that scripture relates death to resurrection. Barth protested that this is what comes from assuming that theology must always replace an outdated worldview with a new one: "To speak of the 'rise of the Easter faith' in the first disciples is a good thing. But we cannot pretend that this is an adequate substitute for what is now rejected as the 'mythical' witness to the resurrection of Jesus Christ from the dead."[68]

The echoes of 1 Corinthians 15 were strong whenever Barth spoke of the resurrection: "If Christ has not been raised, then our proclamation has been in vain and your faith has been in vain" (1 Cor. 15:14). Like Paul, Barth had no interest in following Christ if Christ merely exemplified a mythic or moral ideal. Like Paul, he had little interest in religion as such and no interest in comparing Christianity to other religions. Though his later theology softened the antireligion polemics of his second edition *Epistle to the Romans,* Barth steadfastly upheld the Pauline theme that religion itself never saved anyone. With Paul he affirmed that salvation is attainable only through the Lord who wills salvation for all people and who "has put all things in subjection under his feet" (1 Cor. 15:27). The notion that Christian theology should affirm all world religions as equal means of salvation was therefore absurd to him. There is no point in trying to find points of agreement among religions regarding salvation, he reasoned, since religion does not bring salvation. To Barth it was possible to speak of true religion "only in the sense in which we speak of a 'justified sinner.' "[69]

Just as Hegel played upon the ambiguity of the German verb *Aufhebung* in developing his dialectic, Barth played upon the dialectical character of the same term in establishing the relation between revelation and religion. In Hegelian usage, the term implies not only negation or abolition, but also the process of overcoming. In Barth's appropriation of Hegelian dialectic, the status of religion was analogous to the status of the unjustified sinner. When a person is justified by faith through grace, he reasoned, the person does not leave behind the condition of being a sinner. He or she brings this condition forward—as negated and overcome—into her new life as a justified sinner. In Hegelian terms, justification is not simply a positive good, but the negation of the negative. Barth's view of religion followed the same logic. All religion stands under judgment, including Christianity, just as all sinners stand under judgment. A religion can *become* true only in the same way that a sinner can become justified, he argued, for "the true religion, like the justified human being, is a creature of *grace*."[70]

It followed for him that most of the energies of modern interreligious dialogue were focused on a false problem. Only God can make God known, and only God can save humankind. The hope of the world is not religion, but God's ever-gracious mercy. That is, the hope of the world is the ever-gracious Word, Jesus Christ, who elects all people to salvation.[71] Christ is the only Way and Truth that we need. Christianity needs no other foundation or apparatus to justify its claims. Barth never worked out the implications of his suggestion that non-Christian religions might be used by God as vehicles of God's unlimited justifying grace. This shortcoming derived as much from his lack of personal interest in other religions as from the logic of his Christocentric emphasis. Even his nearly-explicit universalism was chastened by the hedge that we cannot know for sure whether the Pauline vision of the universal eschatological triumph of grace should be taken literally. In Romans 5:18–19, 1 Corinthians 15:22, and 2 Corinthians 5:17–19, Paul states that Christ has reconciled all persons to God through his saving death. Colossians 1:20 remarks that God has determined through his Son as his image and as the firstborn of the whole creation to "reconcile to himself all things." Barth held out for the literal universality of these statements without claiming to know for certain that Paul or the author of Colossians was a universalist. He exhorted that, at the very least, Christians should consider whether these statements "could not perhaps have a good meaning." The Pauline image of a wholly reconciled creation in which God is "all in all" seems to exclude the notion of a realm of eternal separation from God depicted in other New Testament texts, he judged.[72]

He was considerably more decisive and strenuous in resisting the judgment that the New Testament is also ambiguous in its witness to faith and revelation alone. This insistence applied especially to Paul. Barth admonished that the claims of Easter faith are inherently unverifiable from the standpoint of critical history. The "non-historical" nature of the Easter event and the lack of "public" witnesses to it preclude any possible claim to critical historicity; we know nothing about the witnesses to the resurrection apart from the partisan faith-testimonies of the New Testament; and the act of divine intervention claimed by Easter faith cannot be verified by an understanding of history that excludes divine intervention as a hypothetical cause. These considerations reinforced his contention that theology must begin with revelation, not with religious questions or philosophical arguments or historical evidence. Faith is not the end of an argument. To establish or support faith with an appeal to outside evidence is to undermine faith in the revealed Word, which is its own basis.

Does this mean that no appeal to evidence can be legitimate even as a factor that confirms or supports one's faith? Is it true that we cannot believe in Christ "and still want to know" whatever can be known about God or Jesus on the basis of reason? Barth's Herrmannian answer pressed the Pauline doctrine of faith to an extreme that Paul might not have recognized, given his predisposition to persuade people with whatever evidence he possessed that Christ was the resurrected Son of God. Though he may have wished that the resurrected Jesus had appeared to Pilate or the Roman senate, the fact that Paul could not produce any "neutral" or outside witnesses to the resurrection did not prevent him from appealing to the testimonies of the witnesses that he knew. Since all of the witnesses to the resurrection were believers, the concept of a "non-believing witness" would have made little sense to him. When he heard that even some church members in Corinth did not believe in the resurrection, Paul sought to convince them otherwise by appealing to a list of witnesses who saw Jesus after his crucifixion.

The evidence that he presented included fragments of what was undoubtedly a very early Christian creed—"For I handed on to you as of first importance what I in turn had also received" (1 Cor. 15:3)—and which was already stylized, through repetition, when he wrote 1 Corinthians in the early 50s.[73] It included the teaching that Jesus appeared first to Cephas, "then to the twelve. Then he appeared to more than five hundred brothers and sisters at one time, most of whom are still alive, though some have died. Then he appeared to James, then to all the apostles. Last of all, as to one untimely born, he appeared also to me" (1 Cor. 15: 5–8). Paul's reference to the five hundred and his clinching reference to his own experience were undoubtedly meant to convince skeptics inside and outside the church alike with evidence. If the skeptics did not believe the church's preaching about Christ's resurrection, he implied, they should speak to the witnesses, most of whom were still alive.

Bultmann straightforwardly judged that this appeal to historical evidence was ill-advised and anti-kerygmatic. "I can understand the text only as an attempt to make the resurrection of Christ credible as an objective historical fact," he remarked. "And I see only that Paul is betrayed by his apologetic into contradicting himself." That is, Paul's appeal to rationally convicting evidence betrayed his evangelical appeal to revelation. The resurrection as an eschatological event cannot be claimed in faith if the resurrection is an objective historical fact, Bultmann insisted. By referring to historical evidence to establish his faith in the eschatological victory of Christ over the powers of death, Paul undermined his appeal to the convicting power of the Word that is knowable only through faith.[74]

This was not a tolerable verdict for Barth, however. He could not take the view that Paul was simply wrong about such a crucial matter. He therefore denied that 1 Corinthians 15 contained an appeal to evidence. "An 'evidence' would be a witness *outside* the Church," he contended. "Here Paul is just showing the unity of the Church in the resurrection faith."[75] The witnesses were believers whose testimony is part of the gospel message. If Paul had appealed (or been able to appeal) to evidence for the resurrection brought by a true outsider, this would have represented a claim based on historical evidence. But no such claim was either possible or desirable, Barth insisted, for historical evidence does nothing to strengthen true Christian faith. Like the proofs of God's existence, arguments from historical evidence encourage Christians to put their faith in the evidence rather than God's revelation. Christian faith is thus reduced to an opinion about relative historical matters, just as Herrmann warned. The upshot is that one is led to believe in a crutch instead of revelation. In the case of the resurrection, Barth admonished, if one could historically demonstrate that the resurrection of Christ must have occurred, the thing that would be proven would not be the resurrection, for historical reason can demonstrate only that which it controls.

DIALECTICS OF THE WORD

Barth once remarked that Herrmann was an independent thinker who was always strongest when he spun his own thread.[76] As a church theologian Barth resisted the verdict that the same was true of him, but to a considerable extent, especially on the topics that this study has highlighted, it was. His arguments against natural revelation and apologetics were always stronger than his claim that he was merely explicating the views of Calvin and Paul. He might have convinced more theologians to follow his approach to theology had he come clean on the difference. Barth's appeal to the spirit of Calvin and Paul was fundamentally warranted, but he pressed the logic of this position to an extreme that was not compatible with Calvin's (very limited) conception of natural revelation or Paul's (equally limited) appeals to outside evidence. This distinction could have been pressed to support a "faith seeking understanding" form of apologetics that considered and defended evidentialist judgments *without* basing faith claims on reasons prior to faith. Having committed himself to a thoroughly exclusionary position on this question, however, Barth was forced to distort Paul's argument to make Paul agree with him. While it is undoubtedly correct to judge that Paul was chiefly concerned in 1 Corinthians 15 to show the unity of the church in the resurrection faith, it is not plausible that Paul made such arguments only with insiders or for the purpose of illustration. 1 Corinthians 15 made apologetic claims that Paul undoubtedly employed to persuade skeptical outsiders and wavering insiders that Christ really did rise from the dead.

Moreover, even Barth could not deny that the Gospel writers occasionally made appeals to evidence to support their kerygmatic claims. He admitted that Matthew offered "feeble evidence" for the resurrection in his story about the chief priests and elders paying the guards of Jesus' tomb not to reveal what had taken place (Matt. 28: 11–15). He was driven to distinguish between "persuasive events" and "rational persuasion as proof" in explaining the Gospel references to miracles of Jesus that "caused many to believe." Barth claimed that the miracles of Jesus were merely persuasive events, not intended or used as demonstrations of anything. He contended that the reference to the "proofs" of Jesus' resurrection in Acts 1:3 was unfortunate and misleading.[77] Just as he resisted the evidence that much of Christianity is mythical in the ordinary history of religions sense of the term, he strained to deny that the Word is compatible with supportive arguments for it, even when scripture alludes to them.

Barth always objected that his approach was not fideistic or anti-historical in the narrow sense. He used reason to understand Christian faith in all of its complexity. In principle he believed that the entire arsenal of form critical, redaction critical, and other historiocritical methodologies should be employed as prolegomena to the work of dogmatics. He insisted that the theorizing of dogmatic theologians should always be informed by the historical, literary, and hermeneutical judgments of biblical criticism. He wanted biblical scholars and theologians to work together to deconstruct the biblical text as a first step toward a fuller understanding of scripture as canon in its wholeness. His own work took little note of the biblical scholarship of his time, however. Barth did most of his own exegesis in the *Church Dogmatics* because, as he complained, most biblical scholars were content to take the text apart and leave the reconstructive work of theology to theologians. Barth was too wary of this enterprise to make use of its findings. In 1948 he remarked that "the time does not yet seem to have arrived when the dogmatician can accept with a good conscience and confidence the findings of his colleagues in Old and New Testament studies." Conventional biblical scholarship conceived its task too narrowly for his taste and proceeded without any acknowledgment of its religious assumptions or consequences. As long as this situation obtained among biblical scholars, Barth asserted, "so long as so many still seem to pride themselves on being utterly unconcerned as to the dogmatic presuppositions and consequences of their notions, while unwittingly reading them into the picture, the dogmatician is forced to run the same risk as the non-expert and work out his own proof from Scripture."[78]

As long as biblical critics merely deconstructed the text without any recognition of its character as sacred scripture, no cooperation between biblical criticism and theology was possible for him. As long as biblical scholars read scripture as the product of a mythical or otherwise outdated worldview, the Word-oriented theologian would have to do her own exegesis. Barth's call for a new kind of biblical scholarship helped to inspire the Biblical Theology movement, which heightened Barth's insistence on the history-oriented distinctiveness and anti-mythical character of biblical faith. This movement dominated Old Testament scholarship in England and the United States during the 1940s and 1950s and produced an admirable body of scholarship. Long after the movement lost its hegemonic influence and its movement-character, neoorthodox biblical scholars such as Brevard Childs continued to produce prototypes of the kind of integrative, canonical biblical theology that Barth longed to see.[79]

The Biblical Theology movement exaggerated the distinctiveness of Hebrew religion, however, and it failed to justify its defining claims about the historicity of God's "mighty acts" in biblical history. James Barr shrewdly noted that it relied heavily upon a notion of "biblical history" that was foreign to scripture itself. Barr demolished the Biblical Theology attempt to contrast Hebrew and Greek thought patterns on the basis of purported differences in Hebrew and Greek semantics.[80] During the same period, Langdon Gilkey's pointed questions about what God actually did in the Exodus events proved to be remarkably deflating for what had seemed to be a well-entrenched and certainly dominating biblical studies establishment.[81] The Biblical Theology movement was weakened by its hubris in claiming an historical foundation that it did not possess. Though most of its proponents considered themselves to be "neoorthodox" or even "Barthian" thinkers, they would have done better to actually follow Barth's example. Their movement would not have collapsed so suddenly or with such shattering finality if they had vested their faith in the church-received Word that subverts and transcends all historical categories.

Though he pressed this argument to an extreme conclusion that required tendentious readings of Calvin and certain scriptural passages, Barth was right to insist that the questions of subject position and total context are crucially determinative in all matters pertaining to religious knowledge. He rightly protested that theologians across the religious spectrum routinely defended positions regarding the nature of the Word and the scope of scriptural authority without taking care to address the question of the context in which scripture is properly approached and interpreted. His own discussion of the nature of biblical authority took place within his explication of the threefold doctrine of the Word of God in order to avoid this mistake.

The Word of God revealed is Jesus Christ, he affirmed; the Word of God written is the scriptural witness; the Word of God proclaimed is the preaching of the church. These three forms of God's Word are not separable, yet there is a clear ordering among them. The biblical witness is subordinate to the revealed Word, Jesus Christ, to whom it points, and the church's proclamation is subordinate to the biblical witness. Barth urged that this is the comprehensive context in which the biblical witness must be approached as Christian scripture.[82] Scott Saye observes that Barth's three forms can be thought of as concentric circles with Christ at the center, scripture encircling Christ, and the church's proclamation encircling the biblical witness.[83] The flow of authority is from the center (Christ) through the inner circle (scripture) to the outer circle (church), but the order of knowing moves from the church to scripture to Christ.

Christ can thus be known only in the church through the witness of the church's written Word. More precisely, the Word discloses itself through the power of the Spirit by means of the church's canonical scripture and its proclamation. Therefore we meet the direct Word of God only indirectly. The revealed Word underlies the other forms of the Word, Barth observed, but it "never meets us anywhere in abstract form."[84] Just as scripture must be proclaimed in the church to become God's Spirit-illuminated Word for us, the revealed or "direct" Word of God meets us only in the twofold mediacy of scripture and proclamation.

This is the context in which the charge of *Offenbarungspositivismus* is most appropriately judged. Were Bonhoeffer and so many others right to accuse Barth of reducing theology to like-it-or-lump-it "revelational positivism"? In the broad sense of the phrase, Barth surely was a revelational positivist. He made historical claims on dogmatic grounds and defended certain doctrinal positions—such as his affirmation of the virgin birth of Christ—on exactly the wholistic dogmatic grounds that Bonhoeffer described. In the more precise sense of the phrase, however, Barth was justified in protesting that he was not a revelational positivist. In the early days of his turn to dogmatic theology, he reminded Eduard Thurneysen that their protest against the degeneration of the church had led them first to the Bible and then to the ancient dogmas of the church.[85] This remained the pattern of Barthian theology. Barth corrected liberal theology by appealing to the superior spiritual depth and richness of church dogma, but he claimed no authority for church dogma apart from its faithful witness to scriptural teaching. In the precise sense of the phrase, he was not a revelational positivist because he did not appeal to church-established dogmas of revelation prior to or apart from his exegesis of the inscripturated Word. For all of the scholastic appearances of his massive dogmatic project, it remained something of a misnomer even to speak of "Barthianism" or "Barthian theology," for Barth conceived theology as exegesis and reflection upon a radically open Word of Christ that subverts and transcends all theological systems.

The priority of the Spirit-illuminated Word negated the possibility or even desirability of a definitive system. Barth vigorously affirmed for this reason that his dogmatic project was not a system. He eschewed all attempts to systematize the arguments that he variously propounded over the decades of writing the *Church Dogmatics.* He offered no apology for the numerous shifts in position that his dogmatics contained with regard to the doctrines of humanity, baptism, the humanity of God, the role of narrative in scripture, and other issues. Brunner once observed that the *Church Dogmatics* contained "so many contradictory statements" that it defied all attempts to derive a systematic position from Barth: "Again and again it has occurred to me that you understand Barth best when you take him not so much as a systematic theologian but as one who has first one insight and then another which he puts into words as they come, without worrying whether they fit closely together in a system."[86]

This judgment was rendered at least partly as a reproach, but it actually described reasonably well the way that Barth approached the work of theology, with two critical omissions. The first was that Brunner failed to acknowledge that Barth's succession of insights derived from his continual open-ended struggle to discern the meaning of the inscripturated Word, which does not submit to settled judgments. Barth was unsystematic because he believed that scriptural teaching cannot rightly be reduced to a system. The second missing factor was the crucial question of the context in which theology is appropriately carried out. Barth insisted that the Spirit-illuminated Word is self-authenticating for all authentically Christian proclamation and theology, but he urged with equal force that this process of authentication must never be viewed as coming upon individuals in isolation or abstraction from the church. The Word is always indissolubly unified with the texts, tradition, and present life of the church, he affirmed. At the same time it is always necessary for theology to distinguish between the Word and the text, the text and the Christian community, and the church's present creeds and future possibilities.

No dogmatic system or systematized theological method can rightly deliver the church's collective self-understanding from this paradoxical and relative process. The gospel conveys the radically new possibilities of God, which are glimpsed only indirectly and in fragments. The Word of Christ is an eschatological reality that relativizes all historical possibilities and achievements. In this sense above all others, Barth's theology remained a dialectics of the open Word.

NOTES

Introduction

1. Hans Urs von Balthasar, *The Theology of Karl Barth,* trans. John Drury (New York: Holt, Rinehart & Winston, 1971), 48–150; Thomas F. Torrance, *Karl Barth: An Introduction to His Early Theology, 1910–1931* (London: SCM Press, 1962), 48–198.
2. Eberhard Mechels, *Analogie bei Erich Przywara und Karl Barth: Das Verhältnis von Offenbarungstheologie und Metaphysik* (Neukirchen-Vluyn: Neukirchener Verlag, 1974); Ingrid Spieckermann, *Gotteserkenntnis: Ein Beitrag zur Grundfrage der neuen Theologie Karl Barths* (Munich: Chr. Kaiser Verlag, 1985); Michael Beintker, *Die Dialektik in der 'dialektischen Theologie' Karl Barths* (Munich: Chr. Kaiser Verlag, 1987); Trutz Rendtorff, "Radikale Autonomie Gottes: Zum Verständnis der Theologie Karl Barths und ihre Folgen," in *Theorie des Christentums: Historisch-theologisch Studien zu seiner neuzeitlichen Verfassung* (Gütersloh: Gütersloher Verlagshaus Gerd Mohn, 1972), 164–74; Eberhard Jüngel, "Von der Dialektik zur Analogie: Die Schule Kierkegaards und der Einspruch Petersons," in *Barth-Studien* (Gütersloh: Gütersloher Verlagshaus Gerd Mohn, 1982), 127–79.
3. Bruce L. McCormack, *Karl Barth's Critically Realistic Dialectical Theology: Its Genesis and Development, 1909–1936* (Oxford: Clarendon Press, 1995); George Hunsinger, *How to Read Karl Barth: The Shape of His Theology* (New York: Oxford University Press, 1991); Walter Lowe, *Theology and Difference: The Wound of Reason* (Bloomington, Ind.: Indiana University Press, 1993); Graham Ward, *Barth, Derrida and the Language of Theology* (Cambridge: Cambridge University Press, 1995); William Stacy Johnson, *The Mystery of God: Karl Barth and the Postmodern Foundations of Theology* (Louisville, Ky.: Westminster John Knox Press, 1997); Hans W. Frei, *Types of Christian Theology,* ed. George Hunsinger and William C. Placher (New Haven, Conn.: Yale University Press, 1992), 38–46; David H. Kelsey, *The Uses of Scripture in Recent Theology* (Philadelphia: Fortress Press, 1975), 39–50.
4. Friedrich-Wilhelm Marquardt, *Theologie und Sozialismus: Das Beispiel Karl Barths,* 3rd ed. (Munich: Chr. Kaiser Verlag, 1985). See Helmut Gollwitzer, *Reich Gottes und Sozialismus bei Karl Barth* (Munich: Chr. Kaiser Verlag, 1972); George Hunsinger, ed., *Karl Barth and Radical Politics* (Philadelphia: Westminster Press, 1976).
5. Karl Barth, "How My Mind Has Changed," in *How I Changed My Mind* (Richmond: John Knox Press, 1966), 41. This article appeared, originally, in 1938 in *The Christian Century.*
6. McCormack, *Karl Barth's Critically Realistic Dialectical Theology,* 1–28; Hunsinger, *How to Read Karl Barth,* 3–23.
7. See G. W. F. Hegel, *Phenomenology of Spirit,* trans. A. V. Miller (Oxford: Clarendon Press, 1977), 453–78; Hegel, *Lectures on the Philosophy of Religion,* vol. 3, trans. E. B. Speirs and J. Burdon Sanderson (New York: Humanities Press, 1974), 134–51. On the influence of Hegel and (perhaps) the right-Hegelian Philipp K. Marheineke on Barth's conception of revelation, see Wolfhart Pannenberg, *Revelation as History,* trans. D. Granskou (New York: Macmillan & Co., 1968), 3–6. For definitions of neoorthodoxy, see James Richmond, "Neo-Orthodoxy," in *The Westminster Dictionary of Christian Theology,*

ed. Alan Richardson and John Bowden (Philadelphia: Westminster Press, 1983), 395; Langdon Gilkey, "Neo-orthodoxy," in *A Handbook of Christian Theology,* ed. Marvin Halverson and Arthur A. Cohen (Cleveland: World Publishing Co., 1958), 256–61.

8. Gilkey, "Neo-orthodoxy," 260.
9. Charles E. Raven, *The Gospel and the Church: A Study of Distortion and Its Remedy* (London: Hodder & Stoughton, 1939), 219–21; Gordon H. Clark, *Karl Barth's Theological Method* (Philadelphia: Presbyterian and Reformed Publishing Co., 1963), 109–50, 185–225; Wolfhart Pannenberg, *Systematic Theology* vol. 1, trans. Geoffrey W. Bromiley (Grand Rapids: Wm. B. Eerdmans Publishing Co., 1991), 44–48; David Tracy, *Blessed Rage for Order: The New Pluralism in Theology* (New York: Seabury Press, 1975), 27–31. Tracy argues that the entire neoorthodox movement shared (perhaps only to a lesser degree) in this failing of Barth's.
10. Reinhold Niebuhr, "The Truth in Myths," in *The Nature of Religious Experience: Essays in Honor of Douglas Clyde Macintosh,* ed. J. S. Bixler et al. (New York: Harper & Brothers, 1937), 132–33; Paul Tillich, "What is wrong with the 'dialectic' theology?" *The Journal of Religion* 35, no. 2 (April 1935): 127–45.
11. Hermann Diem, *Dogmatik: Ihr Weg zwischen Historismus und Existenzialismus* (Munich: Chr. Kaiser Verlag, 1955); Otto Weber, *Grundlagen der Dogmatik,* vol. 1 (Neukirchen, Kreis Moers: Verlag der Buchhandlung des Erziehungsvereins, 1955); Alan Richardson, *Christian Apologetics* (London: SCM Press, 1947); William Hordern, *The Case for a New Reformation Theology* (Philadelphia: Westminster Press, 1959); Paul Sevier Minear, *Eyes of Faith: A Study in the Biblical Point of View* (Philadelphia: Westminster Press, 1946).
12. See Langdon B. Gilkey, "Introduction: A Retrospective Glance at My Work," in *The Whirlwind in Culture: Frontiers in Theology,* ed. Donald W. Musser and Joseph L. Price (Bloomington, Ind.: Meyer-Stone Books, 1988), 7–8, 13–16; Gilkey, "An Appreciation of Karl Barth," in *How Karl Barth Changed My Mind,* ed. Donald K. McKim (Grand Rapids: Wm. B. Eerdmans Publishing Co., 1986), 150–52.
13. See Langdon Gilkey, "Cosmology, Ontology and the Travail of Biblical Language," *The Journal of Religion* 41, no. 2 (July 1961): 196–203; James Barr, "Revelation Through History in the Old Testament and in Modern Theology," *Princeton Seminary Bulletin* 56 (1963): 4–14; Barr, *The Semantics of Biblical Language* (London: Oxford University Press, 1961).
14. See Jürgen Moltmann, *Theology of Hope: On the Ground and the Implications of a Christian Eschatology,* trans. James W. Leitch (London: SCM Press, 1967); Wolfhart Pannenberg, *Basic Questions in Theology,* vol. 1, trans. George H. Kihm (Philadelphia: Fortress Press, 1970), esp. 81–95. Citation from author's discussion with Moltmann, October 10, 1997.
15. Sidney E. Ahlstrom, "The Radical Turn in Theology and Ethics: Why It Occurred in the 1960s," *Annals of the American Academy of Political and Social Science* 387 (January 1970): 1–13.
16. On Barth's antifeminism, see Jürgen Moltmann, "Henriette Visser 't Hooft und Karl Barth," in *Gotteslehrerinnen,* ed. Luise Schottroff and Johannes Thiele (Stuttgart: Kreuz Verlag, 1989), 169–79. For other reasons, see Gary Dorrien, *The Word as True Myth: Interpreting Modern Theology* (Louisville, Ky.: Westminster John Knox Press, 1997), 230–31.
17. See Wilhelm Pauck, *Karl Barth: Prophet of a New Christianity?* (New York: Harper & Brothers, 1931); Pauck, *Harnack and Troeltsch: Two Historical The-*

ologians (New York: Oxford University Press, 1968), 43–45; discussion of Pauck in David Tracy, *Blessed Rage for Order,* 27.

18. For example, see Lonnie D. Kliever, *The Shattered Spectrum: A Survey of Contemporary Theology* (Atlanta: John Knox Press, 1981); James M. Wall, ed., *Theologians in Transition: The Christian Century "How My Mind Has Changed" Series* (New York: Crossroad Publishing Co., 1981). Though his major work, *God as the Mystery of the World,* found enough readers to require three editions in its first year, Jüngel noted in the Foreword to the third edition that he had no longer expected to find such readers. The mode of discourse to which it belonged "had largely been forgotten and probably also repressed, if not made quite purposefully the object of suspicion," he judged. See Eberhard Jüngel, *God as the Mystery of the World: On the Foundation of the Theology of the Crucified One in the Dispute between Theism and Atheism,* trans. Darrell L. Guder (Grand Rapids: Wm. B. Eerdmans Publishing Co., 1983), xiii.
19. Tracy, *Blessed Rage for Order,* 28–30. See Tracy, *The Analogical Imagination: Christian Theology and the Culture of Pluralism* (New York: Crossroad Publishing Co., 1981), 14–21.
20. Dietrich Bonhoeffer, *Letters and Papers from Prison: The Enlarged Edition,* ed. Eberhard Bethge, trans. Reginald Fuller et al. (New York: Macmillan & Co., 1971), 286.
21. See Thomas S. Kuhn, *The Structure of Scientific Revolutions,* 2nd ed. (Chicago: University of Chicago Press, 1971); Alasdair MacIntyre, *After Virtue: A Study in Moral Theory,* 2nd ed. (Notre Dame: University of Notre Dame Press, 1984); Richard Rorty, *Philosophy and the Mirror of Nature* (Princeton, N.J.: Princeton University Press, 1979).
22. The key texts of Yale-school "postliberal" or "narrative" theology are Hans W. Frei, *The Eclipse of Biblical Narrative: A Study in Eighteenth and Nineteenth Century Hermeneutics* (New Haven, Conn.: Yale University Press, 1974); Frei, *The Identity of Jesus Christ: The Hermeneutical Bases of Dogmatic Theology* (Philadelphia: Fortress Press, 1975); George A. Lindbeck, *The Nature of Doctrine: Religion and Theology in a Postliberal Age* (Philadelphia: Westminster Press, 1984).

Chapter 1. Twilight of the Gods

1. Karl Barth to A. Graf, 18 March 1955, quoted in Eberhard Busch, *Karl Barth: His Life from Letters and Autobiographical Texts,* trans. John Bowden (London: SCM Press, 1976), 44. Harvey Cox posed the question at Tillich's last Harvard seminar in 1962. My sources for Tillich's answer are Cox and Max Stackhouse, both of whom were present.
2. See Adolf von Harnack, *What Is Christianity?* trans. Thomas Bailey Saunders (Philadelphia: Fortress Press, 1957); Agnes von Zahn-Harnack, *Adolf von Harnack* (Berlin: Walter de Gruyter, 1951).
3. Busch, *Karl Barth,* 40–44. See Eberhard Jüngel, *Karl Barth, A Theological Legacy,* trans. Garrett E. Paul (Philadelphia: Westminster Press, 1986), 23; Theodor Häring, *The Christian Faith: A System of Dogmatics,* 2 vols., trans. John Dickie and George Ferries (London: Hodder & Stoughton, 1913).
4. "Teacher" quote in Karl Barth, "The Principles of Dogmatics According to Wilhelm Herrmann," in *Theology and Church: Shorter Writings 1920–1928,* trans. Louise Pettibone Smith (New York: Harper & Row, 1962), 238. "Absorbed Herrmann" quote in appendix to *Karl Barth-Rudolf Bultmann Letters, 1922–1966,*

trans. Geoffrey W. Bromiley (1971; reprint, Grand Rapids: Wm. B. Eerdmans Publishing Co., 1981), 153. For biographical details, see Busch, *Karl Barth,* 43–44.

5. See Ernst Troeltsch, "Historical and Dogmatic Method in Theology," trans. Ephraim Fischoff, in Troeltsch, *Religion in History,* ed. James Luther Adams (Minneapolis: Fortress Press, 1991), 11–32; Troeltsch, "The Dogmatics of the History-of-Religions School," trans. Walter E. Wyman, Jr., in ibid., 87–108; Troeltsch, *Die Absolutheit der Christentums und die Religionsgeschichte* (1902; reprint, Tübingen: J. C. B. Mohr [Paul Siebeck], 1912).
6. See Hans-Georg Drescher, *Ernst Troeltsch: His Life and Work,* trans. John Bowden (Minneapolis: Fortress Press, 1992), 70–97; Joachim Wach, "Introduction: The Meaning and Task of the History of Religions (Religionswissenschaft)," in *The History of Religions: Essays on the Problem of Understanding,* ed. Joseph M. Kitagawa (Chicago: University of Chicago Press, 1967); Helmut Koester, "Early Christianity from the Perspective of the History of Religions: Rudolf Bultmann's Contribution," in *Bultmann: Retrospect and Prospect,* ed. Edward. C. Hobbs (Philadelphia: Fortress Press, 1985), 63–67.
7. Gustav Ecke, *Die theologische Schule Albrecht Ritschls und die Evangelische Kirche der Gegenwart* (Berlin: Reuther & Reichard, 1897). Ecke distinguished three periods in the history of the Ritschlian school: (1) 1874–1880, founding and earlier development; (2) 1880–1889, pluralization of the school, with competing factions led by Herrmann, Troeltsch, Theodor Häring, Julius Kaftan, and others; (3) 1889–1897, outright factional rivalry, with a further developed Ritschlian mainstream led by Harnack; see 74–78. See Johannes Rathje, *Die Welt des freien Protestantismus: Ein Beitrag zur deutsch-evangelischen Geistesgeschichte, dargestellt an Leben und Werk von Martin Rade* (Stuttgart: Ehrenfried Klotz Verlag, 1952), 102–3; and Bruce L. McCormack, *Karl Barth's Critically Realistic Dialectical Theology: Its Genesis and Development 1909–1936* (New York: Oxford University Press, 1995), 40–41.
8. Ernst Troeltsch, "Christianity and the History of Religion," trans. James Luther Adams, in Troeltsch, *Religion in History,* 77.
9. On the early mythical school tradition, see Christian Hartlich and Walter Sachs, *Der Ursprung des Mythosbegriffes in der modernen Bibelwissenschaft* (Tübingen: J. C. B. Mohr [Paul Siebeck], 1952); and David Friedrich Strauss, *The Life of Jesus Critically Examined,* trans. George Eliot (1892; reprint, Ramsey, N.J.: Sigler Press 1994), 39–92.
10. See Rathje, *Die Welt des freien Protestantismus,* 103. On the development of F. C. Baur's Tübingen-school historicism and its influence on Ritschl, who studied under Baur, see Peter C. Hodgson, *The Formation of Historical Theology: A Study of Ferdinand Christian Baur* (New York: Harper & Row, 1966).
11. Terrence N. Tice, "Interviews with Karl Barth and Reflections on His Interpretations of Schleiermacher," in *Barth and Schleiermacher: Beyond the Impasse?* ed. James O. Duke and Robert F. Streetman (Philadelphia: Fortress Press, 1988), 46.
12. Wilhelm Herrmann, "Der evangelische Glaube und die Theologie Albr. Ritschls," in *Gesammelte Aufsätze,* ed. F. W. Schmidt (Tübingen: J. C. B. Mohr [Paul Siebeck], 1923), 1–25. On Herrmann's influence over Ritschl regarding the relationship between theology and metaphysics, see Hermann Timm, *Theorie und Praxis in der Theologie Albrecht Ritschls und Wilhelm Herrmanns: ein Beitrag zur Entwicklungsgeschichte des Kulturprotestantismus* (Gütersloh: Gütersloher Verlagshaus Gerd Mohn, 1967), 98.
13. Wilhelm Herrmann, *Die Metaphysik in der Theologie* (Halle: Max Niemeyer, 1876); Herrmann, *Die Religion im Verhältnis zum Welterkennen und zur Sittlichkeit* (Halle: Max Niemeyer, 1879).

14. See Albrecht Ritschl, *Die christliche Lehre von der Rechtfertigung und Versöhnung,* 3 vols. (Bonn: Adolph Marcus, 1870–1874); Rolf Schafer, *Ritschl* (Tübingen: J. C. B. Mohr [Paul Siebeck], 1968); Otto Ritschl, *Albrecht Ritschls Leben,* 2 vols. (Freiburg: J. C. B. Mohr, 1892, 1896).
15. See Wilhelm Herrmann, "Albrecht Ritschl, seine Größe und seine Schranke," in *Festgabe von Fachgenossen und Freunden A. von Harnack zum seibzigsten Geburtstag dargebracht,* ed. Karl Holl (Tübingen: J. C. B. Mohr [Paul Siebeck], 1921), 405–6.
16. Albrecht Ritschl, "Theology and Metaphysics," trans. Philip Hefner, in Ritschl, *Three Essays* (Philadelphia: Fortress Press, 1972), 164, 179.
17. See Wilhelm Herrmann, "Kants Bedeutung für das Christentum," in *Schriften zur Grundlegung der Theologie,* vol. 1, ed. Peter Fischer-Appelt (Munich: Chr. Kaiser Verlag, 1966), 104–22; Theodor Mahlmann, "Das Axiom des Erlebnisses bei Wilhelm Herrmann," in *Neue Zeitschrift für systematische Theologie,* 4 (1962): 11–18; Peter Fischer-Appelt, *Metaphysik im Horizont der Theologie Wilhelm Herrmanns* (Munich: Chr. Kaiser Verlag, 1965); Immanuel Kant, *Religion Within the Limits of Reason Alone,* trans. Theodore M. Greene and Hoyt H. Hudson (Chicago: Open Court Publishing Co., 1934).
18. See Wilhelm Herrmann, "Hermann Cohens Ethik," in Schriften zur Grundlegung der Theologie, vol. 2 (Munich: Chr. Kaiser Verlag, 1967), 88–113; Herrmann, "Die Auffassung der Religion in Cohens und Natorps Ethik," in ibid., 206–32; and Herrmann, "Der Begriff der Religion nach Hermann Cohen," in ibid; 318–23. On Marburg neo-Kantianism, see Simon Fisher, *Revelatory Positivism? Barth's Earliest Theology and the Marburg School* (Oxford: Oxford University Press, 1988), 7–71; and McCormack, *Karl Barth's Critically Realistic Dialectical Theology,* 42–49.
19. See Wilhelm Herrmann, "Die Auffassung der Religion in Cohens and Natorps Ethik," in *Gesammelte Schriften,* ed. Friedrich Wilhelm Schmidt (Tübingen: J. C. B. Mohr [Paul Siebeck], 1923), 377–405; Paul Natorp, *Religion innerhalb der Grenzen der Humanität,* 2nd ed. (Tübingen: J. C. B. Mohr [Paul Siebeck], 1908); Hermann Cohen, *Reason and Hope: Selections from the Jewish Writings of Hermann Cohen,* trans. E. Jospe (New York: W. W. Norton & Co., 1971); Friedrich Schleiermacher, *On Religion: Addresses in Response to its Cultured Critics,* trans. Terrence N. Tice (Richmond: John Knox Press, 1969), 69–157; Schleiermacher, *The Christian Faith,* ed. H. R. Mackintosh and J. S. Stewart (Edinburgh: T. & T. Clark, 1989), 5–31. For a thorough discussion of Herrmann's relation to Natorp and Cohen, see Fisher, *Revelatory Positivism?* 72–169.
20. See Herrmann, "Kants Bedeutung für das Christentum," in *Schriften zur Grundlegung der Theologie,* vol. 2, 104–23; Herrmann, "Die religiöse Frage in der Gegenwart," in ibid., 114–49; and Hermann, "Die Auffassung der Religion in Cohens and Natorps Ethik," in ibid., 206–32.
21. This theme pervaded Herrmann's lectures on dogmatics for many years, including the period in which Barth studied under Herrmann. The final edition of these lectures (given in 1916) was published in 1925 as *Dogmatik* (Stuttgart: Verlag Friedrich Andres Perthes, 1925). The English edition was titled *Systematic Theology,* trans. Nathaniel Micklem and Kenneth A. Saunders (New York: & Macmillan Co., 1927). Herrmann would not have objected to the change in title effected by his English translators, since he viewed dogmatics as a relic of Catholicism and Protestant Scholasticism. "For with us there cannot be a systematic but only a historical science of dogma, since Evangelical Christianity cannot have any dogmas in the old sense of the term," he explained. He used the word only because "there is no point in unnecessarily abandoning a

familiar term" (16). On religion as an independent saving power, see Herrmann, "Kants Bedeutung für das Christentum," 119–22, and Herrmann, "Religion," in Herrmann, *Schriflen zur Grundlegung der Theologie,* vol. 1, 282–97. On the experience of moral conflict as a precondition for saving faith, see Wilhelm Herrmann, *Ethik,* 5th ed. (1913; reprint Tübingen: J. C. B. Mohr [Paul Siebeck], 1921), 90–96. Closing quote in Wilhelm Herrmann, "Zur theologischen Darstellung der christlichen Erfahrung," in *Gesammelte Aufsätze,* 245, quoted in McCormack, *Karl Barth's Critically Realistic Dialectical Theology,* 55–56; see Herrmann, *Systematic Theology,* 18, 26–27, 33–35.

22. Barth, "The Principles of Dogmatics According to Wilhelm Herrmann," 258.
23. Autobiographical sketch of Karl Barth from the faculty album of the faculty of evangelical theology at Münster in *Karl Barth-Rudolf Bultmann Letters, 1922–1966,* ed. Bernd Jaspert, trans. Geoffrey W. Bromiley (Edinburgh: T. & T. Clark, 1982), 153.
24. Albrecht Ritschl, *The Christian Doctrine of Justification and Reconciliation,* ed. H. R. Mackintosh and A. B. Macaulay (Edinburgh: T. & T. Clark, 1902), 3.
25. Wilhelm Herrmann, *The Communion of the Christian with God: Described on the Basis of Luther's Statements,* 2nd English ed., trans. J. Sandys Stanyon (1906; reprint, Philadelphia: Fortress Press, 1971, 36–37, 59–60). The 2nd English edition, of 1906, was revised in accordance with the fourth German edition of 1903. See Herrmann, "Der evangelische Glaube und die Theologie Albrecht Ritschls," *Schriften zur Grundlegung der Theologie* vol. 1, 11–25; Herrmann, "Der geschichtliche Christus der Grund unseres Glaubens," in ibid., 149–85.
26. See Wilhelm Herrmann, "Albrecht Ritschl, seine Größe und seine Schranke," 405–6; discussion in McCormack, *Karl Barth's Critically Realistic Dialectical Theology,* 53.
27. Wilhelm Herrmann, "Die Absolutheit des Christentums und die Religionsgeschichte," in *Schriften zur Grundlegung der Theologie,* vol. 1, 193–99; citations from Ferdinand Kattenbusch concerning Herrmann's regard for Schleiermacher quoted in Barth, "The Principles of Dogmatics According to Wilhelm Herrmann," 246.
28. Herrmann, *The Communion of the Christian with God,* 19–49.
29. For an especially pointed affirmation that Christian faith requires the historical fact of Jesus, see Wilhelm Herrmann, "Warum bedarf unser Glaube geschichtlicher Tatsachen?" in *Schriften zur Grundlegung der Theologie,* vol. 1, 81–103.
30. Herrmann, *The Communion of the Christian with God,* lxv–lxvi, 5, 37–48.
31. Ibid., lxvii, 7; on Pietist accounts of faith, see Herrmann, *Systematic Theology,* 34–36, 43–47.
32. *Herrmann, The Communion of the Christian with God,* 49–51.
33. Ibid., 14–15.
34. Ibid., 17, 42.
35. Ibid., 45.
36. Ibid., 36–37.
37. See Ludwig Feuerbach, *The Essence of Christianity,* trans. George Eliot (New York: Harper & Brothers, 1957). Herrmann, *The Communion of the Christian with God,* 37, 48.
38. G. E. Lessing, *Lessing's Theological Writings,* ed. Henry Chadwick (Stanford, Calif: Stanford University Press, 1957), 12–13. Herrmann, *The Communion of the Christian with God,* 70, 72.
39. Herrmann, *The Communion of the Christian with God,* 69–70.
40. Closing quote in Herrmann, "Die Lage und Aufgabe der evangelischen Dogmatik in der Gegenwart," in *Gesammelte Aufsätze,* 117–19; earlier quotes in

Herrmann, *The Communion of the Christian with God,* 74–75; see Herrmann, "Warum bedarf unser Glaube geschichtlicher Tatsachen?" 94–101.

41. Herrmann, *The Communion of the Christian with God,* 75.
42. Barth, "The Principles of Dogmatics According to Wilhelm Herrmann," 248, 257, 267. See Julius Kaftan, *Dogmatik* (Freiburg: J. C. B. Mohr, 1897); Theodor Häring, *zur Versöhnungslehre, eine dogmatische Utersuchung* (Göttingen: Vandenhoeck und Ruprecht, 1893).
43. Karl Barth, "Moderne Theologie und Reichgottesarbeit," *Zeitschrift für Theologie und Kirche* 19 (1909): 317–20.
44. Ibid., 320–21.
45. See Hans Frei, "The Doctrine of Revelation in the Thought of Karl Barth, 1909 to 1922" (Ph.D. diss., Yale University, 1956), 14; Barth to Martin Rade, *Karl Barth-Martin Rade: Ein Briefwechsel,* ed. Christoph Schwöbel (Gütersloh: Gütersloher Verlagshaus Gerd Mohn, 1981), 70; McCormack, *Karl Barth's Critically Realistic Dialectical Theology,* 70.
46. Quoted in Tice, "Interviews with Karl Barth and Reflections on His Interpretations of Schleiermacher," 46.
47. Herrmann, *Schriften zur Grundlegung der Theologie,* vol. 1, 193–200.
48. Barth, "Moderne Theologie und Reichgottesarbeit," 321. See discussion in Hendrikus Berkhof, *Two Hundred Years of Theology: Report of a Personal Journey,* trans. John Vriend (Grand Rapids: Wm. B. Eerdmans Publishing Co., 1989), 180–81.
49. See Ernst Christian Achelis, "Noch einmal: Moderne Theologie und Reichgottesarbeit," *Zeitschrift für Theologie und Kirche* 19 (1909): 406–10; Paul Drews, "Zum dritten Mal: Moderne Theologie und Reichgottesarbeit," *Zeitschrift für Theologie und Kirche* 19 (1909): 475–79. Achelis and Drews were Ritschlian practical theologians whose arguments with Barth (somewhat unwittingly) reflected differences between the "older Ritschlians" and Herrmann. For Barth's defense of his article, which leaned heavily on Schleiermacher's account of the origins of doctrine in religious experience, see Karl Barth, "Antwort an D. Achelis und D. Drews," *Zeitschrift für Theologie und Kirche* 19 (1909): 479–86.
50. Barth to Adolf Keller, 20 May 1956, quoted in Busch, *Karl Barth,* 54; quotations from Barth's sermons of 1910–1911 quoted in ibid.
51. Karl Barth, "Der christliche Glaube und die Geschichte," *Schweizerische theologische Zeitschrift* 2 (1912): 1–18, 49–72 (quote on 3). See Wilhelm Herrmann, "Die Bedeutung der Geschichtlichkeit Jesu für den Glauben; Eine Besprechung des gleichnamigen Vortrags von Ernst Troeltsch," in *Schriften zur Grundlegung der Theologie,* vol. 2, 287–89.
52. Barth, "Der christliche Glaube und die Geschichte," 53–54, 63–67. See discussions in Simon Fisher, *Revelatory Positivism?* 226–33; McCormack, *Karl Barth's Critically Realistic Dialectical Theology,* 74–77; and Jüngel, *Karl Barth, A Theological Legacy,* 28–30.
53. Barth to Helmut Thielicke, 7 November 1967, quoted in Busch, *Karl Barth,* 57.
54. See Karl Barth, *Predigten 1913,* ed. Nelly Barth and Gerhard Sauter (Zurich: TVZ, 1976); Jochen Fähler, *Der Ausbruch des 1. Weltkrieges in Karl Barths Predigten, 1913–1915* (Frankfurt: Peter Lang, 1979); Cornelis van der Kooi, *Anfängliche Theologie: Der Denkweg des jungen Karl Barths* (Munich: Chr. Kaiser Verlag, 1987); Busch, *Karl Barth,* 61–63; Arthur C. Cochrane, "The Sermons of 1913 and 1914," *Karl Barth in Re-View: Posthumous Works Reviewed and Assessed,* ed. H. Martin Rumscheidt (Pittsburgh: Pickwick Press, 1981), 1–5.
55. Quoted in Busch, *Karl Barth,* 64; closing quote, in Barth to Eduard Thurneysen, 13 June 1925, *Revolutionary Theology in the Making: Barth-Thurneysen Correspondence, 1914–1925,* trans. James D. Smart (Richmond: John Knox Press, 1964), 230.

56. Hermann Kutter, *Sie Müssen! Ein offenes Wort an die christliche Gesellschaft* (Berlin: Hermann Walther Verlagsbuchhandlung, 1904); Kutter, *They Must; or, God and the Social Democracy,* American edition (Chicago: Co-operative Printing Co., 1906), quote on 176.
57. Karl Barth, "Rückblick," in *Karl Barth: Offene Briefe, 1945–1968,* ed. Diether Koch (Zurich: TVZ, 1984), 189, quoted in McCormack, *Karl Barth's Critically Realistic Dialectical Theology,* 85.
58. Harnack, *What is Christianity?* 88–91, 115–16.
59. Wilhelm Herrmann, "The Moral Teachings of Jesus," in Adolf Harnack and Wilhelm Herrmann, *Essays on the Social Gospel,* trans. G. M. Craik (New York: G. P. Putnam's Sons, 1907), 218.
60. Ibid., 207, 218. See Friedrich Naumann, *Briefe über Religion,* (Berlin: Buchverlag der *Hilfe,* 1903), 41–48.
61. Harnack, *What is Christianity?* 89. See Wilhelm Herrmann, "Religion und Sozialdemokratie," in *Gesammelte Aufsätze,* 463–89.
62. Barth, autobiographical sketch of Karl Barth from the faculty album of the faculty of evangelical theology at Münster, (1927), 154.
63. This exchange appears in *Karl Barth and Radical Politics,* ed. and trans. George Hunsinger (Philadelphia: Westminster Press, 1976), 19–45.
64. Kutter, *They Must; or, God and the Social Democracy,* 88.
65. "Great word" quote in Barth, "Concluding Unscientific Postscript on Schleiermacher," in *The Theology of Schleiermacher,* trans. Geoffrey W. Bromiley (Grand Rapids: Wm. B. Eerdmans Publishing Co., 1982), 263; "realm of the church" quote in Karl Barth, *Church Dogmatics: The Doctrine of the Word of God* I:1, trans. G. T. Thomson (Edinburgh: T. & T. Clark, 1936), 82.
66. Kutter, *They Must; or, God and the Social Democracy,* 89. See Hermann Kutter, Jr., *Hermann Kutters Lebenswerk* (Zurich: EVZ, 1965); Leonhard Ragaz, *Der Kampf um das Reich Gottes in Blumhardt Vater und Sonhund Weiter!* (Erlenbach-Zurich: Rotapfel Verlag, 1922); Andreas Lindt, *Leonhard Ragaz: Eine Studie zur Geschichte und Theologie des religiösen Sozialismus* (Zollikon: Evangelischer Verlag, 1957).
67. Karl Barth, "Jesus Christ and the Movement for Social Justice," in *Karl Barth and Radical Politics,* 19–46.
68. Kutter, *They Must; or, God and the Social Democracy,* 120–21.
69. Barth, *Predigten 1913,* 67–68, 166–68, 224–25, 251–52.
70. See Gary Dorrien, *Reconstructing the Common Good: Theology and the Social Order* (Maryknoll, N.Y.: Orbis Books, 1992), 16–47. Rauschenbusch's debt to the German liberal tradition was expressed most explicitly in his last book; see Walter Rauschenbusch, *A Theology for the Social Gospel* (1917; reprint, Nashville: Abingdon Cokesbury Press, 1945), 23–37.
71. Barth, *Predigten 1913,* 91, 94; "let the war rage" quote in Busch, *Karl Barth,* 81.
72. Barth to Martin Rade, 31 August 1914, *Karl Barth-Martin Rade: Ein Briefwechsel,* 96, quoted in McCormack, *Karl Barth's Critically Realistic Dialectical Theology,* 111.
73. Barth to Thurneysen, 4 September 1914, in *Revolutionary Theology in the Making,* 26; Barth to Rade, 1 October 1914, quoted in McCormack, *Karl Barth's Critically Realistic Dialectical Theology,* 114. This section includes material adapted from my earlier book, *The Word as True Myth: Interpreting Modern Theology* (Louisville, Ky.: Westminster John Knox Press, 1997), 75–76.
74. Text of the manifesto reprinted in H. Martin Rumscheidt, *Revelation and Theology: An Analysis of the Barth-Harnack Correspondence of 1923* (Cambridge: Cambridge University Press, 1972), 202–3.

75. Belgian invasion quote in Barth, "Concluding Unscientific Postscript on Schleiermacher," 263; "hopelessly compromised" recollection in Barth, autobiographical sketch of Karl Barth from the faculty album of the faculty of evangelical theology at Münster, 154; "presuppositions" statement quoted in Busch, *Karl Barth,* 81; "suddenly realized" quote from Karl Barth, *The Humanity of God,* trans. John Newton Thomas and Thomas Wieser (Richmond: John Knox Press, 1960), 14. Barth's various recollections of the manifesto stated mistakenly that it was issued on the same day as the Kaiser's call to war, a mistake that confuses much of the literature on this subject, including Busch's account. In some of his later recollections (such as the account in *The Humanity of God*) Barth also tended to exaggerate the suddenness and categorical finality of his break from theological liberalism in 1914.
76. Barth to Herrmann, 4 Nov. 1914; Rade to Barth, 5 Sept. [Oct.] 1914; Barth to Rade, 23 Nov. 1914; in *Karl Barth–Martin Rade,* 115, 110, 120. See quotes and discussion in McCormack, *Karl Barth's Critically Realistic Dialectical Theology,* 113, 114. For a representative example of Rade's theological Ritschlianism, see Martin Rade, *Die Wahrheit der christlichen Religion* (Tübingen: J. C. B. Mohr, 1900)
77. Barth, "Concluding Unscientific Postscript on Schleiermacher," 264; "any future" quote in Barth, *The Humanity of God,* 14.
78. Barth to Thurneysen, 5 February 1915, *Revolutionary Theology in the Making,* 28.
79. See *Signs of the Kingdom: A Ragaz Reader,* trans. Paul Bock (Grand Rapids: Wm. B. Eerdmans Publishing Co., 1984); Hermann Kutter, *Wir Pfarrer* (Leipzig: H. Haessel Verlag, 1907); Harry W. Laidler, *A History of Socialist Thought* (New York: Thomas Y. Crowell Co., 1933), 295–347.
80. See Markus Mattmüller, *Leonhard Ragaz und der religiöse Sozialismus* (Zollikon: EVZ, 1968); Hermann Kutter, *Ich kann mir nicht helfen . . . , Auch ein Wort an die deutschen Freunden der Religiös-sozialen* (Zurich: Orell Füssli, 1915); McCormack, *Karl Barth's Critically Realistic Dialectical Theology,* 119–20.
81. Karl Barth, *Predigten 1914,* ed. Ursula and Jochen Fähler (Zurich: TVZ, 1974), 447; *Karl Barth–Eduard Thurneysen: Briefwechsel, vol. 1: 1913–1921,* ed. Eduard Thurneysen (Zurich, TVZ, 1973), 48, 449; both cited in McCormack, *Karl Barth's Critically Realistic Dialectical Theology,* 121.
82. "Blumhardt always begins" quote in Karl Barth, *Action in Waiting* (Rifton, N.Y.: Plough Publishing House, 1969), 23–24. See Eduard Buess and Markus Mattmüller, *Prophetischer Socialismus: Blumhardt, Ragaz, Barth* (Freiburg, Schweiz: Edition Exodus, 1986); *Karl Barth–Eduard Thurneysen: Briefwechsel,* vol. 1, 29–33; Eduard Thurneysen, *Christoph Blumhardt* (Munich: Chr. Kaiser Verlag, 1926); Karl Barth, "Past and Future: Friedrich Naumann and Christoph Blumhardt," in *The Beginnings of Dialectic Theology,* ed. James M. Robinson, trans. Keith R. Crim and Louis De Grazia (Richmond: John Knox Press, 1968), 35–45.
83. Barth to Thurneysen, 8 September 1915, *Revolutionary Theology in the Making,* 30–31.
84. See Barth, "Concluding Unscientific Postscript on Schleiermacher," 264.
85. Barth to Thurneysen, 6 August 1915, *Karl Barth–Eduard Thurneysen: Briefwechsel,* vol. 1, 69–70.
86. Ingrid Spieckermann, *Gotteserkenntnis: Ein Beitrag zur Grundfrage der neuen Theologie Karl Barths* (Munich: Chr. Kaiser Verlag, 1985), 69–70.
87. Barth, "Concluding Unscientific Postscript on Schleiermacher," 265.
88. Tice, "Interviews with Karl Barth and Reflections on His Interpretations of Schleiermacher," 47. See Herrmann, *Systematic Theology,* 27–29.
89. See Schleiermacher, *On Religion,* 49, 63–64; *The Life of Schleiermacher as Unfolded in his Autobiography and Letters,* vol. 2, trans. Frederica Rowan (London:

Smith, Elder & Co., 1860), 203–4; Barth, "Concluding Unscientific Postscript on Schleiermacher," 264.

90. Barth, "Concluding Unscientific Postscript on Schleiermacher," 264.
91. *Karl Barth–Eduard Thurneysen: Briefwechsel,* vol. 1, 489–92.
92. Karl Barth, *The Epistle to the Romans,* trans. of 6th ed., Edwyn C. Hoskyns (London: Oxford University Press, 1933, reprint 1975), 225.
93. Barth, "Concluding Unscientific Postscript on Schleiermacher," 264. 94. Barth, *The Theology of Schleiermacher,* xiii.
95. Ibid., xv.
96. *Friedrich Schleiermachers Briefwechsel mit J. Chr. Gass,* ed. Wilhelm Gass (Berlin: G. Reimer, 1852), 195.
97. Barth, *The Theology of Schleiermacher,* xiv–xv. See Georg Wobbermin, *Systematische Theologie nach religionspsychologischer Methode* 3 vols., (Leipzig: J. C. Hinrichs, 1913).
98. Barth to Thurneysen, 5 February 1924, *Revolutionary Theology in the Making,* 168. Herrmann died in 1922, and Troeltsch the year after.
99. Barth, *The Theology of Schleiermacher,* 257–59.
100. Barth, *The Epistle to the Romans,* 43.
101. Barth, *The Theology of Schleiermacher,* 259–60; see Barth to Thurneysen, 4 March 1924, *Revolutionary Theology in the Making,* 175.
102. Quoted in John McConnachie, *The Significance of Karl Barth* (London: Hodder & Stoughton, 1931), 43.
103. See Barth to Thurneysen, 2 April 1922, *Revolutionary Theology in the Making,* 95; Paul Tillich, "Kairos," in *The Protestant Era,* trans. and ed. James Luther Adams (London: Nisbet & Co., 1951), 37–58.
104. Barth, *The Theology of Schleiermacher,* 260.

Chapter 2. Dialectics of the Word Crisis Theology

1. Karl Barth, "Biblical Questions, Insights, and Vistas" in *The Word of God and the Word of Man,* trans. Douglas Horton (Gloucester, Mass.: Peter Smith, 1978), 80.
2. See Karl Barth, "The Strange New World Within the Bible," in *The Word of God and the Word of Man,* 28–50.
3. See Ingrid Spieckermann, *Gotteserkenntnis: Ein Beitrag zur Grundfrage der neuen Theologie Karl Barths* (Munich: Chr. Kaiser Verlag, 1985), 67–88; Bruce L. McCormack, *Karl Barth's Critically Realistic Dialectical Theology: Its Genesis and Development 1909–1936* (Oxford: Oxford University Press, 1995), 129–83; Gary Dorrien, *The Word as True Myth: Interpreting Modern Theology* (Louisville, Ky.: Westminster John Knox Press, 1997), 75–86.
4. Karl Barth to Eduard Thurneysen, 1 January 1916, *Revolutionary Theology in the Making: Barth-Thurneysen Correspondence, 1914–1925,* trans. James D. Smart (Richmond: John Knox Press, 1964), 35–36.
5. Closing quote in ibid., 36. See Eberhard Busch, *Karl Barth: His Life from Letters and Autobiographical Texts,* trans. John Bowden (London: SCM Press, 1976), 75, 87; *Karl Barth-Eduard Thurneysen: Briefwechsel, i. 1913–1921* (Zurich: TVZ, 1973), 103.
6. Barth to Thurneysen, 27 July 1916, *Revolutionary Theology in the Making,* 38. On Beck's relation to Barth's family, see Eberhard Jüngel, *Karl Barth, a Theological Legacy,* trans. Garrett E. Paul (Philadelphia: Westminster Press, 1986), 23.
7. Barth, "The Strange New World Within the Bible," 33–34.

8. Ibid., 34, 37.
9. Ibid., 41.
10. Ibid., 43–45.
11. Barth to Thurneysen, 1 January 1916, *Revolutionary Theology in the Making,* 36. See Eberhard Busch, *Karl Barth und die Pietisten: Die Pietismuskritik des jungen Karl Barths und ihre Erwiderung* (Munich: Chr. Kaiser Verlag, 1978).
12. Barth to Thurneysen, 20 November 1916, *Revolutionary Theology in the Making,* 39–40.
13. "Demon" quote in Karl Barth, *Der Römerbrief* (Bern: G. A. Baschlin, 1919; reprint, Zurich: Evangelischer Verlag, 1963), 216; "Strike the blow" quote in Barth to Thurneysen, 1 January 1916, *Revolutionary Theology in the Making,* 36; Barth, "The Righteousness of God," in *The Word of God and the Word of Man,* 10–11.
14. Barth to Thurneysen, 11 November 1918, 45, *Revolutionary Theology in the Making;* Barth, "The Strange New World Within the Bible," 45.
15. Barth's sermon "The Pastor Who Pleases the People" was published without his consent in *Die christliche Welt* 14 (1916): 262–65. See James D. Smart, *The Divided Mind of Modern Theology: Karl Barth and Rudolf Bultmann, 1908–1933* (Philadelphia: Westminster Press, 1957), 77–78; Arthur C. Cochrane, "The Sermons of 1913 and 1914," in *Karl Barth in Re-View: Posthumous Works Reviewed and Assessed,* ed. H. Martin Rumscheidt (Pittsburgh: Pickwick Press, 1981), 1–5.
16. Barth, *Der Römerbrief,* 1–22.
17. Ibid., 321–27.
18. Barth, *Der Römerbrief,* 1. Parts of this section are adapted from my earlier book *The Word as True Myth,* 78–79.
19. Barth, *Der Römerbrief,* 420. For discussions of Barth's early expressionism, see Hans Urs von Balthasar, *The Theology of Karl Barth,* trans. John Drury (New York: Holt, Rinehart & Winston, 1971), 70–71; Wilhelm Pauck, *Karl Barth: Prophet of a New Christianity?* (New York: Harper & Brothers, 1931), 19–20; Hans Frei, "An Afterword: Eberhard Busch's Biography of Karl Barth," in *Karl Barth in Re-View, Posthumous Works Reviewed and Assessed,* 98–102; Stephen H. Webb, *Re-Figuring Theology: The Rhetoric of Karl Barth* (Albany, N.Y.: State University of New York Press, 1991), 8–18.
20. Barth, *Der Römerbrief,* 64–66, 86.
21. Barth, *Der Römerbrief,* 48–49, 76–86, 321–28. See discussion of these arguments in McCormack, *Karl Barth's Critically Realistic Dialectical Theology,* 142–43; Smart, *The Divided Mind of Modern Theology,* 83–84.
22. Barth, *Der Römerbrief,* 186. Barth later characterized his shift away from the conceptuality of his first-edition *Romans* as a "shift from Osiander to Luther." See Barth to Thurneysen, 3 December 1920, *Revolutionary Theology in the Making,* 55. On Osiander, see David Steinmetz, *Reformers in the Wings* (Philadelphia: Westminster Press, 1971), 91–99.
23. Barth, *Der Römerbrief,* 105, 308.
24. Philipp Bachmann, "Der Römerbrief verdeutscht und vergegenwärtigt: Ein Wort zu K. Barths Römerbrief," *Neue kirchliche Zeitschrift* 32 (1921): 518; Emil Brunner, "*The Epistle to the Romans* by Karl Barth: An Up-to-Date, Unmodern Paraphrase," in *The Beginnings of Dialectic Theology,* ed. James M. Robinson, trans. Louis De Grazia and Keith R. Crim (Richmond: John Knox Press, 1968), 63; Adolf Jülicher, "A Modern Interpreter of Paul," in *The Beginnings of Dialectic Theology,* 72.
25. Jülicher, "A Modern Interpreter of Paul," 79.
26. Ibid., 78–79.

27. Rudolf Bultmann, "Ethical and Mystical Religion in Primitive Christianity," in *The Beginnings of Dialectic Theology,* 221–35, quotes on 230, 232; Barth to Thurneysen, 14 July 1920, *Revolutionary Theology in the Making,* 52–53.
28. Barth, "The Christian's Place in Society," in *The Word of God and the Word of Man,* 272–327, quotes on 277, 286.
29. See Friedrich Naumann, *Jesus als Volkmann* (Göttingen: Vandenhoeck und Ruprecht, 1894); Adolf Stöcker, *Sozialdemokratie und Sozialmonarchie* (Leipzig: Verlag von Fr. Wilh. Grunow, 1891); Stöcker, *Predigten von Stöcker* (Berlin: Buchhandlung der Berliner Stadmission, 1890); Stöcker, *Das moderne Judenthum in Deutschland, besonders in Berlin: zwei Reden in der christlich-sozialen Arbeiterpartei* (Berlin: Weigandt und Grieben, 1880); James Bentley, *Between Marx and Christ: The Dialogue in German-Speaking Europe, 1870–1970* (London: New Left Books, 1982), 18–22; Claude Welch, *Protestant Thought in the Nineteenth Century: Volume 2, 1870–1914* (New Haven, Conn.: Yale University Press, 1985), 242–45.
30. Friedrich Naumann, *Briefe über Religion* (Berlin: Buchverlag *Die Hilfe,* 1903), 41–48. For a discussion that appropriates much of Naumann's argument while carefully dissenting from his judgments about the meaning of "complete Christianity," see Wilhelm Herrmann, "The Moral Teachings of Jesus," in Adolf Harnack and Wilhelm Herrmann, *Essays on the Social Gospel,* trans. G. M. Craik (New York: G. P. Putnam's Sons, 1907), 207–22. On Naumann and his legacy, see Karl Barth, "'*Die Hilfe* 1913," *Die Christliche Welt* 28 (15 August 1914): 776; Andreas Lindt, *Leonhard Ragaz: Eine Studie zur Geschichte und Theologie des religiösen Sozialismus* (Zollikon: Evangelischer Verlag, 1957), 205–16; McCormack, *Karl Barth's Critically Realistic Dialectical Theology,* 107–11.
31. Karl Barth, "Past and Future: Friedrich Naumann and Christoph Blumhardt," in *The Beginnings of Dialectic Theology,* 35–39.
32. Friedrich Gogarten, "The Holy Egoism of the Christian: An Answer to Jülicher's Essay: 'A Modern Interpreter of Paul,' " in *The Beginnings of Dialectic Theology,* 83–84.
33. Gogarten, "The Holy Egotism of the Christian," 84–87.
34. Friedrich Gogarten, "Between the Times," in *The Beginnings of Dialectic Theology,* 277–79.
35. Friedrich Gogarten, "The Crisis of Our Culture," in *The Beginnings of Dialectic Theology,* 283–300, quotes on 300. See Gogarten, "The Religious Crisis: An Open Letter to Emil Fuchs," in ibid., 301–05.
36. Barth to Thurneysen, 27 October 1920, *Revolutionary Theology in the Making,* 53.
37. Barth, "Biblical Questions, Insights, and Vistas," 53, 66, 73–74.
38. Ibid., 86.
39. Quoted in Agnes zon Zahn-Harnack, *Adolf von Harnack* (Berlin: Walter de Gruyter, 1951), 415.
40. Barth to Thurneysen, 20 April 1920, *Revolutionary Theology in the Making,* 50.
41. Barth to Thurneysen, 27 October 1920, *Revolutionary Theology in the Making,* 53.
42. For Barth's account of these influences on his rethinking, see "The Preface to the Second Edition" in Barth, *The Epistle to the Romans* 2–5.
43. Barth to Thurneysen, 27 October 1920, 53.
44. For example, see Eberhard Jüngel, "Von der Dialektik zur Analogie: Die Schule Kierkegaards und der Einspruch Pertersons," in *Barth-Studien* (Gütersloh: Gütersloher Verlagshaus Gerd Mohn, 1982), 127–79; Thomas F. Torrance,

Karl Barth: An Introduction to His Early Theology, 1910–1931 (London: SCM Press, 1962), 44–45.

45. For readings that downplay the influence of Kierkegaard on Barth, see Gerhard Sauter, "Die 'dialektische Theologie' und das Problem der Kialektik in der Theologie," in *Erwartung und Erfahrung: Predigten, Vorträge und Aufsätze* (Munich: Chr. Kaiser Verlag, 1972), 126; McCormack, *Karl Barth's Critically Realistic Dialectical Theology,* 216–40. McCormack's work contains an extensive review of the debate.
46. See Dorrien, *The Word as True Myth,* 80–83.
47. See Karl Barth, *Vom christliche Leben* (Munich: Chr. Kaiser Verlag, 1926), 445–47.
48. Emil Brunner, "*Der Römerbrief* von Karl Barth," *Kirchenblatt für die Reformierte Schweiz* 34 (1919): 29–32.
49. Barth, "Biblical Questions, Insights, and Vistas," 74.
50. Franz Overbeck, *Christentum und Kultur: Gedanken und Anmerkungen zur modernen Theologie,* ed. Carl Albrecht Bernoulli (Basle: Benno Schwabe & Co., 1919), "gentle fading" quote on 68, discussion of *Urgeschichte* from 20–28. This posthumously published collection of Overbeck's notes is the volume that Barth read.
51. Ibid., 54–63.
52. See Niklaus Peter, *Im Schatten der Modernität: Franz Overbecks Weg zur 'Christlichkeit unserer heutigen Theologie'* (Stuttgart: J. B. Metzler Verlag, 1992).
53. Overbeck, *Christentum und Kultur,* 148–59, 274–75; Karl Barth, "Unsettled Questions for Theology Today," in *Theology and Church: Shorter Writings 1920–1928,* trans. Louise Pettibone Smith (New York: Harper & Row, 1962), 66–68.
54. Barth, "Unsettled Questions for Theology Today," 64–65. See Soren Kierkegaard, *Attack Upon "Christendom,"* trans. Walter Lowrie (Princeton, N.J.: Princeton University Press, 1944).
55. Barth, "Unsettled Questions for Theology Today," 57–58.
56. Overbeck, *Christentum und Kultur,* 9–10, 242. See Barth's discussion in ibid., 61–62; Franz Overbeck, *Über die Christlichkeit unserer heutigen Theologie,* 2nd ed. (Leipzig: C. G. Naumann, 1903), 25–32.
57. Barth, "Unsettled Questions for Theology Today," 60–61.
58. Overbeck, *Christentum und Kultur,* 7; cited in Barth, "Unsettled Questions for Theology Today," 61.
59. See Eduard Thurneysen, *Dostoiewski* (Munich: Chr. Kaiser Verlag, 1921); Thurneysen, *Christoph Blumhardt* (Munich: Chr. Kaiser Verlag, 1926). Barth later recalled that it was Thurneysen who first "put me on the trail" not only of Kutter, but also Blumhardt and Dostoevsky. See *Revolutionary Theology in the Making,* 72.
60. Overbeck, *Christentum und Kultur,* 16; Jüngel, *Karl Barth, A Theological Legacy,* 55.
61. Barth, "Unsettled Questions for Theology Today," 56.
62. Barth, "The Christian's Place in Society," 282–83.
63. Ibid., 287.
64. Barth, "Past and Future: Friedrich Naumann and Christoph Blumhardt," 44.
65. Ibid., 44–45.
66. Barth, "Biblical Questions, Insights, and Vistas," 80.
67. Barth, *The Epistle to the Romans,* 38.
68. Ibid., 37.

69. Ibid., 36.
70. Ibid., 39, 42.
71. See Soren Kierkegaard, *Practice in Christianity,* trans. Howard V. Hong and Edna V. Hong (Princeton, N.J.: Princeton University Press, 1991), 81–83, 94–101, 124–44.
72. Barth, *The Epistle to the Romans,* 98–99, 105.
73. Ibid., 100.
74. Ibid., 108–9, 116.
75. Ibid., 141–42.
76. Ibid., 225.
77. Ibid., 30.
78. Barth, "The Preface to the Second Edition," in *the Epistle to the Romans,* 10.
79. Kierkegaard, *Practice in Christianity,* 201–32, closing quote on 225. See Niels Thulstrup, *Kierkegaard's Relation to Hegel,* trans. George L. Stengren (Princeton, N.J.: Princeton University Press, 1980), 350–81.
80. Jüngel, "Von der Dialektik zur Analogie," 127–79.
81. See von Balthasar, *The Theology of Karl Barth,* 48–100; Torrance, *Karl Barth: An Introduction to his Early Theology,* 48–147.
82. For example, see Karl Barth, *Anselm: Fides Quarerens Intellectum,* trans. Ian W. Robertson (London: SCM Press, 1960), 11.
83. John D. Godsey, ed., *Karl Barth's Table Talk* (Edinburgh: Oliver & Boyd, 1963), 24.
84. See Karl Barth, *The Göttingen Dogmatics: Instruction in the Christian Religion* trans. Geoffrey W. Bromiley (Grand Rapids: Wm. B. Eerdmans Publishing Co., 1991), 3–22; *Die christliche Dogmatik im Entwurf, I: Die Lehre vom Worte Gottes. Prolegomena zur christlichen Dogmatik* (Munich: Chr. Kaiser Verlag, 1927), vii–x; Barth, "The Word in Theology from Schleiermacher to Ritschl," *Theology and Church,* 215–16; *Karl Barth/Rudolf Bultmann Letters, 1922–1966,* ed. Bernd Jaspert, trans. Geoffrey W. Bromiley (Edinburgh: T. & T. Clark, 1982), 32–45. See Spieckermann, *Gotteserkenntnis: Ein Beitrag zur Grundfrage der neuen Theologie Karl Barths;* Michael Beintker, *Die Dialektik in der 'dialektischen Theologie' Karl Barths* (Munich: Chr. Kaiser Verlag, 1987); Eberhard Jüngel, "Von der Dialektik zur Analogie" 127–89.
85. For Barth's analogies between the relationships of the three forms of the Word of God and the inner-Trinitarian communion of persons in God, see Barth, *The Göttingen Dogmatics,* 15, 37, 270.
86. McCormack, *Karl Barth's Critically Realistic Dialectical Theology,* 239.
87. Barth, "Biblical Questions, Insights, and Vistas," 73–74.
88. Barth, *The Epistle to the Romans,* 512.
89. Autobiographical sketch of Karl Barth from the faculty album of the faculty of evangelical theology at Münster, 156.
90. Barth to Thurneysen, 20 March 1924, *Revolutionary Theology in the Making,* 176.
91. The original edition of Heppe's *Reformierte Dogmatik* appeared in 1861 as the second volume of his collection of writings on reformed theology. Quote from Karl Barth, "Foreword," in Heinrich Heppe, *Reformed Dogmatics,* trans. G. T. Thomson (London: Allen & Unwin, 1950), v.
92. Ibid.; closing quote in Karl Barth and Eduard Thurneysen, *Briefwechsel Karl Barth-Eduard Thurneysen, II: 1921–1930* (Zurich: Evangelischer Verlag, 1974), 328–29.
93. Strictly speaking, Barth rejected the notion that there could be such a thing as a *Reformed* dogmatics or a *Roman Catholic* dogmatics. Against his Lutheran colleagues at Göttingen, who disputed his right to teach dogmatics, Barth ar-

gued that dogmatics must be, in principle, a *Christian* discipline that is carried out within different confessional traditions. See Barth, *Göttingen Dogmatics,* 292–93.

94. Autobiographical sketch of Karl Barth from the faculty album of the faculty of evangelical theology at Bonn, in *Karl Barth-Rudolf Bultmann Letters,* 158.
95. Barth, "Foreword," in Heppe, *Reformed Dogmatics,* v.; closing quote in *Karl Barth-Edward Thurneysen Briefwechsel,* vol. 2, 328–29.
96. See Rudolf Bultmann, "Karl Barth's *Epistle to the Romans* in its Second Edition," in *The Beginnings of Dialectical Theology,* 100–120.
97. Hermann Kutter to Eduard Thurneysen, 5 February 1925, in *Revolutionary Theology in the Making,* 210.
98. Thurneysen to Barth, 11 June 1925, *Revolutionary Theory in the Making,* 226–27.
99. Kutter to Thurneysen, 5 February 1925, 211.
100. Thurneysen to Kutter, 11 February 1925, *Revolutionary Theory in the Making,* 212–15.
101. See Emil Brunner, *Truth As Encounter,* 2nd rev. ed. trans. Amandus W. Loos and David Cairns (Philadelphia: Westminster Press, 1964), 41–46. The original edition of this book was published in 1938 as *Wahrheit als Begegnung* (Zurich: Zwingli Verlag), but without the attack on Barth.
102. Barth to Thurneysen, 4 March 1925, *Revolutionary Theology in the Making,* 215–16.
103. Barth, *The Göttingen Dogmatics,* vol. 1, 386.
104. Barth to Thurneysen, 28 May 1924, *Revolutionary Theology in the Making,* 185.
105. Barth, *The Göttingen Dogmatics,* vol. 1, 15.
106. See Francis Turretin, *Institutes of Elenctic Theology,* vol. 1, trans. George Musgrave Giger (Phillipsburg, N.J.: Presbyterian and Reformed Publishing Co., 1992), 55–167.
107. Barth, *The Göttingen Dogmatics,* vol. 1, 18–20.
108. Ibid., 91–92.
109. Ibid., 219–22. See Karl Barth, *The Theology of John Calvin,* trans. Geoffrey W. Bromiley (Grand Rapids: Wm. B. Eerdmans Publishing Co., 1995), 53–54, 158–64.
110. Barth, *The Göttingen Dogmatics,* 58–59, 216–18.
111. Ibid., 3.
112. Ibid., 15.
113. Ibid., 15–16.
114. Adolf von Harnack, "Open Letter to Professor Karl Barth," in *Adolf von Harnack: Liberal Theology at its Height,* trans. and ed. Martin Rumscheidt (Minneapolis: Fortress Press, 1991), 91–92, 94. This debate is also reprinted in *The Beginnings of Dialectic Theology,* 161–87; and in H. Martin Rumscheidt, *Revelation and Theology: An Analysis of the Barth-Harnack Correspondence of 1923* (London: Cambridge University Press, 1972), 29–53.
115. Karl Barth, "An Answer to Professor Adolf von Harnack's Open Letter" in *Adolf von Harnack: Liberal Theology at its Height.*
116. Adolf von Harnack, "A Postscript to My Open Letter to Professor Karl Barth" in *Adolf von Harnack: Liberal Theology at its Height,* in ibid., 105–06.
117. Barth, "An Answer to Professor Adolf von Harnack's Open Letter," 96–97. For a more extensive discussion of this debate, see Dorrien, *The Word as True Myth,* 86–90.
118. Barth, *The Göttingen Dogmatics,* 16, 28.
119. Ibid., 63–64.

120. See Emil Brunner, *The Philosophy of Religion from the Standpoint of Protestant Theology,* trans. A. J. D. Farrer and Bertram Lee Woolf (Cambridge: James Clarke & Co., 1958), 31–36.
121. Barth, *The Göttingen Dogmatics,* 59.
122. Ibid., 109.

Chapter 3. Self-Authenticating?

1. Paul Schempp, "Marginal Glosses on Barthianism," in *The Beginnings of Dialectic Theology,* ed. James M. Robinson, trans. Louis De Grazia and Keith R. Crim (Richmond: John Knox Press, 1968), 191.
2. Karl Barth, *Die christliche Dogmatik im Entwurf, I: Die Lehre vom Worte Gottes. Prolegomena zur christlichen Dogmatik* (Munich: Chr. Kaiser Verlag, 1927).
3. See Karl Barth, *The German Church Conflict,* trans. P. T. A. Parker (Richmond: John Knox Press, 1965). For the text of the Barmen Declaration, see Arthur C. Cochrane, *The Church's Confession under Hitler* (1962; reprint, Pittsburgh: Pickwick Press, 1976), 237–47.
4. Karl Barth, "How My Mind Has Changed," in *How I Changed My Mind* (Richmond: John Knox Press, 1966), 41.
5. Karl Barth, *Church Dogmatics: The Doctrine of the Word of God,* I: 1, trans. G. T. Thomson (Edinburgh: T. & T. Clark, 1936), vii.
6. Ibid., ix.
7. Quoted in Eberhard Busch, *Karl Barth: His Life from Letters and Autobiographical Texts,* trans. John Bowden (London: SCM Press, 1976), 223.
8. See Paul Tillich, "Critical and Positive Paradox: A Discussion with Karl Barth and Friedrich Gogarten," in *The Beginnings of Dialectic Theology,* 133–41; Karl Barth, "The Paradoxical Nature of the 'Positive Paradox': Answers and Questions to Paul Tillich," in ibid., 142–54. In the same article, Barth further protested against Tillich's "broad, general steamroller of faith and revelation, which, when I read Tillich, I cannot help seeing affecting everything and nothing as it rolls over houses, men, and beasts as if it were self-evident that everywhere, everywhere, judgment and grace reigned, that everything, simply everything, 'is' drawn into the strife and peace of the 'positive paradox.' "
9. March 1964 conversation with Tübingen students quoted in Busch, *Karl Barth,* 145.
10. Barth to Thurneysen, 7 October 1922, *Revolutionary Theology in the Making: Barth-Thurneysen Correspondence, 1914–1925,* trans. James D. Smart (Richmond: John Knox Press, 1964), 110.
11. Barth to Thurneysen, 16 October 1922, in *Revolutionary Theology in the Making,* 114.
12. Barth to Thurneysen, 21 July 1924, in *Revolutionary Theology in the Making,* 188.
13. Barth letter to Thurneysen, 15 February 1925, in *Revolutionary Theology in the Making,* 206.
14. Rudolf Bultmann, "Karl Barth's *Epistle to the Romans* in its Second Edition," in *The Beginnings of Dialectic Theology,* 100–120.
15. See Rudolf Bultmann, "Ethical and Mystical Religion in Primitive Christianity," in *The Beginnings of Dialectic Theology,* 221–35.
16. Rudolf Bultmann, *The History of the Synoptic Tradition,* trans. John Marsh (New York: Harper & Row, 1963).
17. Karl Barth, "The Preface to the Third Edition," in *The Epistle to the Romans,* 6th ed., trans, of 6th ed., Edwyn C. Hoskyns (London: Oxford University Press, 1935; reprint 1975), 16–17.

18. Ibid., 17.
19. Ibid., 18.
20. Karl Barth, "The Preface to the Second Edition," in *The Epistle to the Romans,* 13.
21. Bultmann, "Karl Barth's *Epistle to the Romans* in its Second Edition," 119–20.
22. Barth, "The Preface to the Third Edition," 18–19.
23. Ibid., 19.
24. Bultmann, "Karl Barth's *Epistle to the Romans* in its Second Edition," 120.
25. See Rudolf Bultmann, "New Testament and Mythology," in *Kerygma and Myth: A Theological Debate,* vol. 1, ed. Hans-Werner Bartsch, trans. Reginald H. Fuller (London: SPCK, 1953), 1–44; Karl Barth, "Rudolf Bultmann: An Attempt to Understand Him," in *Kerygma and Myth: A Theological Debate,* vol. 2 (London: SPCK, 1962), 83–132; Bultmann, *Jesus Christ and Mythology* (New York: Charles Scribner's Sons, 1958).
26. See Bultmann, "Karl Barth's *Epistle to the Romans* in its Second Edition," 102, 113–16.
27. See Rudolf Bultmann, "Historical and Supra-historical Religion in Christianity," in *Faith and Understanding,* trans. Louise Pettibone Smith (Philadelphia: Fortress Press, 1987, 95–115, and Bultmann, "The Significance of the Historical Jesus for the Theology of Paul," in ibid., 220–46.
28. Rudolf Bultmann, "Liberal Theology and the Latest Theological Movement," in *Faith and Understanding,* 50–52.
29. Ibid., 52.
30. Rudolf Bultmann, "What Does it Mean to Speak of God?" in *Faith and Understanding,* 60.
31. Martin Heidegger, *Being and Time,* trans. John Macquarrie and Edward Robinson (New York: Harper & Row, 1962); see Heidegger, *The Basic Problems of Phenomenology,* trans. Albert Hofstadter (Bloomington, Ind.: Indiana University Press, 1988); Karsten Harries, "Fundamental Ontology and the Search for Man's Place," in *Heidegger and Modern Philosophy: Critical Essays,* ed. Michael Murray (New Haven, Conn.: Yale University Press, 1978), 65–79.
32. Rudolf Bultmann, "The Significance of 'Dialectical Theology' for the Scientific Study of the New Testament," in *Faith and Understanding,* 160; See Heidegger, *Being and Time,* 93.
33. Barth to Thurneysen, 15 February 1925, *Revolutionary Theology in the Making,* 206.
34. Bultmann to Barth, 6 January 1927, in *Karl Barth/Rudolf Bultmann Letters, 1922–1966,* ed. Bernd Jaspert, trans. Geoffrey W. Bromiley (Edinburgh: T. & T. Clark, 1982), 30–31; Barth to Bultmann, 28 April 1927, in *Karl Barth/Rudolf Bultmann Letters,* 32–33.
35. See Rudolf Bultmann, *Jesus and the Word,* trans. Louise Pettibone Smith and Erminie Huntress Lantero (New York: Charles Scribner's Sons, 1934); Barth to Paul Althaus, 30 May 1928, cited in Bruce L. McCormack, *Karl Barth's Critically Realistic Dialectical Theology: Its Genesis and Development, 1909–1936* (Oxford: Clarendon Press, 1995), 394.
36. Barth to Bultmann, 28 April 1927, 32–33.
37. Barth, *Die christliche Dogmatik im Entwurf,* vol. 1, v.
38. Ibid., 25.
39. Ibid., 16.
40. Ibid., viii–ix.
41. Bultmann to Barth, 8 June 1928, *Karl Barth/Rudolf Bultmann Letters,* 38.
42. Ibid., 38–39.

43. Barth to Bultmann, 12 June 1928, *Karl Barth/Rudolf Bultmann Letters,* 40–42.
44. Karl Barth, "Fate and Idea in Theology," in *The Way of Theology in Karl Barth: Essays and Comments,* ed. H. Martin Rumscheidt, trans. George Hunsinger (Allison Park, Pa.: Pickwick Publications, 1986), 29–30.
45. Ibid., 51–52.
46. Ibid., 32–33. See Erich Przywara, "Gott in uns oder Gott über uns? (Immanenz und Transzendenz im heutigen Geistesleben)," *Stimmen der Zeit* 105 (1923): 343–62; Przywara, "Das katholische Kirchenprinzip," *Zwischen den Zeiten* 7 (1929): 277–302.
47. Barth, "Faith and Idea in Theology." 38–40.
48. Ibid., 42–43.
49. Ibid., 45–47.
50. Ibid., 47–48.
51. Ibid., 48–51.
52. Erich Przywara, "Metaphysik, Religion, Analogie," in *Analogia entis; Schriften* 3 (Einsiedeln: Johannes Verlag, 1962), 334–35; see Przywara, "Das katholische Kirchenprinzip," 277–302; B. Gertz, *Glaubenswelt als Analogie; Die theologische Analogie-Lehre Erich Przywaras und ihr Ort in der Auseinandersetzung um die analogia fidei* (Düsseldorf: Patmos-Verlag, 1969), 251–59.
53. Hans Urs von Balthasar, *The Theology of Karl Barth,* trans. John Drury (New York: Holt, Rinehart & Winston, 1971), 249–50, 269–70.
54. Eberhard Jüngel, *God as the Mystery of the World: On the Foundation of the Theology of the Crucified One in the Dispute between Theism and Atheism,* trans. Darrell L. Guder (Grand Rapids: Wm. B. Eerdmans Publishing Co., 1983), 282–83; see Michael Beintker, *Die Dialektik in der 'dialektischen Theologie' Karl Barths* (Munich: Chr. Kaiser Verlag, 1987), 246–51.
55. McCormack, *Karl Barth's Critically Realistic Dialectical Theology,* 388–89.
56. Barth to Thurneysen, 29 April 1929, *Karl Barth-Eduard Thurneysen: Briefwechsel, ii., 1921–1930,* ed. Eduard Thurneysen (Zurich: TVZ, 1974), 660; Erich Przywara, *Religionsphilosophie katholischer Theologie* (Munich: Druck und Verlag von R. Oldenbourg, 1926).
57. Barth to Paul Althaus, 14 September 1929, cited in McCormack, *Karl Barth's Critically Realistic Dialectical Theology,* 390.
58. Przywara, *Religionsphilosophie katholischer Theologie,* 22; Karl Barth, *The Holy Spirit and the Christian Life: The Theological Basis of Ethics* trans. R. Birch Hoyle (Louisville, Ky.: Westminster John Knox Press, 1993), 5.
59. Barth, *The Holy Spirit and the Christian Life,* 5–6; see McCormack's discussion, *Karl Barth's Critically Realistic Dialectical Theology,* 389–91.
60. See Barth, *Church Dogmatics* I/1, x–xi.
61. See Robert P. Ericksen, *Theologians under Hitler: Gerhard Kittel/Paul Althaus/Emanuel Hirsch* (New Haven, Conn.: Yale University Press, 1985), 79–119. In 1927, Barth had joined Althaus and Karl Heim as a coeditor of the journal *Forschungen zur Geschichte und Lehre des Protestantismus.*
62. Barth to Bultmann, 5 February 1930, *Karl Barth/Rudolf Bultmann Letters,* 49.
63. Ibid., 50.
64. Bultmann to Barth, 16 February 1930, *Karl Barth/Rudolf Bultmann Letters,* 51–52; Barth to Bultmann, 17 February 1930, ibid., 52–53.
65. Barth to Bultmann, 30 September 1930, *Karl Barth/Rudolf Bultmann Letters,* 55; Bultmann to Barth, 2 October 1930, ibid., 56; Barth to Bultmann, 3 October 1930, ibid., 56–57.
66. Barth to Bultmann, 27 May 1931, *Karl Barth/Rudolf Bultmann Letters,* 58–59.
67. Bultmann to Barth, 14 June 1931, *Karl Barth/Rudolf Bultmann Letters,* 61.

68. Barth to Bultmann, 20 June 1931, *Karl Barth/Rudolf Bultmann Letters,* 64–65.
69. Barth, "How My Mind Has Changed," 43.
70. Barth, *Die christliche Dogmatik im Entwurf,* 135–36.
71. Ibid., 131.
72. Karl Barth, *Anselm: Fides Quaerens Intellectum. Anselm's Proof of the Existence of God in the Context of His Theological Scheme,* trans. Ian W. Robertson (London: SCM Press, 1960), 18.
73. Ibid., 29.
74. Ibid., 73–171.
75. See St. Anselm, *Basic Writings,* trans. S. N. Deane (La Salle, Ill.: Open Court Publishing Company, 1962); John H. Hick and Arthur C. McGill, eds., *The Many-Faced Argument: Recent Studies on the Ontological Argument for the Existence of God* (New York: Macmillan & Co., 1967).
76. Barth, "Preface to the Second Edition," in *Anselm: Fides Quaerens Intellectum,* 11–12.
77. Ibid., 38–47; see McCormack's discussion of this point, *Karl Barth's Critically Realistic Dialectical Theology,* 431–32.
78. Barth, *Church Dogmatics,* I/1, ix–x.
79. Karl Barth, "Zwischenzeit," *Kirchenblatt für die reformierte Schweiz* 118 (1962): 38–39.
80. Barth to Thurneysen, 18 August 1928, *Karl Barth/Eduard Thurneysen: Briefwechsel,* vol. 2, 607.
81. Quotations in Busch, *Karl Barth,* 217.
82. Barth to Hans Asmussen, 14 January 1932, quoted in McCormack, *Karl Barth's Critically Realistic Dialectical Theology,* 414.
83. Barth to Bultmann, 18 October 1931, *Karl Barth/Rudolf Bultmann Letters,* 70; Günther Dehn, *Kirche und Völkerversöhnung. Dokumente zum Halleschen Universitätskonflikt* (Berlin: Furche-Verlag, 1931), 49–56.
84. Bultmann to Barth, 18 October 1931, *Karl Barth/Rudolf Bultmann Letters,* 72; Barth articles in *Frankfurter Zeitung* (15 February 1932) and *Zofinger Zentralblatt* (December 1931) quoted in Busch, *Karl Barth,* 218.
85. Busch, *Karl Barth,* 222–24, 229–30.
86. See Ernst Christian Helmreich, *The German Churches Under Hitler: Background, Struggle, and Epilogue* (Detroit: Wayne State University Press, 1979); Barth, *The German Church Conflict,* 13–46.
87. Karl Barth, *Theologische Existenz heute,* vol. 1 (Munich: Chr. Kaiser Verlag, 1933), 2–24, 30–46.
88. See Barth to Bultmann, 17 November 1933, *Karl Barth/Rudolf Bultmann Letters,* 71; K. Kupisch, "Zur Genesis des Pfarrernotbundes," *Theologische Literaturzeitung* 91 (1966): 730.
89. Bultmann to Barth, 13 July 1933, *Karl Barth/Rudolf Bultmann Letters,* 69; Bultmann to Barth, 7 July 1934, ibid., 75.
90. Barth to Bultmann, 10 July 1934, *Karl Barth/Rudolf Bultmann Letters,* 76.
91. Bultmann to Barth, 10 December 1935, *Karl Barth/Rudolf Bultmann Letters,* 82–83.
92. Barth to Bultmann, 22 December 1935, *Karl Barth/Rudolf Bultmann Letters,* 84.
93. Karl Barth, "The First Commandment as an Axiom of Theology," in Rumscheidt, ed., *The Way of Theology in Karl Barth,* 63–70.
94. Ibid., 72–73.
95. Quoted in appendix to Karl Barth, *God In Action: Theological Addresses,* trans. E. G. Homrighausen and Karl J. Ernst (Edinburgh: T. & T. Clark, 1937), 134–35.
96. Ibid., 137–39.

97. Barth, "How My Mind Has Changed," 41–42; Barth, "The First Commandment as an Axiom of Theology," 73–76; Ernst Wolf to Bultmann, 21 June 1934, appendix to *Karl Barth/Rudolf Bultmann Letters,* 131; Hans von Soden to Gerhard Kittel, 25 June 1934, ibid., 131–33; Wolf to Bultmann, 29 June 1934, ibid., 133; Barth to von Soden, 5 December 1934, ibid., 136–39.
98. Barth, "How My Mind Has Changed," 42; Barth, "The First Commandment as an Axiom of Theology," 76.
99. Emil Brunner, "Spiritual Autobiography,“ *Japan Christian Quarterly* 21 (July 1955): 238–44; Brunner, "Intellectual Autobiography," in *The Theology of Emil Brunner,* ed. Charles W. Kegley (New York: Macmillan & Co., 1962), 3–20.
100. Emil Brunner, *Das Symbolische in der religiösen Erkenntnis* (Tübingen: J. C. B. Mohr (Paul Siebeck), 1914).
101. Brunner, "Intellectual Autobiography," 5.
102. Ibid., 5–6; Brunner, "Spiritual Autobiography," 239–40.
103. Brunner, "Intellectual Autobiography," 7.
104. Emil Brunner, "*The Epistle to the Romans* by Karl Barth: An Up-to-Date, Unmodern Paraphrase," in *The Beginnings of Dialectic Theology,* 63–71, quote on 69.
105. Brunner, "Intellectual Autobiography," 8–9.
106. See Barth to Thurneysen, 16 February 1923, *Karl Barth/Eduard Thurneysen: Briefwechsel,* vol. 2, 145.
107. Emil Brunner, *Die Mystik und das Wort* (Tübingen: J. C. B. Mohr [Paul Siebeck], 1924).
108. Barth, *The Epistle to the Romans,* 225.
109. Karl Barth, *The Theology of Schleiermacher,* trans. Geoffrey W. Bromiley (Grand Rapids: Wm. B. Eerdmans Publishing Co., 1982), xvi.–xvii; Barth, "Brunners Schleiermacherbuch," *Zwischen den Zeiten* 2 (1924): 49–64; Barth, "Schleiermacher," in *Theology and Church: Shorter Writings 1920–1928,* trans. Louise Pettibone Smith (New York: Harper & Row, 1962), 199.
110. Barth, "Brunners Schleiermacherbuch," 60–61.
111. See Barth, "Schleiermacher," *Theology and Church,* 159, 166, 181; Barth, *The Theology of Schleiermacher,* xiii–xv; Barth, "Concluding Unscientific Postscript on Schleiermacher," in *The Theology of Schleiermacher,* 274–79.
112. Quoted in Terrence N. Tice, "Interviews with Karl Barth and Reflections on His Interpretations of Schleiermacher," in *Barth and Schleiermacher: Beyond the Impasse?* ed. James O. Duke and Robert F. Streetman (Philadelphia: Fortress Press, 1988), 50.
113. Brunner, *Die Mystik und das Wort,* 298–99.
114. Karl Barth, "No! Answer to Emil Brunner," in *Natural Theology: Comprising "Nature and Grace" by Professor Dr. Emil Brunner and the Reply "No!" by Dr. Karl Barth,* trans. Peter Fraenkel (London: Geoffrey Bles, 1946), 69. For a recent reprinting of the preface and sections 2 and 3 of Barth's response, see Karl Barth, "No! Answer to Emil Brunner," in *Karl Barth: Theologian of Freedom,* ed. Clifford Green (Minneapolis: Fortress Press, 1991), 151–67, quote on 153.
115. Brunner to Barth, n. d. (summer 1924), cited in McCormack, *Karl Barth's Critically Realistic Dialectical Theology,* 397–98.
116. Ibid., 398–99; Barth to Thurneysen, 26 November 1924, *Karl Barth/Eduard Thurneysen: Briefwechsel,* vol. 2, 293.
117. Emil Brunner, *Religionphilosophie protestantischer Theologie* (Munich: R. Oldenbourg, 1927); Brunner, *The Philosophy of Religion from the Standpoint*

of Protestant Theology, 2nd English ed., trans. A. J. D. Farrer and Bertram Lee Woolf (London: James Clarke & Co., 1958).

118. Emil Brunner, *The Theology of Crisis* (New York: Charles Scribner's Sons, 1929).
119. Emil Brunner, *The Mediator: A Study of the Central Doctrine of the Christian Faith,* trans. Olive Wyon (Philadelphia: Westminster Press, 1947).
120. On the docetic aspects of Brunner's early Christology, see Georges Florovsky, "The Last Things and the Last Events," in *The Theology of Emil Brunner,* ed. Charles W. Kegley (New York: Macmillan & Co., 1962), 212–16; Emil Brunner, "Reply to Interpretation and Criticism," in ibid., 344.
121. Brunner, *The Philosophy of Religion from the Standpoint of Protestant Theology,* 32; see G. W. F. Hegel, *The Phenomenology of Mind,* trans. J. B. Baillie (New York: Macmillan & Co., 1949), 757–59.
122. Brunner, *The Philosophy of Religion from the Standpoint of Protestant Theology,* 35–36, 155.
123. Ibid., 34–35; see Brunner, *The Theology of Crisis,* 19–20.
124. Brunner, *The Theology of Crisis,* 2.
125. Ibid., 7–10.
126. Ibid., 37–38.
127. John Calvin, *Institutes of the Christian Religion,* I/7/5, trans. Ford Lewis Battles (Philadelphia: Westminster Press, 1975), 80.
128. Brunner, *The Theology of Crisis,* 37–38.
129. Ibid., 141–42.
130. Adolf Keller, "The Theology of Crisis, 2," *The Expositor,* 9th ser., 3, no. 4 (April 1925): 245–60. See Keller, "The Theology of Crisis, 1," *The Expositor,* 9th ser., 3, no. 3 (March 1925): 164–75.
131. Among Gogarten's writings during the period of the dialectical theology movement, see especially Friedrich Gogarten, *Illusionen, Eine Auseinandersetzung mit dem Kulturidealismus* (Jena: Eugen Diederichs, 1926); Gogarten, *Ich glaube an den dreieinigen Gott. Eine Untersuchung über Glaube und Geschichte* (Jena: Eugen Diederichs, 1926); Gogarten, *Glaube und Wirklichkeit* (Jena: Eugen Diederichs, 1928); Gogarten, *Politische Ethik* (Jena: Eugen Diederichs, 1932). On the I-Thou concept, see Friedrich Gogarten, *Von Glauben und Offenbarung, Vier Vorträge* (Jena: Eugen Diederichs, 1923); Martin Buber, *I and Thou,* trans. Walter Kaufmann (New York: Charles Scribner's Sons, 1970).
132. See Emil Brunner, *Man in Revolt: A Christian Anthropology,* trans. Olive Wyon (Philadelphia: Westminster Press, 1947).
133. See Friedrich Gogarten, *Entmythologisierung und Kirche* (Stuttgart: Friedrich Vorwerk, 1953); Gogarten, *Verhängnis und Hoffnung der Neuzeit, Die Säkularisierung als Theologisches Problem* (Stuttgart: Friedrich Vorwerk, 1953); Gogarten, *Die Wirklichkeit des Glaubens; Zum Problem des Subjektivismus in der Theologie* (Stuttgart: Friedrich Vorwerk, 1957).
134. See Ernst Fuchs, *Hermeneutik* (Bad Cannstatt: R. Müllerschön, 1954); Fuchs, *Begegnung mit dem Wort. Eine Rede für Friedrich Gogarten* (Bad Cannstatt: R. Müllerschön, 1955); Fuchs, "Entmythologisierung und Säkularisierung," *Theologische Literaturzeitung* 79 (1954): 723–32; Gerhard Ebeling, *Word and Faith,* trans. James W. Leitch (Philadelphia: Fortress Press, 1963); Ebeling, *The Nature of Faith,* trans. Ronald Gregor Smith (Philadelphia: Muhlenberg Press, 1961).
135. Friedrich Gogarten, "Karl Barth's Dogmatik," *Theologische Rundschau,* Neue Folge, 1 (1929): 65–68.
136. Barth, *Church Dogmatics,* I/1, 39–41, 194–96.

137. Gogarten, *Politsche Ethik,* 113.
138. Karl Barth, "Abschied," *Zwischen den Zeiten* 11 (1933): 538–41. Gogarten never supported the German Christian campaigns to eliminate the Old Testament from the Bible or to exclude people of Jewish blood from the church. He made these positions known as early as mid-November 1933. In 1936 he signed a statement (also signed by Bultmann and Althaus) that rejected German Christianity outright. See Theodor Strohm, *Konservative politische Romantik in den theologischen Frühschriften Friedrich Gogartens* (Berlin: Freie Universität Berlin, 1961), 190–92; Larry Shiner, *The Secularization of History: An Introduction to the Theology of Friedrich Gogarten* (Nashville: Abingdon Press, 1966), 208–09.
139. Emil Brunner, "Nature and Grace: A Contribution to the Discussion with Karl Barth," in *Natural Theology,* 15.
140. Emil Brunner, "Die andere Aufgabe der Theologie," *Zwischen den Zeiten* 7 (1929): 255–74. See McCormack's extensive discussion of this essay, *Karl Barth's Critically Realistic Dialectical Theology,* 402–7. For Brunner's subsequent elaboration of his position, which emphasized that all natural knowledge of God is essentially knowledge of the wrath of God, see Brunner, "Die Frage nach dem 'Anknüpfungspunkt' als Problem der Theologie," *Zwischen den Zeiten* 10 (1932): 505–32.
141. Brunner, "Nature and Grace," 15–17.
142. Ibid., 20–21.
143. Ibid., 22–34.
144. Ibid., 35–47.
145. Ibid., 48.
146. See Barth, *Church Dogmatics,* I/1, 123–24.
147. Brunner, "Nature and Grace," 49–50.
148. See Barth, *Church Dogmatics,* I/1, x.
149. Ibid., 134–35, 274–83.
150. Brunner, "Nature and Grace," 54–58, quotes on 58.
151. Karl Barth, "No! Answer to Emil Brunner," in *Natural Theology,* 67–69, 72.
152. Ibid., 70–72. The latter reference was to Ulrich Zwingli's fateful debate with Martin Luther, which sealed the divide between the Reformed and Lutheran forms of Protestantism. Barth's estimate that Brunner made his decisive turn in 1929 was correct in the sense that Brunner began to *publish* arguments on this theme in that year.
153. Ibid., 74–77, 105.
154. Ibid., 78–82.
155. Emil Brunner, *Natur und Gnade,* 2nd ed. (1935) (Zürich: Zwingli Verlag, 1938), 3–10.
156. Barth, "No! Answer to Emil Brunner," 80–87.
157. Ibid., 88–92.
158. Brunner, "Nature and Grace," footnote 9, 61.
159. See Calvin, *Institutes of the Christian Religion,* ed. John T. McNeill, trans. Ford Lewis Battles (Philadelphia Westminster Press, 1975), II:2:10–24, 267–84.
160. Barth, "No! Answer to Emil Brunner," 108.
161. Calvin, *Institutes of the Christian Religion,* II:2:25, 285.
162. Ibid., 284–86.
163. Barth, "No! Answer to Emil Brunner," 95–97; Thomas Aquinas, *Summa Theologica,* I.q.1.8, trans. Fathers of the English Dominican Province (Westminster, Md.: Christian Classics, 1991), 6.
164. For example: "Now that inward law, which we have described above as written, even engraved, upon the hearts of all, in a sense asserts the very same

things that are to be learned from the two Tables. For our conscience does not allow us to sleep a perpetual insensible sleep without being an inner witness and monitor of what we owe God, without holding before us the difference between good and evil and thus accusing us when we fail in our duty. But man is so shrouded in the darkness of errors that he hardly begins to grasp through this natural law what worship is acceptable to God. . . . Accordingly (because it is necessary both for our dullness and for our arrogance), the Lord has provided us with a written law to give us a clearer witness of what was too obscure in the natural law, shake off our listlessness, and strike more vigorously our mind and memory." Calvin, *Institutes of the Christian Religion,* I:8:1, 367–68.

165. Peter Barth, "Das Problem der natürlichen Theologie bei Calvin," in *Theologische Existenz Heute* vol. 18 (Munich: Chr. Kaiser Verlag, 1935); Peter Brunner, "Allgemeine und besondere Offenbarung in Calvins Institutio," *Evangelische Theologie,* 1 no. 5 (August 1934): 189–215; Günter Gloede, *Theologia Naturalis bei Calvin* (Stuttgart: W. Kohlhammer, 1935).
166. Edward A. Dowey, Jr., *The Knowledge of God in Calvin's Theology* 3rd. ed. (Grand Rapids: Wm. B. Eerdmans Publishing Co., 1994); T. H. L. Parker, *Calvin's Doctrine of the Knowledge of God,* 2nd ed. (Edinburgh: Oliver & Boyd, 1969). Especially recommended among recent treatments of this topic are: William Klempa, "Calvin on Natural Law," in *John Calvin and the Church: A Prism of Reform,* ed. Timothy George (Louisville Ky.: Westminster John Knox Press, 1990), 72–90; Susan E. Schreiner, "Calvin's Use of Natural Law," in *A Preserving Grace: Protestants, Catholics and Natural Law,* ed. Michael Cromartie (Grand Rapids: Wm. B. Eerdmans Publishing Co., 1997), 51–76; and Schreiner, *The Theater of His Glory: John Calvin and the Natural Order* (Grand Rapids: Baker Book House, 1995).
167. On his initial misgivings, see Karl Barth, *Church Dogmatics: The Doctrine of Creation,* 3/1, trans. J. W. Edwards, O. Bussey, and Harold Knight (Edinburgh: T. & T. Clark, 1958), ix–x.
168. Karl Barth, *Church Dogmatics: The Doctrine of Creation,* 3/2, trans. Harold Knight et. al. (Edinburgh: T. & T. Clark, 1960), 274–85, 316–24.
169. Karl Barth, *Church Dogmatics: The Doctrine of Reconciliation,* 4/3, 1, trans. G. W. Bromiley (Edinburgh: T. & T. Clark, 1961), 113–35, quotes on 115, 117.
170. Karl Barth, *The Humanity of God,* trans. Thomas Wieser and John Newton Thomas (Atlanta: John Knox Press, 1960), 37–65.
171. Brunner, "Reply to Interpretation and Criticism," 328; Brunner, "Intellectual Autobiography," 12; see Emil Brunner, "The New Barth," *Scottish Journal of Theology* 4 (June 1951): 123–35.
172. Emil Brunner, *The Christian Doctrine of God: Dogmatics,* vol. 1, trans. Olive Wyon (Philadelphia: Westminster Press, 1949), 235–36.
173. Brunner, "Reply to Interpretation and Criticism," 328; Emil Brunner, *Truth as Encounter,* trans. David Cairns (Philadelphia: Westminster Press, 1964), 45.
174. Barth, "No! Answer to Emil Brunner," 104.

Chapter 4. Otherworldly Positivism?

1. Karl Barth, *Church Dogmatics: The Doctrine of the Word of God,* I/1, trans. G. T. Thomson (Edinburgh: T. & T. Clark, 1936), x.
2. Paul Tillich, "Critical and Positive Paradox: A Discussion with Karl Barth and Friedrich Gogarten," in *The Beginnings of Dialectic Theology,* ed. James M. Robinson, trans. Louis De Grazia and Keith R. Crim (Richmond: John Knox Press, 1968), 138–41.

3. Paul Tillich, "Answer to Karl Barth," in *The Beginnings of Dialectic Theology,* 157.
4. Paul Tillich, "What is Wrong with the 'Dialectic' Theology?" in *Paul Tillich: Theologian of the Boundaries,* ed. Mark Kline Taylor (Minneapolis: Fortress Press, 1991), 104–16.
5. Paul Tillich, *A History of Christian Thought from its Judaic and Hellenistic Origins to Existentialism,* ed. Carl E. Braaten (New York: Simon & Schuster, 1968), 536–38.
6. Helmut Thielicke, *Notes from a Wayfarer: The Autobiography of Helmut Thielicke,* trans. David R. Law (New York: Paragon House, 1995), 66–67, 69.
7. Tillich, *A History of Christian Thought,* 538–39.
8. Paul Tillich, "Trends in Religious Thought that Affect Social Outlook," in *Religion and the World Order,* ed. F. Ernest Johnson (New York: Harper & Brothers, 1944), 24–25. "Neoorthodox" statement in Paul Tillich, *Systematic Theology,* vol. 1 (Chicago: University of Chicago Press, 1951), 5. See Karl Barth, *This Christian Cause: A Letter to Great Britain from Switzerland* (New York: Macmillan & Co., 1941).
9. Thielicke, *Notes from a Wayfarer,* 67–68.
10. Karl Barth, "Amsterdamer Fragen und Antworten," *Theologische Existenz heute* 15 (1949): 3–7. An edited version of this speech (featuring a somewhat problematic translation provided by the World Council of Churches staff) was published under the title, "No Christian Marshall Plan," in *The Christian Century* 65 (8 December 1948), 1330–33.
11. Karl Barth, "Continental vs. Anglo-Saxon Theology: A Preliminary Reply to Reinhold Niebuhr," *The Christian Century* (16 February 1949), 201.
12. For extensive discussions of these themes, see Gary Dorrien, *Soul in Society: The Making and Renewal of Social Christianity* (Minneapolis: Fortress Press, 1995), 84–161, 308–10, 343–50.
13. Reinhold Niebuhr, "We Are Men and Not God," *The Christian Century* (27 October 1948), 1138–40.
14. See Emil Brunner, "An Open Letter to Karl Barth," in Karl Barth, *Against the Stream: Shorter Post-War Writings, 1946–52,* 113–15, trans. E. M. Delacour and Stanley Godman (London: SCM Press, 1954), 106–13.
15. See Karl Barth, "The Christian Community in the Midst of Political Change," in *Against the Stream,* 113–15.
16. Ibid., 114–15.
17. Ibid., 116–18.
18. Reinhold Niebuhr, "An Answer to Karl Barth," *The Christian Century* (23 February 1949), 234.
19. See Karl Barth, *The Humanity of God,* trans Thomas Wieser and John Newton Thomas (Atlanta: John Knox Press, 1960); Barth, "Rudolf Bultmann—An Attempt to Understand Him," in *Kerygma and Myth: A Theological Debate,* vol. 2, ed. Hans-Werner Bartsch, trans. Reginald H. Fuller (London: SPCK, 1962), 83–132.
20. Karl Barth, "How My Mind Has Changed," in *How I Changed My Mind* (Richmond: John Knox Press, 1966), 62–67, quotes on 63, 66. See Barth, "The Church Between East and West," in *Against the Stream,* 127–46.
21. Karl Barth, "Karl Barth's Own Words: Excerpts from the Swiss theologian's letter to an East German pastor," *The Christian Century,* trans. RoseMarie Oswald Barth, LXXVI (March 25, 1959), 353, 355. Reprinted as "Letter to a Pastor in the German Democratic Republic," in *How to Serve God in a Marxist Land,* ed. Robert McAfee Brown (New York: Association Press, 1959), 54–58. On Barth's

theme regarding communism as a product of modern Western history, see Barth, "How My Mind Has Changed," 63–65.

22. Barth, "Karl Barth's Own Words: Excerpts from the Swiss Theologian's Letter to an East German Pastor," 353–55.
23. Ibid., 354–55.
24. Reinhold Niebuhr, "Barth's East German Letter," *The Christian Century* 76 (11 February 1959), 167–68. Ten years later, sick at heart over America's war in Vietnam, Niebuhr had second thoughts about his debate with Barth. He remarked that while he still did not share Barth's "sneer at the 'fleshpots of Germany and America,' I must admit that our wealth makes our religious anti-Communism particularly odious. Perhaps there is not so much to choose between Communist and anti-Communist fanaticism, particularly when the latter, combined with our wealth, has caused us to stumble into the most pointless, costly, and bloody war in our history." Reinhold Niebuhr, "Toward New Intra-Christian Endeavors," *The Christian Century* 86 (31 December 1969), 1662–63.
25. Reinhold Niebuhr, "The Truth in Myths," in *The Nature of Religious Experience: Essays in Honor of Douglas Clyde Macintosh,* ed. J. S. Bixler, et al. (New York: Harper & Brothers, 1937), 133.
26. Reinhold Niebuhr, "The Quality of Our Lives," *The Christian Century* 77 (11 May 1960), 568.
27. Emil Brunner, *Wahrheit als Begegnung: Sechs Vorlesungen über das christliche Wahrheitsverständnis* (Berlin: Furche-Verlag, 1938; reprint, Zurich: Zwingli-Verlag, 1941); Brunner, *The Divine-Human Encounter,* trans. Amandus W. Loos (Philadelphia: Westminster Press, 1943).
28. Emil Brunner, *Truth as Encounter,* 2nd ed., trans. Amandus W. Loos and David Cairns (Philadelphia: Westminster Press, 1964), 46–49.
29. Ibid., 47–49. For Brunner's early critique of Bultmann's Heideggerianism, see Emil Brunner, "Theologie und Ontologie—oder die Theologie am Scheidewege," *Zeitschrift für Theologie und Kirche,* Neue Folge 12 (1931): 2.
30. Brunner, *Truth as Encounter,* 41–43.
31. Ibid., 42.
32. Ibid., 43.
33. Ibid., 43–44.
34. Ibid., 44. Brunner's quotes from Barth were taken from Karl Barth, *Die Kirchliche Dogmatik: Die Lehre von der Versöhnung,* IV/1 (Zurich: Evangelischer Verlag 1953), 828–29.
35. Brunner, *Truth as Encounter,* 44–45.
36. Karl Barth, *Brief an einen Pfarrer in der Deutschen Demokratischen Republik* (Zollikon: Evangelischer Verlag, 1958), 30–32.
37. See discussion in Eberhard Busch, *Karl Barth: His Life from Letters and Autobiographical Texts,* trans. John Bowden (London: SCM Press, 1976), 246–48, quote on 248; "somewhat reluctant" quote in Karl Barth, *Karl Barth zum Kirchenkampf: Beteiligung, Mahnung, Zuspruch* (Munich: Chr. Kaiser, 1956), 91.
38. See Karl Barth, *The German Church Conflict* (Richmond: John Knox Press, 1965); Barth, *The Church and the Political Problem of our Day* (New York: Charles Scribner's Sons, 1939); Barth, *Der Deinst der Kirche an der Heimat* (Zollikon: Evangelischer Verlag, 1940); Barth, *Unsere Kirche und die Schweiz in der heutigen Zeit* (St. Gallen: Verlag der Evangelischen Gesellschaft, 1941).
39. Barth to Hermann Albert Hesse, 30 June 1935, quoted in Busch, *Karl Barth,* 261.
40. Barth, *Der Deinst der Kirche an der Heimat;* Barth, *This Christian Cause: A Letter to Great Britain from Switzerland* (N.Y.: Macmillan, 1941).

41. Karl Barth, *The Germans and Ourselves* (London: Nisbet & Co., 1945), 34–41.
42. Barth, "Continental vs. Anglo-Saxon Theology," 202.
43. Interview with Margareta Deschner, 26 April 1956, quoted in John Deschner, "Karl Barth as Political Activist," *Union Seminary Quarterly Review* 28 (Fall 1972): 55. This article contains an excellent summary of Barth's later political activism. See Margareta Deschner, "Karl Barth 70 vuotta," *Kotimaa* (May 1956); and Barth's essays, "Evangelium und Gesetz," "Rechtfertigung und Recht," and "Christengemeinde und Bügergemeinde" in *Community, State, and Church: Three Essays,* trans. A. M. Hall, G. Ronald Howe, and Stanley Godman (Garden City, N.Y.: Anchor Books, 1960).
44. Karl Barth, "How My Mind Has Changed," 57. See Barth, "How My Mind Has Changed," 62–63; Barth, "The Christian Community in the Midst of Political Change", 53–124; Barth, "The Church Between East and West," 125–46; Georges Casalis, *Portrait of Karl Barth* (Garden City, N. Y.: Doubleday & Co., 1963), 74; Deschner, "Karl Barth as Political Activist," 59–60.
45. Barth to Pastor Hans Heinrich Brunner, 11 November 1963, *Letters 1961–1968,* ed. Jürgen Fangmeier and Hinrich Stoevesandt, trans. Geoffrey W. Bromiley (Edinburgh: T. & T. Clark, 1981), 140; Barth to Hans Heinrich Brunner, 21 November 1963, ibid., 140–41.
46. Hans Urs von Balthasar, *The Theology of Karl Barth,* trans. John Drury (New York: Holt, Rinehart & Winston, 1971), 73–150; Karl Barth, *Anselm: Fides Quaerens Intellectum,* trans. of 2nd. ed., Ian W. Robertson (London: SCM Press, 1960). For a standard neoorthodox treatment of Barth's movement "from dialectical to dogmatic thinking," see Thomas F. Torrance, *Karl Barth: An Introduction to His Early Theology, 1910–1931* (London: SCM Press, 1962), 48–132.
47. Karl Barth, *The Göttingen Dogmatics: Instruction in the Christian Religion,* vol. 1, ed. Hannelotte Reiffen, trans. Geoffrey W. Bromiley (Grand Rapids: Wm. B. Eerdmans Publishing Co., 1991), 37, 94, 270; Barth to Thurneysen, 20 March 1924, *Revolutionary Theology in the Making: Barth-Thurneysen Correspondence, 1914–1925,* trans. James D. Smart (Richmond: John Knox Press, 1964), 176.; Barth, *The Göttingen Dogmatics,* vol. 1, 95–109. On Barth's theological development, see his "Preface to the Second Edition" of *Anselm: Fides Quaerens Intellectum,* 11–12.
48. Brunner, *Truth as Encounter,* 42–43.
49. Barth, *The Göttingen Dogmatics,* vol. 1, 156–60. Barth's chief guides to Protestant orthodoxy were Heinrich Heppe's *Reformed Dogmatics* (London: Allen & Unwin, 1950); and Heinrich Schmid's *The Doctrinal Theology of the Evangelical Lutheran Church* (Philadelphia: Fortress Press, 1899).
50. Ibid., 160–61.
51. Ibid., 163. See Adolf von Harnack, *Marcion: Das Evangelium vom fremden Gott* (Leipzig: , 1921), 101, 186–187.
52. Barth, *The Göttingen Dogmatics,* 163–64.
53. Ibid., 164.
54. Ibid., 167.
55. Barth, *Church Dogmatics,* I/1, x–xi; Barth, *The Göttingen Dogmatics,* vol. 1, 167.
56. Karl Barth, *Credo* (1935; reprint, New York: Charles Scribner's Sons, 1962), vii; Busch, *Karl Barth,* 203, 267.
57. See Karl Barth, "Rechtfertigung und Recht," in *Theologische Studien,* vol. 1 (Zurich: Evangelischer Verlag, 1938). Other contributors to this series included Pierre Maury, Oscar Cullmann, Günther Dehn, Markus Barth, Walter Klaas, Karl Ludwig Schmidt, and Wilhelm Vischer.

58. Dietrich Bonhoeffer, *Gesammelte Schriften,* vol. 1, ed. Eberhard Bethge (Munich: Chr. Kaiser Verlag, 1972), 19.
59. Quoted in Eberhard Bethge, *Dietrich Bonhoeffer: Theologian, Christian, Contemporary,* trans. Eric Mosbacher, et al. (New York: Harper & Row, 1970), 132.
60. Bonhoeffer to Barth, 24 October 1933, in Dietrich Bonhoeffer, *A Testament to Freedom: The Essential Writings of Dietrich Bonhoeffer,* rev. ed., ed. Geffrey B. Kelly and F. Burton Nelson (New York: Harper San Francisco, 1995); 390–92.
61. Bonhoeffer to Barth, 17 May 1942, *A Testament to Freedom,* 432. For discussions of this relationship, see John Godsey, "Barth and Bonhoeffer: The Basic Difference," *Quarterly Review* 7 (Spring 1987): 15–17; Charles Marsh, *Reclaiming Dietrich Bonhoeffer: The Promise of His Theology* (New York: Oxford University Press, 1994), 6–7; Paul Lehmann, "The Concreteness of Theology: Reflections on the Conversation Between Barth and Bonhoeffer," in *Footnotes to a Theology: The Karl Barth Colloquium of 1972,* ed. H. Martin Rumscheidt (Waterloo, Ontario: Wilfrid Laurier University Press, 1974).
62. Dietrich Bonhoeffer, *Sanctorum Communio: A Dogmatic Inquiry into the Sociology of the Church,* trans. Ronald Gregor Smith (London: William Collins Sons & Co., 1963).
63. Karl Barth, *Die christliche Dogmatik im Entwurf, I: Die Lehre vom Worte Gottes. Prolegomena zur christlichen Dogmatik* (Munich: Chr. Kaiser Verlag, 1927), 284–88, 295, 357–58. Bonhoeffer also referred to actualist statements in Barth's essay, "Schicksal und Idee in der Theologie," in *The Way of Theology in Karl Barth: Essays and Comments,* ed. H. Martin Rumscheidt, trans. George Hunsinger (Allison Park, Pa: Pickwick Publications, 1986), 53–59.
64. Dietrich Bonhoeffer, *Act and Being,* trans. Bernard Noble (New York: Octagon Books, 1983), 81–82, 89–91.
65. Ibid., 80, 83–85.
66. Ibid., 90.
67. Ibid., 90–91.
68. Barth, *The Göttingen Dogmatics,* vol. 1, 102–9, 131.
69. Karl Barth, *Church Dogmatics: The Doctrine of God,* II/1, ed. G. W. Bromiley and T. F. Torrance, trans. T. H. L. Parker, et al. (Edinburgh: T. & T. Clark, 1957), 16–17.
70. Ibid., 262–63.
71. Marsh, *Reclaiming Dietrich Bonhoeffer.* For readings that interpret Bonhoeffer as a "christomorphic" (Ott) or "christocratic" (Rasmussen) theologian, see Heinrich Ott, *Reality and Faith: The Theological Legacy of Dietrich Bonhoeffer,* trans. Alex A. Morrison (Philadelphia: Fortress Press, 1972); Larry Rasmussen, *Dietrich Bonhoeffer: Reality and Resistance* (Nashville: Abingdon Press, 1972).
72. See Dietrich Bonhoeffer, *Christ the Center,* ed. Eberhard Bethge, trans. Edwin H. Robertson (New York: Harper & Row, 1978); Bonhoeffer, *The Cost of Discipleship,* trans. R. H. Fuller (New York: Macmillan & Co., 1963); Bonhoeffer, *Ethics,* ed. Eberhard Bethge, trans. Neville Horton Smith (New York: Macmillan & Co., 1955).
73. Karl Barth, *Church Dogmatics: The Doctrine of Creation,* III/1, ed. G. W. Bromiley and T. F. Torrance, trans. J. W. Edwards, Ol Bussey, and Harold Knight (Edinburgh: T. & T. Clark, 1958), 194–96. See Dietrich Bonhoeffer, *Creation and Fall: A Theological Interpretation of Genesis 1–3,* trans. John C. Fletcher, published together with *Temptation,* ed. Eberhard Bethge, trans. Kathleen Downham (New York: Macmillan & Co., 1966).
74. Karl Barth, *Church Dogmatics: The Doctrine of Creation,* III/4, ed. G. W.

Bromiley and T. F. Torrance, trans. A. T. Mackay, et al. (Edinburgh: T. & T. Clark, 1961), 19–23. See Dietrich Bonhoeffer, *Ethics,* ed. Eberhard Bethge, trans. Neville Horton Smith (New York: McMillan & Co., 1961), 73–78, 252–67, 308–10.

75. Karl Barth, *Church Dogmatics: The Doctrine of Reconciliation,* IV/1, ed. G. W. Bromiley and T. F. Torrance, trans. G. W. Bromiley (Edinburgh: T. & T. Clark, 1956), 70.
76. Karl Barth, *Church Dogmatics: The Doctrine of Reconciliation,* IV/2, ed. G. W. Bromiley and T. F. Torrance, trans. G. W. Bromiley (Edinburgh: T. & T. Clark, 1958), 533–34.
77. Dietrich Bonhoeffer to Eberhard Bethge, 8 June 1944, *Letters and Papers from Prison,* ed. Eberhard Bethge, trans. Reginald Fuller, et al. (New York: Macmillan & Co., 1971), 327.
78. Ibid., 327–28.
79. Ibid., 328–29.
80. Bonhoeffer to Bethge, 5 May 1944, *Letters and Papers from Prison,* 286.
81. Ibid., 286–87; Bonhoeffer to Bethge, 8 June 1944, ibid., 329.
82. Bonhoeffer to Bethge, 5 May 1944, 286.
83. Dietrich Bonhoeffer, *Ethics,* 21. On Bonhoeffer's religion-opposing Christological focus, see Gerhard Ebeling, *Word and Faith,* trans. James W. Leitch (Philadelphia: Fortress Press, 1963), 106–10; John A. Phillips, *The Form of Christ in the World: A Study of Bonhoeffer's Christology* (London: William Collins Sons & Co., 1967).
84. "Intellectual honesty" quote, dated 24 March 1942, in Bonhoeffer, *Gesammelte Shriften,* 4 vols. (Munich: Chr. Kaiser, 1958–61), III: 45; "fresh air," in Bonhoeffer, *Bonhoeffer Auswahl* (Munich: Chr. Kaiser, 1964), 537. Cited in Ott, *Reality and Faith,* 58; closing quote from "Outline for a Book," in Bonhoeffer, *Letters and Papers from Prison,* 382.
85. Karl Barth to P. Walter Herrenbrück, 21 December 1952, "From a Letter to Superintendent Herrenbrück," in *World Come of Age,* ed. R. G. Smith (Philadelphia: Fortress Press, 1967), 90; Barth to Eberhard Bethge, 22 May 1967, *Letters 1961–1968,* 250–53.
86. Karl Barth to Hanfried Müller, 7 April 1961, quoted in Busch, *Karl Barth,* 381.
87. Barth to J. Glenthøj, 7 September 1956, and conversation with pastors and laypeople from the Pfalz, September 1953, quoted in *Karl Barth,* 381.
88. Barth to Herrenbrück, 90.
89. Karl Barth, "Concluding Unscientific Postscript on Schleiermacher," in *The Theology of Schleiermacher,* ed. Dietrich Ritschl, trans. George Hunsinger (Grand Rapids: Wm. B. Eerdmans Publishing Co., 1982), 271.
90. Karl Barth to Eberhard Bethge, 22 May 1967, *Letters 1961–1968,* 250–52. See Eberhard Bethge, *Dietrich Bonhoeffer: Man of Vision, Man of Courage,* ed. Edwin H. Robertson, trans. Eric Mosbacher, et al. (New York: Harper & Row, 1970).
91. Barth to Bethge, 22 May 1967, 252.
92. See John A. T. Robinson, *Honest to God* (London: SCM Press, 1963); Harvey Cox, *The Secular City* (New York: Macmillan & Co., 1965); William Hamilton, *The New Essence of Christianity* (New York: Association Press, 1961); Thomas J. J. Altizer and William Hamilton, eds., *Radical Theology and the Death of God* (Indianapolis: Bobbs-Merrill Co., 1966).
93. See Gerhard Ebeling, *Theology and Proclamation: A Discussion with Rudolf Bultmann,* trans. John Riches (London: Williams Collins Sons & Co., 1966); Ernst Fuchs, *Zum hermeneutischen Problem in der Theologie; Die existentiale Interpretation* (Tübingen: J. C. B. Mohr [Paul Siebeck], 1959); James M. Robin-

son and John B. Cobb, Jr., eds., *New Frontiers in Theology,* vol. 2: *The New Hermeneutic* (New York: Harper & Row, 1964); Schubert M. Ogden, *Christ Without Myth: A Study Based on the Theology of Rudolf Bultmann* (New York: Harper & Row, 1961).

94. Barth quoted in John D. Godsey, "Epilogue: Barth's Life After 1958," in Barth, *How I Changed My Mind,* 82–83; see author's foreword in Karl Barth, *Rudolf Bultmann: Ein Versuch, ihn zu verstegen; Christus und Adam nach Röm. 5: Zwei theologische Studien* (Zurich: EVZ-Verlag, 1964).
95. Barth to Bethge, 22 May 1967, 252.
96. See Alan Richardson, *Christian Apologetics* (London: SCM Press, 1947); Richardson, *History Sacred and Profane* (Philadelphia: Westminster Press, 1964); Richardson and W. Schweitzer, eds., *Biblical Authority for Today* (Philadelphia: Westminster Press, 1951); H. H. Rowley, *The Faith of Israel: Aspects of Old Testament Thought* (London: SCM Press, 1956); G. Ernest Wright, *God Who Acts: Biblical Theology as Recital* (London: SCM Press, 1952).
97. Ott, *Reality and Faith,* 137–38. See Karl Barth, *Homiletics,* trans. Geoffrey W. Bromiley and Donald E. Daniels (Louisville, Ky.: Westminster John Knox Press, 1991), 44–90.
98. Ott, *Reality and Faith,* 129–38, 153–54.
99. Karl Barth, *Church Dogmatics: The Doctrine of Reconciliation: The Christian Life* IV:4 (Fragment), ed. G. W. Bromiley and T. F. Torrance, trans. G. W. Bromiley (Edinburgh: T. & T. Clark, 1969); see Karl Barth to Karl Rahner, 7 April 1968, *Letters 1961–1968,* 287–88.
100. Barth, *Church Dogmatics,* IV:4, vii; Godsey, "Epilogue: Barth's Life After 1958," 85–86.
101. Karl Barth to Helmut Gollwitzer, 31 July 1962; and Barth letter to C. H. Ratschow, 2 January 1958, quoted in Busch, *Karl Barth,* 461, 488; author's foreword in Barth, *Rudolf Bultmann . . . Christus und Adam,* vi.
102. Karl Barth to Jürgen Moltmann, 17 November 1964, *Letters 1961–1968,* 174–76. Barth's reference to the "eternally rich God" was a favorite phrase from the second verse of M. Rickart's hymn, "Now Thank We All Our God." For his discussions of threefold time and the threefold Parousia of Christ, see Barth, *Church Dogmatics: The Doctrine of Creation* III:2, trans. Harold Knight, G. W. Bromiley, J. K. S. Reid, and R. H. Fuller (Edinburgh: T. & T. Clark, 1960), 437–640; and Barth, *Church Dogmatics: The Doctrine of Reconciliation* IV:3,1, trans. G. W. Bromiley (Edinburgh: T. & T. Clark, 1961), 274–367. See Jürgen Moltmann, *Theology of Hope: On the Ground and Implications of a Christian Eschatology,* trans. James W. Leitch (London: SCM Press, 1965); and Ernst Bloch, *Das Prinzip Hoffnung,* 3 vols. (Frankfurt: Surkamp Verlag, 1959).
103. Barth to W. Herrenbrück, 13 July 1963, quoted in Busch, *Karl Barth,* 488; Karl Barth, "Remembrances of America," *The Christian Century,* 80 (January 2, 1963): 1, 7–8.
104. See Eberhard Jüngel, *Barth-Studien* (Gütersloh: Gütersloher Verlagshaus Gerd Mohn, 1982); Jüngel, *God as the Mystery of the World: On the Foundation of the Theology of the Crucified One in the Dispute between Theism and Atheism,* trans. Darrell L. Guder (Grand Rapids: Wm. B. Eerdmans Publishing Co., 1983); T. H. L. Parker, *Karl Barth* (Grand Rapids: Wm. B. Eerdmans Publishing Co., 1970); Parker, "Learning the Meaning of What I Believe," in *How Karl Barth Changed My Mind,* ed. Donald K. McKim (Grand Rapids: Wm. B. Eerdmans Publishing Co., 1986), 79–85; Robert W. Jenson, *God after God: The God of the Past and the Future as Seen in the Work of Karl Barth*

(Indianapolis: Bobbs-Merrill Co., 1969); Thomas F. Torrance, *Karl Barth, Biblical and Evangelical Theologian* (Edinburgh: T. & T. Clark, 1990).

105. Thomas F. Torrance, "My Interaction with Karl Barth," *How Karl Barth Changed My Mind,* 52–53, 56; essay reprinted in Torrance, *Karl Barth, Biblical and Evangelical Theologian,* 121–35. See Torrance, *Theological Science* (London: Oxford University Press, 1969), 106–40.
106. Thomas F. Torrance, *Space, Time and Incarnation* (Edinburgh: T. & T. Clark, 1997), 54.
107. Thomas F. Torrance, *Transformation and Convergence in the Frame of Knowledge: Explorations in the Interrelations of Scientific and Theological Enterprise* (Grand Rapids: Wm. B. Eerdmans Publishing Co., 1984), ix–x, 285–301.
108. Ibid., x; Torrance, *Theological Science,* 307–8. See Thomas F. Torrance, *God and Rationality* (Edinburgh: T. & T. Clark, 1997), 3–25.
109. Torrance, *Theological Science,* 308, 341–42, 352; quote from Barth in Max Zellweger-Barth, *My Father-In-Law: Memories of Karl Barth,* trans. H. Martin Rumscheidt (Allison Park, Pa: Pickwick Publications, 1986), 17.
110. Thomas F. Torrance, *Karl Barth,* 96, 144–45; see Torrance, *Karl Barth, Biblical and Evangelical Theologian,* 83–120.
111. Thomas F. Torrance, *Reality and Evangelical Theology* (Philadelphia: Westminster Press, 1982), 31–34; Torrance, *Transformation and Convergence in the Frame of Knowledge,* 287–301. On Barth's development, see Torrance, *Karl Barth,* 48–132. On realism and idealism, see Karl Barth, "Fate and Idea in Theology," in *The Way of Theology in Karl Barth: Essays and Comments,* ed. H. Martin Rumscheidt (Allison Park, Pa: Pickwick Publications, 1986), 25–61.
112. Torrance, *Space, Time and Resurrection,* 6; Barth, "Fate and Idea in Theology," 47.
113. George Hunsinger, *How to Read Karl Barth: The Shape of His Theology* (New York: Oxford University Press, 1991), 11–12.
114. For evangelical appeals to Barth's position, see Bernard Ramm, *After Fundamentalism: The Future of Evangelical Theology* (San Francisco: Harper & Row, 1983), and, more cautiously, Donald G. Bloesch, *A Theology of Word and Spirit: Authority and Method in Theology* (Downers Grove, Ill: InterVarsity Press, 1992). For neoorthodox accounts, see Eberhard Jüngel, *Karl Barth: A Theological Legacy,* trans. Garrett E. Paul (Philadelphia: Westminster Press, 1986); and most of the essays in *Theology Beyond Christendom: Essays on the Centenary of the Birth of Karl Barth, May 10, 1886,* ed. John Thompson (Allison Park, PA: Pickwick Publications, 1986).
115. See Eberhard Mechels, *Analogie bei Erich Przywara und Karl Barth: Das Verhältnis von Offenbarungstheologie und Metaphysik* (Neukirchen-Vluyn: Neukirchener Verlag, 1974); Ingrid Spieckermann, *Gotteserkenntnis: Ein Beitrag zur Grundfrage der neuen Theologie Karl Barths* (Chr. Kaiser Verlag, 1985); Michael Beintker, *Die Dialektik in der 'dialektischen Theologie' Karl Barths* (Munich: Chr. Kaiser Verlag, 1987).
116. See Friedrich-Wilhelm Marquardt, *Theologie und Sozialismus: Das Beispiel Karl Barths* (Munich: Chr. Kaiser Verlag, 1985); Ulrich Dannemann, *Theologie und Politik im Denken Karl Barths* (Munich: Chr. Kaiser Verlag, 1977); George Hunsinger, ed., *Karl Barth and Radical Politics* (Philadelphia: Westminster Press, 1976).
117. See Trutz Rendtorff, "Radikale Autonomie Gottes: Zum Verständnis der Theologie Karl Barths und ihre Folgen," in *Theorie des Christentums* (Gütersloh: Gütersloher Verlagshaus Gerd Mohn, 1972), 164–74.
118. See Bruce L. McCormack, *Karl Barth's Critically Realistic Dialectical Theology: Its Genesis and Development, 1909–1936* (Oxford: Clarendon Press, 1995);

McCormack, "Revelation and History in Transfoundationalist Perspective: Karl Barth's Theological Epistemology in Conversation with a Schleiermacherian Tradition," *The Journal of Religion* 78 (January 1998): 18–37.

119. See Hans W. Frei, *Types of Christian Theology,* ed. George Hunsinger and William C. Placher (New Haven, Conn.: Yale University Press, 1992); George W. Stroup, *The Promise of Narrative Theology: Recovering the Gospel in the Church* (Atlanta: John Knox Press, 1981); Hunsinger, *How to Read Karl Barth.*
120. Walter Lowe, *Theology and Difference: The Wound of Reason* (Bloomington, Ind.: Indiana University Press, 1993); William Stacy Johnson, *The Mystery of God: Karl Barth and the Postmodern Foundations of Theology* (Louisville, Ky.: Westminster John Knox Press, 1997), quote on 2–3; Graham Ward, *Barth, Derrida and the Language of Theology* (Cambridge: Cambridge University Press, 1995).
121. McCormack, *Karl Barth's Critically Realistic Dialectical Theology,* 1–20; see Eberhard Jüngel, "Von der Dialektik zur Analogie: Die Schule Kierkegaards und der Einspruch Petersons," in *Barth-Studien* (Gütersloh: Gutersloher Verlagshaus Gerd Mohn, 1982), 127–79.
122. See Henriette Visser 't Hooft, "Is There a Woman's Problem?" *The Student World* 27 (1934), 12–15.
123. W. A. Visser 't Hooft, *The Fatherhood of God in an Age of Emancipation* (Geneva: World Council of Churches, 1982), 58–59; Moltmann, "Henriette Visser 't Hooft," 170–72; Karl Barth, *Church Dogmatics: The Doctrine of Creation,* III:4, trans. A. T. Mackay et al. (Edinburgh T. T. Clark, 1961), 116–240, quotes 171, 173. This article and the correspondence between Barth and Henriette Visser 't Hooft are described in Jürgen Moltmann, "Henriette Visser 't Hooft," in *Gotteslehrerinnen,* eds. Luise Schottroff and Johannes Thiele (Stuttgart: Kreuzz Verlag, 1989), 169–79; See Niebuhr, "An Answer to Karl Barth." 235.

Chapter 5. Theology Without Weapons History and the Open Word

1. Karl Barth to Eduard Thurneysen, 15 February 1925, *Revolutionary Theology in the Making: Barth-Thurneysen Correspondence, 1914–1925,* trans. James D. Smart (Richmond: John Knox Press, 1964), 203–04.
2. "Gigantic swindle" remark in Barth to Thurneysen, 5 February 1924, *Revolutionary Theology in the Making,* 168.
3. Wilhelm Herrmann, *Christlich-protestantische Dogmatik,* (1906) reprinted in Paul Hinneberg, ed., *Die Kultur der Gegenwart: Ihre Entwicklung und ihre Ziele* I: IV, 2 (Berlin und Leipzig: Druck und Verlag von B. G. Teubner 1909), 129–80; and Herrmann, *Schriften zur Grundlegung der Theologie,* vol. 1 ed., Peter Fischer-Appelt, (Munich: Chr. Kaiser Verlag, 1966), 298–58; Herrmann, "Der evangelische Glaube und die Theologie Albr. Ritschls," in Herrmann, *Gesammelte Aufsätze,* ed. F. W. Schmidt (Tübingen: J. C. B. Mohr [Paul Siebeck], 1923), 1–25; Herrmann, "Die religiöse Frage in der Gegenwart," in Herrmann, *Schriften zur Grundlegung der Theologie,* vol. 2, ed. Peter Fischer-Appelt (Munich: Chr. Kaiser Verlag, 1967), 114–149; Karl Barth, "The Principles of Dogmatics According to Wilhelm Herrmann" in Barth, *Theology and Church: Shorter Writings 1920–1928,* trans. Louise Pettibone Smith (New York: Harper & Row, 1962), 247–48. Herrmann's first edition of *Der Verkehr des Christen mit Gott* was published in 1886; revised editions were published in 1892, 1896, 1903, 1908 (5th and 6th eds.), and 1921. The J. Sandys Stanyon-R. W. Stewart second English edition was based on the fourth German edition.

4. Wilhelm Herrmann, "Die Absolutheit des Christentums und die Religionsgeschichte: Eine Besprechung des gleichnamigen Vortrags von Ernst Troeltsch," in *Schriften zur Grundlegung der Theologie,* vol. 1, 193–99; Herrmann, *Christlich-protestantische Dogmatik* (1906), in Hinneberg, *Kultur der Gegenwart* I: IV, 2, 604–24; Herrmann, "Der Widerspruch im religiösen Denken und seine Bedeutung für das Leben der Religion," in Herrmann *Schriften zur Grundlegung der Theologie,* vol. 2, 233–46; James M. Robinson, *Das Problem des Heiligen Geistes bei Wilhelm Herrmann* (Marburg: K. Gleiser, 1952), 16–22.
5. Ernst Troeltsch, "Half a Century of Theology: A Review" in *Ernst Troeltsch: Writings on Theology and Religion,* trans. and ed. Robert Morgan and Michael Pye (Louisville, Ky.: Westminster John Knox Press, 1990), 58, 66, 75.
6. Ernst Troeltsch, "The Significance of the Historical Existence of Jesus for Faith," in *Ernst Troeltsch,* 191–92.
7. Wilhelm Herrmann, "Die Bedeutung Der Geschichtlichkeit Jesu Für Den Glauben: Eine Besprechung des gleichnamigen Vortrags von Ernst Troeltsch," in *Schriften zur Grundlegung der Theologie,* vol. 2, 282–89. See Herrmann, "Die Lage und Aufgabe der evangelischen Dogmatik in der Gegenwart," in *Gesammelte Aufsätze,* 95–96, 126–38; reprinted in Herrmann, *Schriften zur Grundlegung der Theologie,* vol. 1, 1–89. Page citations from former source.
8. Wilhelm Herrmann, *Systematic Theology (Dogmatik),* trans. Nathaniel Micklem and Kenneth A. Saunders (New York: Macmillan & Co., 1927), 21. These lectures were published shortly after Herrmann's death by Martin Rade in the form in which Herrmann last presented them, which was during the winter semester of 1915/1916. To read these lectures in German, see Herrmann, *Dogmatik* (Stuttgart: Verlag Friedrick Andres Perthes, 1925).
9. Herrmann, *Systematic Theology,* 26–29. See Friedrich Schleiermacher, *The Christian Faith,* ed. H. R. Mackintosh and J. S. Stewart (Edinburgh: T. & T. Clark, 1989), 142–256; Herrmann, "Die Lage und Aufgabe der evangelischen Dogmatik in der Gegenwart," 106–22.
10. Herrmann, *Systematic Theology,* 35.
11. Wilhelm Herrmann, "Hermann Cohens Ethik," in *Schriften zur Grundlegung der Theologie,* vol. 2, 108–09.
12. Herrmann, *Systematic Theology,* 35–37.
13. Wilhelm Herrmann, "The Moral Teachings of Jesus," in Adolf von Harnack and Wilhelm Herrmann, *Essays on the Social Gospel,* ed. Maurice A. Canney, trans. G. M. Craik (New York: G. P. Putnam's Sons, 1907), 175–85.
14. Herrmann, *Systematic Theology,* 44; Herrmann, "The Moral Teachings of Jesus," 206–25.
15. Herrmann, *Systemaatic Theology,* 51, 54.
16. Wilhelm Herrmann, "Die Auffassung der Religion in Cohens und Natorps Ethik," in *Schriften zur Grundlegung der Theologie,* vol. 2, 208.
17. Herrmann, *Systematic Theology,* 58–59, 62, 84. Though there is little direct evidence of a Kierkegaardian influence upon him, Herrmann knew enough about Kierkegaard to at least mention him, on occasion, in this connection, as in Herrmann, "Die Lage und Aufgabe der evangelischen Dogmatik in der Gegenwart," *Gesammelte Aufsätze,* 96.
18. Herrmann, *Systematic Theology,* 125–27. Harnack's distinction between the Easter faith and the Easter message advanced much of the same argument with cleaner categories. Against the background of his governing distinction between gospel kernel and husk, he identified the Easter faith as the "kernel" faith in Christ's victory over death and the Easter message as the church's various attempts to codify and defend Easter faith. This distinction could be used to ex-

plicate much of Herrmann's argument, but Herrmann's argument was not quite as schematically compartmentalized as Harnack's. Herrmann placed within the assured core of Christian faith a historical dimension of the Christian story that Harnack assigned to gospel husk. See Adolf von Harnack, *What Is Christianity?* trans. Thomas Bailey Saunders (Philadelphia: Fortress Press, 1986), 160–63.

19. Herrmann, *Systematic Theology,* 127.
20. Barth, "The Principles of Dogmatics According to Wilhelm Herrmann," 256–69.
21. Ibid., 265.
22. Herrmann, *Systematic Theology,* 152.
23. Barth, "The Principles of Dogmatics According to Wilhelm Herrmann," 269.
24. Karl Barth, *Church Dogmatics: The Doctrine of the Word of God,* I/1, trans. G. T. Thomson (Edinburgh: T. & T. Clark, 1936), 96; Barth, *Church Dogmatics: The Doctrine of Creation,* III/4, trans A. T. Mackay et al. (Edinburgh: T. & T. Clark, 1961), 307, 326, 457, 516, 526; Barth, *Church Dogmatics: The Doctrine of Reconciliation,* IV/1, trans. G. W. Bromiley (Edinburgh: T. & T. Clark, 1956), 287, 755, 761.
25. For an interpretation that insightfully and, I believe, rightly emphasizes Herrmann's influence over Barth and Bultmann, see Hendrikus Berkhof, *Two Hundred Years of Theology: Report of a Personal Journey,* trans. John Vriend (Grand Rapids: Wm. B. Eerdmans Publishing Co., 1989), 163–207.
26. See Karl Barth, *Protestant Theology in the Nineteenth Century: Its Background and History* (Valley Forge, Pa.: Judson Press, 1973), 266–312; John D. Godsey, ed., *Karl Barth's Table Talk* (Edinburgh: Oliver & Boyd, 1963), 61.
27. See Joachim Wach, "Introduction: The Meaning and Task of the History of Religions (Religionswissenschaft)," in *The History of Religions: Essays on the Problem of Understanding,* ed. Joseph M. Kitagawa (Chicago: University of Chicago Press, 1967), 1–19; Wach, *Types of Religious Experience: Christian and Non-Christian* (Chicago: University of Chicago Press, 1972), 3–29; Helmut Koester, "Early Christianity from the Perspective of the History of Religions: Rudolf Bultmann's Contribution," in *Bultmann: Retrospect and Prospect,* ed. Edward C. Hobbs (Philadelphia: Fortress Press, 1985), 59–74.
28. Ernst Troeltsch, "The Dogmatics of the 'Religionsgeschichtliche Schule,'" *The American Journal of Theology* 17 (January 1913): 4. See Troeltsch, *Religion in History,* trans. James Luther Adams and Walter F. Bense (Minneapolis: Fortress Press, 1991).
29. Karl Barth to Eduard Thurneysen, 1 January 1916, *Revolutionary Theology in the Making,* 36.
30. Rudolf Bultmann, *The History of the Synoptic Tradition,* trans. John Marsh (New York: Harper & Row, 1968), esp. 150–66. Marsh translated the second German edition of Bultmann's work.
31. See Wilhelm Herrmann, *The Communion of the Christian With God: Described on the Basis of Luther's Statements,* ed. Robert T. Voelkel, trans. J. Sandys Stanyon (Philadelphia: Fortress Press, 1971), 72–75, 87. See editor's discussion, 361.
32. Martin Heidegger, *Holzwege* (Frankfurt: Klostermann, 1950), 61; Heidegger, *Poetry, Language, Thought,* trans. Albert Hofstadter (New York: Harper & Row, 1971), 189. See Ernst Fuchs, *Zum hermeneutischen Problem in der Theologie; Die existentiale Interpretation* (Tübingen: J. C. B. Mohr [Paul Siebeck], 1959); Fuchs, "The New Testament and the Hermeneutical Problem," in *New Frontiers in Theology,* vol. 2: *The New Hermeneutic,* ed. James M. Robinson and John B. Cobb, Jr. (New York: Harper & Row, 1964), 111–46; Gerhard Ebeling, *The Nature of Faith,* trans. Ronald Gregor Smith (Philadelphia: Muhlenberg Press, 1961), 44–71; Ebeling, *Word and Faith,* trans. James W. Leitch

(Philadelphia: Fortress Press, 1963), 201–46, 288–304; Ebeling, *Theology and Proclamation: A Discussion with Rudolf Bultmann,* trans. John Riches (London: William Collins Sons & Co., 1966), 32–81; James M. Robinson, "The German Discussion of the Later Heidegger," in *The Later Heidegger and Theology,* vol. 1: *New Frontiers in Theology,* ed. Robinson and John B. Cobb, Jr. (New York: Harper & Row, 1963), 3–76.

33. On the Fuchs/Ebeling new hermeneutic, see Rudolf Bultmann, "The Primitive Christian Kerygma and Historical Jesus," in *The Historical Jesus and the Kerygmatic Christ,* ed. Carl E. Braaten and Roy A. Harrisville (Nashville: Abingdon Press, 1964), 24; Bultmann, *Des Verhältnis der urchristlichen Christusbotschaft zum historischen Jesus, Sitzungsberichte der Heidelberger Akadamie der Wissenschaften* (Heidelberg: Carl Winter Universitätsverlag, 1960), 17–25. On Herrmann, see Bultmann, "On the Question of Christology," in *Faith and Understanding,* trans. Louise Pettibone Smith (Philadelphia: Fortress Press, 1987), 132–44.
34. Karl Barth, *Church Dogmatics: The Doctrine of Creation,* III:1, trans. J. W. Edwards et al. (Edinburgh: T. & T. Clark, 1958), 82.
35. Ibid., 80–81.
36. Ibid., 82.
37. Ibid., 85–86.
38. Ibid., 87.
39. See Barth, *Church Dogmatics,* III:2, 446–47.
40. Quoted in Godsey, ed., *Karl Barth's Table Talk,* 23.
41. See Karl Barth, "Wolfgang Amadeus Mozart," trans. Walter M. Mosse, in *Religion and Culture: Essays in Honor of Paul Tillich,* ed. Walter Leibrecht (New York: Harper & Brothers, 1959), 61–78.
42. Karl Barth, *The Göttingen Dogmatics: Instruction in the Christian Religion,* vol. 1, ed. Hannelotte Reiffen trans. Geoffrey W. Bromiley (Grand Rapids: Wm. B. Eerdmans Publishing Co., 1991), 33–34.
43. Karl Barth, *Church Dogmatics: The Doctrine of Creation,* III:3, trans. G. W. Bromiley and R. J. Ehrlich (Edinburgh: T. & T. Clark, 1960), 403; see Barth, *Church Dogmatics: The Doctrine of Reconciliation,* IV:3,1, trans. G. W. Bromiley (Edinburgh: T. & T. Clark, 1961), 109.
44. Rudolf Bultmann, "New Testament and Mythology," in *New Testament and Mythology and Other Basic Writings,* trans. and ed. Schubert M. Ogden (Philadelphia: Fortress Press, 1984), 2–9, 36–41.
45. Barth, *The Epistle to the Romans,* 194–207, quote on 195.
46. Karl Barth, *Die Auferstehung der Toten* (Munich: Chr. Kaiser Verlag, 1924), 143; see Barth, *The Epistle to the Romans,* 30.
47. Rudolf Bultmann, "Karl Barth, *The Resurrection of the Dead,*" in *Faith and Understanding,* trans. Louise Pettibone Smith (Philadelphia: Fortress Press, 1987), 66–94, quote on 94.
48. Karl Barth, *Church Dogmatics: The Doctrine of God,* II:1, trans. T. H. L. Parker et al. (Edinburgh: T. & T. Clark, 1957), 179–204, quote on 199.
49. Ibid., 199.
50. Ibid., 202, 204–5.
51. Karl Barth, *Church Dogmatics: The Doctrine of Reconciliation,* IV: 2, trans. G. W. Bromiley (Edinburgh: T. & T. Clark, 1958), 143.
52. Ibid., 209–10.
53. Barth, *Church Dogmatics,* IV:3, 298.
54. Barth, *Church Dogmatics,* III:2, 446; on modern historiography, see Frederick J. Teggart, *Theory and Processes of History* (Berkeley, Calif.: University of Cal-

ifornia Press, 1977); Edward Hallett Carr, *What Is History?* (London: Macmillan & Co., 1961); Van Austen Harvey, *The Historian and the Believer: The Morality of Historical Knowledge and Christian Belief* (New York: Macmillan & Co., 1966).

55. For examples, see Marcus J. Borg, *Jesus: A New Vision: Spirit, Culture, and the Life of Discipleship* (San Francisco: Harper San Francisco, 1987); John Dominic Crossan, *The Historical Jesus: The Life of a Mediteranean Jewish Peasant* (San Francisco: Harper San Francisco, 1992); Burton L. Mack, *The Lost Gospel: The Book of Q and Christian Origins* (San Francisco: Harper San Francisco, 1993).
56. See Bultmann, *New Testament and Mythology and Other Basic Writings,* 2–42.
57. Barth, *Church Dogmatics,* III:2, 446.
58. Barth, *Church Dogmatics,* III:1, 81, 84.
59. Barth, *Church Dogmatics,* III:2, 446.
60. Ibid., 443.
61. Bultmann, "New Testament and Mythology," 39.
62. Karl Barth, "Rudolf Bultmann—An Attempt to Understand Him," in *Kerygma and Myth: A Theological Debate,* vol. 2, ed. Hans-Werner Bartsch, trans. Reginald H. Fuller (London: SPCK, 1962), 101–2.
63. Bultmann, "New Testament and Mythology," 1–8.
64. Ibid., 4. See Rudolf Bultmann, *Jesus Christ and Mythology* (New York: Charles Scribner's Sons, 1958), 11–21.
65. Barth, *Church Dogmatics,* III:2, 446–47.
66. Ibid., 447; on the analogy of truth, see Barth, *Church Dogmatics: The Doctrine of God,* II:1, 230–36.
67. For an instructive example of a Christianization of outdated science (in this case Lamarckian evolutionary theory), see Pierre Teilhard de Chardin, *The Phenomenon of Man,* trans. Bernard Wall (New York: Harper & Brothers, 1959); Teilhard de Chardin, *The Future of Man,* trans. N. Denny (New York: Harper & Row, 1964).
68. Barth, *Church Dogmatics,* III:2, 446–47.
69. Barth, *Church Dogmatics,* I:2, 280–361, esp. 297–324; quote on 325.
70. Ibid., 325–26; see Garrett Green, "Challenging the Religious Studies Canon: Karl Barth's Theory of Religion," *The Journal of Religion* 75, no. 4 (October 1995): 477–82; Ingolf U. Dalferth, "Karl Barth's Eschatological Realism," in *Karl Barth: Centenary Essays,* ed. S. W. Sykes (Cambridge: Cambridge University Press, 1989), 39–41.
71. Barth, *Church Dogmatics,* I:2, 326.
72. Karl Barth, *The Humanity of God,* trans. John Newton Thomas and Thomas Wieser (Atlanta: John Knox Press, 1960), quote on 61–62; Barth, *Church Dogmatics: The Doctrine of God,* II:2, trans. G. W. Bromiley et al. (Edinburgh: T. & T. Clark, 1957), 145–81.
73. See Reginald H. Fuller, *The Formation of the Resurrection Narratives* (Philadelphia: Fortress Press, 1980), 9–49; Willi Marxsen, *The Resurrection of Jesus of Nazareth,* trans. Margaret Kohl (Philadelphia: Fortress Press, 1970), 80–97; Pheme Perkins, *Resurrection: New Testament Witness and Contemporary Reflection* (New York: Doubleday & Co., 1984), 88–91; Gerd Luedemann, *The Resurrection of Jesus: History, Experience, Theology,* trans. John Bowden (Minneapolis: Fortress Press, 1994), 33–108.
74. Bultmann, "Karl Barth, *The Resurrection of the Dead,*" 83–84.
75. Godsey, ed., *Karl Barth's Table Talk,* 60.
76. Barth, "The Principles of Dogmatics According to Wilhelm Herrmann," 267.

77. Godsey, ed., *Karl Barth's Table Talk,* 59–60.
78. Barth, *Church Dogmatics,* III:2, ix.
79. See Brevard S. Childs, *Biblical Theology in Crisis* (Philadelphia: Westminster Press, 1970); Childs, *Introduction to the Old Testament as Scripture* (Philadelphia: Fortress Press, 1979); Childs, *Biblical Theology of the Old and New Testaments: Theological Reflection on the Christian Bible* (Minneapolis: Fortress Press, 1992).
80. See James Barr, *The Semantics of Biblical Language* (London: Oxford University Press, 1961); Barr, *Old and New in Interpretation: A Study of the Two Testaments* (New York: Harper & Row, 1966); Barr, "Revelation Through History in the Old Testament and in Modern Theology," *Princeton Seminary Bulletin* 56 (1963): 4–14.
81. See Langdon Gilkey, "Cosmology, Ontology, and the Travail of Biblical Language," *The Journal of Religion* 41 (July 1961): 194–205. On the downfall of the Biblical Theology movement, see Brevard S. Childs, *Biblical Theology in Crisis;* Gary Dorrien, *The Word as True Myth: Interpreting Modern Theology* (Louisville, Ky.: Westminster John Knox Press, 1997), 143–53.
82. Karl Barth, *Church Dogmatics: The Doctrine of the Word of God,* I:1, 98–140.
83. Scott C. Saye, "The Wild and Crooked Tree: Barth, Fish, and Interpretive Communities," *Modern Theology* 12 (October 1996): 443–44.
84. Barth, *Church Dogmatics,* I:1, 121.
85. Barth to Thurneysen, 4 March 1925, *Revolutionary Theology in the Making,* 216.
86. Emil Brunner, "The New Barth: Observations on Karl Barth's *Doctrine of Man,*" trans. John C. Campbell, *Scottish Journal of Theology,* 4 (1951): 124.

INDEX